Praise for *Security Chaos Engineering*

Security Chaos Engineering is a must read for technology leaders and engineers today, as we operate increasingly complex systems. *Security Chaos Engineering* presents clear evidence that systems resilience is a shared goal of both ops and security teams, and showcases tools and frameworks to measure, design, and instrument systems to improve the resilience and security of our systems.

10/10 strong recommend (kidding but also not).

—*Dr. Nicole Forsgren, lead author of* Accelerate *and partner at Microsoft Research*

Shortridge weaves multiple under-served concepts into the book's guidance, like recognizing human biases, the power of rehearsals, org design, complex systems, systems thinking, habits, design thinking, thinking like a product manager and a financial planner, and much more.

This book brings the reader in on a well-kept secret: security is more about people and processes than about technology. It is our mental models of those elements that drive our efforts and outcomes.

—*Bob Lord, former Chief Security Officer of the DNC and former Chief Information Security Officer of Yahoo*

As our societies become more digitized then our software ecosystems are becoming ever more complex. While complexity can be considered the enemy of security, striving for simplicity as the sole tactic is not realistic. Rather, we need to manage complexity and a big part of that is chaos engineering. That is testing, probing, modeling, and nudging complex systems to a better state. This is tough, but Kelly and Aaron bring immense cross-domain, practical real-world experience to this area in a way that all security professionals should find accessible and fascinating.

—*Phil Venables, Chief Information Security Officer, Google Cloud*

Security Chaos Engineering provides a much-needed reframing of cybersecurity that moves it away from arcane rules and rituals, replacing them with modern concepts from software and resiliency engineering. If you are looking for ways to uplift your security approaches and engage your whole engineering team in the process, this book is for you.

—*Camille Fournier, engineering leader and author,* The Manager's Path

We as defenders owe it to ourselves to make life as hard for attackers as possible. This essential work expertly frames this journey succinctly and clearly and is a must read for all technology leaders and security practitioners, especially in our cloud native world.

—*Rob Duhart, Jr., VP, Deputy Chief Information Security Officer and Chief Information Security Officer eCommerce at Walmart*

Security Chaos Engineering is an unflinching look at how systems are secured in the real world. Shortridge understands both the human and the technical elements in security engineering.

—*George Neville-Neil, author of the Kode Vicious column in* ACM Queue Magazine

Security masquerades as a technical problem, but it really cuts across all layers: organizational, cultural, managerial, temporal, historical, and technical. You can't even define security without thinking about human expectations, and the dividing line between "flaw" and "vulnerability" is non-technical. This thought-provoking book emphasizes the inherent complexity of security and the need for flexible and adaptive approaches that avoid both box-ticking and 0day-worship.

—*Thomas Dullien, founder, security researcher, and performance engineer*

Security Chaos Engineering

Sustaining Resilience in Software and Systems

Kelly Shortridge
with Aaron Rinehart

Beijing · Boston · Farnham · Sebastopol · Tokyo

Security Chaos Engineering

by Kelly Shortridge with Aaron Rinehart

Published by O'Reilly Media, Inc., 1005 Gravenstein Highway North, Sebastopol, CA 95472.

O'Reilly books may be purchased for educational, business, or sales promotional use. Online editions are also available for most titles (*http://oreilly.com*). For more information, contact our corporate/institutional sales department: 800-998-9938 or *corporate@oreilly.com*.

Acquisitions Editor: John Devins
Development Editor: Michele Cronin
Production Editor: Clare Laylock
Copyeditor: Nicole Taché
Proofreader: Audrey Doyle

Indexer: Sue Klefstad
Interior Designer: David Futato
Cover Designer: Karen Montgomery
Illustrator: Kate Dullea
Chapter-Opener Image Designer: Savannah Glitschka

March 2023:   First Edition

Revision History for the First Edition
2023-03-30:   First Release

See *http://oreilly.com/catalog/errata.csp?isbn=9781098113827* for release details.

The O'Reilly logo is a registered trademark of O'Reilly Media, Inc. *Security Chaos Engineering*, the cover image, and related trade dress are trademarks of O'Reilly Media, Inc.

978-1-098-11382-7

[LSI]

Table of Contents

Preface

In Life's wave, in action's storm,
I float, up and down,
I blow, to and fro!
Birth and the tomb,
An eternal flow,
A woven changing,
A glow of Being.
Over Time's quivering loom intent,
Working the Godhead's living garment.
    — Faust

If you've worked with computers in a professional setting at any point since the dawn of the millennia, you've probably heard that security is important. By now, you've also probably realized cybersecurity is broken. Humans are entrusting us, as people working with software, with more and more of their lives and we are failing to keep that trust. Year after year, the same sorts of attacks ravage the coasts and heartlands of our ever-growing digital territories.

Meanwhile, the security industry accumulates power and money, indulging in newer, shinier technology and oft deepening their sanctimonious effrontery. Success outcomes remain amorphous; and in the background slinks an existential dread that security can't "keep up" with software. Fingers point and other fingers point back. Our security programs coagulate into performative rituals—a modern humoralism based in folk wisdom and tradition rather than empiricism. Software engineering teams simmer in resentment, yearning for answers on how to keep their systems safe without requiring ritual sacrifices. We know we can do better, but we struggle to chart a course when immersed in the murky obliqueness that is cybersecurity today.

A fundamental shift in both philosophy and practice is nigh. Cybersecurity must embrace the reality that failure will happen. Humans will click on things and sometimes it will be the wrong thing. The security implications of simple code changes won't be clear to developers. Mitigations will accidentally be disabled. Things will break (and are, in fact, breaking all the time). This shift requires us to transform toward resilience—the ability to recover from failure and adapt as our context changes.

This book is an attack on current cybersecurity strategy and execution. To evoke author and activist Jane Jacobs, this attack is on the principles and aims that have shaped traditional cybersecurity strategy and execution, not quibbles about specific methods or design patterns.

We call this transformation "Security Chaos Engineering," the subject of this tome. Security Chaos Engineering (SCE) is a sociotechnical transformation that drives value to organizations through an ability to respond to failure and adapt to evolving conditions with speed and grace. To set this transformation up for success, we will draw on interdisciplinary insights regarding the resilience of complex systems. In essence, we can copy the homework of other problem domains to make solving our computer and software problems clearer.

We, as humanity, have gotten quite good at software. Most software is now part of distributed systems. Transformational technology shifts such as cloud computing, microservices, and continuous delivery have each flowered enhancements in customer value but, in turn, have effloresced a new series of challenges too. Primary among those challenges is that we've reached a state where the systems we build have become impossible for our minds to conceive in totality. What starts as our little software seedling grows to something astonishing and impossible to mentally model, should it succeed.

Throughout this book, we cover the philosophies, practices, and principles that will help you achieve outcome-driven security and transform toward resilience. We will discuss far more than just the art of conducting chaos experiments—although the scientific method is essential for our quest. SCE is our ambitious extension of the practice of chaos engineering, which began with the goal of promoting systems resilience from a performance perspective rather than a security perspective. Chaos engineering is the practice of continual experimentation to validate that our systems operate the way we believe they do. These experiments help uncover systemic weaknesses or gaps in our understanding, informing improved design and practices that can help the organization gain more confidence in their behavior.

The aim of chaos engineering is to fix things in production, not break them. There is little point to suffering, in any domain, if we cannot learn from it and devise a constructive course for improvement. Throughout the book, we've taken great care to avoid any analogies related to warfare or violence—the kind you usually find in cybersecurity and that insinuate that militaristic, disciplinary solutions are needed to solve our problems. Instead, we hope to inspire the industry with analogies from nature, ecology, and other domains that involve nurturing, nourishing, and supporting humans in achieving their goal outcomes. We can be creators rather than castigators. We can succeed in our security aims without dehumanizing users, treating them like objects to control lest they thwart our zealous ambitions.

By the end of the book, you—no matter your role—will understand how to sustain resilience in your software and systems so your organization can thrive despite the presence of attackers. You will learn how to adapt to adversity and maintain continuous change as the world evolves around you and your systems. You'll discover that security can escape the dark ages and enter the enlightenment era by embracing empiricism and experimentation. We hope this ignites a meta-transformation away from a security status quo—one that served us before we learned better—toward resilience so we can, at last, outmaneuver attackers and get real stuff done.

Who Should Read This Book?

If your responsibility is to design, develop, build, deploy, deliver, operate, recover, manage, protect, or secure systems that include software, then this book is for you. This book is for humans involved in software and systems engineering across titles and focal areas—software engineers, software architects, security engineers, and security architects; site reliability engineers; platform engineering teams and their leaders; infrastructure, cloud, or DevOps engineers and the directors and VPs of those teams; CTOs, CIOs, and CISOs; and, of course, students who aspire to leave an indelible mark through their work, making the software footprint of humanity better in any way they can.

This book is especially relevant if your software, services, and systems are complex—which is most software, services, and systems that are internet-connected and the byproduct of many minds over many years. No matter where you sit in the software delivery lifecycle—or outside of it, as an administrator, manager, or defender—this book offers you wisdom on how to support your systems' resilience to attack and other adverse conditions from your sphere of influence.

You should have a basic understanding of what software is and how organizations use it. Some practical experience either designing, delivering, or operating software systems or else implementing a security program is helpful—but we recognize that few people possess experience in both. This book is explicitly designed to teach software people about security and security people about software while extending and enriching existing experts' knowledge too.

If any of the following outcomes compel you, then you'll find this book valuable:

- Learn how to design a modern security program.
- Make informed decisions at each phase of software delivery to nurture resilience and adaptive capacity.
- Understand the complex systems dynamics upon which resilience outcomes depend.
- Navigate technical and organizational trade-offs that distort decision making in systems.
- Explore chaos experimentation to verify critical assumptions about software quality and security.
- Learn how major enterprises leverage security chaos engineering.

As we'll emphasize, and reemphasize, your strategy for nourishing your systems' resilience to attack depends on your specific context. Every organization, no matter the size, age, or industry, can benefit from investing in resilience via the SCE transformation we'll describe in these pages. This book is explicitly *not* written only for hyperscalers and Fortune 100 organizations; the content is simply too valuable.

Scope of This Book

This book does not prescribe specific technologies nor does it detail instructions on how to implement the opportunities described in code. We encourage you to peruse relevant documentation for such details and to exercise the unique skills you bring to your organization. Our goal is to discuss the principles, practices, and trade-offs that matter when we consider systems resilience, offering you a cornucopia of opportunities across your software activities from which you can pluck the patterns you feel will most likely bear fruit for your organization.

Outline of This Book

We begin our journey in Chapter 1, "Resilience in Software and Systems", by discussing resilience in complex systems, how failure manifests, how resilience is maintained, and how we can avoid common myths that lead our security strategy astray.

In Chapter 2, "Systems-Oriented Security", we explore the needed shift toward systems thinking in security, describing how to refine mental models of systems behavior and perform resilience assessments before comparing SCE to traditional cybersecurity ("security theater").

The structure for Chapters 3 to 6 acts as a reference guide you can pull out at each stage of software delivery. Chapter 3, "Architecting and Designing", starts in the "first" phase of software delivery: architecting and designing systems. We think through how to invest effort based on your organization's specific context before describing opportunities to invest in looser coupling and linearity.

In Chapter 4, "Building and Delivering", we map the five features that define resilience to activities we can pursue when developing, building, testing, and delivering systems. The ground we cover is expansive, from code reviews, standardization of "raw materials," automating security checks, and Configuration as Code, to test theater, type systems, modularity, and so much more (this chapter is perhaps the most packed full of practical wisdom).

Chapter 5, "Operating and Observing", describes how we can sustain resilience as our systems run in production—and as we operate and observe our systems. We reveal the overlap between site reliability engineering (SRE) and security goals, then discover different strategies for security observability before closing with a discussion of scalability's relevance to security.

In Chapter 6, "Responding and Recovering", we move on to what happens after an incident, digging into the biases that can distort our decision making and learning during this phase—including action bias, hindsight bias, outcome bias, and the just-world hypothesis. Along the way, we propose tactics for countering those biases and supporting more constructive efforts, particularly with an eye to eradicating the especially unproductive blame game of declaring "human error" as the "root cause" of incidents.

Chapter 7, "Platform Resilience Engineering", introduces the concept of platform resilience engineering and describes how to implement it in practice within any organization. We cover the process for creating security solutions for internal customers (like engineering teams), including defining a vision, defining a user problem, designing a solution, and implementing a solution. The Ice Cream Cone Hierarchy of Security Solutions, which we cover in this chapter, is especially tasty (and practical) wisdom.

In Chapter 8, "Security Chaos Experiments", we learn how to conduct experiments and paint a richer picture of our systems, which in turn helps us better navigate strategies to make them more resilient to failure. We outline the end-to-end experimentation process: how to set your experiments up for success; designing hypotheses; designing experiments and writing experiment specifications; conducting experiments and collecting evidence; and analyzing and documenting evidence.

Finally, in Chapter 9, "Security Chaos Engineering in the Wild", we learn from chaos experiments conducted in the wild. Real organizations that have adopted SCE and have conducted chaos experiments generously impart their wisdom through a series of case studies. We'll learn from UnitedHealth Group, Verizon, OpenDoor, Cardinal Health, Accenture Global, and Capital One.

Conventions Used in This Book

The following typographical conventions are used in this book:

Italic

   Indicates new terms, URLs, email addresses, filenames, and file extensions.

`Constant width`

   Used for program listings, as well as within paragraphs to refer to program elements such as variable or function names, databases, data types, environment variables, statements, and keywords.

This element signifies a tip or suggestion.

This element signifies a general note.

This element indicates a warning or caution.

O'Reilly Online Learning

 For more than 40 years, *O'Reilly Media* has provided technology and business training, knowledge, and insight to help companies succeed.

Our unique network of experts and innovators share their knowledge and expertise through books, articles, and our online learning platform. O'Reilly's online learning platform gives you on-demand access to live training courses, in-depth learning paths, interactive coding environments, and a vast collection of text and video from O'Reilly and 200+ other publishers. For more information, visit *https://oreilly.com*.

How to Contact Us

Please address comments and questions concerning this book to the publisher:

O'Reilly Media, Inc.
1005 Gravenstein Highway North
Sebastopol, CA 95472
800-998-9938 (in the United States or Canada)
707-829-0515 (international or local)
707-829-0104 (fax)

We have a web page for this book, where we list errata, examples, and any additional information. You can access this page at *https://oreil.ly/SecurityChaosEngineering*.

Email *bookquestions@oreilly.com* to comment or ask technical questions about this book.

For news and information about our books and courses, visit *https://oreilly.com*.

Find us on LinkedIn: *https://linkedin.com/company/oreilly-media*.

Follow us on Twitter: *https://twitter.com/oreillymedia*.

Watch us on YouTube: *https://youtube.com/oreillymedia*.

Acknowledgments

From Aaron: We would like to acknowledge the SCE community contributions made to this body of work by the following individuals. These early pioneers of Security Chaos Engineering have helped shape the community and the craft that exists today. Thank you so much for all the sacrifices and support!

- Brian Bagdzinski
- Jamie Dicken
- Rob Duhart, Jr.
- Troy Koss
- Matas Kulkovas
- David Lavezzo
- Omar Marrero

- Charles Nwatu
- Mario Platt
- Kennedy Torkura
- Dan Walsh
- Jerome Walters
- James Wickett
- Sounil Yu

From Kelly: This book weaves together threads of thought across countless disciplines, scholars, and practitioners. I lost count of the papers, blog posts, books, and conversations I inhaled before and during the course of writing this book—and this is reflected in the references through the book, of which there are many. It is especially through insights from other problem domains that we can break free from traditional cybersecurity's stifling insularity; there is much we can learn from others' mistakes, stumbles, and successes, even if their quests did not involve computers.

In truth, it would be challenging to enumerate each source of inspiration in the book, especially those lacking a traditional citation. If we've ever challenged the status quo wisdom of systems security together in fervent conversation, I extend my gratitude—including Allan Alford, Geoff Belknap, Juan Pablo Buriticá, Lita Cho, Erinn Clark, Tasha Drew, Rob Duhart, Jr., Thomas Dullien, Dr. Josiah Dykstra, Camille Fournier, Dr. Nicole Forsgren, Jessie Frazelle, Eitan Goldstein, Bea Hughes, Kyle Kingsbury, Julia Knecht, Toby Kohlenberg, Mike Leibowitz, Kelly Lum, Caitie McCaffrey, Fernando Montenegro, Christina Morillo, Renee Orser, Ryan Petrich, Greg Poirier, Alex Rasmussen, Dr. Andrew Ruef, Snare, Inés Sombra, Jason Strange, James Turnbull, Phil Vachon, and Sounil Yu. I'm especially grateful to the entire Rantifesto crew (you know who you are) and Doctor Animal for their computer wisdom—may I continue to learn from you and throw shade with you.

A few chosen humans, our technical reviewers, were especially valuable in shaping this book. Thank you for devouring all this material in such a short period of time, providing constructive feedback and, in some places, proffering inspiration for new content. This book is stronger as a direct result of your efforts: Juan Pablo Buriticá, Will Gallego, Bea Hughes, Ryan Petrich, Alex Rasmussen, and Jason Strange.

To Aaron Rinehart, my unindicted co-conspirator in promulgating the resilience transformation, I am forever indebted that you DM'd me asking if I wanted to work on a book with you.

For her endless patience with my frenetic writing patterns, strange requests, and oft overwrought literary references, I am grateful to our editor, Michele Cronin. To our production editor, Clare Laylock, and copyeditor, Nicole Taché, I am appreciative of their tireless efforts in ensuring a speedy, smooth production process—and their patience with my perfectionism. And thanks to the team at O'Reilly and John Devins for allowing all these words to exist outside the confines of my brain.

Special thanks are due to Savannah Glitschka, who brought Chaos Kitty to life and infused each chapter with magical illustrations. And for giving me the space-time to devote to writing, supporting my challenge of the security status quo, and being a thoughtful teacher, I thank Sean Leach.

In the realm of the personal, I'd like to extend my deepest appreciation to myself for their resilience in the months spent pouring their soul into these pages. Congrats on not totally losing it! To Sotha Sil—the Tinkerer and Clockwork God—I extend my eternal gratitude for your existence; you are my favorite partner in thought crimes and a cherished sounding board for my tonal architecture. To Geralt "Mr. Boopkin" Shortridge, your impossibly soft tummy fluff and blissful, blithe trills were welcome respite from writing.

Finally, I'd like to thank Michael Crichton for introducing baby me to complex systems and my dad for his patience with and nurturing of my scientific curiosity. May we all connect with our inner child and find a fathomless fascination with the world, never hesitating to ask, "But why?"

CHAPTER 1

Resilience in Software and Systems

The world stands on absurdities, and without them perhaps nothing at all would happen.
—Fyodor Dostoevsky, *The Brothers Karamazov*

In our present reality, cybersecurity is more of an arcane art than science—an inscrutable, often excruciating, sequence of performative rituals to check boxes[1] that affirm you've met the appropriate (and often arbitrary) regulatory or standards requirement. In terms of systems security, the ideal state is one of resilience—ensuring that systems can operate successfully now and in the future despite the dangers lurking in our digital world. To sustain resilience, we must understand how all the system's machines and humans interact in pursuit of a common goal and how they respond to disruption.[2] Knowing the intricacies of cybersecurity isn't enough. We must understand the system's resilience (or lack thereof) if we hope to protect it, which involves understanding the system's dynamics, as we'll explore in this chapter. This is why, throughout this book, we treat security as a subset of resilience.

This book is a practical guide for how to design, build, and operate systems that are more resilient to attack. We will prioritize progress over perfection. We will draw on lessons from other complex systems domains, like healthcare, aerospace, disaster recovery, ecology, urban infrastructure, and psychology; indeed, the rich discourse on resilience in these other domains is another reason why resilience is the foundation of Security Chaos Engineering (SCE). "Security" is an abstract, squishy concept that is largely self-contained within the cybersecurity (or "infosec") industry, with occasional appropriations of concepts from physical safety, law enforcement, and, rather

---

1 George V. Neville-Neil, "Securing the Company Jewels," *Communications of the ACM* 65, no. 10 (2022): 25-26.

2 Richard J. Holden, "People or Systems? To Blame Is Human. The Fix Is to Engineer," *Professional Safety* 54, no. 12 (2009): 34.

infamously, warfare. With resilience, however, there's much we can learn from other disciplines to help us in our quest to operate our systems safely, reducing the amount of work and "thinky thinky" required for us to succeed.

As we shift our focus from security to resilience, we gain a superpower: we invest our time, energy, and other resources on *outcome-driven activities* rather than wasting those resources on performative work that may *feel* productive, but does not, in reality, protect our systems. Resilience matters in any complex system and is especially illuminating in complex systems involving humans, inspiring us to change what we can to prepare for success in an uncertain future. This is our vision for security programs, which may become *resilience* programs going forward. If you join the SCE movement, you can protect your organization's ability to thrive now and in the future. All that's required for you to join is an openness to new perspectives and new ways of achieving security outcomes, which is the focus of this book.

SCE seeks to uncover, through experimental evidence, whether our systems are resilient to certain conditions so we can learn how to make them even more resilient. Failure is a normal condition of system operation. SCE offers organizations a pragmatic set of principles and practices for proactively uncovering unknown failure within their systems before it manifests into customer-facing and business-impacting problems. Those practicing SCE eschew waiting to passively witness how things break in production, morphing from a reactive stance to a proactive one.

These are just some of the transformative outcomes possible by adopting a resilience-based approach to systems security through SCE. Before we embark on our quest, we must—like any noble scientist—absorb the foundational concepts that will pave our journey. What is a complex system? What is failure? What is resilience? And how does SCE fit in? This chapter answers all of those questions. A lot of traditional infosec folk wisdom will be challenged and discarded in favor of hard-earned, empirical lessons from resilience across domains. We invite you, like Neo in *The Matrix*, to free your mind and take a leap with us into the real world where resilience is not just how we survive, but how we thrive.

What Is a Complex System?

A *complex system* is one in which a bunch of components interact with each other and generate nonlinear behavior as a result. Humans deal with complex systems constantly, from global supply chains to national economies to cities to our own bodies and our own brains. But before we explore complex systems in more depth, we should probably understand what complexity is.

Complexity is formally defined as a summary term for the properties that emerge from interrelations between variables in a system.[3] As system capabilities increase, interdependencies between these variables extend, deepen, and become more obscure. These interdependencies can lead to a domino effect where disturbances diffuse from one variable to others connected to it. This is referred to as a "contagion effect" and is seen across domains like financial markets,[4] psychology,[5] and, of course, biological viruses.[6] In distributed systems, you're likely to hear this same phenomenon referred to as "cascading failure" (which we will explore in more depth in Chapter 3).

What makes a system complex in practice? Well, let's think about simple systems first. Linear systems are easy. If something bad happens, you just make sure the system is robust enough to bounce back to its status quo. Consider Mr. Potato Head; there is a clear, direct cause and effect between you plugging in his eyeballs and the eyeballs residing on his face. If you plug his ear into his arm socket instead, it is easy to revert to the intended layout—and this mistake does not cause problems with his eyes, feet, hat, mouth, or iconic mustache. The potato "head" base interacts with the appendage components in an extremely predictable, repeatable fashion. But linear systems like Mr. Potato Head[7] are more likely found in textbooks and contrived hypotheticals rather than the real world, which is messy. To adapt the classic wisdom for computer systems (*https://oreil.ly/blgY5*), "No 'perfect' software service survives first contact with production traffic."

Where do complex systems and linear systems most diverge? To answer that question, let's explore the nature of complex systems, including variety, adaptability, and holisticness.

Variety Defines Complex Systems

Variety is perhaps the defining element of complexity; what we tend to describe as "complex" systems are those with a great degree of variety. Systems are replete with all

---

3 David D. Woods, "Engineering Organizational Resilience to Enhance Safety: A Progress Report on the Emerging Field of Resilience Engineering," *Proceedings of the Human Factors and Ergonomics Society Annual Meeting* 50, no. 19 (October 2006): 2237-2241.

4 Dirk G. Baur, "Financial Contagion and the Real Economy," *Journal of Banking & Finance* 36, no. 10 (2012): 2680-2692; Kristin Forbes, "The 'Big C': Identifying Contagion," *National Bureau of Economic Research*, Working Paper 18465 (2012).

5 Iacopo Iacopini et al., "Simplicial Models of Social Contagion," *Nature Communications* 10, no. 1 (2019): 2485; Sinan Aral and Christos Nicolaides, "Exercise Contagion in a Global Social Network," *Nature Communications* 8, no. 1 (2017): 14753.

6 Steven Sanche et al., "High Contagiousness and Rapid Spread of Severe Acute Respiratory Syndrome Coronavirus 2," *Emerging Infectious Diseases* 26, no. 7 (2020): 1470.

7 A modern Diogenes might hold up Mr. Potato Head and declare, "Behold! A linear system!"

kinds of variety: the variety of components, the variety of interactions between those components, and the variety of potential outcomes in the system. Our computer systems involve a lot of variables and components—wetware (our brains), software, hardware—and thus offer a large variety of potential future states too.

Because complex systems involve a veritable festival of variables cavorting and gallivanting together in often unconventional ways, they can present a large variety of possible states.[8] Safety research organization Jepsen notes (*https://oreil.ly/AFa5x*) that distributed systems "have a logical state which changes over time" and all types of complex computer systems are no different. This is why prediction is perceived as an extravagant distraction in a resilience paradigm. With so many possible future states within the system, there is never just one path that will lead to a particular outcome.[9] Even trickier, performing the same sequence of actions in the system may result in different outcomes. Getting from point A to point B in a complex system is less "as the crow flies" and more "as the cat wanders (or zoomies)."

Complex Systems Are Adaptive

Importantly, complex systems are *adaptive*; they change and evolve over time and space, especially in response to changes in their external environment. Our software systems are complex adaptive systems and, as some computer people sometimes forget, they are *socio*technological in nature. Both machines and humans qualify as components of our tech systems, whether production systems or corporate IT systems. The cybersecurity ecosystem is a complex adaptive system in itself, consisting of not only a huge variety of machines, but also developers, defenders, end users, government regulators, government-sponsored attackers, criminal organizations, auditors, and countless other human stakeholders.

Complex systems are adaptive because change cannot be stopped—and therefore failure cannot be stopped from ever occurring. A *resilient complex system* is one that can handle this failure gracefully, adapting its behavior to preserve its critical functions.[10] Understanding the transitions between the variety of potential future states—how a system adapts to ongoing changes—is key to understanding your system's resilience and security over time.

We also must appreciate how humans are a source of strength when a system nears the boundary between success and failure; humans are, in many cases, our mechanism for adaptation in the face of adverse and evolving conditions due to their natural tendency

---

8 Amy Rankin et al., "Resilience in Everyday Operations: A Framework for Analyzing Adaptations in High-Risk Work," *Journal of Cognitive Engineering and Decision Making* 8, no. 1 (2014): 78-97.

9 Rankin, "Resilience in Everyday Operations," 78-97.

10 Joonhong Ahn et al., eds., *Reflections on the Fukushima Daiichi Nuclear Accident: Toward Social-Scientific Literacy and Engineering Resilience* (Berlin: Springer Nature, 2015).

---

to be curious about the problems they face.[11] In healthcare, for example, emergency departments are often brittle due to management-driven changes imposed by financial and operational pressures, making them less resilient in the face of "accumulating or cascading demands" that push them beyond their known-safe capacity.[12] The emergency department system therefore must "stretch" in the face of greater demands on its operation so individual failures—like necessary activities falling through the cracks—do not accumulate and tip the overall system into failure. How does this stretching happen? The humans in the system are the ones who enable this stretching. Humans can work harder, adjust their strategies, and scour for extra resources, like asking other humans to come help out to provide additional adaptive capacity.[13]

The Holistic Nature of Complex Systems

The complexity of a system—and its behavior—is defined holistically; little can be gleaned from the behavior of individual constituent components.[14] Systems thinking is not natural to most humans and security professionals aren't exempt. The cybersecurity industry has trended toward componentization, even down to specific tooling and environments. Unfortunately, this component-based focus restricts your ability to understand how your slice of security relates to all the other components, which together shape how the system operates. Only looking at one component is like a narrow viewing frustum—or, if you prefer, like a cone collar that makes it difficult to navigate nimbly about the world. Nancy G. Leveson, professor of aeronautics and astronautics at MIT, cautions us that "a narrow focus on operator actions, physical component failures, and technology may lead to ignoring some of the most important factors in terms of preventing future accidents."[15]

Attackers perceive the holistic nature of systems, routinely taking advantage of interrelations between components. They look for how interactions within a system can give them an advantage. All the attack phase "lateral movement" means is leveraging the connection between one component in a system to others within the system. Defenders, however, traditionally conceive security in terms of whether individual components are secure or whether the connections between them are secure. Status

---

11 Nick Chater and George Loewenstein, "The Under-Appreciated Drive for Sense-Making," *Journal of Economic Behavior & Organization* 126 (2016): 137-154.

12 Institute of Medicine, *Hospital-Based Emergency Care: At the Breaking Point* (Washington, DC: The National Academies Press, 2007).

13 Christopher Nemeth et al., "Minding the Gaps: Creating Resilience in Health Care," in *Advances in Patient Safety: New Directions and Alternative Approaches*, Vol. 3: Performance and Tools (Rockville, MD: Agency for Healthcare Research and Quality, August 2008).

14 Len Fisher, "To Build Resilience, Study Complex Systems," *Nature* 595, no. 7867 (2021): 352-352.

15 Nancy G. Leveson, *Engineering a Safer World: Systems Thinking Applied to Safety* (Cambridge, MA: MIT Press, 2016).

quo security thinks in terms of lists rather than graphs, whereas attackers think in graphs rather than lists (*https://oreil.ly/XC9sl*). There is a dearth of systems knowledge in traditional cybersecurity defense, which attackers are all too happy to exploit.

The high-profile SolarWinds compromise highlights this dynamic well. The Russian Foreign Intelligence Service (SVR) had a particular objective in mind: gaining access to federal agencies and Fortune 500 companies alike for (presumably) espionage purposes. One way they could achieve this outcome was by looking for any components and subsystems these target systems had in common. SolarWinds' Orion platform, offering infrastructure monitoring and management, was a tool that was not only used by many federal agencies and large enterprises, but also possessed functionality that granted it access to customers' internal infrastructure. Through this lens, attackers exploited interrelations and interactions at multiple levels of abstraction.

A holistic systems perspective must not be limited to specific technology, however. The way in which organizations *use* technology also involves economic and social factors, which are all too frequently ignored or overlooked by traditional enterprise cybersecurity programs. Economic factors in an organization include revenue and profit goals, how compensation schemes are structured, or other budgetary decisions. Social factors in an organization include its key performance indicators, the performance expectations of employees, what sort of behavior is rewarded or reprimanded, or other cultural facets.

As an industry, we tend to think of vulnerabilities as things borne by flaws in software, but vulnerabilities are borne by incentive paradigms too. We overlook the vulnerability in incentivizing employees to do more work, but faster. We overlook the vulnerability in giving bonuses to "yes" people and those who master political games. These vulnerabilities reduce the organization's resilience to failure just the same as software flaws, but they rarely appear in our threat models. Occasionally, we will identify "disgruntled employees" as a potential insider threat, without exploring the factors that lead them to be disgruntled.

These "layer 8" (human) factors may be difficult to distinguish, let alone influence, in an organization. But when we consider how failure manifests, we must nevertheless take them into account.

What Is Failure?

Failure refers to when systems—including any people and business processes involved—do not operate as intended.[16] A service that does not complete communication with another service on which it depends would count as a failure.

---

16 Pertinent domains include disaster management (e.g., flood resilience), climate change (e.g., agriculture, coral reef management), and safety-critical industries like aviation and medicine.

Similarly, we can consider it a failure when security programs do not achieve security objectives. There are more possible failures in software than we could hope to enumerate: abuse of an API, which results in a leak of user data that provokes anxiety and requires users to purchase credit monitoring services; a denial-of-service (DoS) attack, which lasts long enough to violate service-level agreements (SLAs) and trigger revenue refunds; repetitive, tedious, and manual tasks with unclear outcomes, which result in burned out, resentful human operators. And so on, into infinity.

Failure is inevitable and happening all the time. It is a normal part of living and operating in a complex system, and our decisions—successful or not—influence the outcomes. Regardless of the domain of human activity, avoiding failure entirely is possible only by avoiding the activity entirely: we could avoid plane crashes by never flying planes; avoid deaths during surgery by never undergoing surgery; avoid financial crashes by never creating a financial system; or, in the realm of cybersecurity, avoid software failure by never deploying software. This sounds silly, and it is, but when we aim for "perfect security," or when the board of directors demands that we *never* experience a security incident, we are setting ourselves up (ironically) for failure. Since the status quo goal of security programs is to "prevent incidents," it's no wonder practitioners feel engaged in a battle they're constantly losing.

Despite its common characterization in cybersecurity, security failure is never the result of one factor. A failure is never solely because of one vulnerability's existence or the dismissal of a single alert. Failure works like a symphony, with multiple factors interacting together in changing harmonies and discords. As such, we must adopt a systems perspective when seeking to understand security failure, expanding our focus to look at relationships between components rather than pinning the blame to a singular cause; this systems perspective will be the focus of Chapter 2.

When we think about security failure, we also tend to think about situations that occur once systems are deployed and running in production—like data breaches. But the conditions of security failure are sowed much earlier. Failure is a result of interrelated components behaving in unexpected ways, which can—and almost always do—start much further back, in how systems are designed and developed and in other activities that inform how our systems ultimately look and operate.

Failure is a learning opportunity. It is a chance to untangle all the factors that led to an unwanted event to understand how their interaction fomented failure conditions. If you do not understand the goals, constraints, and incentives influencing a system, you will struggle to progress in making the system more resilient to attack.

Acute and Chronic Stressors in Complex Systems

When we think about security incidents, we may tend to blame the incident on an acute event—like a user double-clicking on a malicious executable or an attacker executing a crypto miner payload. In resilience lingo, these acute events are known as pulse-type stressors. *Pulse-type stressors* are negative inputs to the system that occur over a short duration, like hurricanes in the context of ecological systems. *Press-type stressors*, in contrast, are negative inputs that occur over longer periods of time; in ecological systems, this can include pollution, overfishing, or ocean warming. For clarity, we'll call pulse-type stressors "acute stressors" and press-type stressors "chronic stressors" throughout the book.

The problem with a myopic focus on acute stressors in any complex system is that those events will not tip the system over into failure modes on their own. The background noise of chronic stressors wears down the resilience of the system over a longer period of time, whether months or years, so when some sort of acute event does occur, the system is no longer able to absorb it or recover from it.

What do chronic stressors look like in cybersecurity? They can include:

- Regular employee turnover
- Tool sprawl and shelfware
- Inability to update systems/software
- Inflexible procedures
- Upgrade-and-patch treadmill
- Technology debt
- Status quo bias
- Employee burnout
- Documentation gaps
- Low-quality alert signals
- Continuous tool maintenance
- Strained or soured relationships across the organization
- Automation backlog or manual procedure paradigm
- Human-error focus and blame game
- Prevention mindset

And acute stressors in cybersecurity can include:

- Ransomware operation
- Human mistake
- Kernel exploit
- New vulnerability
- Mergers, acquisitions, or an IPO event

- Annual audit
- End-of-life of critical tool
- Outage due to security tool
- Log or monitoring outage
- Change in compliance standard
- New product launch
- Stolen cloud admin credentials
- Reorg or personnel issues
- Contractual changes (like SLAs)

While recovery from acute stressors is important, understanding and handling chronic stressors in your systems will ensure that recovery isn't constrained.

Surprises in Complex Systems

Complex systems also come with the "gift" of sudden and unforeseen events, referred to as "surprises" in some domains. Evolutionary biologist Lynn Margulis eloquently described the element of surprise as "the revelation that a given phenomenon of the environment was, until this moment, misinterpreted."[17] In the software domain, the surprises we encounter come from computers and humans. Both can surprise us in different ways, but we tend to be less forgiving when it's humans who surprise us. It's worth exploring both types of surprises because accepting them is key to maintaining resilience in our complex software systems.

Computer surprises

Computers surprise us in a vexing variety of ways. Kernels panic, hard disks crash, concurrency distorts into deadlocks, memory glitches, and networks disconnect (or worse, network links flap!). Humanity is constantly inundated with computer surprises.[18] An eternal challenge for programming is how to ensure that a program behaves exactly as its designer intended.

When we encounter computer surprises, our instinct (other than cursing the computer) is to eliminate the potential for the same surprise in the future. For hardware, we might enable Trusted Platform Modules (TPMs) in an attempt to better secure

---

17 Lynn Margulis and Dorion Sagan, *What Is Life?* (Berkeley and Los Angeles, CA: University of California Press, 2000).

18 As just one example, Facebook published a study of memory errors at scale (*https://oreil.ly/YwY3s*) and found that 9.62% of servers experienced correctable memory errors (cumulatively across all months)—leading them to "corroborate the trend that *memory errors are still a widespread problem in the field*" (emphasis theirs).

cryptographic keys, or we might add redundancy by deploying additional physical replicas of some components. For software, we might add a vulnerability scanner into our development pipeline or institute a requirement for manual security review before a push to production. If you can remove all bugs from software before it reaches production environments, then you can minimize computer surprises, right?

Of course, none of these responses—nor any response—will eradicate the phenomenon of computer surprises. Surprises, like failures, are inevitable. They're an emergent feature of complex systems.

Yet some computer surprises are rather dubious in the context of security. Attackers using software like NetWire (*https://oreil.ly/O5PY7*), a public remote administration tool first seen in 2012 and still seen as of the end of 2022, should not be surprising. The reality is that the "fast and ever-evolving attacker" narrative is more mythology than reality (a particularly convenient myth for security vendors and defenders wanting to avoid accountability). Attackers evolve only when they *must* because their operational strategy, tooling, or infrastructure no longer provides the desired outcomes; we'll discuss their calculus in Chapter 2.

 Complexity adds vivacity, novelty, and significance to our lives. Without complexity, we wouldn't have communities, economies, or much progress at all. If we attempt to expunge all complexity from our sociotechnical systems, we may banish adverse surprises at the expense of ostracizing pleasant surprises. The innovation and creativity we cherish is often stifled by "streamlining."

How can we encourage opportunities to flourish instead—to enliven rather than deaden our systems? We must enhance, rather than impede, complexity[19] by preserving possibilities and minimizing the disruption begotten by complexity. Meanwhile, we can find the right opportunities to make parts of our systems more linear—more independent components with more predictable, causal influence on outcomes—so that we can expend more effort nourishing plasticity. We'll navigate how to pursue these opportunities across the software delivery lifecycle in Chapters 3 through 7.

Human surprises

Even though most kindergarteners understand that making mistakes is an inevitable part of life, the traditional cybersecurity industry seems to believe that human mistakes can be eliminated from existence. This magical thinking manifests in status quo security strategies that are extremely brittle to human surprises (which is often correlated with brittleness to computer surprises too). A human clicking on a link in

---

19 Jane Jacobs, *The Death and Life of Great American Cities* (New York: Vintage Books, 1992).

an email, an activity they perform thousands of times in a year without incident, should perhaps be the least surprising event of all. A human procrastinating on patching a server because there are a dozen change approval steps required first is also not surprising. And yet both events are still frequently blamed as the fundamental cause of security incidents, as if the failure is in the human exhibiting very normal human behavior rather than a security strategy that explicitly chooses to be ignorant about normal human behavior.

Systems that maintain the greatest resilience to human surprises combine approaches, recognizing that there is no "one size fits all." One element is designing (and continuously refining) systems that fit the human, rather than forcing the human to fit the system through stringent policies. In this mindset, user experience is not a nice-to-have, but a fundamental trait of resilient design (which we'll explore in Chapter 7). Another element is pursuing a learning-led strategy, where mistakes are opportunities to gain new knowledge and inform improvements rather than opportunities to blame, scapegoat, or punish.

We cannot remove the human from our systems anytime soon, and therefore the human element is relevant to all parts of SCE—and to how we nourish resilience in our systems.

What Is Resilience?

Resilience is the ability for a system to adapt its functioning in response to changing conditions so it can continue operating successfully. Instead of attempting to prevent failure, resilience encourages us to handle failure with grace. More formally, the National Academy of Sciences defines resilience as "the ability to prepare and plan for, absorb, recover from, and more successfully adapt to adverse events."[20] In their journal article "Features of Resilience," the authors outline the five common features that define resilience:[21]

1. Critical functionality

2. Safety boundaries (thresholds)

3. Interactions across space-time

4. Feedback loops and learning culture

5. Flexibility and openness to change

---

20 Susan L. Cutter et al., "Disaster Resilience: A National Imperative," *Environment: Science and Policy for Sustainable Development* 55, no. 2 (2013): 25-29.

21 Elizabeth B. Connelly et al., "Features of Resilience," *Environment Systems and Decisions* 37, no. 1 (2017): 46-50.

All of these features—which we've correlated to the ingredients of our resilience potion below—are relevant to SCE and will reprise as a reinforcing motif throughout the book. Let's discuss each of them in more detail.

Resilience Potion Recipe

Reagents:

1. **Milk** for defining the critical functions of the system: pour 2 cups (16 oz) of your preferred milk to serve as your beverage's base (macadamia nut milk is recommended).

2. **Dried hibiscus** for defining the safe boundaries of the system: find a hibiscus flower and harvest 3 of its calyxes, the protective shell around the bud, and dry them.

3. **Cacao beans** for observing system interactions across space-time: ferment the beans for some time and grind into 2 tablespoons (32 ml) cocoa powder (or chop 3 oz of dark chocolate if more sweetness is desired).

4. **Chili peppers** for feedback loops and learning culture: grind this versatile, self-pollinating plant into 1/4 teaspoon (1–2 ml) of powder.

5. **Marshmallow** for flexibility and willingness to change: place 1 squishy marshmallow on top, toasted to your taste.

Combine the first four reagents in a cauldron (or saucepan) on medium-high heat. Mix together with a whisk until the potion is hot, but not boiling. Pour into a vial (or mug) of your choosing and place the marshmallow on top. Stir with a cinnamon stick and drink deep.

Critical Functionality

If you want to understand a system's resilience, you need to understand its critical functionality—especially how it performs these core operations while under stress from deleterious events. Simply put, you can't protect a system if you don't understand its defining purpose.

Defining the system's *raison d'être* is an essential requirement to articulate a system's resilience. The goal is to identify the resilience of what, to what, and for whom. Without this framing, our notion of the system's resilience will be abstract and our strategy aimless, making it difficult to prioritize actions that can help us better sustain resilience.

This foundational statement can be phrased as "the resilience of *<critical functionality>* against *<adverse scenario>* so that *<positive customer (or organization) outcome>*."

For a stock market API, the statement might read: "The resilience of providing performant stock quotes against DoS attacks for financial services customers who require real-time results." For a hospital, the statement might read: "The resilience of emergency room workstations against ransomware so healthcare workers can provide adequate care to patients." Defining what is critical functionality, and what is not, empowers you during a crisis, giving you the option to temporarily sacrifice noncritical functionality to keep critical functionality operational.

This illustrates why the status quo of security teams sitting in an ivory tower silo won't cut it for the resilience reality. To design, build, and operate systems that are more resilient to attack, you need people who understand the system's purposes and how it works. Any one person's definition of a system's critical functions will be different from another person's. Including stakeholders with subjective, but experience-informed, perceptions of the system becomes necessary. That is, "defenders" must include a blend of architects, builders, and operators to succeed in identifying a system's critical functions and understanding the system's resilience. The team that manages security may even look like a platform engineering team—made up of software engineers—as we'll explore in depth in Chapter 7.

Safety Boundaries (Thresholds)

Our second resilience potion ingredient is safety boundaries, the thresholds beyond which the system is no longer resilient to stress. We'll avoid diving too deep into the extensive literature[22] on thresholds[23] in the context of system resilience.[24] For SCE purposes, the key thing to remember about safety boundaries is that any system can absorb changes in conditions only up to a certain point and stay within its current, healthy state of existence (the one that underlies our assumptions of the system's behavior, what we call "mental models"). Beyond that point, the system moves into a different state of existence in which its structure and behavior diverge from our expectations and intentions.[25]

---

22 Jens Rasmussen, "Risk Management in a Dynamic Society: A Modelling Problem," *Safety Science* 27, nos. 2-3 (1997): 183-213.

23 K. J. Willis et al., "Biodiversity Baselines, Thresholds and Resilience: Testing Predictions and Assumptions Using Palaeoecological Data," *Trends in Ecology & Evolution* 25, no. 10 (2010): 583-591.

24 Didier L. Baho et al., "A Quantitative Framework for Assessing Ecological Resilience," *Ecology & Society* 22, no. 3 (2017): 17.

25 This is known as the "collapse" or "confusion" part of the adaptive cycle. Brian D. Fath et al., "Navigating the Adaptive Cycle: An Approach to Managing the Resilience of Social Systems," *Ecology & Society* 20, no. 2 (2015): 24.

A classic example of safety boundaries is found in the book *Jurassic Park*.[26] When the protagonists start their tour of the park, the system is in a stable state. The dinosaurs are within their designated territories and the first on-rail experience successfully returns the guests to the lodge. But changes in conditions are accumulating: the lead geneticist fills in gaps in velociraptors' DNA sequences with frog DNA, allowing them to change sex and reproduce; landscapers plant West Indian lilacs in the park, whose berries stegosauruses confuse for gizzard stones, poisoning them; a computer program for estimating the dinosaur population is designed to search for the expected count (238) rather than the real count (244) to make it operate faster; a disgruntled employee disables the phone lines and the park's security infrastructure to steal embryos, causing a power blackout that disables the electrical fences and tour vehicles; the disgruntled employee steals the emergency Jeep (with a rocket launcher in the back), making it infeasible for the game warden to rescue the protagonists now stranded in the park. These accumulated changes push the park-as-system past its threshold, moving it into a new state of existence that can be summarized as chaos of the lethal kind rather than the constructive kind that SCE embraces. Crucially, once that threshold is crossed, it's nearly impossible for the park to return to its prior state.

Luckily with computer systems, it's a bit easier to revert to expected behavior than it is to wrangle dinosaurs back into their designated pens. But only a bit. *Hysteresis*, the dependence of a system's state on its history,[27] is a common feature of complex systems and means there's rarely the ability to fully return to the prior state. From a resilience perspective, it's better to avoid passing these thresholds in the first place if we can. Doing so includes continual evolution of the system itself so its safety boundaries can be extended to absorb evolving conditions, which we'll explore later in our discussion of flexibility and openness to change.

If we want our systems to be resilient to attack, then we need to identify our system's safety boundaries before they're exceeded—a continuous process, as safety boundaries change as the system itself changes. Security chaos experiments can help us ascertain our system's sensitivity to certain conditions and thereby excavate its thresholds, both now and as they may evolve over time. With an understanding of those safety boundaries, we have a better chance of protecting the system from crossing over those thresholds and tipping into failure. As a system moves toward its limits of safe operation, recovery is still possible, but will be slower. Understanding thresholds can help us navigate the tricky goal of optimizing system performance (gotta go fast!) while preserving the ability to recover quickly.

---

26 The book delves surprisingly deep into nonlinear systems theory, while the movie only scratches the surface.

27 Arie Staal et al., "Hysteresis of Tropical Forests in the 21st Century," *Nature Communications* 11, no. 4978 (2020).

By conducting chaos experiments regularly—or, even better, continuously—experimental outcomes should reveal whether your systems (from a sociotechnical perspective) seem to be drifting toward thresholds that might make them less resilient in the face of a sudden impact. This drift could indicate the presence of chronic stressors, which are worth taking the time to dig into and uncover so you can nurse the systems (and the team) back to a healthier operational baseline. (We'll discuss chaos experimentation for assessing resilience in Chapter 2.)

Finally, remember that complex systems are nonlinear. What may seem like a minor change can be the proverbial final straw that pushes the system past its resilience threshold. As eloquently stated by ecological resilience scholars, "relatively small linear changes in stressors can cause relatively abrupt and nonlinear changes in ecosystems."[28] It is never just one factor that causes failure, but an accumulation that breaches the boundaries of the system's safe operation.

Interactions Across Space-Time

Because complex systems involve many components interacting with each other, their resilience can only be understood through system dynamics across space and time. As variables (not the programming kind) within your system interact, different behaviors will unfold over time and across the topology of the system. The temporal facets of resilience include the timing of an incident as well as the duration between the incident occurring and recovery of system functionality. The spatial facet is the extent of the incident's impact—the resulting state of the system across its components, functionality, and capability.

For instance, when considering the resilience of a consumer-facing application against a distributed denial-of-service (DDoS) attack, one or some or all services might be affected. The attack can happen during peak traffic hours, when your servers are already overwhelmed, or during sleep time for your target customers, when your servers are yawning with spare capacity. Recovery to acceptable performance standards might be milliseconds or hours. A long outage in one service can degrade performance in other services to which it's connected. And an outage across all services can lead to a longer recovery time for the system as a whole. As this example shows, time and space are inherently entwined, and you must consider both when assessing resilience.

---

28 Craig R. Allen et al., "Quantifying Spatial Resilience," *Journal of Applied Ecology* 53, no. 3 (2016): 625-635.

There's one caveat to the notion of "time" here (other than the fact that humanity still doesn't understand what it really is).[29] Time-to-recovery is an important metric (which we'll discuss in Chapter 5), but as we learned in our discussion of safety boundaries, it's equally important to consider that there might be preferable alternative states of operation. That is, continually recovering to the current equilibrium is not always desirable if that equilibrium depends on operating conditions that don't match reality. As in our example of dinosaurs gone wild in *Jurassic Park*, sometimes you simply can't return to the original equilibrium because reality has changed too much.

Feedback Loops and Learning Culture

Resilience depends on remembering failure and learning from it. We want to handle failure with ease and dignity rather than just prevent it from occurring; to do so, we must embrace failure as a teacher. Feedback loops, in which outputs from the system are used as inputs in future operations, are therefore essential for system resilience. When we observe an incident and remember the system's response to it, we can use it to inform changes that will make the system more resilient to those incidents in the future. This process of learning and changing in response to events is known as adaptation, which we introduced earlier in the chapter and will cover in more detail shortly. Unfortunately, we often hear the infosec folk wisdom of how quickly attackers adapt to defenses, but there isn't as much discussion about how to support more adaptation in our defenses (outside of hand-wavy ballyhoo about AI). SCE aims to change that.

The importance of operational memory for resilience is seen across other domains too. For instance, ecological memory, the ability of the past to influence an ecosystem's present or future responses,[30] involves both informational and material memory. Informational memory includes adaptive responses while material memory includes new structures, like seeds or nutrients, that result from a disturbance.[31]

Maintaining this memory is nontrivial, but diversity within a system helps. Socioecological systems that adapt through modular experimentation can more effectively reorganize after a disturbance.[32] When a system's network of variables is more diverse and the connections between them more modular, failure is less likely to reach *all*

---

29 Carlo Rovelli, "The Disappearance of Space and Time," in *Philosophy and Foundations of Physics: The Ontology of Spacetime*, 25-36 (Amsterdam and Oxford, UK: Elsevier, 2006).

30 Terry P. Hughes et al., "Ecological Memory Modifies the Cumulative Impact of Recurrent Climate Extremes," *Nature Climate Change* 9, no. 1 (2019): 40-43.

31 Jill F. Johnstone et al., "Changing Disturbance Regimes, Ecological Memory, and Forest Resilience," *Frontiers in Ecology and the Environment* 14, no. 7 (2016): 369-378.

32 Fath, "Navigating the Adaptive Cycle."

functions within a system. This ability to reorient in the face of failure means that fewer variables and connections between them are lost during a disturbance—preserving more memories of the event that can be used as inputs into feedback loops.

As an example, the urbanization of Constantinople was successful in part because the community learned from repeated sieges upon the city (on average every half-century).[33] These repeated incidents, write archaeology and urban sustainability scholars, "generated a diversity of socioecological memories—the means by which the knowledge, experience, and practice of how to manage a local ecosystem were stored and transmitted in a community." It wasn't just historians preserving these memories. Multiple societal groups maintained memories of the siege, leading to adaptations like decentralization of food production and transportation into smaller communities that were less likely to be disrupted by a siege—conceptually akin to a modular, service-oriented architecture that isolates disruption due to a resource spike in one component. Defensive walls were actually *moved* to make space for this new agricultural use as well as for gardens. These walls served as visual reminders of the lessons learned from the siege and protected those memories from dissolving over time.

As we will continue to stress throughout the book, our computer systems are sociotechnical in nature and therefore memory maintenance by communities is just as essential for systems resilience in our world as it was for Constantinople. No matter who is implementing the security program in your organization, they must ensure that insights learned from incidents are not only stored (and in a way that is accessible to the community), but also leveraged in new ways as conditions change over time. We're all too familiar with the phenomenon of a company being breached by attackers and suddenly investing a mountain of money and a flurry of energy into security. But, as memory of the incident fades, this enhanced security investment fades too. Reality doesn't take a break from changing, but not experiencing a shocking event for a while can reduce the need to prepare for them in the future.

A learning culture doesn't just happen after an incident. Feedback loops don't happen once, either. Monitoring for changes in critical functions and system conditions is complementary to preserving incident memories. Incidents—whether caused by attackers or security chaos experiments—can provide a form of sensory input that helps us understand causal relationships within our systems (similar to touching a hot stove and remembering that it leads to "ouch"). Monitoring, logging, and other forms of sensing help us understand, based on those causal relationships, whether our systems are nearing the boundaries of safe operation. While past behavior isn't an indicator of future behavior, the combination of learning from memories, collecting

---

33 John Ljungkvist et al., "The Urban Anthropocene: Lessons for Sustainability from the Environmental History of Constantinople," in *The Urban Mind: Cultural and Environmental Dynamics*, 367-390 (Uppsala, Sweden: Uppsala University Press, 2010).

data on system behavior, and conducting experiments that simulate failure scenarios can give us far more confidence that when the inevitable happens, we'll be prepared for it.

Flexibility and Openness to Change

Finally, maintaining flexibility across space-time is an essential part of resilience. This is often referred to as "adaptive capacity" in resilience engineering.[34] *Adaptive capacity* reflects how ready or poised a system is for change—its behaviors, models, plans, procedures, processes, practices—so it can continue to operate in a changing world featuring stressors, surprises, and other vagaries.[35] We must sustain this flexibility over time too, which can get tricky in the face of organizational social dynamics and trade-offs.[36]

As we mentioned with learning cultures and feedback loops (and will discuss more in Chapter 4), modularity can support resilience. Keeping the system flexible enough to adapt in response to changes in operating conditions is one element of this. The system must be able to stretch or extend beyond its safety boundaries over space and time. (Hopefully you're starting to see how all the ingredients in our resilience potion complement each other!) Another way to think about this, as David D. Woods pithily puts it (*https://oreil.ly/UOdVf*), we must "be prepared to be surprised."

As always, the human element is poignant here too. We, as stakeholders who wish to keep our systems safe, *also* need to be open to change within ourselves (not just in our machines). We might be wedded to the status quo or we may not want to change course because we've already invested so much time and money. Maybe something was our special idea that got us a promotion. Or maybe we're worried change might be hard. But this cognitive resistance will erode your system's ability to respond and adapt to incidents. A good decision a year ago might not be a good decision today; we need to be vigilant for when our assumptions no longer ring true based on how the world around us has changed.

There's never just one thing that will affect your systems; *many* things will continue to surprise or stress the system, constantly shifting its safety boundaries. Flexibility is the essential property that allows a system to absorb and adapt to those events while still maintaining its core purpose. We'll never cultivate complete knowledge about a

---

34 Nick Brooks et al., "Assessing and Enhancing Adaptive Capacity," in *Adaptation Policy Frameworks for Climate Change: Developing Strategies, Policies and Measures*, 165-181 (New York and Cambridge, UK: UNDP and Cambridge University Press, 2005).

35 Carl Folke et al., "Resilience and Sustainable Development: Building Adaptive Capacity in a World of Transformations," *AMBIO: A Journal of the Human Environment* 31, no. 5 (2002): 437-440.

36 Shana M. Sundstrom and Craig R. Allen, "The Adaptive Cycle: More Than a Metaphor." *Ecological Complexity* 39 (August): 100767.

system, no matter how much data we collect. Even if we could, reducing uncertainty to zero may help us understand the system's state right now, but there would still be plenty of ambiguity in how a particular change will impact the system or which type of policy or procedure would enhance the system's resilience to a particular type of attack. There are simply too many factors and interconnections (*https://oreil.ly/MQzgj*) at play.

Because we live in this indeterministic reality, we must preserve an openness to evolution and discard the rigidness that status quo security approaches recommend. Building upon the feedback loops and learning culture we discussed, we must continue learning about our systems and tracking results of our experiments or outcomes of incidents to refine our understanding of what a truly resilient security program looks like for our systems. This continual adaptation helps us better prepare for future disruptions and gives us the confidence that no matter what lies ahead, it is within our power to adjust our response strategies and ensure the system continues to successfully fulfill its critical function.

What Is Brittleness?

How do we describe a system that is *not* doing resilience? The answer is *brittleness*— the inability to adapt to surprises, to flounder in the face of new situations that challenge underlying assumptions and boundaries.[37] Brittleness represents the precipitous collapse of performance begotten by stressors, which push the system beyond its ability to manage disturbances and variations gracefully (i.e., beyond the system's boundaries of safe operation (*https://oreil.ly/SoKcw*)).

Brittleness can be best understood at a systems level. What we *don't* want in our complex, adaptive systems is brittleness. A brittle system is one that is on the knife's edge of operating as intended or falling over into failure. The degree of brittleness in a system is determined by how close it is to the boundaries of expected function or operation—and what surprises will push it beyond those boundaries into failure.

The concept of brittleness spans different domains that feature complex systems—like your own brain. If you only slept three hours last night, didn't eat breakfast, and there's construction happening right outside your window, you're probably going to be super brittle to stress. When a small disturbance crops up at work, you might not be able to respond to it adequately—even if you are usually able to respond gracefully to even *bigger* stressors when well-rested, fed, and in a quiet environment. The exhaustion, hunger, and sensory intrusion push your physiological system to (or beyond) the boundaries of its safe operation, causing performance degradations and failure in the face of stressful events.

---

37 Woods, "Engineering Organizational Resilience to Enhance Safety," 2237-2241.

Brittleness is pernicious because a system can seem reliable and yet simultaneously creep toward brittleness. But, by nourishing curiosity, we can support studying how the system in question behaves with brittleness. If humans are curious about how the systems under their purview are operating, but system feedback is inaccessible or opaque, this weak observability will undermine resilience and accelerate brittleness.[38] We can study the impact of brittleness by conducting experiments to excavate the boundaries of the system and observe how it behaves near those boundaries when surprises—*vis á vis* a chaos experiment—occur.

Because brittleness can sneak up on us, we must remember that maintaining resilience is an active process—that resilience is a verb.

Resilience Is a Verb

"Resilient" or "safe" or "secure" is an *emergent* property of systems, not a static one.[39] As a subset of resilience, security is something a system *does*, not something a system *has*. As such, security can only be revealed in the event stream of reality. Resilience not only represents the ability to recover from threats and stressors, but also the ability to perform as needed under a variety of conditions and respond appropriately to both disturbances as well as opportunities. Resilience is not solely about weathering tempests. It's also about innovation—spotting opportunities to evolve your practices to be even better prepared for the next storm. Resilience should be thought of as a proactive and perpetual cycle of system-wide monitoring, anticipating disruptions, learning from success and failure, and adapting the system over time.[40] While "resiliencing" would be the most appropriate term to use to capture the action-verb nature of resilience, we will use turns of phrase like "sustain resilience" or "maintain resilience" throughout the book for clarity.

Similarly, security is a value we should continually strive to uphold in our organizations rather than treat as a commodity, destination, or expected end state. We must think in terms of helping our systems exist resiliently and securely in the capricious wilds of production, rather than "adding security" to systems. This perspective helps us understand how failure unfolds across a system, which allows us to identify the points at which this failure might have been stopped or diverted. This ultimately helps inform which signals can help us identify failure earlier, continuing the cycle.

---

38 Nemeth, "Minding the Gaps."

39 J. Park et al., "Integrating Risk and Resilience Approaches to Catastrophe Management in Engineering Systems," *Risk Analysis* 33, no. 3 (2013): 356-366.

40 Connelly, "Features of Resilience," 46-50.

Viewing security as something a system *does* rather than *has* also positions you to anticipate conditions for failure that might emerge in the future. Human factors and systems safety researchers Richard Cook and Jens Rasmussen note in their journal article "Going Solid" that as a system continues to operate over time, it has "a tendency to move incrementally towards the boundaries of safe operations"[41]—those thresholds we discussed earlier. Productivity boosts due to technology rarely manifest in shorter work hours or a newfound capacity to improve security. Organizations will always want to perform their activities with less expense and greater speed, and this desire will manifest in its systems.

Continually evolving and adapting systems provides emergent job security for those responsible for resilience and security. If the security program can help the organization anticipate new types of hazards and opportunities for failure as the organization evolves its systems, then security becomes invaluable. This is often what cybersecurity writ large thinks it does, but in reality it tends to anchor the organization to the past rather than look ahead and carve a safe path forward. What other misperceptions slink within the common cybersecurity conversation? Next, we'll explore other myths related to resilience.

Resilience: Myth Versus Reality

Aristotle argued that to understand anything, we must understand what it is *not*.[42] This section will cover the myths and realities of resilience with the goal of helping you be more resilient to snake oil around the term.

Myth: Robustness = Resilience

A prevalent myth is that resilience is the ability of a system to withstand a shock, like an attack, and revert back to "normal." This ability is specifically known as *robustness* in resilience literature. We commonly see resilience reduced to robustness in the cybersecurity dialogue, especially in overzealous marketing (though cybersecurity is not the only domain felled by this mistake). The reality is that a resilient system isn't one that is robust; it's a system that can *anticipate* potential situations, *observe* ongoing situations, *respond* when a disturbance transpires, and *learn* from past experiences.[43]

---

41 Richard Cook and Jens Rasmussen, "Going Solid: A Model of System Dynamics and Consequences for Patient Safety," *BMJ Quality & Safety* 14, no. 2 (2005): 130-134.

42 Alan Lightman, *Probable Impossibilities: Musings on Beginnings and Endings* (New York: Pantheon Books, 2021).

43 Rankin, "Resilience in Everyday Operations," 78-97.

A focus on robustness leads to a "defensive" posture. Like the giant oak of Aesop's fable (*https://oreil.ly/LTwJA*), robustness tries to fight against the storm while the reeds—much like adaptive systems—humbly bend in the wind, designed with the assumption that adverse conditions *will* impact them. As a result, the status quo in cybersecurity aims for perfect prevention, defying reality by attempting to keep incidents from happening in the first place. This focus on preventing the inevitable distracts us from *preparing* for it.

Robustness also leads us to prioritize restoring a compromised system back to its prior version, despite it being vulnerable to the conditions that fostered compromise.[44] This delusion drives us toward technical or punitive controls rather than systemic or design mitigations, which in turn creates a false sense of security in a system that is still inherently vulnerable.[45] Extracting a lesson from the frenetic frontier of natural disasters, if a physical barrier to flooding is added to a residential area, more housing development is likely to occur there—resulting in a higher probability of catastrophic outcomes if the barrier fails.[46] To draw a parallel in cybersecurity, consider brittle internal applications left to languish with insecure design due to belief that a firewall or intrusion detection system (IDS) will block attackers from accessing and exploiting it.

The resilience approach realizes that change is the language of the universe. Without learning from experience, we can't adapt to reality. Resilience also recognizes that thriving is surviving. Robustness, the ability to withstand an adverse event like an attack, is not enough.

Myth: We Can and Should Prevent Failure

The traditional cybersecurity industry is focused on preventing failure from happening. The goal is to "thwart" threats, "stop" exploits, "block" attacks, and other aggressive verbiage to describe what ultimately is prevention of attackers performing any activity in your organization's technological ecosystem. While illuminating incident reviews (sometimes called "postmortems") on performance-related incidents are often made public (*https://oreil.ly/O6g5z*), security incidents are treated as shameful affairs that should only be discussed behind closed doors or among fee-gated

---

44 Adriana X. Sanchez et al., "Are Some Forms of Resilience More Sustainable Than Others?" *Procedia Engineering* 180 (2017): 881-889.

45 This is known as the "safe development paradox": the anticipated safety gained by introducing a technical solution to a problem instead facilitates risk accumulation over time, leading to larger potential damage in the event of an incident. See Raymond J. Burby, "Hurricane Katrina and the Paradoxes of Government Disaster Policy: Bringing About Wise Governmental Decisions for Hazardous Areas," *The ANNALS of the American Academy of Political and Social Science* 604, no. 1 (2006): 171-191.

46 Caroline Wenger, "The Oak or the Reed: How Resilience Theories Are Translated into Disaster Management Policies," *Ecology and Society* 22, no. 3 (2017): 18.

information-sharing groups. Failure is framed in moral terms of "the bad guys winning"—so it's no wonder the infosec industry discourse often feels so doom-and-gloom. The goal is to somehow prevent all problems all the time, which, ironically, sets the security program up for failure (not to mention smothers a learning culture).

Related to this obsession with prevention is the more recent passion for prediction. The FAIR methodology, a quantitative risk analysis model designed for cybersecurity, is common in traditional security programs and requires assumptions about likelihood of "loss event frequency" as well as "loss magnitude." The thinking goes that if you can predict the types of attacks you'll experience, how often they'll occur, and what the impact will be, you can determine the right amount to spend on security stuff and how it should be spent.

But accurate forecasting is impossible in complex systems; if you think security forecasting is hard, talk to a meteorologist. Our predilection for prediction may have helped *Homo sapiens* survive by solving linear problems, like how prey will navigate a forest, but it arguably hurts more than it helps in a modern world replete with a dizzying degree of interactivity. Since resilience is something a system does rather than has, it can't be quantified by probabilities of disruptive events. As seismologist Susan Elizabeth Hough quipped in the context of natural disasters, "A building doesn't care if an earthquake or shaking was predicted or not; it will withstand the shaking, or it won't."[47]

Attempting to prevent or predict failure in our complex computer systems is a costly activity because it distracts us and takes away resources from actually preparing for failure. Treating failure as a learning opportunity and preparing for it are more productive and pragmatic endeavors. Instead of spending so much time predicting what amount of resources to spend and where, you can conduct experiments and learn from experience to continually refine your security program based on tangible evidence. (And this approach requires spending much less time in Excel, which is a plus for most.)

The "bad guys"[48] will sometimes win. That's just a dissatisfying part of life, no matter where you look across humanity. But what we can control is how much we suffer as a result. Detecting failures in security controls early can mean the difference between an unexploited vulnerability and having to announce a data breach to your customers. Resilience and chaos engineering embrace the reality that models will be incomplete, controls will fail, mitigations will be disabled—in other words, things will fail

---

47 Susan Elizabeth Hough, *Predicting the Unpredictable*, reprint ed. (Princeton, NJ: Princeton University Press, 2016).

48 We will not use the term *bad guys* or *bad actors* throughout this book for a variety of reasons, including the infantile worldview it confesses. Nevertheless, you are likely to encounter it in typical infosec discourse as an attempt at invective against attackers broadly.

and continue failing as the world revolves and evolves. If we architect our systems to expect failure, proactively challenge our assumptions through experimentation, and incorporate what we learn as feedback into our strategy, we can more fully understand how our systems actually work and how to improve and best secure them.

Instead of seeking to stop failure from ever occurring, the goal in resilience and chaos engineering is to handle failure gracefully.[49] Early detection of failure minimizes incident impact and also reduces post-incident cleanup costs. Engineers have learned that detecting service failures early—like plethoric latency on a payment API—reduces the cost of a fix, and security failure is no different.

Thus we arrive at two core guiding principles of SCE:

1. Expect security controls to fail and prepare accordingly.
2. Do not attempt to completely avoid incidents, but instead embrace the ability to quickly and effectively respond to them.

Under the first principle, systems must be designed under this assumption that security controls will fail and that users will not immediately understand (or care about) the security implications of their actions.[50] Under the second principle, as described by ecological economics scholar Peter Timmerman, resilience can be thought of as the building of "buffering capacity" into a system to continually strengthen its ability to cope in the future.[51]

It is essential to accept that compromise and mistakes will happen, and to maintain a focus on ensuring our systems can gracefully handle adverse events. Security must move away from defensive postures to resilient postures, letting go of the impossible standard of perfect prevention.

Myth: The Security of Each Component Adds Up to Resilience

Because resilience is an emergent property at the systems level, it can't be measured by analyzing components. This is quite unfortunate since traditional cybersecurity is largely grounded in the component level, whether evaluating the security of components or protecting components. Tabulating vulnerabilities in individual components is seen as providing evidence of how secure the organization is against attacks. From

---

49 See Bill Hoffman's tenets of operations-friendly services, by way of James R. Hamilton, "On Designing and Deploying Internet-Scale Services," *LISA* 18 (November 2007): 1-18.

50 "End users" and "system admins" are continually featured as "top actors" involved in data breaches in the annual editions of the Verizon Data Breach Investigations Report (DBIR) (2020 Report) (*https://oreil.ly/MRuLD*).

51 Peter Timmerman, "Vulnerability, Resilience and the Collapse of Society," Environmental Monograph No. 1 (1981): 1-42.

a resilience engineering perspective, that notion is nonsense. If we connect a frontend receiving input to a database and verify each component is "secure" individually, we may miss the potential for SQL injection (*https://oreil.ly/qq6mT*) that arises from their interaction.

Mitigation and protection at the component level is partially due to this myth. Another belief, which practitioners are more reticent to acknowledge, is that addressing security issues one by one, component by component, is comparatively more convenient than working on the larger picture of systems security. Gravitating toward work that feels easier and justifying it with a more profound impetus (like this myth) is a natural human tendency. To wit, we see the same focus on process redesign and component-level safety engineering in healthcare too.[52] The dearth of knowledge and understanding about how complex systems work spans industries.

The good news is we don't really need precise measurement to assess resilience (as we'll detail in Chapter 2). Evaluating both brittleness and resilience comes from observing the system in both adverse and healthy scenarios. This is the beauty of SCE: by conducting specific experiments, you can test hypotheses about your system's resilience to different types of adverse conditions and observe how your systems respond to them. Like tiles in a mosaic, each experiment creates a richer picture of your system to help you understand it better. As we'll explore in Chapter 7, we can even approach security as a product, applying the scientific rigor and experimentation that helps us achieve better product outcomes.

Domains outside software don't have this luxury. We don't want to inject cyclones onto the Great Barrier Reef as an experiment to evaluate its resilience, nor would we want to inject adverse conditions into a national economy, a human body on the operating table, an urban water system, an airplane mid-flight, or really any other real, live system on which humans depend. Since (as far as we know) computers aren't sentient, and as long as we gain consent from human stakeholders in our computer systems, then this domain possesses a huge advantage relative to other domains in understanding systems resilience because we can conduct security chaos experiments.

Myth: Creating a "Security Culture" Fixes Human Error

The cybersecurity industry thinks and talks a lot about "security culture," but this term means different things depending on whom you ask. Infosec isn't alone in this focus; other domains, especially healthcare,[53] have paid a lot of attention to fostering a "safety culture." But at the bedrock of this focus on "culture"—no matter the industry—is its bellicose insistence that the humans intertwined with systems

---

52 Nemeth, "Minding the Gaps."

53 Cook, "Going Solid," 130-134.

must focus more on security (or "safety" in other domains). In cybersecurity, especially, this is an attempt to distribute the burden of security to the rest of the organization—including accountability for incidents. Hence, we see an obsession with preventing users from clicking on things, despite the need in their work to click on many things many times a day. One might characterize the cynosure of infosec "security culture" as preventing people from clicking things on the thing-clicking machine (*https://oreil.ly/hP6CI*)—the modern monomania of subduing the internet era's indomitable white whale.

Discussions about culture offer little impact without being grounded in the reality of the dynamic, complex systems in which humans operate. It is easy to suggest that all would be ameliorated if humans simply paid more attention to security concerns in the course of their work, but such recommendations are unlikely to stick. More fruitful is understanding *why* security concerns are overlooked—whether due to competing priorities, production pressures, attention pulled in multiple ways, confusing alert messages, and beyond. And then, which work do we mean? Paying attention to security means something quite different to a procurement professional, who is frequently interacting with external parties, than it does to a developer building APIs operating in production environments.

Any fruitful discussion in this vein is often stifled by poorly chosen health metrics and other "security vanity" metrics. They simply don't provide the full picture of organizational security, but rather lure practitioners into *thinking* they understand because quantification feels like real science—just as shamanism, humoralism, and astrology felt in prior eras. The percentage of users clicking on phishing links in your organization does not tell you whether your organization will experience a horrific incident if a user ends up clicking something they shouldn't. If the number of vulnerabilities you find goes up, is that good or bad? Perhaps the number of vulnerabilities found in applications matters less than whether these vulnerabilities are being found earlier in the software delivery lifecycle, if they are being remediated more quickly or, even better, if the production environment is architected so that their exploitation doesn't result in any material impact. Needless to say, a metric like the percent of "risk coverage" (the goal being 100% coverage of this phantasmal ectoplasm) is little more than filler to feed to executives and boards of directors who lack technical expertise.

The other distressing byproduct of traditional attempts to foster a "security culture" is the focus on punishing humans or treating them as enemies labeled "insider threats." Status quo security programs may buy tools with machine learning systems and natural language processing capabilities to figure out which employees sound sad or angry to detect "insider threats" early.[54] Or security teams may install spyware[55] on employee equipment to detect if they are looking for other jobs or exhibit other arbitrary symptoms of being upset with the organization. In the security status quo, we would rather treat humans like Schrödinger's attacker than dissect the organizational factors that could lead to this form of vulnerability in the first place. This may placate those in charge, but it represents our failure in fostering organizational security.

Cybersecurity isn't the only problem domain displaying this tendency. Yale sociologist Charles Perrow observed across complex systems that:

> Virtually every system we will examine places "operator error" high on its list of causal factors — generally about 60 to 80 percent of accidents are attributed to this factor. But if, as we shall see time and time again, the operator is confronted by unexpected and usually mysterious interactions among failures, saying that he or she should have zigged instead of zagged is possible only after the fact.[56]

Remarkably, the cybersecurity industry ascribes about the same proportion of failures to "human error" too. The precise contribution of purported "human error" in data breaches depends on which source you view: the 2022 Verizon Data Breach Investigations Report (*https://oreil.ly/kvkqi*) says that 82% of breaches "involved a human element," while another study from 2021 (*https://oreil.ly/Gu4D3*) reported human error as the cause of 88% of data breaches. Of the breaches reported to the Information Commissioner's Office (ICO) between 2017 and 2018, 90% cited human error as the cause (*https://oreil.ly/7Gg26*) too. But if you dig into what those human errors were, they often represent actions that are entirely benign in other contexts, like clicking links, pushing code, updating configurations, sharing data, or entering credentials into login pages.

SCE emphasizes the importance of outside perspectives. We should consider our adversaries' perspectives (as we'll discuss in Chapter 2) and conduct user research (as we'll discuss in Chapter 7), developing an understanding of the perspectives of those who are building, maintaining, and using systems so that the security program is not based on a fantasy. Adopting a systems perspective is the first step in better coping

---

54 There are a few examples of this sort of sentiment analysis to detect "insider threats," one of which is: *https://oreil.ly/qTA76*. See CMU's blog post (*https://oreil.ly/-4EKR*) for the challenges associated with it in practice.

55 Usually vendors won't say "keylogging" explicitly, but will use euphemisms like "keystroke dynamics," "keystroke logging," or "user behavior analytics." As CISA explains in their Insider Threat Mitigation Guide (*https://oreil.ly/rT0Gz*) about User Activity Monitoring (UAM), "In general, UAM software monitors the full range of a user's cyber behavior. It can log keystrokes, capture screenshots, make video recordings of sessions, inspect network packets, monitor kernels, track web browsing and searching, record the uploading and downloading of files, and monitor system logs for a comprehensive picture of activity across the network." See also the presentation "Exploring keystroke dynamics for insider threat detection" (*https://oreil.ly/pAyPr*).

56 Charles Perrow, *Normal Accidents: Living with High-Risk Technologies, Revised Edition* (Princeton, NJ: Princeton University Press, 1999).

with security failure, as it allows you to see how a combination of chronic stressors and acute stressors leads to failure.

With SCE, the security program can provide immense value to its organization by narrowing the gap between work-as-imagined and work-as-performed.[57] Systems will encroach upon their safety thresholds when policies and procedures are designed based on ideal operational behaviors (by humans and machines alike). Expecting humans to perform multiple steps sequentially without any reminders or visual aids is a recipe for mistakes and omissions.

Security programs in SCE are also *curious* about workarounds rather than forbidding them. Workarounds can actually support resilience. Humans can be quite adept at responding to competing pressures and goals, creating workarounds that allow the system to sustain performance of its critical functions. When the workarounds are eliminated, it's harder for humans interacting with the system to use a variety of strategies in response to the variety of behaviors they may encounter during their work. And that erodes resilience. Unlike traditional infosec wisdom, SCE sees work-arounds for what they are: adaptations in response to evolving conditions that are natural in complex systems.[58] Workarounds are worth understanding in devising the right procedures for humans to operate flexibly and safely.

Chapter Takeaways

- All of our software systems are complex. Complex systems are filled with variety, are adaptive, and are holistic in nature.

- Failure is when systems—or components within systems—do not operate as intended. In complex systems, failure is inevitable and happening all the time. What matters is how we prepare for it.

- Failure is never the result of one factor; there are multiple influencing factors working in concert. Acute and chronic stressors are factors, as are computer and human surprises.

- Resilience is the ability for a system to gracefully adapt its functioning in response to changing conditions so it can continue thriving.

- Resilience is the foundation of security chaos engineering. Security Chaos Engineering (SCE) is a set of principles and practices that help you design, build, and operate complex systems that are more resilient to attack.

---

57 Manikam Pillay and Gaël Morel, "Measuring Resilience Engineering: An Integrative Review and Framework for Bench-marking Organisational Safety," *Safety* 6, no. 3 (2020): 37.

58 Rankin, "Resilience in Everyday Operations," 78-97.

- The five ingredients of the "resilience potion" include understanding a system's critical functionality; understanding its safety boundaries; observing interactions between its components across space and time; fostering feedback loops and a learning culture; and maintaining flexibility and openness to change.

- Resilience is a verb. Security, as a subset of resilience, is something a system *does*, not something a system *has*.

- SCE recognizes that a resilient system is one that performs as needed under a variety of conditions and can respond appropriately both to disturbances—like threats—as well as opportunities. Security programs are meant to help the organization anticipate new types of hazards as well as opportunities to innovate to be even better prepared for the next incident.

- There are many myths about resilience, four of which we covered: resilience is conflated with robustness, the ability the "bounce back" to normal after an attack; the belief that we can and should prevent failure (which is impossible); the myth that the security of each component adds up to the security of the whole system; and that creating a "security culture" fixes the "human error" problem.

- SCE embraces the idea that failure is inevitable and uses it as a learning opportunity. Rather than preventing failure, we must prioritize handling failure gracefully—which better aligns with organizational goals too.

CHAPTER 2

Systems-Oriented Security

Understanding is relating; it is fitting things into a context. Nothing can be understood on its own.

—Mary Midgley, *Beast and Man*

In our sociotechnical transformation toward resilience, we must become systems thinkers. We must no longer perceive components as stationary, solitary objects. Within the susurrations of shadows on the wall (*https://oreil.ly/T4i3k*), we can sense their sophisticated symphony—that they coordinate in concert toward a more momentous aspiration, grand in scale. In our day-to-day lives as computer people, we must nurture more holistic views of the technologies we build, operate, and manage if we wish to prepare them for adversity. Like spectators escaping Plato's cave, we must work together—dismantling divisions between teams and services—to probe beyond the shadows and reveal the exquisite complexity of our system's reality.

In this chapter, we will deepen our exploration of security in the resilience era to set the foundation for applying it in practice across the delivery lifecycle. We'll begin with a discussion of our mental models, our omnipresent assumptions about how our systems behave; like shadows in the cave, they can lead us astray and weaken our security outcomes. How can we free ourselves from phantasms and align our mental models with reality? The answer is through resilience stress testing, a pragmatic implementation of our resilience potion recipe. We'll introduce a two-tier approach to resilience assessment—the Evaluate and Experiment (E&E) Approach—that can help us cultivate a systems perspective for security. It's the perfect place to start for security teams seeking to modernize their practices, or platform or software engineering teams wanting pragmatic ways to improve their system's security.

With an understanding of how to assess our system's resilience and excavate its complexity, we gain stable footing on the concept of SCE from which we can pirouette through principles and practices in the rest of the book. To close the chapter, we'll review the unsatisfactory state of security for systems thinking before digging into the differences between SCE and "security theater"—the strategy of the security status quo that stimulates outrage more than outcomes. The end goal is for security, software, and platform teams to grasp how a fortuitous future might look after the SCE transformation.

Mental Models of System Behavior

No matter what stage of a system's lifecycle we are interacting with, we compose a mental model of the system—our assumptions about how the system behaves. *Mental models* are "cognitive representations of external reality."[1] This means we hold, in our brains, a smaller-scale model of how we think a system works. It includes all the assumptions we make about the *why, how,* and *when* behind a system and its components. Naturally, these representations of reality are incomplete and inconsistent; mental models are dynamic, changing as a situation changes, making them dependent on context.

Understanding your system's context is no small feat. It's especially difficult to understand a system that is the result of years of iteration, its tendrils fractalizing and unfurling beyond the bounded expanse of our conception. Your systems will grow. Your teams will look different. Your organization's priorities will shift. To keep up with these changes and adapt to them, a security program must be curious. Curiosity is the antidote to our mental models moldering.

If our systems-oriented security program is curious, we prioritize the right question over a definitive answer. We understand that answers may be ambiguous; we must remain open to change as new evidence emerges—the final ingredient of our resilience potion. Members of a curious security program are eager to *learn* and recognize the fact that knowledge today might be stale tomorrow. As seen in the wild, "animals who experience surprises as pleasure are likely to recognize camouflage and leave more offspring than their less perspicacious brethren."[2] Even the secondary dictionary definition of *curious*—strange, unusual—works here, as a curious security program knows that real-world systems are weird and that unexpected escapades are natural threads woven into the fabric of reality.

---

1 Natalie A. Jones et al., "Mental Models: An Interdisciplinary Synthesis of Theory and Methods," *Ecology and Society* 16, no. 1 (2011).

2 Lynn Margulis and Dorion Sagan, *What Is Life?* (Berkeley and Los Angeles, CA: University of California Press, 2000).

Throughout the book, we use the language of security *programs* rather than security *teams* since a dedicated security team is not required to implement a security program. In fact, we'll describe in Chapter 7 how a Platform Resilience Engineering team might be the most suitable group to implement a security program. Every company—even every human interacting with computers—has a security strategy, even if that strategy is "do nothing about it."

If you can't discern the flows within your system, or the interconnections between things in your system (or between things in your system and other systems), then you sink into quagmire and quandary when attempting to make the system resilient to attacks that take advantage of those flows and interconnections. How can you protect something that you don't understand? You can't (although the traditional cybersecurity industry is content to tilt at these windmills). Attackers will spend the time navigating your system to uncover those complex interactions, generating strategically valuable information asymmetry—one that puts you at a nontrivial disadvantage.

When we say we need to understand the *why* and the *when* of a system to have clear mental models, we don't mean the entire system. Doing so will be absurd unless you constrain your system's growth. It's impossible to completely understand every single flow, interconnection, and interaction in a complex system, especially distributed systems at scale (otherwise we could "just" use formal methods and call it a day). What we need is to keep the parts of the system under our purview simple enough for us to fit it all in our head. Few, if any, NASA engineers have a thorough mental model of a rocket; instead, they have deep knowledge of the components they work on and share that knowledge so operators and managers *can* reason about the rocket as a whole. If you're throwing your hands up and moaning about how the component(s) you work on is too complex, it's a call to action to redesign your part of the system—either break it apart or make it more linear (we'll discuss this more when we turn to coupling and complexity in Chapter 3). Redesign isn't defeat, it's curiosity in action. At the system level, the goal is—by combining knowledge—to be able to mentally model different facets of the system. A single individual can never hope to fully mentally model a complex system; a desire to do so is hubris.

The hard part about computer systems is not that machines are unpredictable. The hard part is that machines are *very* predictable, and their range of behaviors must be anticipated beforehand. If you miss any of the possible behaviors, your software will fail to meet your intentions. People, including technical software people, see weirdness in software and think, "That's just the machine being weird." This is the wrong conclusion. The observed weirdness indicates an incomplete mental model, that someone failed to completely model the problem and come up with a solution for it. Humans have incomplete mental models about everything, but they can adapt when something is unexpected. Computers cannot.

This fate is avoidable. We can learn valuable lessons from how adversaries attack our assumptions and harness the same thinking to improve our mental models, to which we'll now turn.

How Attackers Exploit Our Mental Models

The underlying principle behind attacks is: Attackers search for your hidden assumptions of "this will always be true" and then ask, "you say this will always be true; is that the case?" to break them. Attackers approach this process with a curious mindset, maintaining an open mind that the defenders' assumptions might be right or wrong, but also giving those assumptions a second look just in case. These assumptions can manifest in every part of your stack at every level. "Parsing this string will always be fast." "Messages that show up on this port will always be post-authentication." "An alert will always fire if a malicious DLL appears." And so on.

Attackers will take each assumption in your mental models as an axiom and think about it critically on independent merits, neither accepting it without criticism nor maintaining a myopic focus on breaking it. The attacker thinks, "They say this thing here, but I can show that it isn't quite true. That's interesting. Let's keep looking there and see if they're just a little wrong or really wrong."[3] Attackers will do this broadly and proceed with the first of your assumptions that "gives" a bit (because faster "time to market" applies to attackers too).

A frequent misconception—one that needlessly aggrandizes attackers—is that attackers will find something you think is true and make it false. For instance, the legend goes, an attacker will think, "Well, I can't find a call to this function with this parameter set to null anywhere. *But what if* I could Rowhammer (*https://oreil.ly/SX7nH*) to make that call happen???" Realistically, the attacker will try anything else first (we'll discuss what makes bugs scalable for attackers in the next chapter). Attackers in our world are not like Neo from *The Matrix*, capable of forcing the rules of reality to be rewritten on demand. Attackers are more like lawyers, searching for loopholes and alternative interpretations in our mental models that they can brandish in their favor.

---

3 As an attacker, this is a tricky game to play because you must maintain objectivity. The attacker can tie themselves in knots with the seductive thought of "maybe I can break this property of physics." An attacker could therefore hyperfixate and descend into a rabbit hole, thinking, "Oh no, *really bad* things happen if this parameter is null, so I have to make it happen. Maybe we could use Spectre to make it happen."

Refining Our Mental Models

The "cat and mouse" game of cybersecurity is better characterized as a "Spy vs. Spy" game (*https://oreil.ly/f5OBC*), where each side can inflict harm on each other's mental models through booby traps and other bamboozles. We must prowl our own assumptions for loopholes and alternative interpretations rather than waiting for attackers to take advantage of them. These insights galvanize an advantage whereby we proactively refine our design and architecture before attackers can exploit the difference between our mental models and reality. As is evident, the attacker mindset is ultimately one defined by curiosity. How can we foster such curiosity, nudging ourselves and our teams to challenge assumptions and enrich them with evidence? The answer is experimentation—curiosity in action. When we conduct experiments, we can generate evidence that unmasks blemishes in your mental model of the system, but without the stress and fear that arise when attackers succeed in compromising your systems.

The importance of experimentation is related to Woods' Theorem. In 1988, one of the founders of resilience engineering, David D. Woods, wrote (*https://oreil.ly/VqCJ1*) that as system complexity increases, the accuracy of any single agent's mental model of that system rapidly decreases. Experiments help that single agent gain a more accurate mental model, even in the face of complexity. There is no inherent evil in complexity, but it does make it harder to maintain appropriate mental models of the system, requiring more of our effort. When complex interactions conspire with tight coupling, it is nearly impossible to maintain proper mental models—and catastrophe brews (as we will discuss in the next chapter).

We must discern between how our systems look in reality—the systems that attackers encounter—and our current beliefs about our systems. To unveil the interconnections coiling and roiling throughout our systems, we must conduct experiments. Resilience stress testing can reveal the outcomes of failures in our systems and bestow a blessing in our tussle of "Spy vs. Spy."

Resilience Stress Testing

Our resilience potion isn't complete until we maintain a feedback loop—ensuring that our understanding of the system's critical functions, safety boundaries, and interactions across space-time leads to learning and change. We must adapt to stressors and surprises. But how can we identify whether our system exhibits cascading failures in adverse conditions? How do we know which mitigation and recovery strategies are best? Resilience stress testing gives us a conceptual framework and methodology to discern system behavior under stressors and surprises so we can prioritize actions that will improve resilience.

Resilience stress testing helps us identify the confluence of conditions—described as an *adverse scenario*—where system failure is possible. Resilience stress testing bears a rich precedent across other complex systems domains like financial services (*https://oreil.ly/chH-U*),[4] air transportation,[5] urban planning,[6] healthcare,[7] water management,[8] and more. Rather than varying stress loads on individual components to discern the conditions where failure is possible, resilience stress testing seeks to understand how disruptions impact the *entire* system's ability to recover and adapt.[9] It appreciates the inherent *interactivity* in the system across space-time, conducting system-level adverse scenarios rather than evaluating parts of the system. In the messy reality of complex systems, there is simply not enough time or energy available to stress-test every single component in a system to identify weaknesses (just as we cannot hope to mentally model every single component in our heads). Whether you call it resilience stress testing or chaos experimentation, the point is: We can move fast and observe how failure unfolds in our systems *purposefully* through experiments, allowing us to learn from them, fix flaws, and ameliorate system design.

---

4 Hamed Amini et al., "Stress Testing the Resilience of Financial Networks," *International Journal of Theoretical and Applied Finance* 15, no. 1 (2012): 1250006.

5 Suhyung Yoo and Hwasoo Yeo, "Evaluation of the Resilience of Air Transportation Network with Adaptive Capacity," *International Journal of Urban Sciences* 20, no. 1 (2016): 38-49.

6 Franz van de Ven et al., "Guideline for Stress Testing the Climate Resilience of Urban Areas" (*https://oreil.ly/DMBoL*), (2014); Nazli Yonca Aydin et al.,"Integration of Stress Testing with Graph Theory to Assess the Resilience of Urban Road Networks Under Seismic Hazards," *Natural Hazards* 91 (2018): 37-68.

7 Donald Ruggiero Lo Sardo et al., "Quantification of the Resilience of Primary Care Networks by Stress Testing the Health Care System," *Proceedings of the National Academy of Sciences* 116, no. 48 (2019): 23930-23935; A. S. Jovanović et al., "Assessing Resilience of Healthcare Infrastructure Exposed to COVID-19: Emerging Risks, Resilience Indicators, Interdependencies and International Standards," *Environment Systems and Decisions* 40 (2020): 252-286.

8 Dionysios Nikolopoulos et al., "Stress-testing Framework for Urban Water Systems: A Source to Tap Approach for Stochastic Resilience Assessment," *Water* 14, no. 2 (2022): 154; Christos Makropoulos et al., "A Resilience Assessment Method for Urban Water Systems," *Urban Water Journal* 15, no. 4 (2018): 316-328.

9 Igor Linkov et al., "Resilience Stress Testing for Critical Infrastructure," *International Journal of Disaster Risk Reduction* 82 (2022): 103323.

The software industry is privileged over nearly every other industry when it comes to resilience stress testing. We can, if we so choose, conduct resilience stress tests directly in our real, live production systems. Doing so would be preposterously unethical in other domains, as we discussed in Chapter 1. Even our recovery capacity is enviable; only in urban planners' dreams could they possess the capability to spin up more sewer drains or transmission pipes on demand during a torrential rainstorm.

We must remember that we live in an era of abundance in software and that we are inestimably lucky that, for most of our systems, failure isn't *really* fatal. No one will die or be displaced by a UDP flood like they will in a hurricane flood. It may *feel* like a disaster to us, but we're largely fortunate. We should not waste this privilege— so let's harness experimentation to learn and adapt the way other domains wish they could.

In software systems, resilience stress testing is called "chaos experimentation," but feel free to call chaos experiments "resilience stress tests," if it appeases your executives. *Chaos experiments* simulate adverse conditions to generate evidence of system behavior—especially when this behavior isn't as we intend or desire. This evidence helps us build confidence in the system and iteratively refine it, making chaos experiments an invaluable tool for each stage of the software delivery lifecycle (as we'll explore throughout the rest of this book).

When we use resilience stress testing to identify the adverse attack scenarios where system failure is possible, we call it security chaos experimentation (throughout the book, we'll refer to them as "security chaos experiments" or "chaos experiments," depending on the context). With that said, much of the book will describe how to sustain resilience against all kinds of adverse scenarios, as the conditions present in an attack often overlap with other incidents not incited by attackers.

"Security chaos experiments" refers to any "chaos experiment" that is assessing how the system behaves in response to attack-related conditions specifically. "Chaos experiment" can cover those conditions as well as other adverse conditions.

The status quo in many domains, not just cybersecurity, is to perform *risk-based stress testing*. A load test, for example, is a form of risk-based stress testing, as it varies stress loads on components to understand when they fail—like sending a large volume of queries to a database to see at what point latency spikes. In cybersecurity, there are tests that will attempt to exploit a vulnerability to see whether a component is vulnerable. (Scanning for a vulnerability is a risk-based test, but not really a stress test.)

Risk-based stress testing fails us in complex systems because it focuses on the component level rather than the system level. It's like testing to reveal if a single violin is out of tune rather than to discover if the whole orchestra sounds in tune; even if you test each instrument individually, it is only when observing them *in concert* that you can understand the orchestra's sound quality. As we emphasized in Chapter 1, complex systems possess variegated interactions and it is this interconnected nature that instigates the failures that vex us.

For any software or computer system of sufficient scale, risk-based stress testing will offer convenience more than knowledge. Resilience stress testing, in contrast, can scale as a system grows to continue generating knowledge of the system's behavior—whether it recovers gracefully or fails—when immersed in crises. In Table 2-1, we've summarized how resilience stress tests (i.e., chaos experiments) differ from risk-based tests (whether stress tests or otherwise).

Table 2-1. Chaos experiments versus typical tests

Chaos experiments	Typical tests
Support resilience	Support robustness
*Socio*technical (includes humans as part of the system)	Technical (excludes humans as part of the system)
System-focused	Component-focused
Capable of being run in production	Must run in a development or staging environment
Random or pseudorandom	Scripted
Adverse scenarios	Boolean requirements
Observe and learn from failures	Detect and prevent failures
N-order effects	Direct effects

If you've ever strolled a cybersecurity conference, you know the industry is obsessed with "threats." Risk-based stress testing is obsessed with specific threats too, which limits our ability to scale such approaches and keeps us moored to the past. It leads us to think about incidents in terms of a vulnerability as the cause and a "threat actor" leveraging it—compressing our viewing frustum and frustrating our ability to understand *all* the causal factors present in an incident (without which we cannot inform meaningful change).

The "stress" in resilience stress testing can be either the acute or chronic stressors we discussed in Chapter 1. Really, this assessment approach is "threat-agnostic." We are far more curious about assessing the interconnections and nature of the system—how it behaves in adverse conditions—than we are about how it responds to a specific exploit or malicious change. With resilience stress testing, we want to understand how systems under adverse conditions, like degraded or disrupted functionality, recover and adapt. Adverse conditions can take many guises, and conducting experiments for them will enrich our mental model of our systems. Which experimental scenarios we conduct depends on what resources are at our disposal.

Through chaos experiments, we seek to understand the first three ingredients in our resilience potion—the purpose of the system and its structure, its interconnections and interactions, and where its thresholds lie (beyond which it can tip into failure).

This is the basis of the E&E Approach—evaluation and experimentation—to resilience assessment. You can think of this as a standardized two-tier approach that can help you assess a system's resilience under adverse conditions like stressors and surprises. The first tier is evaluation: a screening assessment describing the system's purpose, the interactions and flows between its components, and its failure thresholds (mapping to the first three ingredients of our resilience potion). The second tier is experimentation: a scenario-based simulation that reveals *how* the sociotechnical system fails when exposed to adverse conditions—including how it recovers, learns, and adapts to continue delivering its critical functionality (mapping to the fourth and fifth ingredients of our resilience potion). The next sections will explore the E&E Approach in depth.

The E&E Resilience Assessment Approach

The most basic resilience metric, adapted from Makropoulos et al.,[10] is the degree to which a system continues to perform its critical functions under disturbance. To assess this, we need both tiers—first evaluating our system to set the foundation for experimenting on it. Crucially, we want to model interconnections and interdependencies. We must understand how failures cascade in the system and what behaviors emerge in different adverse scenarios. Even if you do nothing we describe in later chapters, the E&E Approach can still help you ignite the resilience flywheel in your organization.

A two-tiered approach to resilience assessment helps us incrementally adopt a resilience-based approach to our systems. The goal behind the tiered approach is to establish a transparent, repeatable, and evidence-informed process for resilience assessment. Tier 1 is a readiness phase with no experimentation required—a perfect fit for cautious organizations that want to begin their resilience transformation, but that need a bit more confidence before conducting experiments. Tier 2 builds upon tier 1 by performing chaos experiments.

Evaluation: Tier 1 Assessment

The first tier of our assessment is evaluation. Our goals are to characterize the system's critical functions and interactions across space-time (the flows in the system), as well as forge some idea of the system's safety boundaries. It's a kind of screening

---

10 Makropoulos, "A Resilience Assessment Method for Urban Water Systems," 316-328.

assessment about the system's critical functions and its behavior in response to adverse conditions. These goals align with the first three ingredients of our resilience potion from Chapter 1: critical functions, safety boundaries (thresholds), and interactions across space-time. The last two ingredients—learning and flexibility—represent what you do with this understanding, which aligns with experimentation in tier 2.

We can think of the evaluation tier of the E&E assessment as a readiness phase—building confidence in our mental models and preparing us for resilience stress testing in tier 2—that still rewards us. As part of tier 1, we map the system's critical functionality and interdependencies, allowing us to layer a resilience view over our architecture diagrams. Our requirements and resulting artifacts of tier 1 are thus: a diagram of system flows, documentation of critical functions, and a diagram of failure behaviors.

What are the recommended steps for the evaluation assessment? Let's explore each.

Mapping Flows to Critical Functionality

The most useful place to start in tier 1 is mapping your system's data flow diagrams—interactions across space-time—to its critical functionality, or its reason or purpose for existing. Creating this mapping is important because architecture diagrams can't just be static; they need a layer showing *interactions*—how things flow through components in the system. We need to capture not just what happens, but when.

Many, if not most, humans are focused on their team and its function, so much so that they don't pay much attention to the critical functions of the whole system. They don't understand how the component(s) their team is responsible for helps fulfill the system's critical function (or if it even does). Tier 1 can counter this, which is especially important as systems scale. During tier 1 assessment, we should brainstorm and document our answers to questions like:

- Why is the system important?
- What parts of the system are critical?
- Is it better for our system to be down and safe, or up and compromised?
- What is the impact if the system doesn't perform as expected?
- Where can a human step in if the system malfunctions?
- Which components grant access to other parts of the system?
- Do engineering teams understand the security properties of their software?
- Do we know who would need to be notified for each part of the system that could fail?
- Can we recover the system if it fails, or is it compromised while key people are unavailable?

Mapping the system's critical functionality is crucial for assessing its resilience. For instance, consider a service dashboard with a traffic light system: green indicating healthy, yellow for disrupted, red for down (i.e., not functioning). Even if many things on the dashboard are yellow (disrupted), we want to ensure that the critical functionality is not disrupted. This is precisely what transpires at cloud service providers, who operate at massive scale; things are breaking all the time, but the core functionality they provide is seldom disrupted.

 In the commercial space, Netflix invests notable effort in understanding their topology and flows throughout it (*https://oreil.ly/ guPl1*). Trace IDs are likely the easiest way to start mapping data flows. If you don't have modern tracing tools set up, you can do this manually too—tracing is just an automated trick for it.

Document Assumptions About Safety Boundaries

Once we have mapped flows to critical functionality, we want to document our assumptions about the system's safety boundaries (thresholds). What are the conditions beyond which the system tips into failure? If we can identify our assumptions around the answer to this question, we'll reach our goal in this tier 1 evaluation phase.

Many organizations do a variation of this exercise naturally, like adding an "availability layer"—this is something good software architects will do when their system's success depends on availability. Scaling plays a role here as well. If you're expecting bursts, how much excess capacity do you need to sustain events simultaneously? Today, though, software engineers assess this mostly with back-of-the-napkin gut feelings rather than something structured, like we're proposing.

We can also think ahead as a way to describe our assumptions about our system's resilience. What would happen to our systems if we were to make X change? What properties of the system, if excised, would result in a system that is no longer resilient to attack? For example, changing the contents of a cloud storage bucket from JPEG to PNG would not change its resilience to attack. Adding or removing data stored within the bucket would also not change its resilience to attack. But subtracting the authenticated access requirement for a cloud storage bucket would certainly result in a system state that is not resilient to attack.

We can capture these assumptions about system interactions and behaviors via decision trees, creating a tangible artifact that can support success during experimentation in tier 2. The fabulous thing about decision trees is that they're a convenient and inexpensive place to start because they allow you to run an experiment for "free" in your head—or *heads*, since we highly recommend developing decision trees collaboratively. Carpentering a decision tree allows you to consider whether the system may fail or succeed in a given scenario.

You don't need to run an experiment if you know something is broken; that'd be a waste of time. For example, if the ap-southeast-1a zone (an availability zone in AWS's Singapore region) goes down, you don't need to run an experiment to know your application will be down if it's only hosted in ap-southeast-1a. The actions you could take include hot failover, georouting, multiprimary, edge compute—all of which could make your system more resilient to a number of scenarios. Once you implement one of those actions, you could move on to the tier 2 experimentation assessment.

How do we create decision trees and why are they so vital for security programs that seek to assess resilience—or for anyone wanting to undergo a transformation to SCE? This brings us to a discussion of what decision trees are, a walkthrough of creating one, and their value when applied in practice.

Making Attacker Math Work for You

We need our mental models to match reality as much as they can if we are to design, develop, and operate systems that sustain resilience to attack. How can we start describing our mental models in tier 1 so we can challenge the assumptions within? We start with making attacker math work for us. Thinking through how attackers make choices during their operations is essential for refining our mental models at all stages of the software delivery lifecycle. Pondering them during the tier 1 assessment —or, even better, on a continuous basis when designing and redesigning systems— sets our systems up for success when they are released into the real world.

Articulating our mental models of the system's resilience to attack, framed through the lens of how we think attackers will behave, can expose gaps in our mental models before we even conduct experiments. Understanding the attacker's decision-making process can save us from excess engineering efforts to stop a niche threat and instead focus our efforts on plucking off the low-hanging fruit in our systems that attackers will try to compromise first. As Chief Information Security Officer Phil Venables said (*https://oreil.ly/Nhayc*), "Attackers have bosses and budgets too." Just like any other project, an attack operation is expected to generate a positive return on investment (ROI). This attacker ROI is colloquially referred to as "attacker math." Understanding the attacker math related to your software, services, and systems—and visualizing it as a decision tree—is invaluable in helping you rank which security strategies, mitigations, and practices to implement.

In the context of our E&E resilience assessment, decision trees provide a blueprint for the experiments you should conduct during tier 2. By thinking through the highest ROI options of an attacker, you're discovering which actions they are most likely to take—and thus illuminating what types of adverse conditions you should simulate in your systems to verify their resilience. We will discuss this more later in this chapter (and we'll dig into how to conduct an end-to-end experiment in Chapter 8).

A Crash Course on Attack Terminology

In cybersecurity, there is a lot of terminology from the military sphere, but most organizations are not going to war, they're trying to keep services running or pass their compliance audit. Throughout this book, we've aimed for accessible language to describe attack operations and other security concepts. With that said, there are a few concepts you might want to know as you aspire to maintain resilience to attack in your systems.

Action on target
> Action on target is the *why* behind an attacker gaining access to a system. They usually don't access a system for fun. Around 95% of attackers seem to compromise a system for profit (*https://oreil.ly/kvkqi*)—that is, for financial benefit—while the remaining 5% gain access to a system for other purposes, primarily espionage (hacktivism and fun are negligible at the time of this writing). Financial benefit can take a few forms. *Data exfiltration*, in which attackers retrieve data from the target system, can be remunerative when whatever data that was hoovered out of the system can be sold for profit (such as national identification numbers on dark net markets). Extortion is another way to monetize access to a system; the attacker can hold system availability or data "hostage" through a variety of means and demand payment to relinquish control.

Initial access
> Initial access is what we often call "compromise," when an attacker gains access to a particular resource. This is the attack stage featured the most in media and at industry conferences because it's when an attacker will exploit a vulnerability in a resource to gain access to it. Unfortunately, coverage of this phase is overweight. We should think about initial access as the *start* of the attack, not the end. We'll talk more about security bugs in the next chapter, especially how not all exploits are equal; some system vulnerabilities are extremely difficult to exploit or require considerable "continuation of execution" effort (i.e., surviving a busted or unstable process you've compromised). Social engineering is a prevalent form of initial access, despite it being considered "boring" relative to exploitation. It isn't just your code that attackers want to exploit; if attackers can avoid using a costly exploit, they will.

Persistence
> Persistence is how attackers keep the access to a resource they gained from initial access. Without persistence, an attack operation is unsustainable. Attackers don't want to re-compromise a resource every time it restarts or experiences other changes that might disrupt or cut off their access (like the exploited vulnerability being patched overnight or a network connection randomly dying). If you ask an

---

attacker what makes for a bad day, they'll probably say it's sitting down at their desk in the morning and discovering they've lost their shell on their target overnight (i.e., they no longer have remote access in the target system). Persistence can be harder than initial access in some cases; with social engineering, for example, it's not so easy to advance from "I've compromised a user" to "I possess enough access that is stable enough that I can begin pivoting toward my goal."[11]

Expansion

Expansion is how attackers establish more access to more resources in a target system. This can help them achieve their action on target or to more loosely couple their persistence. Attackers have infrastructure engineers, DevOps practices, and ops tooling too. They'll collect system telemetry and higher-level data (which is its own form of data exfiltration) to inform their next steps toward their action on target (or to ensure they remain undetected). A ransomware operation, for instance, may survey and analyze the system to determine not just which resources are worth encrypting or where to put the ransom note, but also whether the target has a cyber insurance policy (which could result in a bigger ransom payout). Depending on the action on target and resourcing of the attacker, it could take weeks, months, or potentially even years to go from initial access to achieving their action on target. You may sometimes hear this referred to, in part, as "lateral movement."[12]

Finally, it's best to think about attacks as having their own lifecycle (i.e., the Attack Development Lifecycle, or ADLC). Attackers will maintain a feedback loop of persisting, expanding access, exfiltrating information, and using that information to polish persistence, expand access, and so forth (if there were a Gartner for attackers, it might be labeled Continuous Persistence / Continuous Expansion, or CP/CE for short). Disrupting that feedback loop or poisoning it can be invaluable.[13]

Decision trees for mental modeling

As we've discussed, decision trees allow us to capture our mental models of how attackers may behave in our systems and how our systems may respond (including both the socio and technical parts of the system). They are a means to document our assumptions about system behavior for evaluation in tier 2. In our decision tree, we can preserve some elements of a threat model: enumerating the characteristics of a system, product, or feature that could be abused by an adversary. You can think about

---

11 Eugene Spafford et al., *Cybersecurity Myths and Misconceptions: Avoiding the Hazards and Pitfalls that Derail Us* (Boston: Addison-Wesley Professional, 2023).

12 Matthew Monte, *Network Attacks and Exploitation: A Framework* (Hoboken, NJ: Wiley, 2015)

13 Josiah Dykstra et al., "Sludge for Good: Slowing and Imposing Costs on Cyber Attackers," arXiv preprint arXiv:2211.16626 (2022).

decision trees as a form of threat model that incorporates attacker ROI. When we craft a decision tree during a system's design phase, we set the system up for success when it's implemented across subsequent phases. Decision trees also facilitate refinement based on what we learn after the system is deployed to production.

In the context of the E&E assessment, the decision tree elaborates on our mental model of "the resilience of what, to what?" The decision tree covers any attacker actions relevant in our system, even ones that already have mitigations implemented to address them, because contexts change over time. More tactically, a decision tree visualizes system architecture, the current processes used to secure that architecture, and any security gaps that exist.

Combined with our diagram of flows mapped to critical functions, we gain a detailed understanding of the system's architecture. To sufficiently document this understanding, we should include asset inventory and inventory of sensitive data, as well as information about connections to upstream and downstream services—all of the flows within our system. Ideally, we also proffer links to codebases, tools, and tests performed so anyone can better understand it and track progress. In essence, we want to thoroughly portray our mental models and evolve them over time as we learn more, whether from the tier 2 experimentation assessment, continuous experimentation, or real incidents.

Decision trees serve as a visual representation of the different actions an attacker can take at each phase of an attack operation and how our system can respond to each of those attacker actions. When wanting to compromise a specific asset, attackers have multiple avenues and methods at their disposal. Creating decision trees can help you map out these attacker choices and visualize which paths attackers are most likely to take or which methods they are most likely to employ. Keep in mind that our aim here is to document our mental models of potential attacker choices and defense responses to set the stage for proactive experimentation—whether in the tier 2 assessment or continuously. The real-world decisions attackers make may refute parts of our mental model. The point isn't perfection. Rather, it is iteration that keeps us honest about our mental models as they, the system, and the system's context—like attackers—evolve over time. And this encourages earnest evaluation in tier 1.

Before exploring how to get started with your own tree and the other ways they can add value, let's walk through a tangible example of a decision tree to help frame the rest of the chapter. In this example, we will assemble a decision tree for an S3 bucket representing an attacker's ultimate goal of obtaining "sensitive customer data," specifically video recordings.

Decision tree walkthrough: S3 bucket with customer data

We've identified a business priority: securing the cloud storage bucket (Amazon S3, specifically) that contains customer video recordings, which fits the general attacker's goal of retrieving "sensitive customer data that they can monetize." Our next task is brainstorming how an attacker would most easily achieve their goal of accessing and absconding with this data. While it can be tempting to dream up scenarios where Mossad uses thermal side-channel attacks on keyboard input (*https://oreil.ly/bIi9g*)[14] or fluctuates your datacenter's power supply to exfiltrate data bit by bit,[15] determining the least-cost path attackers can take to their goal is the most sensible place to start. Once you determine this, you've begun to set the foundation for the experimentation phase in tier 2.

The easiest way for an attacker to compromise an S3 bucket containing sensitive data would be for the bucket to be configured as public rather than private, allowing the attacker to access it directly without any authorization required. While it may seem contrived, this case is similar to the most common "cloud breaches" in the late 2010s,[16] affecting organizations such as Booz Allen Hamilton (*https://oreil.ly/eL6Td*), Accenture (*https://oreil.ly/D18TT*), and Twilio (*https://oreil.ly/r1uDN*). It divulges the absence of security mechanisms in place—the failure to apply security controls in the first place—which has lovingly been referred to as "yolosec" (*https://oreil.ly/9XztY*) by one of the authors. Starting with the assumption of "yolosec" and how the attacker would take advantage of it is a sensible way to craft the least cost path in your decision tree. In our case, the easiest path for the attacker would be to access the cache of the public bucket, as Figure 2-1 shows.

---

14 Tyler Kaczmarek et al., "Thermal (and Hybrid Thermal/Audio) Side-Channel Attacks on Keyboard Input," arXiv preprint arXiv:2210.02234 (2022).

15 Mordechai Guri et al., "PowerHammer: Exfiltrating Data from Air-Gapped Computers Through Power Lines," *IEEE Transactions on Information Forensics and Security* 15 (2019): 1879-1890.

16 These breaches have decreased since AWS added the "Block Public Access" configuration in 2018 (*https://oreil.ly/ymwL_*). They introduced even more friction in granting storage buckets public access in December 2022 (*https://oreil.ly/j91fx*).

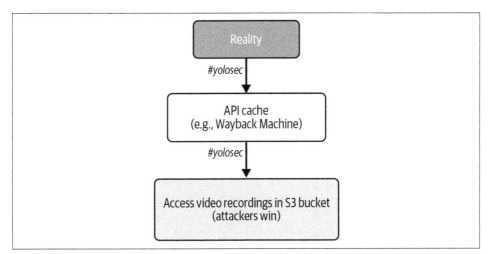

Figure 2-1. The first "branch" of the decision tree demonstrates the easiest path for the attacker to get to their goal (image based on visual from deciduous.app)

Once you have created the first branch of the decision tree—the easiest path for the attacker—add a new branch with the most basic defensive assumption in place. In our case, the easiest mitigation may seem to be ensuring the S3 bucket uses the default of private access with access control lists (ACLs). But the first necessary mitigation is disallowing crawling on site maps (shown with a dashed border in Figure 2-2) to avoid caching any of the data in a public S3 bucket. Next, consider what the attacker will do to evade that requirement. The attacker may have multiple options available to them, with varying degrees of difficulty. For instance, fabricating a phishing email to steal the necessary credentials is usually an easier path than exploiting a vulnerability in the server itself.

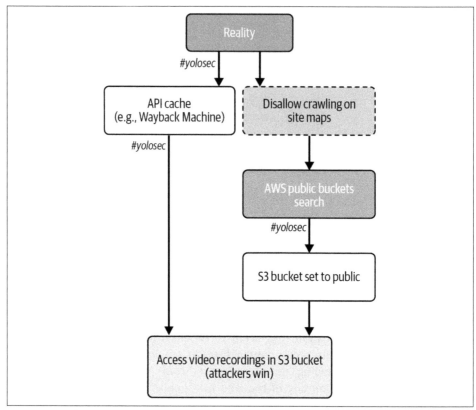

Figure 2-2. The second branch of the decision tree implements the first necessary mitiga-tion and considers how the attacker will subsequently respond to the mitigation (image based on visual from deciduous.app)

To grow your next branch of the decision tree, consider what the attacker would do if the S3 bucket was instead kept private with basic ACLs in place. The easiest sub-branch under phishing would be to compromise user credentials to the web client, and then forage for any misconfigurations that facilitate client-side manipulation leading to S3 bucket access. With the right mitigations in place (shown with dashed borders in Figure 2-3), we can foil the attacker's plans and force them to pursue other phishing methods.

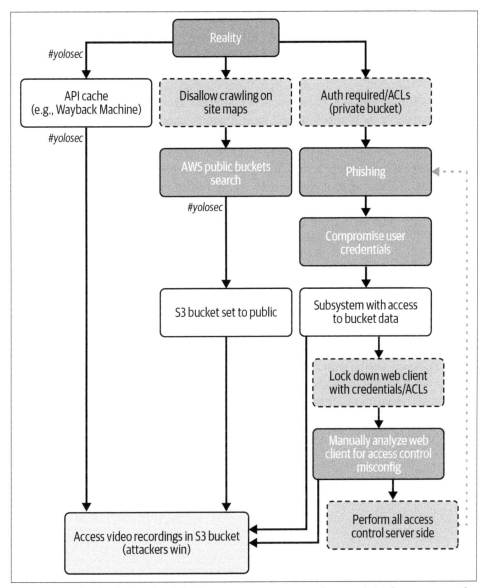

Figure 2-3. The third branch of the decision tree maps out the next initial avenue attackers will explore, what mitigations could be effective, and how the attacker will respond to each mitigation down the branch (image based on visual from deciduous.app)

You and your team should continue this process of considering the attacker's easiest sequence of actions to get to their goal, what you could implement to mitigate it, and how the attacker might adjust their actions to circumvent the mitigation. By the end of the exercise, the hardest path could be exploiting a chain of zero-day vulnerabilities—the "0day path"—as that usually reflects the hardest and most expensive set of challenges for an attacker. There are fewer defenses against zero-day exploits—after all, no one knows about them. But for most organizations, building your defenses to a level where attackers are forced to use zero days will restrict the spectrum of potential attackers, and attacker actions, to only those who are the best resourced and experienced, such as nation-state actors. Remember, you are harnessing attacker math to ensure that an attack against you presents a poor return on their effort.

 Let's say you put a mitigation on the tree because you're sure it's in place. Now, go talk to the engineer of the system and ask them what they think of the mitigation. You might be surprised how often the answer is, "Oh yeah, we planned to do that, but never got around to it." In our own experience building decision trees at organizations, it's amazing how often this exercise uncovers where mitigations are missing—without having to even conduct an experiment.

In our example of customer data stored in an S3 bucket, Figure 2-4 shows how eliminating the low-hanging fruit—the easy paths for attackers—by implementing the mitigations with dashed borders, eventually forces attackers onto the "0day path" we mentioned—the path requiring the most investment by attackers (like finding a zero-day vulnerability and writing an exploit for it). Even nation-state attackers will find the prospect of backdooring supply chains to be frustrating and resource-intensive, so they won't do it unless the target goal is extremely valuable to their mission.

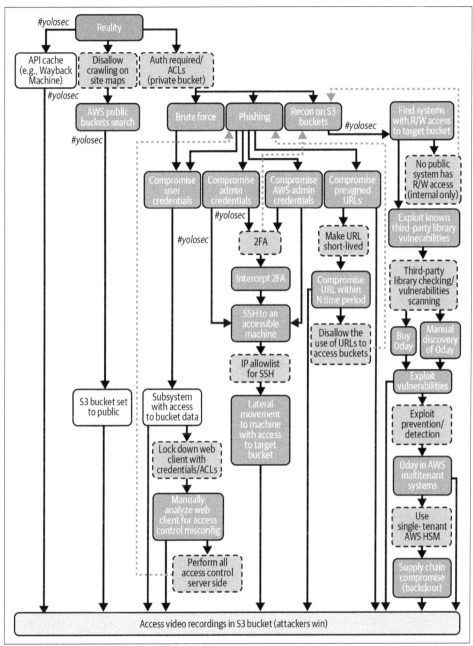

Figure 2-4. The full decision tree maps out the range of actions attackers are likely to take to reach their goal, from easiest path to hardest. It includes potential mitigations you can deploy to thwart these actions and how attackers will respond to these mitigations, which can inform what strategies and tools you need to implement to raise the cost of attack (image based on visual from deciduous.app)

Outthinking your adversaries.   As you can see in this example, an important benefit of decision trees is that they help you think ahead of your adversaries' decision making by proactively refining your mental models, whether for the tier 1 assessment or continual use (like during the design phase). Decision trees encourage you to perform second-order thinking—or, even more powerfully, n-order or "k-level" thinking (where n or k is greater than two levels).[17] First-order thinking, which is usually the default mode of operation for human brains, considers the obvious implications of an action—mentally modeling one step of the interaction at hand.[18] N-order thinking, in contrast, considers cascading implications. If you think in terms of a game like chess, n-order thinking considers how decisions made in the current round will impact future rounds.

The n-order thinking process is the essence of belief prompting.[19] Belief prompting is a tactic to foster strategic thinking by encouraging people in a competitive setting to express their beliefs about their opponents' probable actions.[20] In essence, belief prompting nudges you to articulate your mental models outside the gossamer aether of your mind. By thinking about how your opponent will respond to whatever move you are about to make, experimental evidence suggests that you will make a substantially smarter choice. Even seeing a visual representation of the potential sequence of moves (a specific kind of decision tree referred to as an "extensive-form game tree" in game theory lingo) within a competitive scenario is shown to encourage more rational choices[21]—that is, choices that maximize your chances of winning.[22]

Not only does the exercise of creating the decision tree force you to articulate your beliefs about your opponent's probable moves in response to your own, the resulting graph serves as an ongoing visual reference to inform more strategic decision making—our goal outcome from resilience assessments. When applied to a system's resilience to attack, belief prompting means we must repeatedly ask ourselves what the attacker would do in response to a defensive move. For instance, if we block

---

17 Tomasz Strzalecki, "Depth of Reasoning and Higher Order Beliefs," *Journal of Economic Behavior & Organization* 108 (2014): 108-122.

18 Colin F. Camerer et al., "A Cognitive Hierarchy Model of Games," *The Quarterly Journal of Economics* 119, no. 3 (2004): 861-898.

19 Andrew M. Colman, "Depth of Strategic Reasoning in Games," *Trends in Cognitive Sciences* 7, no. 1 (2003): 2-4.

20 Colin F. Camerer et al., "Behavioural Game Theory: Thinking, Learning and Teaching," *Advances in Understanding Strategic Behaviour: Game Theory, Experiments and Bounded Rationality*, 120-180 (London: Palgrave Macmillan, 2004).

21 Ben Meijering et al., "I Do Know What You Think I Think: Second-Order Theory of Mind in Strategic Games Is Not That Difficult," *Proceedings of the Annual Meeting of the Cognitive Science Society* 33, no. 33 (2011).

22 Andrew Schotter et al., "A Laboratory Investigation of Multiperson Rationality and Presentation Effects," *Games and Economic Behavior* 6, no. 3 (1994): 445-468.

---

outbound direct connections, an attacker might use DNS tunneling to hide their traffic. Whether performing belief prompting or crafting decision trees, these are some of the key questions to ask:

- Which of our organizational assets will attackers want? Enticing assets to attackers could include money, user data, compute power, or intellectual property.
- How does the attacker decide upon their initial access method, and how do they formulate their operation?
- What countermeasures does an attacker anticipate encountering in our environment?
- How would an attacker bypass each of our security controls they encounter on their path?
- How would an attacker respond to our security controls? Would they change course and take a different action?
- What resources would be required for an attacker to conduct a particular action in their attack campaign?
- What is the likelihood that an attacker will conduct a particular action in their attack campaign? How would that change based on public knowledge versus internal knowledge?

When we document our answers to these questions and, more generally, our assumptions about the "Spy vs. Spy" game being played, we support the readiness goal of the tier 1 evaluation assessment.

Getting started on your own decision tree

To craft your own decision tree, start by identifying the priority that poses a potential hazard for your organization—which likely relates to your critical functions (which, as we recommended earlier, you want to define before you proceed to decision trees in the tier 1 assessment). Maybe it's a service that, if disrupted by an attacker, would lead to foregone revenue. Maybe it's a resource that, if accessed by an attacker, violates customers' trust in you. Whatever it is, this will represent the attackers' ultimate goal. There are, of course, a whole range of goals attackers might have across the entirety of your organization's technology footprint, but you should focus on the largest material hazard to your organization—the type that would need to be disclosed to customers, the board, or shareholders, or else would create a tangible financial impact. After all, if it doesn't matter to the business, then why stress about it? You have an endless number of duties, so your time and attention must be respected.

This is your chance to play poet. Constructing myths that warn us about danger is a very human trait seen across countless civilizations and cultures.[23] Human brains latch onto stories in a way that they simply don't with checklists. Traditional security policy is like anti-myth in this sense: it prescribes an action without sharing the tale of *why* the action is necessary. We'll talk more about policies (especially their pitfalls) in Chapter 7, but laying the groundwork for this educational mythology starts when creating decision trees—whether during the tier 1 assessment or each time you're designing and redesigning the system (which we'll explore in the next chapter). By articulating the organizational priority, or value jeopardized by attackers, and then fleshing out the narrative arc of how the foe might try to fell the hero—the attack branches of the trees—and how the hero can vanquish the foe at each turn—the potential mitigations—you are creating an enduring myth that can be far more salient to the humans in your systems than just demanding that they do something because "security is important."

A simple prioritization matrix, as shown in Figure 2-5, can be a valuable precursor to building your decision tree. This matrix simplifies the prioritization problem. By considering the value of an asset to both the organization and the attacker, you can sort out which attacker goals most merit a decision tree. You can even use this prioritization matrix—or at least the *y*-axis of it—when you define your system's critical functions, the first step in the tier 1 assessment.

Importantly, the matrix in Figure 2-5 considers the ultimate goals in an attack (action on target), not assets that can be used as footholds during the expansion phase of an attack operation. A list of employees isn't directly tied to revenue for the organization. The list of employees becomes valuable when used to inform whom to target for social engineering, but isn't so valuable in and of itself. In contrast, money as an asset always matters to both sides of the attack equation—and, ultimately, the impact of most organizational assets being compromised is due to how it affects money. Disruption of service delivery translates into lost revenue. A crypto miner translates to higher compute costs for an organization. Thus, a simple way to think of this matrix is on the spectrum of "How directly does this make money for the organization?" and "How monetizable is this for attackers?"

---

23 Patrick D. Nunn and Nicholas J. Reid, "Aboriginal Memories of Inundation of the Australian Coast Dating from More Than 7000 Years Ago," *Australian Geographer* 47, no. 1 (2016): 11-47; Dorothy B. Vitaliano, "Geomythology: Geological Origins of Myths and Legends," *Geological Society, London, Special Publications* 273, no. 1 (2007): 1-7; Shaiza Z. Janif et al., "Value of Traditional Oral Narratives in Building Climate-Change Resilience: Insights from Rural Communities in Fiji," *Ecology and Society* 21, no. 2 (2016).

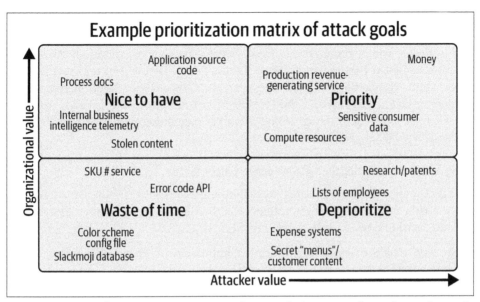

Figure 2-5. Example prioritization matrix of assets relative to attacker value and organizational value

When figuring out where to start with your decision trees, you can focus on the "Priority" box in the matrix (although starting with the critical functions you defined at the beginning of the tier 1 assessment is perfectly fine). Each of the assets in the "Priority" box represents a different decision tree that should be crafted. A decision tree that tries to bundle multiple ultimate goals at once will suffer from visual messiness that is counter to our goal of refining our mental models. Choose a *specific* example of one ultimate outcome. For instance, protecting "sensitive customer data" is a priority goal, but enumerating all the attack paths to every place that data resides in your organization would suffer from complexity overload. Instead, choose something like "An S3 bucket containing customer video recordings," which has a specific location and characteristics for more easily mapped attack paths. Once this specific decision tree is complete, you can extrapolate the mitigations to apply to other resources matching that goal type.

After you've covered the key resources within the "Priority" box with decision trees and any critical functions, you can move on to the "Nice to Haves." These resources and assets more directly contribute to revenue, but are not as easily monetizable by attackers, like business intelligence metrics or documentation around company processes. After crafting decision trees for those, you can optionally move to the "Deprioritize" box, which is full of items that are valuable to attackers, but are only abstractly or indirectly contributing to your organization's success. These deprioritized resources and assets can include expensing systems, secret menus (e.g., Netflix's list of secret titles), or even speculative research.

The example resources and assets we included in each box are for illustrative purposes only. While attacker value stays reasonably constant across industries, it's up to you to decide which resources are most valuable to your organization. Work with your colleagues in business units or in the finance department to understand what drives your organization's revenue and operations. In our view, each matrix will be unique for each company, and thus the decision trees prioritized by each company will likely be different (although some resources containing money or sensitive customer data will likely persist across many industries).

Using decision trees during the software delivery lifecycle

In this chapter, we've introduced systems thinking and the E&E resilience assessment, but the next few chapters cover resilience across the software delivery lifecycle. So how do decision trees apply in those activities?

A decision tree is essential for informing improvements during the initial design phase of a feature or system. But decision trees also shine when used as a tool for continuously informing and refining system architecture to optimize resilience. When thinking through changes to the system or feature, you can consult your decision tree to see how the proposed changes would alter the relevant attacker math—and thereby understand how the system's resilience to attack might change.

Decision trees are also valuable during incident reviews, as we will cover more in Chapters 6 and 8. You can pull up your relevant decision trees and see where your assumptions held true or false. Some of the questions your team should be asking during a retrospective include:

- Did the attackers take any of the branches modeled in the tree? In our example, perhaps log data from historical API logs showed repeated access attempts from the same IP address over a short period of time—suggesting the attacker began by trying the easiest path.

- Did the mitigations alter the attacker's path as anticipated? In our example, maybe implementing 2FA forced attackers to attempt vulnerability exploitation instead.

- What attacker options were missing from your assumptions? Perhaps your application monitoring data shows the attacker tried to exploit a vulnerability in a separate application in an attempt to gain a foothold on your AWS infrastructure.

- Did the attacker encounter any stumbling blocks that you didn't realize served as mitigations? In our example, maybe your use of immutable containers in your AWS infrastructure made it difficult for attackers to find a foothold via SSH and move laterally.

In addition to incident retrospectives, decision trees can be useful for comparing different designs or implementations. An experienced software architect or site reliability engineer in an environment with reasonable ops practices should be able to self-serve decision trees. Or programmers can partner with an SRE or ops colleague to conduct an experiment to test the efficacy of a potential architectural change; even if it isn't a perfect experiment, you can gain a rough evaluation of your architectural hypothesis, which is an improvement on pure conjecture. Software engineers can do the same to see if their draft pull request (PR) matches their expectations and successfully meets requirements. These iterations, in turn, can refine the decision tree and enumerate potential mitigations and their efficacy.

If your security team lacks software engineering expertise, you have two options in order to thrive in the resilience paradigm. The first option is to begin transforming your program and team composition toward the platform engineering model, which involves more programming and programmers (we'll discuss the concept of a Platform Resilience Engineering team in Chapter 7). Your second option is to begin collaborating with your organization's infrastructure or platform engineering team—or whichever team builds the tools, platforms, and practices used by your software engineers—since they can help you with the programming parts.

Realistically, when software is voraciously eating the world and you want to protect said software, you cannot avoid the inevitable need to understand and work with software directly—lest ye be eaten instead.

Starting your experimentation at each functionality point along the easiest branches lets you continuously verify that any low-hanging fruit for attackers is sufficiently addressed. It also demonstrates how the E&E resilience assessment is useful as a feedback loop. Once you feel confident in your system's resilience to the more obvious security failures, you can swing to the branches that require higher attacker effort. Only after an extensive period of security chaos experimentation and strategy refinement (based on the resulting feedback loop) should you move on to tackling the "0day branch"—the branch involving attackers writing and deploying exploits targeting zero-day vulnerabilities, those which were heretofore unknown by the public. It's possible your organization never quite gets there because there are enough ongoing changes to continually experiment against; most organizations will never get there. While conducting continuous experimentation or a tier 2 assessment on the toughest, threatiest threats can feel exhilarating, it won't help your organization if easier attack paths—the ones attackers will pursue first—are left lurking in the dim depths of your mental models, vague and imprecise.

Decision trees for new systems

If you are building a new system or revamping an existing system, how do you apply decision trees? If you have multiple possible designs in mind—or, more accurately, a bunch of trade-offs bouncing around in your head, which informs your eventual design—then decision trees can inform which design you choose. For instance, if you currently offer a free application or service and decide to pivot to a freemium model, then you need to add billing and subscription management. But how do you choose the right way to manage subscriptions and the right billing provider, where "right" includes resilience?

Decision trees help you make better design decisions in this scenario, as well as proactively assess resilience before implementing and deploying the system to production. You don't want to leverage decision trees *before* you draft architecture diagrams, of course, since you need a basis on top of which to formulate hypotheses. But once you have a draft diagram or general sense of how you think the architecture will look, that's when you should start documenting assumptions in your decision tree. Think of it as another part of the discussion about prospective drawbacks of the proposed infrastructure—just about the system's security rather than its performance.

Otherwise, the decision tree creation process is the same. There's probably nothing so drastically new in your proposed architecture that you have zero clue how attackers could take advantage of the components, interactions, and flows throughout the system. If you do have zero clue, playing pretend as your evil alter ego is the right place to start! Perform the brainstorming exercise of how a resentful developer might seize control over the system to knock it offline or steal data from it. Or consider how both your worst and best software engineers, if your organization really angered them, could disrupt or damage the system. If you've exhausted all options after that thought exercise and still have no clue, that's a great time to call on your local security expert or, if it's an especially critical system, hire someone well-versed in attacker thinking and threat modeling who can help.

With that said, if you don't understand the security properties of some part of your architecture, that is perhaps a sign that you don't understand the system's design well enough to use it effectively—and that you need to retry the first steps of the tier 1 assessment (identifying critical functions and flows). There are very few systems for which the security properties are the complicated ones. But, for instance, if you don't understand user accounts in Postgres, chances are you will not be great at building a system on top of Postgres. And attackers will happily take advantage of that naivete in their operations.

Starting the Feedback Flywheel with Decision Trees

Decision trees can help us kick off the feedback flywheel. When we ask neutral practitioner questions, which we'll discuss in Chapter 6, and understand how our collective mental models deviated from reality, we can update our decision trees with this new evidence. If we brainstorm potential mitigations during incident review, we can add those into the decision tree as well for discussion during design refinement (as we'll cover in Chapter 3).

Establishing a maintainable way to update and publish decision trees so teams can access them goes a long way toward promoting curiosity. It also reinforces the idea that incidents are a chance to learn rather than blame, that the goal is to continuously improve resilience against attacks, not stop all attacks from happening. The learning mindset emboldens, while the latter humiliates—and shame is a powerful motivator, one that stifles learning and promotes human behavior designed to avoid punishment rather than uphold resilience.

Moving Toward Tier 2: Experimentation

The tier 1 assessment sets the foundation for the tier 2 assessment. We need an understanding of critical functions, flows within the system, and some idea of failure thresholds before we can gain the most benefit from chaos experiments. Without this understanding, it will be difficult for us to learn from failure and maintain adaptive capacity.

The questions we ask in tier 1 frame our exploration of what failure means for the system, allowing us to excavate the edges where the system can flump into failure. We now must investigate what happens when different stressors and surprises are added—that is, how resilient your systems are to certain kinds of security events—as part of the tier 2 assessment. It doesn't mean much to say, "This system is resilient to attack." What kind of attack? For how long? Under what conditions? As observed of systems resilience in healthcare, "No system has infinite adaptive capacity."[24] Experimentation in tier 2 can reveal the constraints on that capacity.

---

24 Christopher Nemeth et al., "Minding the Gaps: Creating Resilience in Health Care," in *Advances in Patient Safety: New Directions and Alternative Approaches*, Vol. 3: Performance and Tools (Rockville, MD: Agency for Healthcare Research and Quality, August 2008).

Experimentation: Tier 2 Assessment

Experimentation in tier 2 exposes actual system behavior, which we can compare against our assumptions from the evaluation tier. We perform this comparison by conducting resilience stress tests—our chaos experiments. These help us understand interconnections and how they impact critical functionality when the system is experiencing an adverse scenario. When we conduct resilience stress tests we see, in sharp relief, how our system actually behaves in a scenario, not just how we believe it will behave. It elucidates how the system's critical functions can be disrupted by adverse conditions, which allows us to develop action plans for improving system design or otherwise preparing for such scenarios.

The experimentation assessment in tier 2 is where we dig into the details of actual interconnections, especially the hidden or unexpected ones. Chaos experiments can unearth hidden flows and dependencies in your system. They can show you the difference between your data flow map from tier 1 and how data actually flows. For instance, there aren't any trace IDs to correlate with DNS, but if you're dependent on DNS, when it goes down, you go down. A chaos experiment will divulge that dependency, even if your tier 1 assessment does not.

Complexity makes mental models slippery. How can we understand this complexity as it unfolds and evolves? The evaluation assessment in tier 1 gets us partly there. The experimentation assessment, harnessing chaos experiments, exposes complexity and helps us understand how our systems are becoming—an active process of change—in contrast to our beliefs, which are often about its "being." The goal outcome of the tier 2 assessment is to gather sufficient evidence to clarify a course of action; actions are a downstream step from understanding the scenarios being experimented. With tier 2, we seek to produce sufficient context to prioritize actions that improve our system's resilience—to give sufficient detail around *why* so you can strategically determine *what* should be done.

The Value of Experimental Evidence

While we'll explore the practice of conducting chaos experiments in depth in Chapter 8, let's briefly discuss how chaos experiments look to set the stage for how they help us support resilience across the software delivery lifecycle. A useful template for defining experiments is: "In the event of a condition X, we are confident that our system will respond by Y."

An example hypothesis from a real chaos experiment (*https://oreil.ly/sIgiX*), depicted in Figure 2-6, is: "If a user accidentally or maliciously introduced a misconfigured port, we would immediately detect, block, and alert on the event." This hypothesis might be disproved after the experiment. The firewall didn't detect or block the port change. The port change didn't trigger an alert and the log data from the firewall indicated a successful change audit. But we learned—quite unexpectedly—the configuration management tool caught the change and alerted responders.

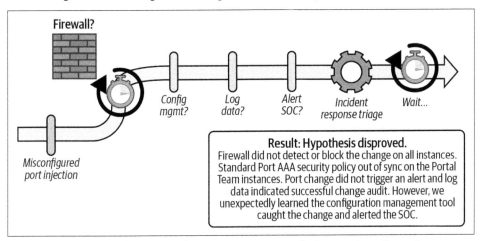

Figure 2-6. An example security chaos experiment simulating a misconfigured port injection scenario

This experiment demonstrates how our mental models can crumble when we conduct experiments; a branch of assumptions we believed to be true may be snapped off at the root. Figure 2-7 depicts how a mental model might be revised after a chaos experiment, drawing on our example in Figure 2-6. Our assumption that the firewall would block the misconfigured port change clashed with reality, but a new opportunity blossomed in the form of using the change configuration management tool as a source of security signal (a surprise, to be sure, but a welcome one).

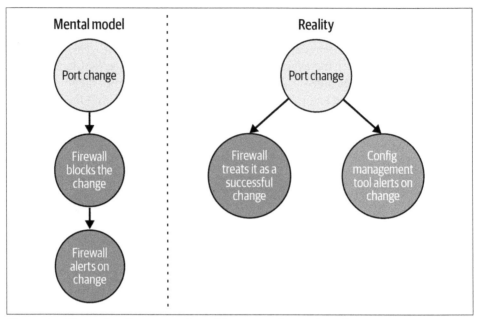

Figure 2-7. Example of how mental models can conflict with reality

The architectural assumptions you challenge with security chaos experiments need not be earth-shattering and colossal in scope. There are even plenty of security-specific aspects to architecture that we often neglect. Is our web application firewall (WAF) effective, blocking the traffic we assume it does? Is our VPC routing set up as per our policy? Does our service mesh log events as we expect it to? If we document our mental models of our systems *and* the attacker behaviors we anticipate, then we can challenge our assumptions with constructive critique.

Experimental evidence helps you chart a course for how to maintain resilience even if stressors increase and surprises sprout. It can also reveal the degree of brittleness in your systems so you can work to diminish it. For example, if you are curious about the impact of a DoS in your service, your extended hypothesis might be: "Our system experiences latency of more than 500 ms during a DoS of more than 5 million requests per second (RPS) in size. Delayed autoscaling or restart queues makes the system more brittle. Configuration problems in our CDN also increase brittleness. Our service-level agreements state that we must respond to 95% of requests within each one-hour period in under 250 ms. We expect our CDN vendor to handle simple DoS attacks up to 5 million RPS and our autoscaling strategy to handle traffic from the CDN at up to 100,000 RPS." From this elaborate hypothesis, you could propose a security chaos experiment for tier 2 or to run on demand, to load-test your infrastructure, specifying that it should fail early if the 99th percentile response time exceeds 175 ms.

Excitingly, combining forward-thinking properties with security chaos experiments is a match made in heaven. The future-factuals that you concoct can be crafted into hypotheses for experiments, allowing you to collect evidence for questions like, "If we subtract X property from the system, is it as resilient to Y type of activity?"

Don't focus solely on the technical systems in your sociotechnical systems when conducting E&E resilience assessments. When you conduct a chaos experiment, how do the humans respond? Do they feel stressed and overwhelmed or composed and confident? Do they burn out quickly or can they gambol between tasks without needing restorative downtime? Does communication flourish or does it splinter and sour? Describing resilience means you must also describe how humans are able to adapt in the face of different types and magnitudes of stressors.

 We can even use experiments to generate evidence-based comparisons between different system architectures, implementations (like specific technologies), and practices—or even administrative and policy decisions. Perhaps we want to understand how one topology might sustain resilience against one particular kind of an attack versus another; we can simulate both and compare responses.

Sustaining Resilience Assessments

The two-tier E&E Approach to resilience assessment helps satisfy our curiosity around sustaining resilience even when stressors (whether acute or chronic) increase—which refines our mental models and strengthens our systems thinking. Coping with stressors involves a complementary mix of experiments, feedback loops, and resilient design. Curiosity inspires thoughtful experiments, analysis of evidence to incorporate into feedback loops, and open-mindedness in designing and revising systems so they sustain resilience. That is, curiosity opens our minds to *adaptation*, to changing our design and strategy as necessary when problems, environments, tech stacks, regulatory regimes, humans, and all the other attributes that make up our organization's context change.

As we will continue to emphasize, there is no such thing as "one size fits all" when it comes to resilience. Your organization's approach to coping with failures and brittleness—how to optimize resilience in your systems—will be built from building blocks and patterns based on your unique context. We'll discuss those building blocks and patterns throughout the book so you can devise your own resilience approach, which will inevitably change bit by bit over time in response to evolving conditions.

"To overcome the risk of brittleness in the face of surprising disruptions," says David D. Woods (*https://oreil.ly/k2t0I*), "requires a system with the potential for adaptive action *in the future* when information varies, conditions change, or when new kinds of events occur, any of which challenge the viability of previous adaptations, models, plans, or assumptions."

A curious security program supports humans reflecting on all the factors that led to a failure from multiple angles, ingesting information from a variety of sources to understand a problem, and brainstorming a diverse range of potential solutions. This continuous thirst for knowledge is an important mindset in security programs, especially among its managers (*https://oreil.ly/guKUS*). (We'll cover curiosity during incident review specifically in Chapter 6.) The E&E resilience assessment should reflect this curiosity in action.

Fail-Safe Versus Safe-to-Fail

Assessing resilience is a worthy first step in your sociotechnical transformation. What comes next? In the remainder of the chapter, we will contrast the antiquated security story—one of prevention, tension, theatrics, and reactions—with the modern SCE story—one of preparation, liberation, confidence, and prudence.

We can characterize the security status quo as the "fail-safe" mindset, reflective of a prevention-driven approach. The status quo in cybersecurity is to stamp out all possible vulnerabilities, "risks," or "threats" before they happen. For all the reasons we described in Chapter 1, this is impossible—and a rather profligate use of an organization's resources. The "fail-safe" logic leads to a false sense of security. It does not care how the system failed or how it recovered from failure, but demonizes that it failed at all.

If we shift toward "safe-to-fail" logic, we transform toward preparation—anticipating failures and investing effort in preparing to recover and adapt to them.[25] Safe-to-fail seeks to understand *how* systems respond to adverse, changing conditions and how they fail in certain scenarios. Does the system recover with speed and grace? Are critical functions affected, or just noncritical ones? These and other questions are respected when we shift to "safe-to-fail" logic.

The fail-safe logic ignores system-level dynamics, instead dwelling at the level of individual components and attempting to portend future failures in them. It ignores cascading uncertainties and the complexity of interactions in the system, offering convenience and a sense of control that is impotent when the inevitable transpires. Perhaps worse, the fail-safe mindset neglects the outcomes of risk mitigations failing

---

25 Jack Ahern, "From Fail-Safe to Safe-to-Fail: Sustainability and Resilience in the New Urban World," *Landscape and Urban Planning* 100, no. 4 (2011): 341-343.

(hence the poor code quality and vulnerabilities we often find in cybersecurity solutions themselves). Overall, the fail-safe mindset generates a false sense of security. They place faith in risk controls and mitigations, hoping that they can thwart failure at every turn. We see this in other domains too; the faith placed in large levees "exacerbated catastrophe" when Hurricane Katrina struck.[26] In a fail-safe security program, surprises are intolerable; the brisk gusts of change bring only catastrophe and calamity; our only hope is to don ornamental armor, constricting ourselves and our reality into torpidity and rigidity under the heraldry of control.

If you optimize for eliminating failure, you won't be taken seriously in business settings where the clear goal is to make more money (whether the thirst is for revenue or profitability). Eliminating failure costs money, but introducing change—by shipping features, launching products, and other activities—*makes* money. Attempting to eliminate failure often costs more money than the amount lost by the failure itself. Actively investing in change is a competitive advantage; a focus on eliminating failure chokes innovation, corroding that advantage. After all, the best way to optimize your Mean Time Between Failure (MTBF) metric in software engineering is to never write software. Software security is solved! The End.

Reality does not match this wishful thinking. We can never fully prevent failure; change is the language of our universe. And because resources are finite, one dollar or one minute spent on futile prevention could have been spent on preparation for the inevitable—on a better understanding of how failures propagate throughout your systems and how your organization handles them. Aside from this opportunity cost, a dollar or minute spent on prevention *also* bears the cost of forgone learning opportunities. Without the benefit of repetition and accumulation, you never build the muscle memory that is essential during incidents.

In contrast, a security program with the safe-to-fail mindset can accept surprises, minimize their impact, and learn from them. It acknowledges the world is absurd and can cope with reality not being a fairy tale with easily defined and enforced "good" and "evil." The safe-to-fail design strategy accepts the inevitability of surprises and focuses system design decisions on its adaptive capacity—its resilience to adverse conditions. As Kim et al. suggest, transitioning from a fail-safe to safe-to-fail design requires a shift in perspective toward the following (adapted for software systems):[27]

---

26 Jeryang Park et al., "Integrating Risk and Resilience Approaches to Catastrophe Management in Engineering Systems," *Risk Analysis* 33, no. 3 (September 2012): 356-367.

27 Yeowon Kim et al., "Fail-Safe and Safe-to-Fail Adaptation: Decision-Making for Urban Flooding Under Climate Change," *Climatic Change* 145, no. 3 (2017): 397-412.

- Focusing on maintaining critical functions and services instead of preventing component failure[28]
- Minimizing the *consequences* of surprises rather than minimizing the *probability* of damages[29]
- Privileging the use of solutions that nurture recovery, adaptability, diversity, cohesion, flexibility, renewability, regrowth, innovation, and transformation
- Designing for decentralized, autonomous agents that respond to local contexts rather than centralized, manual administrative control
- Encouraging communication and collaboration that transcends disciplinary barriers rather than distinct, siloed perspectives[30]

Safe-to-fail chooses efficacy over expediency. It might be nice to wrap an incident up with the shiny bow of surface-level "root cause," but it won't help you achieve palpable security outcomes. If we want to build security programs that meaningfully improve the resilience and security of our systems and nurture the ongoing viability of our organizations, we need to accept and endure failure as a fundamental part of complex systems—and to stay curious about our systems by conducting E&E resilience assessments and, more generally, continuous experimentation.

 Surprises can feel scary, so how do we handle them? The answer is by making investments in things that support adaptive action (*https://oreil.ly/l3QCr*) in the future. If we are so concerned about the so-called rapidly evolving attacker, then defenders should harness rapid evolution too. The rest of the book will cover adaptive security strategies that foster continual evolution toward systems resilience—so that surprises are more *yawn* than *yikes*.

It's counterintuitive to think that probability-based analysis and armor-based design may fail us. This notion may even scare security professionals who were taught to prevent failure as much as possible. When things go wrong, our instinctive response is to implement policies, procedures, or tools meant to decrease the system's rate of failure. This is what we see in the infosec status quo today—the monomaniacal culling of uncertainty to raze the future into a single, legible trajectory in denial that it can never be tamed.

---

28 Niklas Möller and Sven Ove Hansson, "Principles of Engineering Safety: Risk and Uncertainty Reduction," *Reliability Engineering & System Safety* 93, no. 6 (2008): 798-805.

29 Park, "Integrating Risk and Resilience Approaches to Catastrophe Management in Engineering Systems," 356-367.

30 Mari R. Tye et al., "Rethinking Failure: Time for Closer Engineer–Scientist Collaborations on Design," *Proceedings of the Institution of Civil Engineers-Forensic Engineering* 168, no. 2 (2015): 49-57.

Uncertainty Versus Ambiguity

While cybersecurity is often characterized as gloomy and doomy, at its heart lurks the suspicion that we could "solve" security if only we could eliminate uncertainty. This rather utopian (and unearned) optimism supposes that if we can discover all the ways our systems are unsafe, then we can make everything fail-safe. This presents the problem as a matter of information: once we collect enough information about our reality and fix all the unsafe things, then we can avoid any and all incidents.

Yet, even if we had perfect information (which we can never have), we cannot solve the ambiguity pervading our problems. Reality is not composed of a web of objective facts. Information requires interpretation to be meaningful. The same fact, such as "Wildfire is rushing toward us," could result in wildly different interpretations, like "We should run up the hill, away from the fire" or "We should pre-burn some brush to create a safe space from the fire."[31] We can reduce uncertainty by collecting more information, but this is not a substitute for reducing *ambiguity*—the reality that that information can have multiple potential meanings, or even no meaning.[32]

The ambiguity of reality is what torments us in traditional cybersecurity; we cope through excess optimism about our ability to reduce uncertainty, which leads our strategy astray. Other industries struggle with the same unhealthy coping mechanisms too. For example, from the realm of healthcare, tighter procedures meant to improve glycemic (blood sugar) monitoring were introduced as a coping mechanism for uncertainty but they "ironically had the opposite result."[33] Heavier processes and overly restrictive guardrails can result in a system that is precariously balanced on a narrow beam; if any computer or human deviates from the prescribed procedure, things fall apart.

Ambiguity can only be resolved by interaction with the system. Then we manage it on an ongoing basis by gaining more experience with this ambiguous reality to build comfort with responding to ambiguous situations. Experiments are one way we can interact with our systems, nourishing a feedback loop that informs design refinements to make our systems safe-to-fail. In a safe-to-fail mindset, we must accept the ambiguity of reality—that complex systems, by nature of their perpetual fluctuation in a fluxing world, are steeped in ambiguity—and that the only way to preserve our systems is to adapt. In fact, this is a foundational rule of life; the essence of

---

31 Michelle A. Barton et al., "Performing Under Uncertainty: Contextualized Engagement in Wildland Firefighting," *Journal of Contingencies and Crisis Management* 23, no. 2 (2015): 74-83.

32 John S. Carroll, "Making Sense of Ambiguity Through Dialogue and Collaborative Action," *Journal of Contingencies and Crisis Management* 23, no. 2 (2015): 59-65.

33 Shawna Perry et al., "Ironies of Improvement: Organizational Factors Undermining Resilient Performance in Healthcare," *2007 IEEE International Conference on Systems, Man and Cybernetics* (October 2007): 3413-3417.

autopoiesis, the ability for a cellular organism to maintain itself, is "changing to stay the same."[34]

Fail-Safe Neglects the Systems Perspective

The limiting factor for security today isn't budget, people, or tooling (despite what many pundits say). The bigger problems are usually the scale of systems, the complexity of systems, and the speed at which systems are changing. Security tools can be purchased with relative ease, but implementing them, maintaining them, and ensuring they are supporting outcome achievement makes it a more intractable affair. And the rate of change in the world will always be greater than your hiring budget.

The range of things we could protect is vast. Most organizations will operate systems that must integrate with the outside world, through either humans or direct connections to systems operated by other organizations. These systems will use things like data stores and databases; compute and other technologies that process data (search, stream, batch processing); and communication protocols and network technologies. There are also systems used to make the operations of other systems better for purposes like logging, monitoring, load balancing, and policy enforcement.

But describing systems based on their high-level components belies their complexity. When we talk about making a system "secure," we often think in terms of ensuring each component in the system cannot be abused to achieve undesirable outcomes. The power and challenge of systems is that they do not operate in a vacuum; the interconnections between systems and *how* they interact can often be more relevant to the resilience equation than how each individual component looks.

Attackers thrive on these interconnections and frequently target them to maximize the ROI of their attack operations. For instance, attackers targeted Codecov, a code coverage reporting tool, and compromised its bash uploader script in April 2021 (*https://www.cisa.gov/news-events/alerts/2021/04/30/codecov-releases-new-detections-supply-chain-compromise*) because, by design, Codecov can access customers' internal systems to analyze them. And, in the case of the SolarWinds compromise that we discussed in Chapter 1, it is precisely because of SolarWinds' interconnected nature within organizations—by design, the Orion product connects to internal systems to extract data from them—that compromising it and injecting malicious code into Orion's update functionality presented a high ROI for attackers. By pushing this malicious update for SolarWinds' customers to download, the SVR could compromise a range of organizations—from Fortune 500 companies to government agencies. SolarWinds' product by itself when deployed on prem by customers—that is, considering it in isolation as a single component—may not have presented vulnerabilities ready to

---

34 Margulis and Sagan, *What Is Life?*

be exploited, but its interconnectivity with other infrastructure was highly relevant to each customer's resilience against attack.

The Fragmented World of Fail-Safe

We usually think about security strategy based on specific problem areas, like user access to resources, flaws in application code, malware on employee laptops, or harmful network traffic. As of early 2023, Gartner maintains nearly 20 "Magic Quadrants"[35] for different security subsectors, such as Application Security Testing, Endpoint Protection, and Web Application Firewalls. Market maps for cybersecurity tools look like a conspiracy theorist's mindmap board given the bewildering number of categories and subcategories filled with countless venture capital–funded startups and large, publicly traded vendors alike; just look at Figure 2-8 to see what we mean.

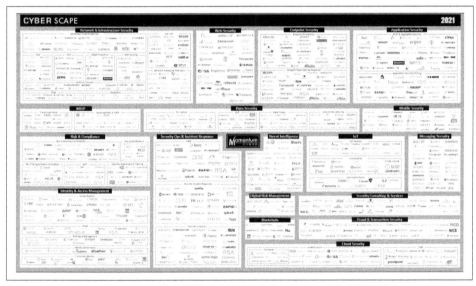

Figure 2-8. Momentum Cyber's "CYBERSCAPE" (https://oreil.ly/PlTYz), a market map of cybersecurity companies across the subsectors they've identified

---

35 As of January 19, 2023, there are 18 "Magic Quadrants" related to cybersecurity (not including segments related to backup and disaster recovery): Access Management, Application Security Testing, Cloud Access Security Brokers, Cloud Web Application & API Protection, Endpoint Protection Platforms, Enterprise Network Firewalls, Identity Governance and Administration, Integrated Risk Management Solutions, Intrusion Detection and Prevention Systems, IT Risk Management, IT Vendor Risk Management, Managed Security Services (Worldwide), Privileged Access Management, Security Information and Event Management, Security Service Edge, Unified Threat Management, Web Application and API Protection, and Web Application Firewalls.

This status quo is fragmented, a sloppy smorgasbord of disparate parts; no wonder the structure of our security program is so often a silo. New tools and subcategories are emerging constantly. You need only pay light attention to news headlines to recognize cybersecurity is a problem. Investors across asset classes are excitedly and collectively pouring billions of dollars into new security companies every year—sometimes even funding solutions tackling problems that don't yet exist.[36] Because these tools are often built for specific or niche slices of bigger security problems, it is challenging to fit all these solutions into traditional categories. For example, is securing the communication between microservices "network security" or "application security" or "access control?" Protecting servers running in production is technically "endpoint security" (since hosts are endpoints), but given those servers are used to run applications, is "application security" a better fit? Industry buzzwords seem to evolve even faster than attack methods. No wonder people working on security challenges feel like it's hard to keep up.

As our computer systems grow in importance, complexity, and size within businesses—combined with the pressures of delivering digital experiences to end users—it's relatively impossible for a single tool to solve all the security needs of the system. In more effective cases, system security needs are decomposed into steps toward a goal outcome, using the right tool for the right step and then coordinating their actions into a cohesive process (through a variety of code-based means). In less effective cases, organizations attempt to retrofit their system security needs into whatever functionality their existing tools can provide, letting the vendor dictate what steps are useful and losing sight of the goal outcome (think traditional antivirus agents in containers). Or, equally ineffective, organizations attempt to stitch multiple security tools together,[37] often lacking API support, and end up with a spaghetti mess of broken noodles.

What gets lost in this sea of security tools dedicated to narrow slices of the security problem set are the inevitable spillover effects. Everything you do in service of your security program affects the systems that fuel business operations. Security tools and procedures have a direct effect on different teams. They invigorate or impede different goals. There is no such thing as a security tool, procedure, policy, or task that exists in total isolation.

Hence, when we talk about security, we must discuss it in the realm of *systems*. While thinking in systems may feel too abstract, a systems perspective keeps you outcome-oriented (rather than out*put*-oriented) and allows you to layer solutions that complement and build upon each other toward a system-level goal. What matters isn't,

---

36 Like "quantum computing threats."

37 George V. Neville-Neil, "What Is a CSO Good For? Security Requires More Than an Off-the-Shelf Solution," *Queue* 17, no. 3 (2019): 32-37.

"Ensure this specific code repo is free of vulnerabilities," but instead, "Ensure this service experiences minimal impact if attacked."

Now that we have a feel for how fail-safe differs from safe-to-fail, let's sharpen this distinction by contrasting security in the SCE world to the status quo world of "security theater."

SCE Versus Security Theater

No one disputes that the security of our data and systems is important. So why are security goals often rendered secondary to other goals? Traditional cybersecurity programs commonly add friction to work being conducted, requiring organizational users of all kinds to jump through extra hoops to achieve their goals. Security thereby serves as a gatekeeper—whether demanding user interaction with security tools for account access or decreeing their rubber stamp essential in approving software releases. Of course, businesses need to make money, so anything standing in the way of making widgets or delivering services to customers is, quite understandably, placed at a lower priority.

The solution seems simple—just ensure security programs are enabling the business rather than slowing it down! But as with many things in life and in technology operations, it's far easier said than done. Some compliance requirements, such as access controls stipulated by PCI and HIPAA, are nonnegotiable if an organization wants to avoid fines and reputational damage. There can be ethical judgments, like preserving privacy over monetizing as much user data as can be collected, that are also irreconcilable. However, many of the constraints espoused as valuable by traditional security programs are artificial in nature—a product of status quo bias ("This is how it's always been done, so it must be right.") and an all-or-nothing mentality.[38]

The principles of SCE lay the foundation for a security program that inherently enables organizations, that demonstrate a safe-to-fail mindset, and that align with the understanding that security must be as convenient as possible. By embracing failure in the safe-to-fail mindset, you will not only consider what types of failure will impact the business the most, but also gain a deeper understanding of the systemic factors that lead to failure. Because of this, it is difficult to stick to absolute notions of what "must" be part of your security program. We should instead focus on what works in practice to reduce security failure and maximize adaptive innovation.

In this section, we'll explore the differences between the security theater of the infosec status quo and an SCE approach. The rest of the book will cover how to shift away from theater and toward resilience.

---

38 Daniel Kahneman et al., "Anomalies: The Endowment Effect, Loss Aversion, and Status Quo Bias," *Journal of Economic Perspectives* 5, no. 1 (1991): 193-206.

What Is Security Theater?

One pillar of the ineffective status quo of security-as-a-gatekeeper is *security theater*: work performed that creates the *perception* of improved security, rather than creating tangible and positive security outcomes. When you perform security theater, you're optimizing, unsurprisingly, for drama. You focus on the "bad apples" cases, contriving processes that affect everyone just to catch the few who may do something seemingly "silly" (deemed as such through the benefit of hindsight) or malicious. Underpinning these theatrics, as award-winning author and speaker Bjarte Bogsnes notes, is the philosophy that "there might be someone who cannot be trusted. The strategy seems to be preventative control on everybody instead of damage control on those few."[39] Naturally, this makes the situation less tolerable for everyone—and this is seen in other areas of tech already, not just cybersecurity.[40] But security theater is also what fuels the reputation of enterprise cybersecurity teams as the "Department of No" and sets up an antagonistic relationship between the security program and the rest of the organization.

Theater of any kind—whether cybersecurity, risk management, or physical security—is, in the words of SRE and author Jez Humble, a "common-encountered control apparatus, imposed in a top-down way, which makes life painful for the innocent but can be circumvented by the guilty."[41] This notion of top-down control is counter to everything we've discussed so far in terms of complex adaptive systems. It is fundamentally incongruent with the need to adopt adaptive security to co-evolve with the changing environment around you. Top-down control—what we (not-so-) affectionately call "gatekeeping"—may create a *feeling* of security, but it is less effective at achieving it than a systems-based approach that embraces experimentation and feedback loops.

How Does SCE Differ from Security Theater?

How does this security theater look in practice? What are the red flags you can spot in your own organization? And, importantly, how does the drama-free approach of SCE look in contrast? Table 2-2 outlines the core differences between the SCE approach

---

39 Bjarte Bogsnes, *Implementing Beyond Budgeting: Unlocking the Performance Potential* (Hoboken, NJ: Wiley, 2016).

40 Garrick Blalock et al., "The Impact of 9/11 on Road Fatalities: The Other Lives Lost to Terrorism," Available at SSRN 677549 (2005).

41 Jez Humble, "Risk Management Theatre: On Show At An Organization Near You" (*https://oreil.ly/B4-9o*) (August 5, 2013).

---

discussed in this book and the traditional security theater approach that creates security-as-gatekeepers in the enterprise.[42]

Table 2-2. Core differences between SCE and security theater

Security chaos engineering	Security theater
Failure is a learning opportunity. Seeks to uncover failure via experimentation as feedback for continual refinement. When incidents occur, conducts a blameless retrospective to understand system-level dynamics and influencing factors to inform improvement.	**Failure is shameful and should be punished.** "Human error" is the root cause of failure. Seeks to prevent humans from causing failure through policy and process enforcement. When incidents occur, investigates who is responsible and punishes them.
Accepts that eventual failure is inevitable as systems evolve. Systems are continually changing, and it's impossible to always be aware of all known and unknown sources of failure. Supports human decision making by evolving practices, technology, and knowledge through continual experimentation and feedback loops.	**Failure can be avoided forever, people have to be perfect, and nothing ever gets to change.** If people always adhere to security policies and procedures, nothing bad can happen. Controls are put in place to manage "stupid," "lazy," or "bad apple" humans. Ignores the fact that policies and procedures are always subject to interpretation and adaptation in reality.
Uses experimentation and transparent feedback loops to minimize failure impact. Understands real-world constraints, and thus the value of continual experimentation and refinement to promote adaptation versus rigid policy enforcement. Prioritizes the ability to recover from incidents and learn from them over finding opportunities to pass blame on to others.	**Uses policies and controls to prevent failure.** By assuming security policies will be followed (perfectly), incidents can be blamed on humans' failure to adhere to policy. Implementing controls helps the security team prove they've "done something" after an incident. Adaptation is restricted, and unknown sources of failure emerge due to the inability to follow global-level policies when performing local-level work under competing pressures.
Aligns security accountability and situational awareness with responsibility. Risk-acceptance decisions are made by the teams performing the work, not the security team. The security program shares its expertise across teams as an advisor, and facilitates knowledge sharing across the organization.	**The security team operates in a silo.** Knowledge is often tribal: undocumented and unshared. Duties are segregated between nonsecurity versus security. Security is removed from the work being conducted, but approves or denies changes. The act of security approval itself is seen as creating security.
Incentivizes collaboration, experimentation, and system-level improvements. Both engineering and security teams collaborate to improve system-level metrics. No rewards for blocking change on individual or function level. Accepts that "locally rational" decisions—ones that are rational in a specific context—can lead to system-level failures.	**Incentivizes saying no and narrow optimization.** The security team creates barriers that discourage adoption of technology that could increase operational quality or performance. Or the product security program optimizes for (perceived) stability at the expense of velocity. Believes there is a "globally rational" decision for every situation—one that is always rational regardless of context.

---

42 There are overlaps between this comparison and Jez Humble's comparison of adaptive risk management versus risk management theater, which is to be expected in applications of resilience to IT domains (especially when it comes to cultural concerns).

Security chaos engineering	Security theater
Creates a culture of continuous learning. Encourages blameless retrospectives after incidents (and experiments) and open discussion of mistakes or oversights. Promotes experimentation to generate knowledge, with the goal of system-level design improvements. Humans interacting with the system feel safe raising issues transparently and early.	**Creates a culture of fear and mistrust.** Encourages finger pointing, passing the blame, and lack of ownership for mistakes or oversights. Hiding issues becomes preferred because raising issues is punished. Antagonistic vibe between the security team and other teams. Humans are incentivized to "CYA," creating an inherently adversarial dynamic.
Principle-based and defaults to adaptation. Guiding principles are applied to new, unfamiliar situations. There is an openness to rethinking and refining security strategy for new or evolving situations. Carefully considers trade-offs and appreciates nuance.	**Rule-based and defaults to the status quo.** When new technologies and practices are encountered, rules are rewritten and the same security controls from prior tech/practices implemented (e.g., "container firewalls"). Often ignores trade-offs; defaults to "security at all costs" rooted in status quo knowledge.
Fast, transparent security verification. Integrates with workflows across the software delivery lifecycle. Provides fast, digestible feedback to engineers on security issues. Facilitates threat models during design phase and continuous refinement of them as experimental data is generated.	**Manual security reviews and assessments.** Releases are blocked until security approvals are received. Reviews are performed by a separate team, often in a separate location with limited information sharing. Delayed and siloed feedback on system-level security impacts.

As you can see, SCE is all about outcomes rather than output, prefers psychological safety to ruling with an iron fist, and experiments with strategies optimized for the real world, not an ideal security-is-the-only-priority world. The simple premise of achieving tangible outcomes rather than performing dramatic motions to give the appearance of "doing something" should be compelling to all stakeholders involved in an organization's security—from the security teams themselves to software engineering and product teams (not to mention company leadership who can start to see more tangible outcomes from the security budget).[43]

While being enabled by security rather than subjected to a "bad apples" approach is already a refreshing value proposition to product and engineering teams, the SCE approach is also more in line with their current way of thinking and working than is security theater. Experimenting with failure crosses over considerably with teams (especially SRE teams) wanting to test for bugs that could lead to performance issues. Many of your organization's engineering teams—perhaps even your own—may already be proactively seeking out bugs and other issues, and thinking of how to improve the tech stack or practices if the current strategy isn't producing results. The shift in thinking required by the SCE approach, therefore, is pretty minimal—we just assume that bugs exist rather than assume the security team checked everything and that things are now perfect.

---

43 Kelly Shortridge, "From Lemons to Peaches: Improving Security ROI Through Security Chaos Engineering," *2022 IEEE Secure Development Conference (SecDev)* (2022): 59-60.

As we'll explore in depth in Chapter 7, policies and prescribed procedures shouldn't be overly relied upon to prevent all possible badness from happening. In particular, policies shouldn't represent punitive measures. We must instead encourage continuous learning, experimentation, and adaptation. Procedures shouldn't serve as "gotchas" that, if not followed, can be used as supporting evidence of someone being fired after a security incident. Anything that ignores human behavior or the workflows of the people to which the policy or procedure applies is doomed, ironically, to fail.

This is precisely how security theater can create a self-fulfilling prophecy. By treating everyone as a potential source of error at which fingers can be pointed, it becomes more likely that mistakes will be covered up, concerns kept quiet, and thus feedback loops dampened. Without feedback loops, it's difficult to continuously improve your security strategy—holding everyone back. And by treating humans like error-generating nuisances, you miss out on harnessing humans' unique ability to adapt in the face of unexpected situations. We pick apart the times that human action leads to unsafe situations, but how often do we appreciate when human action is successful?[44]

How to RAVE Your Way to Resilience

Before we move on to what the SCE transformation looks like at each stage of the software delivery lifecycle, let's examine a few key principles that can help us across all stages of software engineering: repeatability, accessibility, and variability, or RAV Engineering (aka "RAVE"). The rest of this chapter explores these principles and how they're relevant to help security programs scale.

Repeatability: Handling Complexity

In complex adaptive systems, security depends on the ability to handle complexity—to ensure more interconnections don't break our brains and computers alike. Some complexity is accidental, an emergent feature of adding more functionality, scaling out infrastructure, or reorganizing human teams. Remember Woods' Theorem, which we discussed earlier in the chapter? It succinctly describes the primary symptom of complexity in humans: "As the complexity of a system increases, the accuracy of any single agent's own model of that system decreases rapidly."[45] If the mental models of our systems are increasingly inaccurate, then our designs and procedures for those systems will result in computers that are ill-equipped for reality.

Repeatability helps us handle complexity by making workflows more linear, reducing cognitive overload—minimizing mistakes—and freeing up time for strategic work

---

44 Rankin, "Resilience in Everyday Operations," 78-97.

45 Woods' words are cited in this report: *https://oreil.ly/HqcVF*.

that can help us reason more accurately about the system. As the Cybersecurity and Infrastructure Security Agency (CISA) espouses in their Cloud Security Technical Reference Architecture (*https://oreil.ly/enb6b*), repeated activities reduce mistakes and make processes faster and more reliable. Much like the Serenity Prayer, we must reduce complexity in the tasks and objects we can control so we can maintain hope in our ability to adapt gracefully to the things we cannot control.

Of course, there is no true "one size fits all," and customization will be a requirement for some systems. But by making security accessible and repeatable, software engineering teams can implement most security building blocks by themselves—leaving far more time and energy for security experts to advise on new patterns or even build new primitives[46] as necessary for teams. We'll discuss strategies to make security work more repeatable, like standardized templates, API patterns, and policies that treat security as just another nonfunctional requirement, in Chapter 4. And in Chapter 7, we'll explore how systems-oriented security programs can be reified in a platform engineering model that builds those standardized patterns and secure "paved roads."

Accessibility: Making Security Easier for Engineers

If we want to build and operate safer systems, we need to create design-based solutions toward those outcomes that are accessible to stakeholders involved in these systems. One analogy, by way of Security Platforms Engineering Manager Julia Knecht at Netflix, is that engineers need security LEGOs that they can use to build their systems. With these LEGO blueprints, detecting drift or deviation is more straightforward than when security is more ad hoc and manual. These primitives also make security more repeatable.

Documenting security requirements in one place for all teams is an overlooked practice that directly supports accessibility (as well as repeatability). Engineering teams are used to building solutions based on a set of functional and nonfunctional requirements (ideally provided by a product manager). In SCE, a security program should provide similar requirements to engineering teams that support security, but allow room for flexibility in how engineers implement those requirements. The security program defines the *what* and engineering teams figure out the *how*. For example, rather than ad hoc negotiations and siloed conversations around what password policy is best for each external-facing or internal-facing service, describing the requirements in a single wiki page accessible by all teams allows teams to self-start and self-serve because they can now determine a way to meet those requirements that makes sense for *their* service. The security team avoids a ton of back-and-forth between teams, freeing up their time to focus on more valuable work.

---

46 We use the term *primitives* from a systems perspective. Think of patterns like the LEGO blueprint and primitives like the building blocks.

Another part of making security more attainable to software engineers or other relevant stakeholders is avoiding portraying security as an arcane art that only experts can hope to understand and implement. While deep expertise in security can be invaluable in some contexts, like advising on architecture in critical infrastructure domains, it isn't required to achieve safer outcomes in our systems. Security experts can serve as advisors and partners to engineering teams, jumping in when necessary to solve particularly thorny problems or build foundational primitives or tooling to support safer software delivery. Today's security experts should give thoughtful consideration to transforming their skills and adapting to a platform engineering model (more on that in Chapter 7).

Many of the goal outcomes and challenges in the way of achieving them are already quite familiar to software engineers. For instance, if your goal outcome is a highly available service, stability in that service is crucial, and therefore you will design your service to be resilient to activity that can jeopardize that stability. A developer debugging in production is within this "threat model," and extending this performance-related "threat model" to include attackers debugging in production is not much of a leap. The main difference is in motivation; developers want to debug in production because it's easier, while attackers want to debug in production because they can extract secrets or instrument the system to their advantage. But this difference in motivation honestly doesn't matter much in terms of business impact; whether you leak secrets accidentally as a developer or purposefully as an attacker, it still affects system stability and potentially violates compliance.

There are few software engineers who fail to understand why remote code execution in a production system is a big deal. The tricky part for them is figuring out what to do about it. Demystifying security challenges, goals, and processes is an important start. If security improvements aren't accessible to people in the flow of software delivery work, then implementing them will always be unnatural. Combining accessibility with repeatability and variability ensures not only that systems achieve security outcomes, but that the security of these systems can scale more efficiently.

Variability: Supporting Evolution

Our reality is constantly evolving, so our resilience and security requirements are in constant flux too. To sustain resilience on a continuous basis, it isn't enough to ensure our software and computers are robust. Our security programs must evolve, and we must support the human behavior that helps us cope with stressors and surprises too. Humans are still the only entities that can uncover novel problems and respond to them in novel ways outside the confines of existing policies and procedures. Try as we might, it will be impossible to anticipate *everything* that can happen in a complex system and codify it in our workflows, so we need to encourage deviation from those defined workflows that promotes resiliency when the system must "stretch."

This helpful human behavior is sometimes referred to as *variety*, which we discussed in Chapter 1. Cybernetics pioneer W. Ross Ashby's Law of Requisite Variety (*https://oreil.ly/NnD_b*) states: "Any system that governs another, larger complex system must have a degree of complexity comparable to the system it is governing." While Ashby was originally thinking of self-regulating biological systems when defining this law, in software engineering, human systems are usually the ones governing software systems. Ashby's law means that humans must maintain a "repertoire of responses" (*https://oreil.ly/KSCb5*), which are at least as multifarious, intricate, and variegated as the challenges engendered by the system's environment. This is the only way human governors can successfully handle the variability arising from complex computer systems. In essence, the only way to cope with variety is with variety. Hence, our security programs must promote *variability* to gracefully absorb the variability we will encounter in our systems.[47]

For systems-oriented security, we must give individual teams ownership of their system's security and thereby the flexibility needed to support this variability—a decentralized model in which we encourage teams to evolve. The goal of variability is to foster teams trying out new ideas for security practices and sharing the best implementations across the organization to foster learning. Experiments—whether chaos tests or trying out new procedures—that aren't considered successful can be shared too (since failure is a fantastic learning opportunity), but otherwise dropped or replaced so resources are allocated on more constructive experiments.

Unfortunately, variability is an uncommon property of security programs today. The status quo model of organization-wide decrees from an ivory tower not only punishes variability, but also reflects an assumption that there is a single, global rationality. The idea is, no matter the context, there is one correct way to perform work, and deviation from that is irrational and wrong. This assumption of global rationality often also extends to the security program itself. There is a "right way" to do security "properly"—often based on industry folk wisdom or outdated course materials from certification programs—rather than evidence. Hence, security programs are notoriously slow to evolve their procedures, even in the face of weak outcomes (like the infamous bane of corporate employees' existence: password rotation policies). In response to variability from attackers, status quo security programs cling to invariability rather than responding with variability.

The SCE approach, however, embraces variability and aligns with the concept of *local rationality*—that humans generally behave rationally given the goals and constraints in their immediate context. Under the assumption of local rationality, variability is

---

47 Ashby puts it as "variety is necessary to destroy variety," which is a bit more violent in feel than the vibe we're cultivating with SCE.

seen as a necessary part of work, because what choices are "rational" depends entirely on the conditions around the moment of the choice.

Variability is ultimately about supporting adaptation and evolution. Whether conducting a security chaos experiment or experiencing a real incident by an attacker, you will learn a lot about your reality from it. Rigidity, on the other hand, means you can't incorporate that learning into improved design and operation. But supporting variability keeps space open to refine your systems and evolve your procedures based on the evidence you uncover—ensuring you can maintain resilience on an ongoing basis.

We'll now begin our journey through the software delivery lifecycle, exploring the principles, practices, and technologies that can support RAVE, systems-oriented security, and our resilience potion in our noble quest to sustain systems that are resilient to attack.

Chapter Takeaways

- If we want to protect complex systems, we can't think in terms of components. We must infuse systems thinking in our security programs.

- No matter our role, we maintain some sort of "mental model" about our systems—assumptions about how a system behaves. Because our systems and their surrounding context constantly evolve, our mental models will be incomplete.

- Attackers take advantage of our incomplete mental models. They search for our "this will always be true" assumptions and hunt for loopholes and alternative explanations (much like lawyers).

- We can proactively find loopholes in our own mental models through resilience stress testing. That way, we can refine our mental models before attackers can take advantage of inaccuracies in them.

- Resilience stress testing is a cross-discipline practice of identifying the confluence of conditions in which failure is possible; financial markets, healthcare, ecology, biology, urban planning, disaster recovery, and many other disciplines recognize its value in achieving better responses to failure (versus risk-based testing). In software, we call resilience stress testing chaos experimentation. It involves injecting adverse conditions into a system to observe how the system responds and adapts.

- The E&E Approach is a repeatable, standardized means to incrementally transform toward resilience. It involves two tiers of assessment: evaluation and experimentation. The evaluation tier is a readiness assessment that solidifies the first three resilience potion ingredients: understanding critical functions, mapping system flows to those functions, and identifying failure thresholds. The experimentation tier harnesses learning and flexibility: conducting chaos experiments to expose real system behavior in response to adverse conditions, which informs changes to improve system resilience.

- The "fail-safe" mindset is anchored to prevention and component-based thinking. The "safe-to-fail" mindset nurtures preparation and systems-based thinking. Fail-safe tries to stop failure from ever happening (impossible) while safe-to-fail proactively learns from failure for continuous improvement. The fail-safe mindset is a driver of the status quo cybersecurity industry's lack of systems thinking, its fragmentation, and its futile obsession with prediction.

- Security Chaos Engineering (SCE) helps organizations migrate away from the security theater that abounds in traditional cybersecurity programs. Security theater is performative; it focuses on outputs rather than outcomes. Security theater punishes "bad apples" and stifles the organization's capacity to learn; it is manual, inefficient, and siloed. Instead, SCE prioritizes measurable success outcomes, nurtures curiosity and adaptability, and supports a decentralized model for security programs.

- RAV Engineering (or RAVE) reflects a set of principles—repeatability, accessibility, and variability—that support resilience across the software delivery lifecycle. When an activity is repeatable, it minimizes mistakes and is easier to mentally model. Accessible security means stakeholders don't have to be experts to achieve our goal security outcomes. Supporting variability means sustaining our capacity to respond and adapt gracefully to stressors and surprises in a reality defined by variability.

CHAPTER 3

Architecting and Designing

The only thing that makes life possible is permanent, intolerable uncertainty: not knowing what comes next.

—Ursula K. Le Guin, *The Left Hand of Darkness*

When we decide to evolve our systems toward resilience, architecting and designing the system is the first step in what becomes an ineluctable cycle of redesigning the system as it ripens in the runtime of reality. During this phase, we describe the system's functions, features, and relationships in detail to make it clear to software engineers how to build and deliver the system. It is in this phase when we first mold our mental models of system behavior. And it is also in this phase when we cast the initial etch in our system's dragon spiral, as shown in Figure 3-1. With each iteration, our system effloresces, sprouting new interactions and interconnections that obfuscate its simpler "beginning."

Our systems are always *becoming*—an active process of change—in contrast to our beliefs, which are often about our systems being. There is not a perfect architecture we can prescribe for all software systems because, remember, resilience is a verb; the optimal architecture today may impede our systems in the future. As we discussed in Chapter 1, resilience is of what, to what: it depends on context. When we design and architect systems, we must accept that resilient design is context-dependent by nature, making it imperative that we understand that context during this phase. You are a curator of the system across its lifetime, as it and the serpentine circumstances surrounding it unfurl. Your responsibility is not unlike Mother Nature's: to nurture your system so it may recover from incidents, adapt to surprises, and evolve to succeed over time.

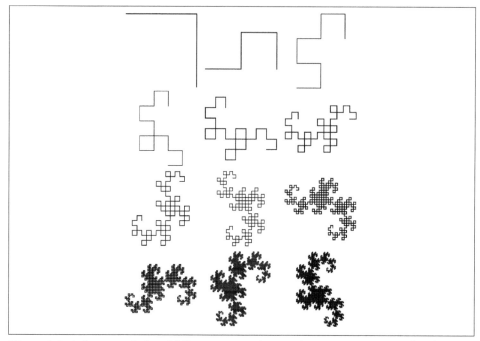

Figure 3-1. A dragon spiral unfolding as system interactions grow more complex (source: Stack Exchange post (https://oreil.ly/qFNKm))

Our goal in this chapter is to help you understand the design patterns and design-based mitigations you can build into your system—all based on your system's local context—to support system resilience in each design iteration. It's quite likely that you already employ some of these design patterns without realizing their resilience benefit. The safe-to-fail design mindset requires accepting that our resources are finite and that we must invest them with prudence; our discussion on the Effort Investment Portfolio will provide a mental framework for this. We'll explore how investing in looser coupling and linearity can help us avoid the "Danger Zone" of catastrophe by traversing trade-offs between resilience and expediency during design and architecture. We'll also present opportunities for introducing looser coupling and linearity in design and architecture to preserve possibilities through the rest of the software delivery lifecycle.

By the end of the chapter, you will understand how you can influence system resilience from its earliest conception and as our creations grow and evolve into prolific dragons.

The Effort Investment Portfolio

The late, legendary computer scientist and Turning award winner Edsger W. Dijkstra (*https://oreil.ly/G3E8h*) declared that "brainpower is by far our scarcest resource…

The competent programmer is fully aware of the strictly limited size of his own skull," but time is a close competitor as our most precious and finite resource. When you combine brainpower with time, you produce effort—the force we exert over time on a particular task or problem. We should protect our pool of potential effort as a dragon might protect a pile of gold, only parting with it for prudent and purposeful plans. When we expend effort, we must allocate it to the most valuable problems and the tasks that best help us solve those problems. That is, we must treat our effort as capital and invest it for the highest return.

The concept of the Effort Investment Portfolio captures this imperative and signals that we must balance our portfolio of effort to meet our goals—in this case, our goal of optimizing our investment for designing and architecting resilient systems. The architecting and designing phase is defined by subtlety and nuance; even a slight difference in requirements between iterations can result in radical change in a design's success. How we invest our effort capital at the beginning of each design iteration directly influences how the dragon spiral of our system unfolds, and whether our system will be resilient to the stressors and surprises it faces in the wilds of production.

 In financial investing, we typically assume a trade-off between return and risk. In the Effort Investment Portfolio, the trade-off is between a resilience return and the risk of excess effort. As we'll discover in this chapter and throughout the book, resilience and efficiency are not at odds. What resilience does require, however, is effort.

We will present copious opportunities to design and architect for resilience in this chapter; alas, you cannot pursue them all. The following section on the Effort Investment Portfolio will provide the mental scaffolding for prioritizing these opportunities based on your organization's goal outcomes and local context.

Allocating Your Effort Investment Portfolio

There are infinite allocations possible for our Effort Investment Portfolios. Somewhere in the distant, darkling reaches of the multiverse, we've perhaps invested all our effort capital in training cats to walk on keyboards as the perfect stochastic fuzzing input.[1] That would likely leave us jobless in our universe. Because we have finite effort capital, we must be thoughtful about our "investment" objectives and select the best distribution of our effort from the astronomical number of available allocations. Are we maximizing for a resilience return? Do we want to minimize downside impact,

---

1 A friend of a friend found a bug that way once, so it is indeed possible, but perhaps not advisable as a continual practice.

like downtime? Defining our objectives will inform how we allocate our effort capital, which, in turn, informs how we design and architect our systems.

When deciding how to expend our effort—in software as in life—we face a continual conundrum: are we trading off convenience today for friction and stress tomorrow? This is the opportunity cost of effort. We can only allocate effort to one thing at one instance in space-time, so we must integrate trade-offs across time when we prioritize. How often have we cursed our past selves for making a decision that requires more effort now from our current selves? That is the opportunity cost in action. Sometimes this trade-off is inexorable. If our monetary capital is light, then we may have to invest excess effort anyway, which means we will have less effort capital to invest in other activities.

From the perspective of this phase—architecting and designing software systems (and IT systems, more generally)—our overarching investment goal is to design systems that maintain their critical function during normal times as well as when experiencing stressors and surprises.[2] The critical function of a system is the one we intend for it to perform, its *raison d'être* (as discussed in Chapter 1). This phase is where we define these critical functions. We must free up time, cognitive effort, and other resources that can be spent on the activities that add value to our organizations the most. Doing so requires consideration of local context.

Investing Effort Based on Local Context

When we allocate our Effort Investment Portfolio during design and architecture, we must consider the local context of the entire sociotechnical system and preserve possibilities for both software and humans within it to adapt and evolve over time. It may feel strange to treat a service or system like an ecosystem or organism, but we should. In a vacuum, a software system can perhaps remain a static entity in its own crystallized space-time. But our systems are always sociotechnical; when they adapt to new challenges, they're no longer the same system afterward.

The related Ship of Theseus thought experiment (*https://oreil.ly/gn2do*) is commonly applied to software. In this experiment, all of the ship's planks are replaced one by one over time until the ship is composed of entirely different planks, yet still resembles the original ship. The piquing question posed by Plutarch (*https://oreil.ly/TNKmC*) still stimulates in software today: is it the same ship? But less common is to consider both the software *and* the humans who interact with the software as planks comprising the ever-evolving ship.

---

2 Emerson Mahoney et al., "Resilience-by-Design and Resilience-by-Intervention in Supply Chains for Remote and Indigenous Communities," *Nature Communications* 13, no. 1 (2022): 1-5.

The Effort Investment Portfolio and Smaller Organizations

The Effort Investment Portfolio especially applies to smaller organizations, which often don't have a dedicated security team. We need to be thoughtful about how those constrained resources are spent toward improving system resilience to attack. We could spend those resources on a prevention tool promising to stop ransomware or malware from happening. Alternatively, we might avail ourselves by migrating to cloud-based systems to outsource prevention to cloud providers, who have far more spare capacity to protect lower layers of the system (or SaaS providers, who likewise have the same in protecting applications).

Our resilience potion recipe from Chapter 1 can elucidate our local context; the first ingredient, critical functionality, is particularly constructive during this phase. Do we understand why we are architecting and designing the system in the first place? Do we understand why we are designing it in a particular way? Do we understand why there are certain interactions and when they happen? Whether we consider software quality or resilience, a shortage of answers to these questions will distort our investments. Investing our effort in a project despite a fuzzy mental model may lower costs in Act One and engender a devastating tragedy in Act Three. Not thinking through the *why* behind our design and architecture can lead us to overlook faster, simpler ways of conceiving systems.

As we'll discuss throughout this chapter, software architecture is rife with ambiguity—and this is why shrewd selection of your Effort Investment Portfolio sets your software up for success. The thorniest brambles we must navigate during this phase are how to model data representation within the system and how data flows throughout the system. Untangling these flows makes it easier to navigate decomposing the design into subsystems, services, components, and smaller units of whatever buzzword is currently trendy (as of this writing, *functions* or *containers*).

From this foundation of flows, we can determine the accuracy and availability each flow requires and appraise rough estimates about their data volumes. These requirements effervesce into the higher-level performance or resilience behaviors necessary at each billow of the system's fractal, from the smallest unit up through the application as a whole. Security is implicit in the resilience requirements for each flow at each fractal stage. We may need to isolate critical flows from each other or at least ensure any flows that receive less attention (i.e., receive less resilience or security care) cannot commingle with critical flows.

What effort capital is required to achieve these desired system behaviors? The answer informs the effort investments we must allocate—but we must enrich this with an understanding of what portfolios are attainable given our available effort capital. Are you investing in the fashionable financial asset of today, even if you lack the necessary pool of effort capital and it's all wrong for your investment objectives? When designing and architecting systems, make investment choices that are appropriate for the systems you're creating based on your local context—including an understanding of the practices available to you and the existing legacy parts you must lug around or else evolve.

How Effort Manifests Across the Software Delivery Lifecycle

When designing systems, you should never assume a perfect human operator who always makes the right call—especially when scrutinized in the harsh interrogation light of hindsight. A person referred to only as "Duskin" (employed by the company ICI) captured this wisdom best during an investigation of a fire at an ammonia plant back in 1979: "If you depend only on well-trained operators, you may fail."[3] This is no less true in our complex software systems.

Any computer system is inherently sociotechnical—humans design, build, and operate them. Our architectures must reflect that. With advances in hardware, and innovation like infrastructure-as-a-service, the emerging (but not yet predominant) trend is for a system's computer costs to represent a smaller portion of budget than the costs of the engineers who build and maintain the system (artisanal lattes and mechanical keyboard hobbies are expensive).

Beyond costs, organizational design strongly influences system design (and we suspect vice versa as well). Conway's Law (*https://oreil.ly/EBVrI*), which states that organizations design systems that mirror their own communication structures, is difficult to fight. When designing a system and allocating your Effort Investment Portfolio, it's important to consider not only the system architecture, but also the structure of the teams that would build, operate, and use the system.

Throughout this chapter—and the rest of the book—think of the principles, practices, and patterns we propose as potential investments you could make in your Effort Investment Portfolio. If your systems are far from resilient today, don't try to allocate all the resources at your disposal at once. Choose the opportunities where your organization has sufficient effort capital to allocate and could invest that effort quickly. As you realize success from those investments, you can grow the portfolio and adopt even more principles, practices, and patterns to sustain resilience even deeper.

In *Jurassic Park*, Dr. Ian Malcolm laments, "Your scientists were so preoccupied with whether or not they could that they didn't stop to think if they should." As scientists stewarding our systems to success, we should always consider whether we should, not just if we could. The Effort Investment Portfolio nudges us to think about our

---

3 F. G. Kokemor, "Synthesis Start-up Heater Failure," *Ammonia Plant Safety* 22 (1980): 162.

objectives across space-time, not just myopic expediency. How do we plan our portfolios for outcomes rather than immediate outputs? We can start by considering the four failure modes that result from system design.

The Four Failure Modes Resulting from System Design

When our systems expand and unfurl into a dragon spiral, but our organization pursues intensifying parsimony and efficiency, our resilience potion can curdle into poison—we lose sight of the system's critical functions; push the system past its safe boundaries; overlook system interactions; struggle to learn and ingest feedback; and ossify. All of this obstructs change. This is the dreaded "Danger Zone," where meltdowns erupt most.[4] This is one of four macro failure modes we might see in a system (across any problem domain, including computer systems), as shown in Figure 3-2.

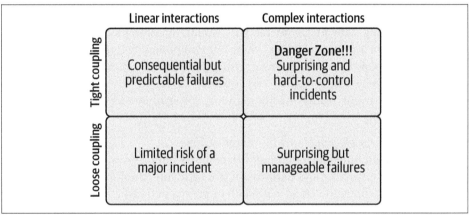

Figure 3-2. Failure modes across coupling and complexity

Each quadrant represents a combination of coupling and complexity. Coupling reflects the degree to which initial failures can concatenate rapidly to bring down other parts of the system—the degree of interdependence between the system's components. As we discussed in Chapter 1, complexity reflects the number and degree of system interconnections. We'll journey through the concepts of coupling and complexity in depth throughout this chapter. For now, let's start by discussing each quadrant and the characteristics of the failures within.

---

4 Charles Perrow, *Normal Accidents*.

Limited risk of a major incident

Linear interactions combined with loose coupling results in a limited risk of a major incident; it is unlikely that one component failing will result in a domino effect, and the interactions between components are unsurprising and relatively trivial to trace.

Surprising but manageable failures

Loose coupling combined with complex interactions results in surprising but manageable failures; it may be harder to trace how components interact, but the impact of a failure in one component is relatively isolated and unlikely to lead to contagion. Loose coupling preserves *slack* (spare resources like time, energy, or compute) and possibilities, the different adaptation paths that reduce incident impact and enable graceful recovery.

Consequential but predictable failures

Tight coupling with linear interactions results in consequential but *predictable* failures; there is a domino effect, where one component failing will cascade to the others, but how it cascades is unsurprising and relatively consistent. Humans like a predictable world, which is why we often gravitate toward tight coupling. Unfortunately, our reality—including most software systems—involves interactive complexity.

Danger Zone—surprising and hard-to-control incidents

When you combine tight coupling with complex interactions, you enter the Danger Zone of surprising and hard-to-control incidents (think nuclear meltdowns); the resulting contagion effect is difficult to predict and just as difficult to contain. It's important to stress that complex interactions on their own may be unintended and confounding, but that does not mean they will cause damage to components or the overall system. It's when there is tight coupling *and* complex interactions that especially insidious or injurious incidents surface.

Reflecting on this chart, you may realize many of your systems are or will be in the Danger Zone. Rather than a reason for nihilism or resignation, think of this as a call to action to invest effort capital in moving away from the Danger Zone. Our Effort Investment Portfolio makes it clear that resources are finite, particularly time (the most treasured of all). We may not be capable of pursuing looser coupling and linearity at the same time—or in all parts of our system—so we should consider opportunity cost and allocate resources to whichever path offers a better resilience return on those resources.

Many systems are like a massy, messy ball of gluten-free spaghetti where critical and noncritical functionality are tangled together, and this commingling encumbers resilience of critical functionality. In this context, the best way for us to quickly and fruitfully allocate our effort capital is by moving critical functionality out of the

Danger Zone, even if we leave everything else within it. We can't move everything out of the Danger Zone or implement every resilient design pattern in this chapter all at once. But we can be thoughtful about which system functionality needs to be resilient against attack (or other disruptions) today and in our future. Then we can incrementally invest our effort capital based on the functionality's priority in our system. Strategic allocation of effort based on the system's anticipated context is the most valuable thing an architect can do to design systems that sustain resilience.

Each quadrant in Figure 3-2 requires different management patterns. Tight coupling needs centralized management. Complex interactivity needs decentralized management. This brews an inherent tension that no amount of managerial magic can fix. How do we invest our effort capital during this phase to avoid this paradox? As a general guideline, we want to trend toward loose coupling to allow *decentralized* management, which we need for our inevitably complex software systems.

This brings us to a deeper discussion of these two key axes of resilient design—coupling and complexity. Exploring these concepts can inform how we allocate our Effort Investment Portfolio and influence our systems away from the Danger Zone.

The Two Key Axes of Resilient Design: Coupling and Complexity

We don't want to roil in turmoil in the Danger Zone, so what paths can we take out of it? Our possible paths toward resilience are paved with two key design metapatterns: loose coupling and linearity. The appropriate blend of each to escape the dastardly darkness of the Danger Zone depends on your incentives, goals, risks, and the teams and resources available to you. Where is the best place to pursue these patterns in the mess of systems you have to maintain? How do you pursue these patterns in practice? Why do these patterns ferry us toward resilience, away from peril? The next few sections will answer these questions and also illuminate how many of the design traits you already use for performance, scalability, or other reasons actually support loose coupling or linearity.

Designing to Preserve Possibilities

If we want to invest in the system's ability to succeed now and in the future, even as the contexts swirling around it morph and pressurize, we must design for resilience. In the SCE transformation, our goal is to design systems that preserve possibilities. Doing so allows us to avoid the trap of rigidity[5] (which paralyzes us during crises) and to remain flexible as the world inevitably evolves past our optimal design. As VP

---

5 Brian D. Fath et al., "Navigating the Adaptive Cycle: An Approach to Managing the Resilience of Social Systems," *Ecology and Society* 20, no. 2 (2015).

of Infrastructure and Google Fellow Eric Brewer noted at the beginning of this century, reducing the frequency of failures may be "more pleasing aesthetically," but reducing the impact of failure—whether the time to fix failures or their scope—is easier to accomplish, especially with evolving systems.[6]

 In general, you can think about resilience similarly to how accessibility features often help improve usability for the entire population. Resilience against attack helps with other use cases too. After all, it isn't like there is "friendly" or "healthy" memory corruption. This is a powerful tool to wield for stakeholder buy-in; if you find other use cases that your security designs or mitigations solve, then the organization will feel more willing to collaborate with you on implementing them. Consider examples such as these:

- Centralized logging increases visibility for developers while also increasing visibility for security to detect nefarious activity.

- Distributed tracing allows developers to find chokepoints, but also allows security to identify real-world code paths for any given API route, which can better inform testing.

- Building a culture of automated patching makes it easier to patch vulnerabilities, which is good for security, while also making it easier to update buggy dependencies and to fix other problems software engineers otherwise must hack around.

- A package repository can perform security scans of dependencies as well as perform software license checks for compliance.

- Fuzzing can find edge case bugs as well as unexpected attack paths in software.

The best organizational and system architecture is one that works now, but can evolve and grow into the system context you expect in a few years—responding to challenges today and adapting to challenges tomorrow. To *preserve possibilities* in this phase is to align software and team design in the possible directions that requirements might shift. The trick is to make the friction of implementing each possibility roughly proportional to its probability. However, probability is a messy business often closer to fortune telling than forecasting; if forecasting future requirements is even possible, it is preposterously difficult. Security chaos experiments can help by exposing where requirements are shifting over time with real-world evidence rather than silicon astrology. We can't predict, but we can adapt.

---

6 Eric Brewer, "Lessons from Giant-Scale Services," *IEEE Internet Computing* 5, no. 4 (2001): 46-55.

Architecting systems with this flexibility occurs at multiple layers of abstraction. We should allow the design to flexibly change over time as stressors change over time (like new attack classes or patterns). We should also design to minimize possibilities for attackers, restricting the functionality they can exploit within our system's flows, interactions, and components. And lastly, we should design to preserve possibilities for operators so they can respond to incidents faster. To draw from author and urban theorist Jane Jacobs' framing of the practice, our goal is to "foreclose as few options as possible."[7]

What we want in our systems is *sustained adaptability*: "The ability to adapt to future surprises as conditions continue to evolve."[8] To achieve this, we must allocate our Effort Investment Portfolio to the right blend of patterns, practices, and tools that preserve possibilities, so that when conditions and information and humans in the system change, the system is not brittle in the face of these surprises. A surprise is, in this context, an open challenge to our mental model of the system, a refutation of our assumptions and a pestilence to our plans. Part of preserving possibilities is considering the perspectives of the people who will build, maintain, and operate the system.

The capacity to adapt and change—the fifth and final ingredient of our resilience potion recipe—brings us to the first axis of resilient design: coupling.

Coupling in Complex Systems

The degree of *coupling* in our systems influences how we can change them, for which we must preserve possibilities. Coupling reflects the degree to which initial failures can concatenate rapidly to bring down other parts of the system. Our definitions of coupling (and complexity) aim to stay true to the complex systems foundations of resilience—and our ability to learn lessons from other domains.

As you might imagine, coupling is less of a binary and more of a spectrum; hence, we describe coupling in terms of *degrees*. As our dragon spiral expands and mutates, it's likely that the degree of coupling will change over time as the machines and humans in the system evolve.

7 Jane Jacobs, *The Death and Life of Great American Cities* (New York: Vintage Books, 1992).

8 David D. Woods, "Four Concepts for Resilience and the Implications for the Future of Resilience Engineering," *Reliability Engineering & System Safety* 141 (2015): 5-9.

Tight coupling reflects a system with mutual dependence (reliance between things) and minimal spare resources, so a failure in one component propagates to other parts of the system. A tightly coupled system is less "forgiving" of failures, so an action will likely lead to a consequence. Tightly coupled systems "have multiple, critical, concatenated dependencies that propagate effects through time and space, often via linkages that are difficult to anticipate."[9]

Loose coupling reflects a system with somewhat to largely independent components and spare resources, so a failure in one component does not propagate to other parts of the system. There are buffers between actions and consequences, making loosely coupled systems more forgiving of failures.

What is the ideal amount of coupling? Our goal is to minimize the amount of the system a human must consider when introducing a change. Thus, to ensure our effort investments pay off for maintaining resilience, we must accurately capture coupling in our mental models—which means we must understand the spectrum of tight and loose coupling when designing and architecting systems. Table 3-1 summarizes the characteristics of tight and loose coupling through the lens of complex systems. Think of this as a "cheat sheet" when you're designing, evaluating, or redesigning your systems.

Table 3-1. Characteristics of tight versus loose coupling[a]

Tight coupling	Loose coupling
Minimal buffering capacity	Can absorb the impact of surprises with spare capacity
Multiple, critical, concatenated dependencies	Flexible dependencies and independent connections
Difficult to analyze after incidents	Easier to untangle interactions after incidents
Difficult to troubleshoot during operation	Easier to debug and troubleshoot at runtime
More efficiency across the system	Efficiency can be suboptimal
Cost-effective over the short term	Cost-effective over the long term
Harder to foresee problems; interactions are less visible	Issues arising from interactions are more visible
Difficult to apply changes without impacting other parts of the system	New changes can be implemented independently with confidence their effects will be isolated
Adding new components increases system brittleness	Adding new components increases system resilience
Operational delays are intolerable, with outcomes disrupted	Processing delays are tolerable, with only delays in intended outcomes
Invariant sequences	Order of sequences can be changed
Only one method to achieve the goal	Alternate methods available to achieve the goal

9 Richard Cook and Jens Rasmussen, "Going Solid: A Model of System Dynamics and Consequences for Patient Safety," *BMJ Quality & Safety* 14, no. 2 (2005): 130-134.

Tight coupling	Loose coupling
Little slack possible in software, machines, personnel	Slack in resources available
Buffers and redundancies are premeditated in design	Buffers and redundancies are natural; emergent from the design
Substitutions of software, machines, personnel are limited and premeditated in design; reduces reusability	Substitutions are natural, available, and extensive (emergent from the design); supports reusability
Transformative changes require herculean, coordinated effort	Transformative changes are performed incrementally and in a decentralized fashion

[a] This table is based on the similar table from Charles Perrow's *Normal Accidents*, which we have adapted for software systems.

As Table 3-1 demonstrates, loose coupling helps us preserve possibilities in a variety of ways. A core benefit of loose coupling is that it can enable the use of off-the-shelf components developed and maintained by others, removing the need for custom software. For example, we could handle bursty traffic that doesn't need immediate processing by splitting the service into a collector and a processor, then sticking a durable queue in between. Loose coupling in this case yields real benefits to availability, cost, and failure tolerance. Maintainers of a loosely coupled system don't have to worry as much about the system as a whole, which, ironically, can make the system easier to understand than a tightly coupled one of equivalent scale. With loose coupling, we can change the system with more freedom and gain the capacity to continuously adapt to evolving conditions.

Buffers are elements or resources that increase capacity in a system, helping to stabilize it. Think about our fluffy-tailed friends, squirrels. When they hoard a trove of nuts in the hollow of a tree, they create buffers that help them be more resilient to seasonal disruptions to food availability.[10] We can think of them as going nuts for looser coupling. These nut buffers—at least in the case of red squirrel caches—can even influence the abundance of other mammals as well as bird species.[11]

The concept of sustained adaptability prompts an important question relevant to our discussion of loose coupling: what is "adaptation" in computer systems? In the strict, tactical sense, adaptation in computer systems is the ability to respond to unexpected input, uncovered design flaws, unexpected failures of components, or unexpected shifts in flows and volumes. However, this definition neglects the human element. In

10 David N. Fisher and Jonathan N. Pruitt, "Insights from the Study of Complex Systems for the Ecology and Evolution of Animal Populations," *Current Zoology* 66, no. 1 (2020): 1-14.

11 Erin E. Posthumus et al., "Red Squirrel Middens Influence Abundance But Not Diversity of Other Vertebrates," *PLoS One* 10, no. 4 (2015): e0123633.

a wider sense, we have sociotechnical systems with humans executing their processes and machines doing the same; both are continually influencing each other. Humans iterate on new and updated programs for the machines based on feedback received from the machines or from other humans asking for the system to function in a different fashion.

When machine processes fail in ways that are noticeable, humans jump in. To a large extent, the humans in the process are the mechanism of adaptation, like genetic mutation in biology. The Log4Shell attack evinces this dynamic. In December 2021, the world learned of a vulnerability in Log4j, a Java logging framework maintained by the Apache Software Foundation, that was present in many Java-based software systems running in production. When the Log4Shell attack unfolded, it was an emergency all-hands-on-deck situation for many organizations, but the real-world harm was low—or at least much lower than it might have been—thanks to the socio part of the sociotechnical system. Those organizations that fixed the vulnerability, or otherwise prepared for Log4Shell attacks with speed and minimal disruption, had systems that not only offered standardized mechanisms to make changes, but also had architectures that helped humans reason about where the attack might be possible.

Simple systems are easier for squishy human brains to reason about, operate, and change safely. So, in an ideal yet tactical sense, the looser the coupling, the better so that we can isolate failures to localized downtime or data loss. If we zoom out to the wider sociotechnical perspective, we can see that some design decisions result in tighter coupling due to the human element and that our effort investments may only be able to achieve a few characteristics of loose coupling at a time. Thus, we must explore the trade-offs of tight coupling to inform our effort investments.

The Tight Coupling Trade-Off

Reality is rarely linear and legible. In the reality of complex systems, tight coupling increases the potential for cascading failure even though it can reduce cost and increase efficiency in the short term. These benefits come with a heavy price tag: interdependencies, often hidden, foment incidents at larger scale that are harder to anticipate and recover from.[12] When surprises do happen, tight coupling makes it harder to troubleshoot the system and adapt to those surprises—whether naturally or by human design. With tight coupling, any change you make could drastically impact any part of the system, and when something goes wrong, it becomes harder to untangle *how* the failure unfolded. It's harder to recover from it too, since recovery almost always involves some sort of system change.

---

12 Igor Linkov et al., "Resilience Stress Testing for Critical Infrastructure," *International Journal of Disaster Risk Reduction* 82 (2022): 103323.

Because organizations and computer systems are both complex, adaptive systems, it is crucial to think of the *interconnections* between components when pondering the right design. Most of the quirky failures that are difficult to debug happen in the boundaries between components, not in the components themselves (and arguably this is also true for human components in the system). Incidents that span teams are more difficult and cumbersome to triage. An unexpected interaction is an opportunity for an unexpected failure.

The effects of tight coupling can creep up on you as the system grows larger, glutting itself on your effort capital until you have little left for anything but "Keep the Lights On" work. András Tilcsik calls this dynamic the "Paradox of Progress" (*https:// oreil.ly/ZxC7y*), observing that "complex systems enable us to do all sorts of innovative things, and tight coupling often arises because we are trying to make a system leaner and more efficient. That is the paradox of progress: We often do these things for good economic reasons; but, at the same time, we are pushing ourselves into the danger zone without realizing it."

Once you become aware of tight coupling, you can't "unsee" it. Even supposedly simple activities like making a holiday dinner are tightly coupled.[13] Many holidays fall on a specific day each year, so there is no flexibility to just try again tomorrow if something goes wrong. And since most homes only have one oven to cook their entree of choice, it's difficult to recover the dinner if you mess up that step.

Even we, as humans, can be analyzed through this lens of coupling. A normal human features very complex interactions, but is, on balance, loosely coupled. Generally, we can sustain an injury or modification in one area without concatenated failure. A patient under the effect of anesthesia, however, becomes more tightly coupled on top of being naturally complex. The self-regulating subsystems of the body become controlled by the anesthesia, which has "suspended, altered, or taken over" those subsystems.[14] When the body is tightly coupled with this technology, it requires far more oversight to succeed—hence, it is more likely to succumb to a catastrophic failure.

We shouldn't feel discouraged because tight coupling is everywhere. Rather, we must understand how tight coupling manifests so we can incite change to loosen coupling in our systems where it befits the trade-off between frugality, efficiency, and resilience. Let's explore an example from ecology that illuminates the trade-offs we discussed and the differing outcomes between tight and loose coupling in complex systems.

---

13 Chris Clearfield and András Tilcsik, *Meltdown: Why Our Systems Fail and What We Can Do About It* (London: Penguin Press, 2018).

14 Craig S. Webster et al., "The Challenges of Technological Intensification," *APSF Newsletter* 24 (2009): 33-35.

The Dangers of Tight Coupling: Taming the Forest

In nearly every problem domain, humans create tight coupling in the pursuit of parsimony and short-term efficiency. One notable example of this is documented in James C. Scott's book *Seeing Like a State*, which describes how early German forestry science created a hyper-streamlined "Normalbaum." The "chaotic, old-growth" forest was transformed into a "new, more uniform" forest that was more convenient for administrators to understand and manipulate.[15] They achieved this by clearing underbrush, reducing the number of species, and planting trees in straight rows for navigation and ease of visual assessment. In essence, the forest managers forced the existing loosely coupled, complex forest to not just more closely match their mental models, but also make it easier to mentally model.

This introduction of tight coupling resulted in tangible cost and "legibility" gains. Managing linear rows of same-age and mostly monocropped trees became more routine, which meant training protocols were easier to write and apply. It was also easier to forecast logging yields since logs were now of a uniform width and length (making it easier to market to buyers). With a forest of same-age, single-species, geometrically planted trees, the forest managers had achieved the Pyrrhic victory of simplicity—a "legible" forest with variables held in artificial stasis.[16]

Of course, the radically simplified forest now had nature as its enemy. As Scott wrote in *Seeing Like a State*,

> Unauthorized disturbances—whether by fire or by local populations—were seen as implicit threats to management routines. The more uniform the forest, the greater the possibilities for centralized management; the routines that could be applied minimized the need for the discretion necessary in the management of diverse old-growth forests.

This passage may feel familiar in its appeal. If only we can make our software and systems more uniform, more inspectable, more neatly fitting our mental models, then we can centrally manage them and achieve optimal efficiency! Even better, we can remove the need for human judgment![17] In nearly every sense, this quest for tight coupling in the forest was at the expense of diversity—and that diversity is indispensable when things go wrong.

And things went quite wrong in the Normalbaum. Tight coupling works well in the sandbox of our imagination, but not so well in the messy reality of complex systems. The dangers of tight coupling encroach while luring us into a sense of success and safety. In the Normalbaum, the first generation of trees—taking nearly a century to

---

15 James C. Scott, *Seeing Like a State* (New Haven, CT: Yale University Press, 2008).

16 James C. Scott, "State Simplifications: Nature, Space, and People," *NOMOS* 38 (1996): 42-85.

17 Theodore M. Porter, "Trust in Numbers," in *Trust in Numbers* (Princeton, NJ: Princeton University Press, 1996).

realize (trees do not grow as quickly as software)—seemed like a smashing success, offering a convincing illusion of progress. But surprises are inevitable and forests are not exempt; fire, storms, climactic changes will rage despite our human desires.

It was not until planting the second generation of uniform trees that the Normal-baum's negative consequences finally manifested: the rows of trees retrogressed, resulting in a production loss of 20% to 30%. The term *Waldsterben* (forest death) was even introduced into the language due to this failure. Why did this reversal of fortune happen? The administrators had streamlined a process—but that process involved a variety of components and activities for a reason. Nature involves a symbiosis between soil, nutrient uptake, fungi, insects, mammals, and flora[18]—all of which administrators tried to remove for the sake of streamlining. They thought they were achieving more linear interactions—taming the complexity of the forest—but all they achieved was tight coupling, which conduces cascading failures. Controlling variables into "generalized" processes meant any variable out of whack caused problems for the whole system.

Even in the face of failure, forest managers denied the pervading dynamic: what sustained the forest was diversity and the loose coupling between components within the forest. It was better, in their minds, to attempt a "virtual" ecology rather than lose the promise of efficiency from the monoculture (which was, of course, now irreparably gone).

The key takeaways from this story are:

- Attempting to "solve" complex interactions or "streamline" variables—the interrelations and processes between things in a system that are difficult to mentally model—may overlook their necessity in sustaining the system; attempting linearity at the level of a multipurpose system results in problems.

- Humans will pursue legibility and frugality with a myopic focus, not thinking about second-order effects—thus prioritizing short-term streamlining over long-term resilience and sustainability.

- Tight coupling may *appear* to "solve" complexity by giving the illusion of more linear interactions; the undesirable consequences of tight coupling may be distant in time; what feels like a more manageable and orderly system may just reflect concatenated dependencies.

- Loose coupling liberates more slack in the system, or the ability to absorb surprises due to spare capacity. Loose coupling keeps the complexity from spiraling into a devastating failure; the underbrush, wildlife, weeds, and other natural

---

18 James Wells and Vincent Varel, "Symbiosis of Plants, Animals and Microbes," in *Animal Welfare in Animal Agriculture: Husbandry, Stewardship and Sustainability in Animal Production*, 185-203 (New York: CRC Press, 2011).

elements forest managers removed felt like unnecessary detritus, but were, in fact, factors in promoting system resilience.

- The hardest problem we face is finding the balance between short-term streamlining and legibility and long-term resilience; the best solutions we find will be those that foster more resilience while finding opportunities to improve efficiency from the status quo.

Investing in Loose Coupling in Software Systems

For all the reasons the forest case study highlights, we want to invest in loose coupling in our software systems so that a failure in one part of the system does not concatenate into other parts of the system. What opportunities exist for us to invest in looser coupling? Let's start with some considerations first.

For any given service or system, we are unlikely to achieve all outcomes of loose coupling—nor do we necessarily need to do so to receive resilience returns. It's also impossible to dissolve all instances of tight coupling; we may as well try to boil the ocean. If our service is written in Go, we're tightly coupled to the language and its ecosystem. If instead we pursued a polyglot approach in our current context, the outcome would vaporize efficiency. Writing services in multiple languages by default would be inefficient, unpleasant, and prone to influencing failures at boundaries. But we can mimic nature's approach and accept that standardized materials—like elements, DNA, water, and so forth—are necessary for sustainable systems.

 Loose coupling doesn't mean there is no *determinacy*—no clear causal links—between any elements. We aren't saying you should design for *de*coupled or *un*coupled systems, but instead that you should design for loosely coupled ones. This means our systems preserve some degree of independence and indeterminacy, but components will still be linked and there will always be some degree of dependence.

In their journal article "Loosely Coupled Systems: A Reconceptualization," organizational theorists Orton and Weick summarized the outcomes of tight and loose coupling by comparing responsiveness and distinctiveness: "If there is responsiveness without distinctiveness, the system is tightly coupled. If there is distinctiveness without responsiveness, the system is decoupled. If there is both distinctiveness and responsiveness, the system is loosely coupled."[19]

---

19 J. Douglas Orton and Karl E. Weick, "Loosely Coupled Systems: A Reconceptualization," *Academy of Management Review* 15, no. 2 (1990): 203-223.

Rather than attempting to decouple everything, our goal is to prioritize outcomes—as enumerated earlier in Table 3-1—and invest our effort capital in architecting and designing for them. Where can we afford tighter coupling so we can invest in loose coupling elsewhere? Reasoning about this question involves contemplating the implicit contracts of loose coupling, which we'll now explore.

Implicit contracts of loose coupling

Earlier, we mentioned a durable queue as one tactic for achieving looser coupling. But this pattern results in more overhead in maintaining the system—which requires more effort capital. We must now understand, evolve, and operationalize not just the additional durable queue, but also the communication glue that interacts with it and all the other tooling that allows engineers to develop and debug the system.

One way to think about this trade-off is through the framing of implicit contracts. In our durable queue example, there are implicit contracts that form between the thing writing into the collector, the thing writing into the queue, and the processor reading from it. That contract can be subtle, and neither side really knows exactly what is going to happen should the other party violate it (unless they go out of their way to test it). The two sides may have subtle differences in their interpretation of the contract—in the vein of Hyrum's law (*https://oreil.ly/JCw2z*)—and when something goes awry, there are more pieces that are interacting together. From a resilience perspective, it's worth it. Smoothing out spiky loads and fortifying durability to crashes—not to mention enabling greater scale—may be worth it to the organization if resilience and reliability are held as important values.

As our systems become more loosely coupled, it may begin to feel like mentally modeling how they work is a matter of contract law (with implicitly specified contracts) and estimating how likely all the parties are to conform to the contract. Most problems become distributed systems problems, which require more effort to understand and debug. Loose coupling allows us to *achieve* the scale of distributed systems that tight coupling would suppress. If we attempted the same outcome with a tightly coupled system, we would not even be aware of those boundaries; it would be like one giant kingdom where boundaries between cities and towns and villages are invisible and squabbles between one entity and another result in ruin for everyone. A village itself might work fine as a tightly coupled system, but a kingdom cannot. Blaming the problems of a kingdom on loose coupling ignores the impossibility of maintaining the kingdom over time *without* that loose coupling.

Whether in the sense of cognitive overhead or machine overhead, investing in loose coupling can require more effort capital. For instance, you can migrate a program onto another computer to remove the shared dependency, but now the programs must talk to each other over a network that has delays and is lossy (*https://oreil.ly/Zx1X5*). Whether your organization believes that this loss of efficiency is made up for by the benefits loose coupling provides—like more adaptive response or saving overall effort long term—depends entirely on its preferences (usually collective preferences across company leadership). As with any thorny problem, the answer to the optimal amount of coupling is: It depends. The ad absurdum of perfect uncoupling means we will likely dissatisfy shareholders (who expect short-term economic performance) and therefore have less financial *and* effort capital at our disposal to absorb surprises and stressors—ultimately *reducing* slack in the system (becoming the very thing we swore to destroy!). We want enough loose coupling to preserve possibilities and ensure there is sufficient slack in the system. Then we can gracefully recover from adverse conditions and adapt as our local context evolves.

Nature avoids the overhead issue because the components are usually autonomous entities that can adapt on their own and make efficient use of resources by design. Our computers cannot adapt on their own; we've designed them to be dependent on us. That is, we have tightly coupled computers to ourselves and, until a major breakthrough in computer science, we cannot remove that coupling. Therefore, the loose coupling nature can achieve for cheap we must achieve through effort.

Nevertheless, we can still strive toward effort that makes the best use of our energy, time, and money—that minimizes waste while pursuing loose coupling. Many of the real-world examples of resilience-by-design will illustrate that loose coupling still can be achieved with acceptable efficiency—sometimes even greater efficiency than before. We should seize these opportunities, as they reflect the best ways to allocate our effort capital. The next section describes opportunities to introduce looser coupling toward these aims.

Empirical evidence from the 2021 Accelerate State of DevOps report (*https://oreil.ly/-lR-2*) shows that organizations who meet their reliability targets—the "elite" DevOps performers—are three times more likely to employ a loosely coupled architecture than low-performing organizations.

Opportunities for looser coupling by design

When we consider opportunities for looser coupling when architecting and designing systems, there are a few key questions we should contemplate:

- Which parts of our system should be loosely coupled?
- In which dimensions are they coupled and uncoupled?
- What are the characteristics of our coupling and uncoupling?

These answers are rooted in our local context. But, for most systems, we can prioritize looser coupling between critical functionality and noncritical functionality. If you find branches that can be pruned from your critical functions, you can allow those branches to remain tightly coupled without impacting critical functions—and free up effort capital to invest in those critical functions. From there, we can select which characteristics of loose coupling we wish to optimize since, with finite effort capital, we cannot invest in them all.

Perhaps you want to change the system more quickly or isolate failures more frequently. Depending on your priorities, you might need to choose different practices or tools when you allocate your efforts. Chaos experiments can demystify which parts of the system behave in a loosely or tightly coupled way in adverse scenarios, giving us experimental evidence to inform these choices.

The rest of this section divulges different investment options that endow looser coupling. Our goal in not only this chapter, but throughout the book, is to present resilience opportunities that inspire you so you can select the ones that fit best for your systems. In Table 3-2, we enumerate potential design and architecture decisions—as well as other mechanisms across the software delivery lifecycle—that help us realize looser coupling. Remember, it's unlikely you can pursue every opportunity in the table; instead, the opportunities you choose to pursue should make the best use of your effort capital.

Table 3-2. Mechanisms to achieve loose coupling outcomes

Loose coupling outcome	Potential mechanisms
Can absorb the impact of surprises with spare capacity	Buffers, failover, autoscaling, queueing, backpressure, job systems, background/batch processing
Independent, or flexible dependencies	Isolation, declarative dependencies (like infrastructure-as-code)
Easier to untangle interactions after incidents	Isolation, standardization, documentation
Easier to debug and troubleshoot at runtime	Standardization, iterative design, logging, tracing, observability, monitoring, break-glass debugging mechanism with audit
Cost-effective over the long term	Standardization, monitoring
Issues arising from interactions are more visible	Failover, isolation, alerting, monitoring, tracing
Supports reusability	Standardization, documentation, libraries, component model, specifications
New changes can be implemented independently	Isolation, iterative design, documentation
Adding new components increases system resilience	Failover, buffers
Processing delays are tolerable	Isolation, failover, autoscaling, queues, job systems, background/batch processing, asynchronous processing
Order of sequences can be changed	Message passing, queues, background/batch processing
Alternate methods available to achieve the goal	Documentation, standardization, specifications, common protocols

Loose coupling outcome	Potential mechanisms
Slack in resources possible	Autoscaling, spare capacity/failover
Buffers and redundancies are natural; emergent from the design	Message buses, queueing, log-oriented designs, resource pools
Substitutions are natural, available, and extensive; emergent from the design	Failover, standardization, specifications, common protocols

What other opportunities exist for us to invest in looser coupling? The next section elaborates on a design pattern—the D.I.E. pattern—that can help us achieve not only looser coupling but, in some cases, more linear interactions as well.

The Distributed, Immutable, Ephemeral (D.I.E.) design pattern

Some valuable opportunities lie within patterns that may not apply to all systems, but can be worthy investments in looser coupling if applicable to your local context. One such pattern is making custom software or systems distributed, immutable, and ephemeral, and then using common off-the-shelf software for the hard, stateful parts of your architecture (under the assumption that the off-the-shelf software will be more mature and the hard parts will be handled by the vendor by design or via the support contract). Some engineering teams organically follow this pattern as it flowers from their requirements. But we can purposefully use this pattern—the D.I.E. pattern, coined by CISO and author Sounil Yu—to invest our effort capital in looser coupling. By adopting these characteristics—distributed, immutable, and ephemeral—in our infrastructure, we can reduce paths available for attackers to pursue when they attack us (like we discussed in the last chapter). All three of these attributes can also be seen as a form of isolation and therefore a way of infusing linearity in our systems, which we'll cover in the next section.

If we want to build in security by design and our system (or components within) allows us to pursue this pattern, D.I.E. is a way to allocate our effort capital that considers resilience in the broader context of what might jeopardize the system's successful operation. Of course, some of the components in our systems need to store data, so the D.I.E. pattern won't be the best use of your effort capital. This is precisely why our Effort Investment Portfolio depends on local context; what works for some organizations and contexts may not work for yours.

Optimizing for D.I.E. in system design inherently reduces hazards, even when security isn't the explicit ambition. The D.I.E. attributes are all about the system's ability to be resilient and recover effectively in the face of problems, whether hazards to performance or to security. Let's explore each characteristic and why it presents an opportunity for resilience.

Distributed. Distributed infrastructure involves multiple systems that may be in different locations, but support the same overarching goal. Distributed infrastructure, if

---

designed carefully, can loosen coupling (when we tighten coupling in distributed systems, we get brittle systems that are hard to manage). Content delivery networks (CDNs) are a form of distributed infrastructure and their near-ubiquitous adoption among enterprises directly diminished harm by distributed denial-of-service (DDoS) attacks. The rise of ransomware is arguably in part a result of DDoS no longer being a lucrative criminal pursuit (as evidenced by the decline in dark net market prices for DDoS attack services).

More generally, distributed infrastructure softens the severity of service outages because it facilitates high availability, scalability, redundancy, and failure tolerance. The caveat—just as with many loose coupling mechanisms—is it can create overhead[20] in terms of managing lots of machines,[21] which is why many enterprises outsource coordination of those machines to a vendor (or vendors) to reap the benefits with fewer distractions. That is, organizations spend financial capital to free up effort capital.

Immutable. Immutable infrastructure (*https://oreil.ly/VraZ_*) does not change after it's deployed. If a modification or update is necessary, we use a standardized image with appropriate changes to build a new resource (like a server) to replace the old one. Engineers responsible for system operation often prefer immutable infrastructure because it provides more consistency and reliability through a simpler, standardized deployment process—which, along with other outcomes, benefits resilience too.

In the D.I.E. paradigm, servers are no longer closely held and cherished "pets," but instead are disposable "cattle."[22] This framing drastically simplifies incident recovery. Because each base image is validated and version-controlled, we can cull and redeploy each server built from this image without consequence. And, because images are version-controlled, rollbacks become easier, reducing the traditional headaches of the update process.

The resilience (and security) return is considerable with immutable infrastructure. We can perform configuration changes through a standard, automated deployment process rather than engineers logging into servers for manual configuration. This kind of deployment process can create audit trails of who wrote the change, who reviewed the change, who deployed the change, and so on.

---

20 Daniel Abadi, "Consistency Tradeoffs in Modern Distributed Database System Design: CAP Is Only Part of the Story," *Computer* 45, no. 2 (2012): 37-42.

21 Diogo Faustino et al., "Stepwise Migration of a Monolith to a Microservices Architecture: Performance and Migration Effort Evaluation," arXiv preprint arXiv:2201.07226 (2022).

22 Randy Bias, "The History of Pets vs Cattle and How to Use the Analogy Properly" (*https://oreil.ly/MXqgF*), Cloudscaling (posted September 29, 2016).

Immutability also means you can completely restrict shell access to servers, which is a veritable security miracle. If shell access is disabled, it's much harder for attackers to access or modify servers without being noisy in their operations. While indubitably tricky to implement for cultural reasons, banning shell access can ruin an attacker's day…maybe even their week or whole month.

The new mindset is to ask what access is "good enough." For instance, does your beta launch need full integration with your IAM system? Or will MFA suffice to ensure the beta is up and running quickly? Persistent root access is seen as an outdated pattern in this world—whether cloud root, UNIX root, Windows domain root, and so forth. We will describe more modern IAM patterns, which eschew this old paradigm, toward the end of the chapter.

Ephemeral. Ephemeral infrastructure has a tiny lifespan, living only for the duration of a task before dying (in contrast to traditional monolithic applications that can live for thousands of days). This limited lifespan grants looser coupling, limiting the propagation of failure across time—a form of temporal isolation. It also makes better use of capacity and can make software easier to change too (*https://oreil.ly/TTZXh*).

Infrastructure that could die at any moment is a nightmare for attackers. Attackers love a cozy place to kick up their feet and chill out, biding their time until their preferred moment of attack. Ephemerality destroys that dream, generating a formidable level of uncertainty for persistence. Installing a rootkit on a resource that will die within minutes is a waste of effort, which, per the attacker math we learned in Chapter 2, means they're less likely to chase it as an option.

When we automatically kill a resource in response to unintended behavior, ephemerality forces attackers to pivot more quickly to get to their goal. Or it forces attackers to spend time and effort developing automation to continually exploit an ephemeral-but-vulnerable asset. In a sense, either option drains the attacker's Effort Investment Portfolio and doesn't produce immediate returns—very disappointing attacker math for them. If the cost of investment is higher than the likely return from compromise, the attacker is more likely to move on. Ephemerality helps us raise that cost of attacker investment by design.

Chaos Experiments Expose Coupling

Once we've chosen our investments in loose coupling, how do we track our portfolio's performance? Tight and loose coupling can't be measured with a Boolean test like true or false. Loose coupling in your system is *dis*provable, but not provable. The system's true nature is only really revealed at runtime or when the system encounters a surprise—at which point, like a Scooby Doo villain, what looks like loose coupling is unmasked as tight coupling in disguise!

Security chaos experiments can uncover where your system is perched on the spectrum between tight (rigid efficiency) and loose (flexible resilience). These experiments can help us verify whether we have loose coupling or just tight coupling in disguise, because simulating an adverse scenario can expose concatenated dependents and where system components might be codependent.

Consider a manufacturing company that maintains a physical parts database for its manufacturing sites on both the East Coast and West Coast of the United States. Their parts management system runs on the East Coast (making it their primary site) and broadcasts data about the parts to each site via database replication. A core property of replication that organizations usually want to preserve is the ability to operate the system with data that is stale, but not too stale. If replication is 10 seconds behind, that could be acceptable for your needs if it is unlikely that the state will have changed too substantially in those 10 seconds.

For our manufacturing company, the worst-case scenario with laggy replication is that a site assumes they have inventory that they actually don't. When the time window is 10 seconds, the company assumes that it won't happen too frequently and thus the delay is tolerable; after all, most of their parts supply won't be as minimal as one or two items, so when the data is stale, it mostly doesn't matter. But if replication fails and the manufacturing company doesn't notice it for an hour, they're now much more likely to encounter the "phantom inventory" scenario.

Naturally, the manufacturing company wants to understand how their systems behave when replication is severed or when it gets too far behind. Their mental model is that each site can function independently, but how loosely coupled are they in practice? Does the system notice that the data it's operating on is stale? Is someone alerted? Can operators somehow use inventory that doesn't exist, and, if so, what ill effects does that cause? Does it stop the production line?

A chaos experiment can generate evidence to answer these questions. A potential chaos experiment the manufacturing company could conduct involves the adverse condition of severing the database replication between the two sites. When the connection is restored, they want to verify that the secondary site correctly incorporated the changes that were made at the primary site during the outage. Let's say their hypothesis was proven incorrect; replication didn't work and requests continued to be served from the West Coast. Not great! It means there was tighter coupling than they believed and that the site could end up serving a big pile of nothing. This could inform the company's design change of halting the West Coast datacenter (*https:// oreil.ly/n9UlI*) if it isn't caught up to the primary (East Coast) datacenter, rather than letting it proceed and fail (while draining money).

Let's assume they reran the experiment after that design change. This time, they learned a few surprising lessons. The good news is that when they reconnected the sites, the replication caught up quite quickly—in fact, faster than they expected—

suggesting they gained both looser coupling and efficiency from the change. The bad news is that they weren't alerted about the replication lag (that data wasn't up to date), even though they thought they had alerting for that scenario. Their mental model was violated, presenting another opportunity to redesign and refine—and then run the experiment again.

When analyzing the results of a chaos experiment or a real security incident, we should apply the lens of coupling to determine whether tight coupling contributed to conditions that allowed or encouraged failures. When we incorporate this feedback into our design, we should serve as advocates for loose coupling. The loose coupling patterns can even help us generate hypotheses to inform new security chaos experiments. For instance, if a workload is configured to be immutable, a hypothesis could be: "If a user attempts to alter the workload at runtime, we would block, detect, and alert on the attempt."

 If we want to get fancy, we can even replicate prospective designs through the same process used to create deception environments (*https://oreil.ly/8_jFg*)—using IaC and traffic generation to emulate a real system—and then conduct security chaos experiments in this replica environment. This can give us rapid validation on our design assumptions, like how data flows through the system, before deploying into production environments interacting with real users. We'll talk more about deception environments in Chapter 5.

Now that we're inspired to invest in loose coupling and we know some of the worthy opportunities available to us, let's turn to the second axis of resilient design: complexity.

Complexity in Complex Systems

Gall's Law (*https://oreil.ly/-QHW2*) states that a complex system that works is invariably found to have evolved from a simple system that worked. This law implies that even linear software systems eventually evolve into ones with more complex interactions (like our dragon spiral). How do we invest our effort to nourish innovation rather than vexation? In this section, we will discover how to cope with complexity and why investing in linearization—when it befits our local context—augments our resilience returns in conjunction with looser coupling.

According to systems theorist Niklas Luhmann, security efforts should specifically aim to curtail the complexity of the world.[23] The entire world is a bit more ambitious

---

[23] Stefan Kaufmann and Ricky Wichum, "Risk and Security: Diagnosis of the Present in the Context of (Post-) Modern Insecurities," *Historical Social Research/Historische Sozialforschung* (2016): 48-69.

than our purview, which is our organization's systems. Our goal is to help our organizations feel more confident in their ongoing success because we manage complexity. That is, we make effort investments that enhance an innovation engine, which is fueled by complexity, while curtailing the less savory ways it surprises us.

Consider our favorite complex systems example from Chapter 1: *Jurassic Park*. You can design buffers, failover mechanisms, standardized vehicles and rails, isolated paddocks, and other loose coupling patterns, but dinosaurs will still find a way to do dinosaur things, like eating humans. It's difficult to conceive a linear park since dinosaurs—inherently complex creatures—are a core requirement. The closest comparison in software systems is perhaps C code. No matter how many precautions you've taken and how careful you are, there's still danger that you only *think* you've avoided. The irreducible complexity—the essential complexity we'll discuss next—is still ready to pounce and ruin your fun time, or, in the case of software, runtime.

Understanding Complexity: Essential and Accidental

When we invest our effort capital in system resilience, there are two specific types of complexity to consider: essential and accidental.

Essential complexity includes the interactions begotten by the critical functions of the system, the parts of the process that must happen for the system to perform its correct function. As we discussed in Chapter 1, understanding critical functions is the first ingredient in our resilience potion. When we are designing systems, we must think about what functionality, if disrupted, would result in the system not fulfilling its purpose.

For example, if the wrong font is loaded in a webpage, then that may degrade the user experience, but not disrupt their ability to stream a video. But if the API call to the video database fails, then the user will experience a lag in their video playback and may resort to refreshing the page—or giving up entirely and switching to an alternative service. So, one of the most important things you can do to architect resilient systems is to explicitly define and document critical functions, as they directly inform what is top priority to keep safe (whether through protection or monitoring).

Noncritical, but designed, functionality can also constitute essential complexity. For instance, consider a product or accounting team that wants metrics about which users are actively engaging with which parts of the service. This team may be comfortable with the data being slow or missing sometimes, which means that we can sacrifice this noncritical functionality—investing less of our effort capital in making it resilient—to extricate effort capital and other necessary resources for our critical functionality.

Accidental complexity refers to the unintended interactions that manifest during system operation, those arising from the manner in which the system was modeled and the precise implementation of that modeling. In the realm of physical systems, nuclear power plants depend on pipes to pump in water to cool down nuclear reactors, but accidental complexity emerges when other components of the environment swim into the pipes. In 1980, clams clogged the Arkansas Nuclear One power plant's internal cooling pipes and forced operators to shut it down (*https://oreil.ly/Z2_p7*). More recently, in 2013, *Aurelia aurita* (known as the moon jellyfish) swam into Sweden's biggest nuclear reactors' cooling water inlet and blocked it, requiring operators to shut down the plant (*https://oreil.ly/gZ5NB*). The designers of these nuclear power plants certainly did not intend for local aquatic inhabitants to swim into the reactor's cooling pipes, but these interactions emerged anyway. ("Life finds a way," as Ian Malcolm says in *Jurassic Park*.) Thus, we can define these unintended interactions that only manifested once the design became operational reality as accidental complexity.

Software engineers luckily don't have to contend with clams or jellyfish clogging their software or data pipelines. But in your career, you've likely encountered an unexpected interaction in one of your organization's systems that led you to wonder, "How could we have ever anticipated *that*?"

Chaos experiments and accidental complexity

Luckily, security chaos experiments help you uncover those metaphorical jellyfish before they result in an outage for your computer systems. Chaos experiments can reveal accidental complexity and potential failure outcomes. Given an architecture, what failures in one component will result in what potential failures elsewhere? Experimentation can be tool-assisted too: you can collect the architecture from a deployed system or reconstruct it from deployment templates.

How could an experiment to ferret out our metaphorical jellyfish look in practice? No matter the industry, organizations likely have a system with scheduled processes—often in the form of scheduled jobs to inform business decisions, like calculating inventory or profitability. And it's quite common to schedule these processes with the assumption that their prerequisites will finish before the scheduled process starts. Let's say you have a chain of data processing jobs that delivers a daily report. You schedule the first stage at midnight, the second stage at 01:00, and the third stage at 02:00, leaving an hour buffer between each. But one early morning while you're dreaming in cron jobs, one of these stages is delayed. The job doesn't fail, but it exceeds its allocated time budget—which causes cascading failures. A chaos experiment—like injecting the adverse condition of a delay—will expose this accidental complexity and inspire the necessary redesign to avoid such contagion.

As this example suggests, experiments close the feedback loop that is crucial to our resilience potion. They help ground the software architect—who, like an astronaut, sometimes floats up in space while making proclamations about how the system should be—as well as the engineer building the system who must pay lip service to those proclamations while still getting things done. When you perform chaos experiments over time, you may learn general principles of design that you then apply to new systems. We must disseminate this knowledge by documenting your findings and sharing learnings internally. Of course, just because you tell a young child not to touch a hot stove doesn't mean they will avoid it. They must learn through practice. This is the value of ongoing experiments: to teach by doing.

As we mentioned in Chapter 2, chaos experiments expose complexity and help us understand how our systems are becoming—an active process of change—in contrast to our beliefs, which are often about its "being."[24] Chaos experiments show us how dragon-like the system has spiraled since we conceived our intentions when designing and architecting the system. This is perhaps where SCE can contribute the most toward resilient architecture: exposing the delta between designed (idealized) and deployed (implemented) architectures, and better understanding the trade-offs of those architectures.

Complexity and Mental Models

As we've seen, architecting systems often involves a common issue: you have a mental model of how the system will behave based upon your design, but that model may clash with reality. You don't design certain interactions, but they happen in production nevertheless. Across a variety of complex system domains, the system incidents that are most damaging—and those where response and recovery is slower—happen when the system fails in a way that our mental models do not allow (or that they overlook). This is where data and metrics and observability cannot save us; our interpretation of system signals is biased by our mental models of what is possible and probable.

We too often see what we expect to see rather than what is. The case of Apollo 13 is a harrowing tale of precisely this dynamic, which we'll examine next.

When designers' mental models and reality collide: Apollo 13

Apollo 13 (*https://oreil.ly/NWy8M*) was a crewed NASA mission meant to land on the moon. Unfortunately, an oxygen tank exploded two days into the mission, thwarting these lunar ambitions. What followed was a dire predicament—would the astronauts return home alive? The Apollo 13 mission demonstrates the hazard of designers' and managers' reluctance to let go of their mental models in the face of failure. There are two key lessons we can learn from the story:

---

24 Hannah Arendt, *The Life of the Mind: The Groundbreaking Investigation on How We Think* (New York: Harcourt, 1978).

- Designers have a different notion of the system than operators—and no one's view is complete. We can gain a more comprehensive perspective when designers are involved in operation and vice versa.

- Correlated failures are pernicious. Adding security devices and redundancy may make them worse, rather than mitigate them.

Let's explore these lessons in more detail. In the prelude to the Apollo 13 mission, designers and managers—what we'll call Mission Control—attempted to optimize the design so operators were inessential. A contributing factor to this design decision was the insidious framing—seen in so many complex systems domains—of operators as "error producers." What is neglected in this framing is the acknowledgment that operators help the system recover when things go wrong—including adverse conditions due to design mistakes. An even bigger omission in this mental model is that designers can also be "error producers" (although we prefer referring to it as "capable of making mistakes"). The difference is the outcomes of designers' mistakes are delayed until the design is reified and runs in reality.

Because of this mental model—where operators are problematic and designs sacrosanct—designers are often tempted to introduce tighter coupling to enable more centralized control. The resulting "streamlining" means we feel comfortable adding more things into the system since they're under our control. This pushes the system into the Danger Zone, requiring quick intervention to avoid catastrophe; alas, in a stroke of irony, operators—like astronauts—become even more essential.

Apollo 13's designers optimized for centralized control and this tighter coupling made the spaceship's behaviors even more baffling. Designers added redundancy that was defeated by design and contributed to the failure: They added a second oxygen tank for redundancy, but placed the tanks near each other physically. Thus, when one oxygen tank exploded, the other was damaged and subsequently leaked.

Correlated failures are pernicious and do not care about our best intentions during design. As space reporter Henry S.F. Cooper observed in *The New Yorker* (*https://oreil.ly/Q9Q70*), "Everyone placed particular faith in the spacecraft's redundancy: there were two or more of almost anything." Seventeen minutes elapsed—while astronauts' life support systems were depleting—as the humans in Mission Control resisted a fundamental challenge to their mental models since it was "inconceivable" that the "heart" of the spaceship might be broken. The scenario, "in the event of a short in an oxygen tank, we may not receive a signal of its malfunction," was simply unfathomable to the humans designing the spaceship.

We don't want to fall into this same trap. Software is full of correlated failures and software engineers often like to assume redundancy will mitigate them. It does not; it can even intensify failure. We don't want to take for granted that security mechanisms—whether design-based mitigations, security devices, warning systems, or behavior-based controls—are working as expected. Explicitly spelling out our assumptions, especially those of the "this will always be true" variety, can help us identify the most impervious parts of our mental models, the ones we're most likely to cling to when something goes wrong.

Once Mission Control acknowledged the incident, they created slack in the system by ordering the astronaut crew to turn equipment off. However, they exempted any equipment that might still allow them to complete the mission of landing on the moon (it took another 28 minutes for Mission Control to give up on the lunar landing). Despite this misprioritization, there was an emergent safety mechanism: the lunar module. Even though the designers hadn't planned its resilience benefits, the loosely coupled and linear design allowed the astronauts to get home. The outcomes achieved by linear and loosely coupled systems support resilience by design, but the more tightly coupled the complex system—the closer it is to the Danger Zone—the less likely those unplanned resilience gifts will emerge.

In the spirit of security chaos experiments, every recovery step Mission Control created was simulated before astronauts tried it out on the real thing. Without that experimentation capability on the ground, the recovery would have been much less reliable. Mission Control improvised a checklist based on their knowledge of the system's critical functions, then swiftly moved to more loosely couple the lunar module and introduce linearity. The socio part of the system discarded all superfluous components (like television coverage) to make the technical part of the system simpler and single-purpose. They also focused on iterative refinements, preserving possibilities for both the controllers and astronauts to make adjustments at subsequent stages—loosening coupling in the socio part of the system too. While they reduced slack in the system, they loosened coupling around the system's critical functionality, conserving resources to fulfill those critical functions—which is why it's so important for us to understand what they are and for them to guide our Effort Investment Portfolio.

Introducing Linearity into Our Systems

We should think creatively about opportunities to invest in design patterns that introduce linearity during this phase, and implement them where we see the highest potential return. This section will explore opportunities to invest our effort capital to procure more linear systems. Certain architectural choices require continued investment to maintain. Designing for different types of isolation or deploying more units of a service requires effort investments to cope with those choices. Whether the return is worth the investment is entirely situation-dependent. Hence, we must think in terms of balancing our Effort Investment Portfolio.

There are a few "linearity mitigations" to keep in mind when architecting and designing systems:

- Choosing "boring" technology
- Common "raw" software materials (languages, libraries, tooling, protocols, data formats)
- Documentation
- Fast, easy change paths
- Functional diversity
- Logical isolation: virtualization, sandboxing, physical
- Machine-verifiable schemas and protocol definitions
- Modularity
- Resource limits/allocation
- Standardization

As we can see from Table 3-3, isolation is a mechanism to introduce linearity in a few dimensions (like those enumerated in the column "Linear systems"), making it a potent tool for our complex software systems. But there are other mechanisms to introduce linearity that might be less obvious. Standardization helps us achieve a more extensive understanding of our system and lowers the learning curve too. We mostly think of documentation as a necessary evil, but it is, in fact, a blessing for us because it introduces linearity—and powers feedback loops, an important ingredient in our resilience potion.

Table 3-3. Differences between complex and linear software systems, and mechanisms to introduce linearity

Complex systems	Linear systems	Mechanisms to introduce linearity
Logical proximity	Logical isolation	Sandboxing/virtualization, physical isolation
Shared resources with interference effects	Dedicated resources	Virtualization, resource limits/allocation, physical isolation, functional diversity
Interconnected subsystems	Isolated subsystems	Sandboxing/virtualization
Limited substitutions	Easy substitutions	Fast, easy change paths; standardization; machine-verifiable schemas and protocol definitions, functional diversity
Surprising causal chains	Few surprising causal chains	Standardization, choose "boring" technology
Multiple and interacting controls	Single-purpose, isolated controls	Virtualization; modularity, functional diversity
Indirect, inferential information	Direct, documented information	Documentation
Limited understanding	Extensive understanding	Standardization, choose "boring" technology, common "raw" software materials (languages, libraries, tooling, protocols, data formats), documentation

We will discuss modularity, sharing knowledge through documentation, and standardized patterns in the next chapter on building and delivering software, which is where those patterns are typically implemented. For the rest of this section, we will cover isolation, choosing "boring" technology, and functional diversity as opportunities to consider when designing and architecting systems.

Isolation for linearity and looser coupling

In software systems, parts are brittle. They can crack easily. If you haven't designed isolation into your systems, failures in small components can snowball into large impacts and lead to cascading failures. Isolation reduces interactions between a failing component and other components, so we treat it as a mechanism for infusing linearity into the system. Isolation also reduces the capability for contagion, granting us looser coupling.

Isolation is one of nature's favored features to foster resilience, reflective of her superlative prudence. Life quite literally emerged due to isolation. All life relies on a membrane partially severing a living being from its environment;[25] as biophysicist Harold Morowitz summarily states, "The necessity of thermodynamically isolating a subsystem is an irreducible condition of life."[26] Nature was the original architect of nested isolation, long before we conceived the transistor.

There are different forms of isolation we should consider when architecting systems. Runtime isolation is one way we can introduce linearity, allowing us to wrap specific software components in a membrane. It is a form of decentralized response to failures wrought by interactive complexity because resilience is spread across the population (just like each cell has a membrane). Runtime isolation is a form of *fault isolation*.[27] It ensures that when something goes wrong in a component, its effects don't leak out to affect other components. Fault isolation is a key benefit of sandboxing, which raises the cost of attack by only allowing an attacker to control whatever is within the sandbox after successful exploitation of a vulnerability.[28]

Sandboxing is nearly ubiquitous in browsers, cloud workloads, serverless functions, and other critical software because of the resilience benefits of fault isolation. Sandboxing is actually "boring" technology; the idea is far from new (and it's far more

---

25 We use the term *sandbox* to describe a software isolation mechanism, but the more appropriate term might be *membrane* since, if we contemplate living beings, we can observe this membrane-based isolation as a leitmotif across scales and levels of integration.

26 Harold J. Morowitz, *Beginnings of Cellular Life: Metabolism Recapitulates Biogenesis* (New Haven, CT: Yale University Press, 2004).

27 Robert Wahbe et al., "Efficient Software-Based Fault Isolation," *Proceedings of the 14th ACM Symposium on Operating Systems Principles* (Asheville, NC: December 5-8, 1993): 203-216.

28 Exploiting the sandbox layer itself is possible and is referred to as a "sandbox escape."

boring to run services as nonroot than as root). Its resilience benefits extend beyond just ruining attackers' days: a "normal" software bug in a component designed with failure isolation is drastically less likely to cause contagion. We discussed immutability and ephemerality in the context of loose coupling, but they're also mechanisms for infusing more linearity into your systems through fault isolation.

Another type of isolation is *performance isolation*.[29] Consider an assembly line. If there's a failure halfway through its process, it can back up everything before it and create a mess. But putting a temporary store of goods into the faulty slot could keep things flowing instead. This is similar to the benefits of queueing,[30] which offers performance isolation when there's *backpressure*—actions taken by software that resist the intended flow of data (or force it to flow in the opposite direction). The *lack* of performance isolation can also be poignant: a common critique of Kubernetes is that a workload might be put on a host that is already executing other tasks, resulting in degraded performance (a traditional server with a bunch of services mushed together is even worse).

There is also *cost isolation*, which, as any tech leader knows, can be as treasured by organizations as other types of isolation (sometimes even more so). If a system component can consume more resources than its intended budget, it can engender surprise bills and ruin an otherwise lucrative quarter. Cost isolation actually supports system security too. For instance, Kubernetes will autoscale the number of running pods if they aren't meeting their health checks, which is free compute to a clever attacker with a DoS exploit. In the wild, attackers will gladly gobble compute during free trials for tools like continuous integration too.[31] Cost isolation can restrict how much compute attackers can consume.

Isolation is another example of how lucky we are to work with software systems. We can isolate failure to handle unexpected interactions, which you can't do in most other systems; full physical isolation is impossible to achieve on airplanes, in nuclear reactors, in ships or mines or petrochemical plants. We should leverage this blessing to its greatest effect.

---

29 Ben Verghese et al., "Performance Isolation: Sharing and Isolation in Shared-Memory Multiprocessors," *ACM SIGPLAN Notices* 33, no. 11 (1998): 181-192.

30 Kenneth P. Birman and Thomas A. Joseph, "Exploiting Virtual Synchrony in Distributed Systems," *Proceedings of the 11th ACM Symposium on Operating Systems Principles* (Austin, TX: November 8-11, 1987): 123-138.

31 Zhi Li et al., "Robbery on DevOps: Understanding and Mitigating Illicit Cryptomining on Continuous Integration Service Platforms," *2022 IEEE Symposium on Security and Privacy (SP)* (San Francisco, CA: May 23-26, 2022): 2397-2412.

Think like an attacker: Choose "boring" technology

Another opportunity to invest in more linear interactions when architecting and designing systems requires us to adopt a crafty attacker practice, albeit one less sensationalized in industry headlines: choosing "boring" technology. When designing attack plans, attackers will use boring technology that "just works," if they can. Using new or novel technology introduces potential unreliability and distracts from their core mission, whether exfiltrating data, encrypting data for ransom, or disrupting system operations. Some attackers who care more about stealth, like nation-states, will invest more money and effort in novel technology because stealth is akin to a market differentiator for them—but they'll still be intimately familiar with native system services for good reason.

Coupling and Complexity for Attackers

Attackers also face the design considerations of coupling and complexity. Let's consider how they manifest in different types of attacks and attackers.

A crypto mining campaign can be thought of as a form of passive income for cybercriminals (and some nation-states). It's a means to monetize persistence and maintain an automated money printer running in the background while they conduct other activities. A crypto mining campaign is relatively linear and involves two primary steps: exploiting a vulnerability and then dropping a miner. Given they don't necessarily care about stealth—in fact, a machine that is obviously unmonitored is an even better mining spot—the risk of contagion is low. Through automation, they can attack many targets at once, meaning a failure in any one action is unlikely to lead to a catastrophic failure for them. This is especially true given crypto miners at present are considered a "nuisance threat" and therefore don't receive as much law enforcement attention as ransomware.

Ransomware, predominantly conducted by cybercriminals, involves less linear interactions. The sequence of events is to compromise users, figure out what is going on in the systems accessible from their vantage point, perhaps gain domain administrator (DA) rights, then drop their payload. Maybe they'll also search for a cyber insurance policy somewhere in between those steps to determine whether they can milk this target for a larger payout. It's a little more tightly coupled too; if they tip off the company in any one of the preceding steps, then they're potentially less likely to succeed with their aim of dropping the payload. The business model, like crypto mining, incentivizes compromising numerous targets at once, reducing the likelihood of catastrophic failure. Of course, if you target a politically sensitive organization, then you'll attract law enforcement or government agency attention, which does result in a catastrophic failure for the ransomware operator (usually in the form of having financial or infrastructure systems seized).

Finally, a hyperscale, "elite" nation-state likely prioritizes linear interactions.[32] They usually have a single target in mind to accomplish a highly specific mission. They won't "spray and pray" like cybercriminals, but instead painstakingly plan their attack ahead of time. When the time comes to attack, the nation-state's operators will have scripted action on target, their attacks waltzing across the system in a tightly choreographed sequence. Doing so puts them into the zone of consequential, but predictable, failures. This allows them to plan better for when things go wrong, because it would be difficult for them to achieve a significant degree of loose coupling when the target and mission are so tailored.

If the goal of SCE is to nourish our system's resilience to attack, then it behooves us to adopt this same sort of "choose boring" thinking during design and architecture rather than waiting for attackers to do so when attempting to destabilize or co-opt our systems. Does the success of your system depend on it being better in some dimension than another system? If your answer is yes, then perhaps investing in new technology and allocating the necessary effort capital would be useful. But if the system just has to work, then boring tech suffices. For anything that isn't a differentiator, pick boring tech—just like your attackers will. Designing systems that are difficult to maintain or "feed" presents more opportunities for attackers to exploit the inevitable neglect and exhausts our effort capital, constraining our investment opportunities elsewhere.

During the design phase, our goal is to focus on the architectural decisions that matter for this specific project, like "Where is value created?" and "How does the data flow?" For anything that isn't project-specific, we should fall back to organizational conventions—or at least make choices that are easy to refine or unwind to support adaptability and evolvability. By using your organization's conventions to influence architectural decisions, you receive a number of benefits:

- There is existing proof of the convention working in production.
- People already know how to scale it.
- Many of the common pitfalls are already known to people in the organization (probably because they've stumbled upon them).
- New team members can onboard more quickly.

---

32 Not all nation-state attack organizations behave the same. They differ in the resources at their disposal, their skill and experience, their operational goals, and more. There is overlap in capability between the best-resourced criminal organizations, which operate at large scale, and less-resourced nation-states that cannot operate at the same hyperscale. The primary difference is in their objectives, which change the actions they pursue in a decision tree.

- When improvements are made, everyone benefits.
- When there are security problems, there are fewer things to patch.
- …and much more!

If you design everything to be project-specific, rather than taking advantage of some organizational conventions, your Effort Investment Portfolio will be highly concentrated. You'll forego the benefits of repeatability and accessibility that we discussed in Chapter 2 and leave little capital to invest in resilient design patterns.

Functional diversity for software ecology

Finally, we can invest in a more speculative opportunity for introducing linearity: functional diversity. As we saw in the example of Apollo 13, system designers often gravitate toward duplication as a solution for their complexity woes. Duplication can lead us into a false sense of security when we overestimate its resilience benefits; redundancy can help us with uncorrelated failures, but not correlated ones.

 In complex systems, *redundancy* means something slightly different than it does in software engineering colloquial: that there are multiple ways to reach the same goal. "True" redundancy in this sense, with multiple pathways possible to achieve critical functions, is rare in software engineering. Whether it is possible to design such systems at scale remains an exercise for the industry at large.

To achieve greater linearity—and thus more resilient system design—we want *diversity* instead. What we seek is closer to a diverse investment portfolio: influential components overlap and reinforce each other, but each performs a somewhat different function from the others and responds to changes in conditions differently too. At a macro level, we achieve reliable outcomes despite fluctuations in underlying components at the micro level. That is, *functional diversity* is how we can nurture resilience at the system level, just as nature so elegantly achieves it in ecological systems.

Functional diversity emerges when different components performing a similar function exploit different aspects of a system (like different grass species all tapping water in soil, but at different depths).[33] Functional diversity is more closely linked to recovery from disturbances than *species* diversity (or species "richness")[34] and is what drives stability, productivity, balanced resources, and other important dynamics of

---

33 C. S. Holling, "Engineering Resilience Versus Ecological Resilience," *Engineering Within Ecological Constraints* 31 (1996): 32.

34 Sylvain Schmitt et al., "Functional Diversity Improves Tropical Forest Resilience: Insights from a Long-Term Virtual Experiment," *Journal of Ecology* 108, no. 3 (2020: 831-843.

ecosystem functioning.[35] So when we say "functional diversity," we don't mean using something unique for every component in your system. We mean *functionally* disparate components or properties in the system.[36] It means your system has different types of processes that contribute to its structure and dynamic stability by pursuing different, but overlapping, functions and leveraging different resources.[37]

Alas, functional diversity is extremely difficult to achieve given the state of the software industry today—perhaps impossible to realize in full at present. The primary investment opportunity available to us is allocating effort toward single-purpose components—and verifying whether that purpose is fulfilled. In the future, we will perhaps see swapability and the three elements of functional diversity—like richness, evenness, and divergence[38]—seep into software systems.

 Functional diversity and standardization are not inherently incompatible. Much of our DNA is "standardized" across mammals (like eyeballs).[39] It's our *behavior*, our specific functionality, that is diverse. In software land, if you standardize on gRPC or REST to communicate between services and your frontends instead of an obscure, custom protocol, then ease trickles through the system: you can write clients and servers in most common programming languages and use off-the-shelf load balancers and service meshes for communication between them. This enables swapability in the long term because you gain flexibility in designing replacement components in the system, enabling greater diversity.

Other than inspiring a new style of software architecture in the future, how can functional diversity help us in practice today? Investing in functional richness ensures our critical functions aren't serviced by the same unit, or at least that noncritical functionality isn't served in the same unit as critical functionality. Investing in functional evenness ensures whatever is present in our systems serves a clear purpose. If there are lots of vestigial tools barnacled on your system for reasons unknown, or no one

35 Simon A. Levin (ed.), *Encyclopedia of Biodiversity,* 2nd Edition (Amsterdam, Netherlands: Elsevier Academic Press, 2013).

36 Emily A. Martin et al., "Assessing the Resilience of Biodiversity-Driven Functions in Agroecosystems Under Environmental Change," *Advances in Ecological Research* 60 (2019): 59-123.

37 John C. Moore, "Diversity, Taxonomic versus Functional," in *Encyclopedia of Biodiversity*, 2nd ed., ed. Simon A. Levin, 648-656 (Amsterdam, Netherlands: Elsevier Academic Press, 2013).

38 Norman W. H. Mason et al., "Functional Richness, Functional Evenness and Functional Divergence: The Primary Components of Functional Diversity," *Oikos 111*, no. 1 (2005): 112-118.

39 Joram Piatigorsky, "A Genetic Perspective on Eye Evolution: Gene Sharing, Convergence and Parallelism," *Evolution: Education and Outreach* 1, no. 4 (2008): 403-414.

has had a chance to retire them yet, that reflects poor functional evenness. But if each single-purpose service fulfills its function, then we have functional evenness.

The functional diversity framing can guide our data strategy too. Many organizations collect data because it *can* be collected, without having a clear purpose for using it (other than creating jobs for data scientists). Attackers will happily monetize all this data if they can—even if you aren't generating palpable returns from it—making it a form of hazardous waste. Ensuring that the data you collect has a clear, defined purpose can help reduce hazardous materials and encourage healthier ecosystem function.

Designing for Interactivity: Identity and Access Management

As we've already discussed, it is the interactions between things in a system that make systems complex—and that beget opportunities for attackers to seize. In computer systems, identities—whether human users, machine users, API endpoints, servers, and so on—determine how various parts interact with each other. We give some things *permission* to talk to other things, and perhaps only about certain things. In a modern world where we are building distributed systems at scale across multiple environments with a dazzling diversity of underlying components, the identity of these components matters because the system thrives or dies on whether the interactions between all those components work as expected.

The first security chaos experimentation tool, ChaoSlingr (which we will discuss in Chapter 9), conducted an identity and access management (IAM) experiment as part of its chaos test repertoire. It generated misconfigured AWS roles to generate evidence about how the system behaved when injected with those incorrect roles. The mental model you maintain for identities within your system and how they interact may also not align with reality. An abandoned admin account is not as uncommon as you might think. Mistakes aside, allocating effort capital into architecting your system identities and permissions can generate investment returns at runtime in the form of resilience and reliability—especially by reducing the potential for contagion.

IAM presents a spectrum of access that bears trade-offs at each end. Granting too much access creates more opportunities for attackers to misuse credentials and gain access to an organization's critical computer systems, although it is usually more convenient for system users. Granting too minimal access creates friction in legitimate users' workflows, resulting in lower productivity for your organization—the n-order effects of which could be slower revenue growth or smaller profit margins.

Another trade-off dimension when considering IAM is granularity. When two components share the same identity, that identity must be granted the permissions required by both components. But making identities too fine-grained increases complexity and could aggravate operator frustration or confusion.

When designing systems, therefore, it's imperative to consider:

- How legitimate operators (whether human or machine) can access parts of the system to do their work quickly
- How unwanted humans (like attackers, their bots, or misguided developers) can be restricted from interacting with the system

Least privilege is the standard industry default and has been forever.[40] But implementing it in practice, when no organization's *raison d'être* is granting thoughtful permissions, is fraught—people cut corners, things slip through the cracks, and infosec thought leaders on social media shame the company for not knowing better when an incident transpires. Segment, a customer data platform, approached this challenge (*https://oreil.ly/iwI8t*) by implementing time-based, peer-reviewed access—similar to approvals work for pull requests in GitHub. It is a good example of what we mean by designing to preserve possibilities. Their approach, called Access Service, lets them view an entity's access as "amorphous and ever-changing," which allows identities and permissions to be flexible in the face of changing contexts.

Netflix also explicitly states (*https://oreil.ly/R5Dpl*) that authentication is a part of system architecture and their "highest-leverage control." After observing a few unwanted facets of the authentication status quo (auth being a routinely critical issue, service owners struggling to manage tokens, auditing being a pain), Netflix realized it was worth investing in a new initiative to move authentication to the network edge and simplify identity token management. Most notably for the context of this chapter, Netflix realized it could gain much more confidence by making authentication a property of application *architecture* rather than an implementation detail within the app. And it realized that reducing complexity for service owners was a crucial win, because the status quo system was starting to become brittle under the weight of all the complexity due to multiple security protocols and tokens across their ecosystem.

---

40 Jerome H. Saltzer and Michael D. Schroeder, "The Protection of Information in Computer Systems," *Proceedings of the IEEE* 63, no. 9 (1975): 1278-1308.

Thinking back on the Effort Investment Portfolio, we can view Netflix's initiative as reducing effort at the sharp end (the service owners) by adding effort at the blunt end (designing the new auth service). By investing effort capital up front through this new architecture and design paradigm, Netflix was able to drastically reduce effort throughout its ecosystem—thereby pulling back from the precipitous ledge of brittleness and transforming its systems toward resilience.

 Security chaos experiments can expose where humans struggle to handle the complexity they encounter. In the IAM case, injecting a quirky identity into the system can expose where authentication either has been implemented incorrectly or is missing. An outdated credential can also reveal whether any teams are aware when this scenario occurs (not just an alert, but whether the alert is noticed and acted upon).

Navigating Flawed Mental Models

One of our primary goals in SCE is to uncover "baffling interactions," like those encountered in the Apollo 13 mission, by revealing the way the world *actually* exists and how it differs from how we *expect* it to exist. This ability to reconcile our mental models with reality is critical toward continually improving design and ensuring our architecture can meet security needs on an ongoing basis. A considerable portion of incidents in our computer systems are the result of our mental models of the system not aligning with reality—and that is especially true for people designing systems, who are often removed from system operation and therefore not exposed to data about the system's real behavior.

Experiments can generate evidence of how much the designers' mental models deviate from reality (indicating design complexity) as well as how difficult it is for operators to gracefully recover from failure (indicating operational complexity). What experiments *can't* do is write you a neat prescription for what you should do. It is up to the humans designing, building, maintaining, and operating these systems to use *judgment* to decide what is best. No matter the problem area, no metric or measurement will ever serve as a perfect substitute for human judgment.[41]

---

41 Jerry Z. Muller, *The Tyranny of Metrics* (Princeton, NJ: Princeton University Press, 2018).

Loose Coupling at Runtime: Grassland Ecosystems

A helpful analogy for loose coupling at runtime from ecology is fire in grassland ecosystems. Frequent fires, in essence, promote loose coupling. These "small-scale disturbances help to promote diversity by limiting any one node or link from becoming too strong, thus preventing the system from becoming too brittle."[42] Unlike fire-starting, small-scale disturbances via chaos experiments are generally easy to pause or terminate if an operator (or team) deems it necessary. Simulating these adverse scenarios—like a gentle form of shock therapy—can generate evidence and feedback that nurtures adaptation, promoting innovation and consideration of alternate pathways to achieve recovery (and, more generally, resilience) goals.[43]

Understanding system interconnections isn't just important because that's where most of the complexity arises—where things are more likely to go wrong. It's also important because, as we discussed earlier, attackers love to take advantage of interactions between components to compromise a system. Attackers aim to understand information flows, layers of the system's fractal (the dragon curve at the beginning of the chapter), and boundaries and interconnections in order to leverage them for their nefarious schemes.

When a software engineer is told to add a feature or fix a bug, they typically don't (or cannot) understand all the interactions. Given this reality, what can we do? The goal is to understand any relevant system interactions across space-time with sufficient confidence in order to make changes without things blowing up. Trending toward loose coupling—which makes it easier to make independent changes and keep impact independent—and finding opportunities to introduce more linearity in system interactions can help us achieve this goal outcome.

For whatever software we're working on, even a specific line of code, it's safe to assume that we'll eventually need to change it (whether our future selves or a future team member). Thus, we need to understand—and document—*why* our software is built the way it is, *why* it interacts with other software (and, ideally, how), and *why* it is important to the overall system (and, ideally, how it fits in with the rest of the software in the system). A lack of documentation is tightly coupling *yourself* to the system. Since software systems are sociotechnical, we must design them carefully to avoid tight coupling of humans with the system.

---

42 Brian D. Fath et al., "Navigating the Adaptive Cycle: An Approach to Managing the Resilience of Social Systems," *Ecology and Society* 20, no. 2 (2015): 24.

43 C. S. Holling and Lance H. Gunderson (eds.), "Resilience and Adaptive Cycles," in *Panarchy: Understanding Transformations in Human and Natural Systems*, 25-62 (Washington, DC: Island Press, 2002).

It's important to stress that, if you succeed in helping your organization scale its mission through software, the system will grow beyond your individual understanding. Tightly coupling yourself to the system by insisting anything beyond your understanding must be "complex" and "bad" will erode the system's resilience. If your mental model of the system feels overwhelming, that is a call to action—but not in the way many software engineers think. In software engineering, there is often a colloquial, subjective sense of complexity as "anything I don't understand." It isn't defined as nonlinear interactions or baffling interactions or any of the other ways actual complex systems science defines it. It is a suitcase word related to *feelings*. That doesn't mean our feelings aren't important; it means we need to use those feelings as signals and interpret them constructively rather than with a convenient narrative.

The constructive interpretation of "Oh no! This software is way too difficult for me to handle!" is usually a sign that more loose coupling is needed. Complex interactions baffle us, which can feel unsettling, but actual harm from those interactions arises when they are combined with tight coupling. In the next chapter, we'll talk more about loose coupling in "layer 8" (i.e., the human layer), but this concept is highly relevant for design and architecture too.

As we discussed earlier in the chapter, a system with complex interactions requires *decentralized* management. Attempting to be the singular knowledge-holder for a software system or even component is not a decentralized approach. If we are to successfully handle complex systems, we need loose coupling between the *socio* part of the system and the *technical* part of the system, to the extent we can achieve it. Co-dependency with the software we design and architect will only sabotage the system's chance at success; it creates an incentive to resist loose coupling, which is necessary for the system to scale and survive.

Every time you hear, "The system has grown beyond our understanding," in a negative light, it's worth questioning the true source of the complaint. After all, we *want* our systems to grow—it's a sign of success. At its root is often mental model resistance—like forest managers in the Normalbaum and Mission Control in the Apollo 13 story—to update beliefs and accept that we don't understand the entire system the way we thought we did. Our mental models were incomplete, despite our beliefs. We didn't ever *really* understand it, but it now *feels* like we're losing a grip on the understanding we previously held as our system proliferates and as we introduce new mechanisms.

Perhaps we see ourselves as the designer of the system, but the system is outgrowing us. The fact is, in most cases, we didn't actually design most of it. The system was assembled from parts that we then built on top of. It is typical in these epiphanous scenarios that documentation is poor and the system is tightly coupled to the few humans who designed it. This is a very awkward and, for the organization, dangerous phase; for most software systems, this is the phase that many systems never grow out of. Many hit this level and plateau. Others fail and die out. The humans in successful software systems figure out how to graduate this phase and outgrow their creations, even as resources are limited and production pressures are high. The appropriate human and software organizational structures come out of it as the sociotechnical system adapts to its new context.

How we manage this phase of a software system's growth is critical. Effective management relies on the less technical parts of the resilience potion: fostering a learning culture and maintaining a willingness to change. We need to be flexible and appreciate feedback loops, even if they expose how wrong our mental models are. Sometimes experiments (and definitely real incidents) will expose all the suboptimal ways we designed the system, which become especially obvious in the harsh light of hindsight (we'll talk more about hindsight bias in Chapter 6). If we dig in our heels and insist that our design is not the problem, but rather how the engineers built it or deployed it or operated it, then our system will stay brittle and become even more brittle as time goes on, drifting toward failure. If we insist that the system is "too complex" because we're embarrassed that our mental models were off and that we don't understand our own design the way we thought we did, then we will undermine the system's success and ability to scale.

We must embrace the fact that reality is messy and nonlinearity is the nature of things. It goes back to the mindful meditation of: Focus on the things you *can* control. You can introduce loose coupling. You can introduce linearity too. You can ensure that you aren't the gatekeeper of knowledge about the part of the system under your purview in a few ways: documenting why you designed it the way you did, documenting when your assumptions were wrong (why you held those assumptions and why they were wrong), and leveraging iteration and feedback loops so your opinion isn't the only driver of change. There is much we can do to *feel* in control that is far more constructive than the egoism of wanting to feel like the commander of the ship.

In essence, we have very incorrect assumptions, and that is OK. As long as our assumptions are *continuously refined through experimentation* for a "close enough" outcome (which inherently changes over time), we can still sustain systems resilience.

Chapter Takeaways

- Our systems are always "becoming," an active process of change. What started as a simple system we could mental-model with ease will become complex as it grows and the context around it evolves.

- When architecting and designing a system, your responsibility is not unlike that of Mother Nature: to nurture your system so it may recover from incidents, adapt to surprises, and evolve to succeed over time.

- We—as individuals, teams, and organizations—only possess finite effort and must prioritize how we expend it. The Effort Investment Portfolio concept captures the need to balance our "effort capital" across activities to best achieve our objectives.

- When we allocate our Effort Investment Portfolio during design and architecture, we must consider the local context of the entire sociotechnical system and preserve possibilities for both software and humans within it to adapt and evolve over time.

- There are four macro failure modes for complex systems that can inform how we allocate effort when architecting and designing systems. We especially want to avoid the Danger Zone quadrant—where tight coupling and interactive complexity combine—because this is where surprising and hard-to-control failures, like cascading failures, manifest.

- We can invest in looser coupling to stay out of the Danger Zone. We covered numerous opportunities to architect and design for looser coupling; the best opportunities depend on your local context.

- Tight coupling is sneaky and may only be revealed during an incident; systems often inadvertently become more tightly coupled as changes are made and we excise perceived "excess." We can use chaos experiments to expose coupling proactively and refine our design accordingly.

- We can also invest in linearity to stay out of the Danger Zone. We described many opportunities to architect and design for linearity, including isolation, choosing "boring" technology, and functional diversity. The right opportunities depend, again, on your local context.

- Scaling the sociotechnical system is where coupling and complexity especially matter. When immersed in the labyrinthine nest of teams and software interactions in larger organizations, we must tame tight coupling (by investing in looser coupling) and find opportunities to introduce linearity—or else find our forward progress crushed.

- Experiments can generate evidence of how our systems behave in reality so we can refine our mental models during design and architecture. If we do our jobs well, our systems will grow and therefore become impossible to mentally model on our own. We can leverage experimentation to regain confidence in our understanding of system behavior.

CHAPTER 4

Building and Delivering

We delight in the beauty of the butterfly, but rarely admit the changes it has gone through to achieve that beauty.

—Maya Angelou

Building and delivering software systems is complicated and expensive—writing code, compiling it, testing it, deploying it to a repository or staging environment, then delivering it to production for end users to consume. Won't promoting resilience during those activities just increase that complexity and expense? In a word, no. Building and delivering systems that are resilient to attack does not require special security expertise, and most of what makes for "secure" software overlaps with what makes for "high-quality" software too.

As we'll discover in this chapter, if we can move quickly, replace easily, and support repeatability, then we can go a long way to match attackers' nimbleness and reduce the impact of stressors and surprises—whether spawned by attackers or other conspiring influences—in our systems. While this chapter can serve as a guide for security teams to modernize their strategy at this phase, our goal in this chapter is for software or platform engineering teams to understand how they can promote resilience by their own efforts. We need consistency and repeatability. We need to avoid cutting corners while still maintaining speed. We need to follow through on innovation to create more slack in the system. We need to change to stay the same.

We will cover a lot of ground in this chapter—it is packed full of practical wisdom! After we've discussed mental models and ownership concerns, we'll inspect the magical contents of our resilience potion to inform how we can build and deliver resilient software systems. We'll consider what practices help us crystallize the critical functions of the system and invest in their resilience to attack. We'll explore how we can stay within the boundaries of safe operation and expand those thresholds for more leeway. We'll talk about tactics for observing system interactions across space-time—and for making them more linear. We'll discuss development practices that nurture feedback loops and a learning culture so our mental models don't calcify. Then, to close, we'll discover practices and patterns to keep us flexible—willing and able to change to support organizational success as the world evolves.

Mental Models When Developing Software

We talked about good design and architecture from a resilience perspective in the last chapter. There are many ways to accidentally subvert resilient design and architecture once we begin building and delivering those designs. This is the stage where design intentions are first reified because programmers must make choices in how they reify the design, and these choices also influence the degree of coupling and interactive complexity in the system. In fact, practitioners at all phases influence this, but we'll cover each in turn in subsequent chapters. This chapter will explore the numerous trade-offs and opportunities we face as we build and deliver systems.

This phase—building and delivering software—is one of our primary mechanisms for adaptation. This phase is where we can adapt as our organization, business model, or market changes. It's where we adapt as our organization scales. The way to adapt to such chronic stressors is often by building new software, so we need the ability to accurately translate the intent of our adaptation into the new system. The beauty of chaos experiments is that they expose when our mental models digress from reality. In this phase, it means we have an inaccurate idea of what the system does now, but some idea—represented by our design—of how we want it to behave in the future. We want to voyage safely from the current state to the intended future state.

In an SCE world, we must think in terms of systems. This is part of why this phase is described as "building and delivering" and not just "developing" or "coding." Interconnections matter. The software only matters when it becomes "alive" in the production environment and broader software ecosystem. Just because it can survive on your local machine doesn't mean it can survive in the wild. It's when it's delivered to users—much like how we describe a human birth as a delivery—that the software becomes useful, because now it's part of a system. So, while we'll cover ops in the next chapter, we will emphasize the value of this systems perspective for software engineers who typically focus more on the functionality than the environment. Whether your end users are external customers or other internal teams (who are still very much customers), building and delivering a resilient system requires you to think about its ultimate context.

Security chaos experiments help programmers understand the behavior of the systems they build at multiple layers of abstraction. For example, the kube-monkey chaos experimentation tool (*https://oreil.ly/QKH0N*) randomly deletes Kubernetes ("k8s") pods in a cluster, exposing how failures can cascade between applications in a k8s-orchestrated system (where k8s serves as an abstraction layer). This is crucial because attackers think across abstraction layers and exploit how the system actually behaves rather than how it is intended or documented to behave (*https://oreil.ly/lvPPh*). This is also useful for debugging and testing specific hypotheses about the system to refine your mental model of it—and therefore learn enough to build the system better with each iteration.

Who Owns Application Security (and Resilience)?

SCE endorses software engineering teams taking ownership of building and delivering software based on resilient patterns, like those described in this book. This can take a few forms in organizations. Software engineering teams can completely self-serve—a fully decentralized model—with each team coming up with guidelines based on experience and agreeing on which should become standard (a model that is likely best suited for smaller or newer organizations). An advisory model is another option: software engineering teams could leverage defenders as advisors who can help them get "unstuck" or better navigate resilience challenges. The defenders who do so may be the security team, but they could just as easily be the SRE or platform engineering team, which already conducts similar activities—just perhaps not with the attack perspective at present. Or, as we'll discuss in great depth in Chapter 7, organizations can craft a resilience program led by a Platform Resilience Engineering team that can define guidelines and patterns as well as create tooling that makes the resilient way the expedient way for internal users.

If your organization has a typical defender model—like a separate cybersecurity team—there are important considerations to keep in mind when transitioning to an advisory model. Defenders cannot leave the rest of the organization to sink or swim, declaring security awareness training sufficient; we'll discuss why this is anything but sufficient in Chapter 7. Defenders must determine, document, and communicate resilience and security guidelines, remaining accessible as an advisor to assist with implementation as needed. This is a departure from the traditional model of cybersecurity teams enforcing policies and procedures, requiring a mindshift from autocrat to diplomat.

The problem is that traditional security—including in its modern cosmetic makeover as "DevSecOps"—seeks to micromanage software engineering teams. In practice, cybersecurity teams often thrust themselves into software engineering processes however they can to control more of it and ensure it is done "right," where "right" is seen exclusively through the lens of optimizing security. As we know from the world of organizational management, micromanaging is usually a sign of poor managers, unclear goals, and a culture of distrust. The end result is tighter and tighter coupling, an organization as ouroboros.

The goal of good design and platform tools is to make resilience and security background information rather than foreground. In an ideal world, security is *invisible*—the developer isn't even aware of security things happening in the background. Their workflows don't feel more cumbersome. This relates to maintainability: no matter your eagerness or noble intentions, security measures that impede work at this stage aren't maintainable. As we described in the last chapter, our higher purpose is to resist the gravity of production pressures that suck you into the Danger Zone. Organizations will want you to build more software things cheaper and more quickly. Our job is to find a sustainable path for this. Unlike traditional infosec, SCE-based security programs seek opportunities to speed up software engineering work while sustaining resilience—because the fast way will be the way that's used in practice, making the secure way the fast way is often the best path to a win. We will explore this thoroughly in Chapter 7.

It is impossible for all teams to maintain full context about all parts of your organization's systems. But resilient development depends on this context, because the most optimal way to build a system to sustain resilience—remember, resilience is a verb—depends on its context. If we want resilient systems, we must nurture local ownership. Attempts at centralizing control—like traditional cybersecurity—will only make our systems brittle because they are ignorant of local context.

Determining context starts out with a lucid mission: "The system works with the availability, speed, and functionality we intend despite the presence of attackers." That's really open ended, as it should be. For one company, the most efficient way to realize that mission is building their app to be immutable and ephemeral. For another company, it might be writing the system in Rust[1] (and avoiding using the `unsafe` keyword as a loophole…[2]). And for yet another company, the best way to realize this mission is to avoid collecting any sensitive data at all, letting third parties handle it instead—and therefore handling the security of it too.

Lessons We Can Learn from Database Administration Going DevOps

The idea that security could succeed while being "owned" by engineering teams is often perceived as anathema to infosec. But it's happened in other tricky problem areas, like database administration (DBA).

---

1 Rust, like many languages, is memory safe. Unlike many languages, it is also thread safe. But the key difference between Rust and, say, Go—and why people associate Rust with "more secure"—is that Rust is more of a *systems* language, making it a more coherent replacement for C programs (which are *not* memory safe and therefore what people are often looking to replace).

2 Hui Xu et al., "Memory-Safety Challenge Considered Solved? An In-Depth Study with All Rust CVEs," *ACM Transactions on Software Engineering and Methodology* (TOSEM) 31, no. 1 (2021): 1-25; Yechan Bae et al., "Rudra: Finding Memory Safety Bugs in Rust at the Ecosystem Scale," *Proceedings of the ACM SIGOPS 28th Symposium on Operating Systems Principles* (October 2021): 84-99.

DBA has shifted toward the "DevOps" model (and, no, it isn't called DevDBOps). Without adopting DevOps principles, both speed and quality suffer due to:

- Mismatched responsibility and authority
- Overburdened database operations personnel
- Broken feedback loops from production
- Reduced developer productivity

Sound familiar? Like DBA, security programs traditionally sit within a specific, central team kept separate from engineering teams and are often at odds with development work. What else can we learn about applying DevOps to DBA (*https://oreil.ly/jsZK6*)?

- Developers own database schema, workload, and performance.
- Developers debug, troubleshoot, and repair their own outages.
- Schema and data model as code.
- A single fully automated deployment pipeline exists.
- App deployment includes automated schema migrations.
- Automated preproduction refreshes from production.
- Automation of database operations exists.

These attributes exemplify a decentralized paradigm for database work. There is no single team "owning" database work or expertise. When things go wrong in a specific part of the system, the engineering team responsible for that part of the system is also responsible for sleuthing out what's going wrong and fixing it. Teams leverage automation for database work, lowering the barrier to entry and lightening the cognitive load for developers—diminishing the desperate need for deep database expertise. It turns out a lot of required expertise is wrapped up in toil work; eliminate manual, tedious tasks and it gets easier on everyone.

It's worth noting that, in this transformation, toil and complexity haven't really disappeared (at least, mostly); they've just been highly automated and hidden behind abstraction barriers offered by cloud and SaaS providers. And the biggest objection to this transformation—that it would either ruin performance or hinder operations—has been proven (mostly) false. Most organizations simply never run into problems that expose the limitations of this approach.

As data and software engineer Alex Rasmussen notes, this is the same reason why SQL on top of cloud warehouses has largely replaced custom Spark jobs. Some organizations need the power and flexibility Spark grants and are willing to invest the effort in making it successful. But the vast majority of organizations just want to aggregate some structured data and perform a few joins. At this point, we've collectively gained sufficient understanding of this "common" mode, so our solutions that target this common mode are quite robust. There will always be outliers, but your organization probably isn't one.

There are parallels to this dynamic in security too. How many people roll their own payment processing in a world in which payment processing platforms abound? How many people roll their own authentication when there are identity management platform providers? This also reflects the "choose boring" principle we discussed in the last chapter and will discuss later in this chapter in the context of building and delivering. We should assume our problem is boring unless proven otherwise.

If we adapt the attributes of the DBA to DevOps transformation for security, they might look something like:

- Developers own security patterns, workload, and performance.
- Developers debug, troubleshoot, and repair their own incidents.
- Security policies and rules as code.
- A single, fully automated deployment pipeline exists.
- App deployment includes automated security configuration changes.
- Automated preproduction refreshes from production.
- Automation of security operations.

You cannot accomplish these attributes through one security team that rules them all. The only way to achieve this alignment of responsibility and accountability is by *decentralizing* security work. Security Champions programs represent one way to begin decentralizing security programs; organizations that experimented with this model (such as Twilio, whose case study on their program is in the earlier SCE report) are reporting successful results and a more collaborative vibe between security and software engineering. But Security Champions programs are only a bridge. We need a team dedicated to enabling decentralization, which is why we'll dedicate all of Chapter 7 to Platform Resilience Engineering.

What practices nurture resilience when building and delivering software? We'll now turn to which practices promote each ingredient of our resilience potion.

Decisions on Critical Functionality Before Building

How do we harvest the first ingredient of our resilience potion recipe—understanding the system's critical functionality—when building and delivering systems? Well, we should probably start a bit earlier when we decide how to implement our designs from the prior phase. This section covers decisions you should make collectively before you build a part of the system and when you reevaluate it as context changes. When we are implementing critical functionality by developing code, our aim is simplicity and understandability of critical functions; the complexity demon spirit (*https://oreil.ly/nk7K1*) can lurch forth to devour us at any moment!

One facet of critical functionality during this phase is that software engineers are usually building and delivering part of the system, not the whole thing. Neville Holmes (*https://oreil.ly/EXq6F*), author of the column "The Profession" in IEEE's *Computer* magazine, said, "In real life, engineers should be designing and validating the system, not the software. If you forget the system you're building, the software will often be useless." Losing sight of critical functionality—at the component, but especially at the system level—will lead us to misallocate effort investment and spoil our portfolio.

How do we best allocate effort investments during this phase to ensure critical functionality is well-defined before it runs in production? We'll propose a few fruitful opportunities—presented as four practices—during this section that allow us to move quickly while sowing seeds of resilience (and that support our goal of RAVE, which we discussed in Chapter 2).

 If you're on a security team or leading it, treat the opportunities throughout this chapter as practices you should evangelize in your organization and invest effort in making them easy to adopt. You'll likely want to partner with whoever sets standards within the engineering organization to do so. And when you choose vendors to support these practices and patterns, include engineering teams in the evaluation process.

Software engineering teams can adopt these on their own. Or, if there's a platform engineering team, they can expend effort in making these practices as seamless to adopt in engineering workflows as possible. We'll discuss the platform engineering approach more in Chapter 7.

First, we can define system goals and guidelines using the "airlock approach." Second, we can conduct thoughtful code reviews to define and verify the critical functions of the system through the power of competing mental models; if someone is doing something weird in their code—which should be flagged during code review one way or another—it will likely be reflected in the resilience properties of their code. Third, we can encourage the use of patterns already established in the system, choosing "boring" technology (an iteration on the theme we explored in the last chapter). And, finally, we can standardize raw materials to free up effort capital that can be invested elsewhere for resilience.

Let's cover each of these practices in turn.

Defining System Goals and Guidelines on "What to Throw Out the Airlock"

One practice for supporting critical functionality during this phase is what we call the "airlock approach": whenever we are building and delivering software, we need to define what we can "throw out the airlock." What functionality and components can you neglect temporarily and still have the system perform its critical functions? What would you *like* to be able to neglect during an incident? Whatever your answer, make sure you build the software in a way that you can indeed neglect those things as necessary. This applies equally to security incidents and performance incidents; if one component is compromised, the airlock approach allows you to shut it off if it's noncritical.

For example, if processing transactions is your system's critical function and reporting is not, you should build the system so you can throw reporting "out the airlock" to preserve resources for the rest of the system. It's possible that reporting is extremely lucrative—your most prolific money printer—and yet, because timeliness of reporting matters less, it can still be sacrificed. That is, to keep the system safe and keep reporting accurate, you sacrifice the reporting service during an adverse scenario—even as the most valuable service—because its critical functionality can still be upheld with a delay.

Another benefit of defining critical functions as fine as we can is so we can constrain batch size—an important dimension in our ability to reason about what we are building and delivering. Ensuring teams can follow the flow of data in a program under their purview helps shepherd mental models from wandering too far from reality.

This ruthless focus on critical functionality can apply to more local levels too. As we discussed in the last chapter, trending toward single-purpose components infuses more linearity in the system—and it helps us better understand the function of each component. If the critical function of our code remains elusive, then why are we writing it?

Code Reviews and Mental Models

Code reviews help us verify that the implementation of our critical functionality (and noncritical too) aligns with our mental models. Code reviews, at their best, involve one mental model providing feedback on another mental model. When we reify a design through code, we are instantiating our mental model. When we review someone else's code, we construct a mental model of the code and compare it to our mental model of the *intention*, providing feedback on anything that deviates (or opportunities to refine it).

In modern software development workflows, code reviews are usually performed after a pull request ("PR") is submitted. When a developer changes code locally and wants to merge it into the main codebase (known as the "main branch"), they open a PR that notifies another human that those changes—referred to as "commits"—are ready to be reviewed. In a continuous integration and continuous deployment/delivery (CI/CD) model, all the steps involved in pull requests, including merging the changes into the main branch, are automated—except for the code review.

Related to the iterative change model that we'll discuss later in the chapter, we want our code reviews to be small and quick too. When code is submitted, the developer should get feedback early and quickly. To ensure the reviewer can be quick in their review, changes should be small. If a reviewer is assigned a PR including lots of changes at once, there can be an incentive to cut corners. They might just skim the code, comment "lgtm" (looks good to me), and move on to work they perceive as more valuable (like writing their own code). After all, they won't get a bonus or get promoted due to thoughtful code reviews; they're much more likely to receive rewards for writing code that delivers valuable changes into production.

Sometimes critical functions get overlooked during code review because our mental models, as we discussed in the last chapter, are incomplete. As one study found, "the error-handling logic is often simply wrong," and simple testing of it would prevent many critical production failures in distributed systems.[3] We need code reviews for tests too, where other people validate the tests we write.

 Formal code reviews are often proposed after a notable incident in the hopes that tighter coupling will improve security (it won't). If the code in a review is already written and is of significant volume, has many changes, or is very complex, it's already too late. The code author and the reviewer sitting down together to discuss the changes (versus the async, informal model that is far more common) *feels* like it might help, but is just "review theater." If we do have larger features, we should use the "feature branch" model (*https://oreil.ly/vltfC*) or, even better, ensure we perform a design review that informs how the code will be written.

How do we incentivize thoughtful code reviews? There are a few things we can do to discourage cutting corners, starting with ensuring all the nitpicking will be handled by tools. Engineers should never have to point out issues with formatting or trailing spaces; any stylistic concerns should be checked automatically. Ensuring automated tools handle this kind of nitpicky, grunt work allows engineers to focus on higher-value activities that can foster resilience.

---

3 Ding Yuan et al., "Simple Testing Can Prevent Most Critical Failures: An Analysis of Production Failures in Distributed {Data-Intensive} Systems," *11th USENIX Symposium on Operating Systems Design and Implementation (OSDI 14)* (2014): 249-265.

There are many code review antipatterns that are unfortunately common in status quo cybersecurity despite security engineering teams arguably suffering the most from it. One antipattern is a strict requirement for the security team to approve every PR to evaluate its "riskiness." Aside from the nebulosity of the term *riskiness*, there is also the issue of the security team lacking relevant context for the code changes.

As any software engineer knows all too well, one engineering team can't effectively review the PRs of another team. Maybe the storage engineer could spend a week reading the network engineering team's design docs and then review a PR, but no one does that. A security team certainly can't do that. The security team might not even understand the critical functions of the system and, in some cases, might not even know enough about the programming language to identify potential problems in a meaningful way.

As a result, the security team can often become a tight bottleneck that slows down the pace of code change, which, in turn, hurts resilience by hindering adaptability. This usually feels miserable for the security team too—and yet leaders often succumb to believing there's a binary between extremes of manual reviews and "let security issues fall through the cracks." Only a Sith deals in absolutes.

"Boring" Technology Is Resilient Technology

Another practice that can help us refine our critical functions and prioritize maintaining their resilience to attack is choosing "boring" technology. As expounded upon in engineering executive Dan McKinley's famous post, "Choose Boring Technology" (*https://oreil.ly/Muhd1*), boring is not inherently bad. In fact, boring likely indicates well-understood capabilities, which helps us wrangle complexity and reduce the preponderance of "baffling interactions" in our systems (both the system and our mental models become more linear).

In contrast, new, "sexy" technology is less understood and more likely to instigate surprises and bafflements. Bleeding edge is a fitting name given the pain it can inflict when implemented—maybe at first it seems but a flesh wound, but it can eventually drain you and your teams of cognitive energy. In effect, you are adding both tighter coupling and interactive complexity (decreasing linearity). If you recall from the last chapter, choosing "boring" gives us a more extensive understanding, requiring less specialized knowledge—a feature of linear systems—while also promoting looser coupling in a variety of ways.

Thus, when you receive a thoughtful design (such as one informed by the teachings of Chapter 3!), consider whether the coding, building, and delivering choices you make are adding additional complexity and higher potential for surprises—and if you are tightly coupling yourself or your organization to those choices. Software engineers should be making software choices—whether languages, frameworks, tooling, and so forth—that best solve specific business problems. The end user really doesn't care that you used the latest and greatest tool hyped up on HackerNews. The end user wants to use your service whenever they want, as quickly as they want, and with the functionality they want. Sometimes solving those business problems will require a new, fancy technology if it grants you an advantage over your competitors (or otherwise fulfills your organization's mission). Even so, be cautious about how often you pursue "non-boring" technology to differentiate, for the bleeding edge requires many blood sacrifices to maintain.

 One red flag indicating your security architecture has strayed from the principle of "choose boring" is if your threat models are likely to be radically different from your competitors'. While most threat models will be different—because few systems are *exactly* alike—it is rare for two services performing the same function by organizations with similar goals to look like strangers. An exception might be if your competitors are stuck in the security dark ages but you are pursuing security-by-design.

During the build and deliver phase, we must be careful about how we prioritize our cognitive efforts—in addition to how we spend resources more generally. You can spend your finite resources on a super slick new tool that uses AI to write unit tests for you. Or you can spend them on building complex functionality that better solves a problem for your target end users. The former doesn't directly serve your business or differentiate you; it adds significant cognitive overhead that doesn't serve your collective goals for an uncertain benefit (that would only come after a painful tuning process and hair-pulling from minimal troubleshooting docs).

"OK," you're saying, "but what if the new, shiny thing is really really really cool?" You know who else likes really cool, new, shiny software? Attackers. They love when developers adopt new tools and technologies that aren't yet well understood, because that creates lots of opportunities for attackers to take advantage of mistakes or even intended functionality that hasn't been sufficiently vetted against abuse. Vulnerability researchers have resumes too, and it looks impressive when they can demonstrate exploitation against the new, shiny thing (usually referred to as "owning" the thing). Once they publish the details of how they exploited the new shiny thing, criminal attackers can figure out how to turn it into a repeatable, scalable attack (completing the Fun-to-Profit Pipeline of offensive infosec).

Security and observability tools aren't exempt from this "choose boring" principle either. Regardless of your "official" title—and whether you're a leader, manager, or individual contributor—you should choose and encourage simple, well-understood security and observability tools that are adopted across your systems in a consistent manner. Attackers adore finding "special" implementations of security or observability tools and take pride in defeating new, shiny mitigations that brag about defeating attackers one way or another.

Many security and observability tools require special permissions (like running as root, administrator, or domain administrator) and extensive access to other systems to perform their purported function, making them fantastic tools for attackers to gain deep, powerful access across your critical systems (because those are the ones you especially want to protect and monitor). A new, shiny security tool may say that fancy math will solve all your attack woes, but this fanciness is the opposite of boring and can beget a variety of headaches, including time required to tune on an ongoing basis, network bottlenecks due to data hoovering, kernel panics, or, of course, a vulnerability in it (or its fancy collection and AI-driven, rule-pushing channels) that may offer attackers a lovely foothold onto all the systems that matter to you.

For instance, you might be tempted to "roll your own" authentication or cross-site request forgery (XSRF) protection. Outside of edge cases where authentication or XSRF protection is part of the value your service offers to your customers, it makes far more sense to "choose boring" by implementing middleware for authentication or XSRF protection. That way, you're leveraging the vendor's expertise in this "exotic" area.

 Don't DIY middleware.

The point is, if you optimize for the "least-worst" tools for as many of your nondifferentiator problems as you can, then it will be easier to maintain and operate the system and therefore to keep it safe. If you optimize for the best tool for each individual problem, or Rule of Cool, then attackers will gladly exploit your resulting cognitive overload and insufficient allocation of complexity coins into things that help the system be more resilient to attack. Of course, sticking with something boring that is ineffective doesn't make sense either and will erode resilience over time too. We want to aim for the sweet spot of boring and effective.

Standardization of Raw Materials

The final practice we'll cover in the realm of critical functionality is standardizing the "raw materials" we use when building and delivering software—or when we recommend practices to software engineering teams. As we discussed in the last chapter, we can think of "raw materials" in software systems as languages, libraries, and tooling (this applies to firmware and other raw materials that go into computer hardware, like CPUs and GPUs too). These raw materials are elements woven into the software that need to be resilient and safe for system operation.

When building software services, we must be purposeful with what languages, libraries, frameworks, services, and data sources we choose since the service will inherit some of the properties of these raw materials. Many of these materials may have hazardous properties that are unsuitable for building a system as per your requirements. Or the hazard might be expected and, since there isn't a better alternative for your problem domain, you'll need to learn to live with it or think of other ways to reduce hazards by design (which we'll discuss more in Chapter 7). Generally, choosing more than one raw material in any category means you get the downsides of both.

What Is Memory Safety?

Memory safety protects mistakes in memory management in one part of the program from affecting the rest of the program. It makes it so matters of memory resource management are handled by the language and runtime itself.

This capability is a boon for our Effort Investment Portfolio. Memory safety frees developers from most of the cognitive overhead of tracking memory resources, and since memory is the most common resource used in software, this allows developers to dedicate their cognitive effort to other concerns. Other resources—like network sockets, files, locks, threads, hardware resources, and so much more—may still need to be managed by the developer of the program.

The National Security Agency (NSA) officially recommends (*https://oreil.ly/tfwfM*) using memory safe languages wherever possible, like C#, Go, Java, Ruby, Rust, and Swift. The CTO of Microsoft Azure, Mark Russovovich, tweeted more forcefully (*https://oreil.ly/4zNeQ*): "Speaking of languages, it's time to halt starting any new projects in C/C++ and use Rust for those scenarios where a nonGC language is required. For the sake of security and reliability, the industry should declare those languages as deprecated." Memory safety issues damage both the user and the maker of a product or service because data that shouldn't change can magically become a different value. As Matt Miller, partner security software engineer at Microsoft, presented in 2019 (*https://oreil.ly/NgPXt*), ~70% of fixed vulnerabilities with a CVE assigned are memory safety vulnerabilities due to software engineers mistakenly introducing memory safety bugs in their C and C++ code.

When building or refactoring software, you should pick one of dozens of popular languages that are memory safe by default. *Memory unsafety* is mighty unpopular in language design, which is great for us since we have a cornucopia of memory safe options (*https://oreil.ly/vqUVP*) from which to pluck. We can even think of C code like lead; it was quite convenient for many use cases, but it's poisoning us over time, especially as more accumulates.

Ideally, we want to adopt less hazardous raw materials as swiftly as we can, but this quest is often nontrivial (like migrating from one language to another). Full rewrites can work for smaller systems that have relatively complete integration, end-to-end (E2E), and functional tests—but those conditions won't always be true. The strangler fig pattern, which we'll discuss at the end of the chapter, is the most obvious approach to help us iteratively change our codebase.

Another option is to pick a language that integrates well with C and make your app a polyglot application, carefully choosing which parts to write in each language. This approach is more granular than the strangler fig pattern and is similar to the Oxidation project (*https://oreil.ly/WfakR*), Mozilla's approach to integrating Rust code in and around Firefox (which is worth exploring for guidance on how to migrate from C to Rust, should you need it). Some systems may even stay in this state indefinitely if there are benefits to having both high- and low-level languages in the same program simultaneously. Games are a common example of this dynamic: engine code (*https://oreil.ly/i_cEO*) needs to be speedy to control memory layout, but gameplay code needs to be quick to iterate on and performance matters much less. But in general, polyglot services and programs are rare, which makes standardization of some materials a bit more straightforward.

Security teams wanting to drive adoption of memory safety should partner with the humans in your organization who are trying to drive engineering standards—whether practices, tools, or frameworks—and participate in that process. All things equal, maintaining consistency is significantly better for resilience. The humans you seek are within the engineering organization, making the connections, and advocating for the adoption of these standards.

On the flipside, these humans have their own goals: to productively build more software and the systems the business desires. If your asks are insensitive, they will ignore you. So, don't ask for things like disconnecting developer laptops from the internet for security's sake. Emphasizing the security benefits of refactoring C code into a memory safe language, however, will be more constructive, as it likely fits with their goals too—since productivity and operational hazards notoriously sneak within C. Security can have substantial common ground with that group of humans on C since they also want to get rid of it (except for the occasional human insisting we should all write in Assembly and read the Intel instruction manual).

As Mozilla stresses, "crossing the C++/Rust boundary can be difficult." This shouldn't be underestimated as a downside of this pattern. Because C defines the UNIX platform APIs, most languages have robust foreign function interface (FFI) support for C. C++, however, lacks such substantial support as it has way more language oddities for FFI to deal with and to potentially mess up.

Code that passes a language boundary needs extra attention at all stages of development. An emerging approach (*https://oreil.ly/ YDnTZ*) is to trap all the C code in a WebAssembly sandbox with generated FFI wrappers provided automatically. This might even be useful for applications that are entirely written in C to be able to trap the unreliable, hazardous parts in a sandbox (like format parsing).

Caches are an example of a hazardous raw material that is often considered necessary. When caching data on behalf of a service, our goal is to reduce the traffic volume to the service. It's considered successful to have a high cache hit ratio (CHR), and it is often more cost-effective to scale caches than to scale the service behind them. Caches might be the only way to deliver on your performance and cost targets, but some of their properties jeopardize the system's ability to sustain resilience.

There are two hazards with respect to resilience. The first is mundane: whenever data changes, caches must be invalidated or else the data will appear stale. Invalidation can result in quirky or incorrect overall system behavior—those "baffling" interactions in the Danger Zone—if the system relies on consistent data. If careful coordination isn't correct, stale data can rot in the cache indefinitely.

The second hazard is a systemic effect where if the caches ever fail or degrade, they put pressure on the service. With high CHRs, even a partial cache failure can swamp a backend service. If the backend service is down, you can't fill cache entries, and this leads to more traffic bombarding the backend service. Services without caches slow to a crawl, but recover gracefully as more capacity is added or traffic subsides. Services with a cache collapse as they approach capacity and recovery often requires substantial additional capacity beyond steady state.

Yet, even with these hazards, caches are nuanced from a resilience perspective. They benefit resilience because they can decouple requests from the origin (i.e., backend server); the service better weathers surprises but not necessarily sustained failures. While clients are now less tightly coupled to our origin's behavior, they instead become tightly coupled with the cache. This tight coupling grants greater efficiency and reduced costs, which is why caching is widely practiced. But, for the resilience reasons we just mentioned, few organizations are "rolling their own caches." For instance, they often outsource web traffic caching to a dedicated provider, such as a content delivery network (CDN).

Every choice you make either resists or capitulates to tight coupling. The tail end of loose coupling is full swapability of components and languages in your systems, but vendors much prefer lock-in (i.e., tight coupling). When you make choices on your raw materials, always consider whether it moves you closer to or away from the Danger Zone, introduced in Chapter 3.

To recap, during this phase, we can pursue four practices to support critical functionality, the first ingredient of our resilience potion: the airlock approach, thoughtful code reviews, choosing "boring" tech, and standardizing raw materials. Now, let's proceed to the second ingredient: understanding the system's safety boundaries (thresholds).

Developing and Delivering to Expand Safety Boundaries

The second ingredient of our resilience potion is understanding the system's safety boundaries—the thresholds beyond which it slips into failure. But we can also help *expand* those boundaries during this phase, expanding our system's figurative window of tolerance (*https://oreil.ly/98ldr*) to adverse conditions. This section describes the range of behavior that should be expected of the sociotechnical system, with humans curating the system as it drifts from the designed ideal (the mental models constructed during the design and architecture phase). There are four key practices we'll cover that support safety boundaries: anticipating scale, automating security checks, standardizing patterns and tools, and understanding dependencies (including prioritizing vulnerabilities in them).

The good news is that a lot of getting security "right" is actually just solid engineering—things you want to do for reliability and resilience to disruptions other than attacks. In the SCE world, application security is thought of as another facet of software quality: given your constraints, how can you write high-quality software that achieves your goals? The practices we'll explore in this section beget both higher-quality and more resilient software.

We mentioned in the last chapter that what we want in our systems is sustained adaptability. We can nurture sustainability during this phase as part of stretching our boundaries of safe operation too. Sustainability and resilience are interrelated concepts across many complex domains. In environmental science, both resilience and sustainability involve preservation of societal health and well-being in the presence of environmental change.[4] In software engineering, we typically refer to sustainability as "maintainability." It's no less true in our slice of life that both maintainability and

---

4 Xun Zeng et al., "Urban Resilience for Urban Sustainability: Concepts, Dimensions, and Perspectives," *Sustainability*s 14, no. 5 (2022): 2481.

resilience are concerned with the health and well-being of software services in the presence of destabilizing forces, like attackers. As we'll explore throughout this section, supporting *maintainable* software engineering practices—including *repeatable* workflows—is vital for building and delivering systems that can sustain resilience against attacks.

The processes by which you build and deliver must be clear, repeatable, and maintainable—just as we described in Chapter 2 when we introduced RAVE. The goal is to standardize building and delivering as much as you can to reduce unexpected interactions. It also means rather than relying on everything being perfect ahead of deployment, you can cope well with mistakes because fixing them is a swift, straightforward, repeatable process. Weaving this sustainability into our build and delivery practices helps us expand our safety boundaries and gain more grace in the face of adverse scenarios.

Anticipating Scale and SLOs

The first practice during this phase that can help us expand our safety boundaries is, simply put, anticipating scale. When building resilient software systems, we want to consider how operating conditions might evolve and therefore where its boundaries of safe operation lie. Despite best intentions, software engineers sometimes make architecture or implementation decisions that induce either reliability or scalability bottlenecks.

Anticipating scale is another way of challenging those "this will always be true" assumptions we described in the last chapter—the ones attackers exploit in their operations. Consider an eCommerce service. We may think, "On every incoming request, we first need to correlate that request with the user's prior shopping cart, which means making a query to this other thing." There is a "this will always be true" assumption baked into this mental model: that the "other thing" will always be there. If we're thoughtful, then we must challenge: "What if this other thing *isn't* there? What happens then?" This can then refine how we build something (and we should document the *why*—the assumption that we've challenged—as we'll discuss later in this chapter). What if the user's cart retrieval is slow to load or unavailable?

Challenging our "this will always be true" assumptions can expose potential scalability issues at lower levels too. If we say, "we'll always start with a control flow graph, which is the output of a previous analysis," we can challenge it with a question like "what if that analysis is either super slow or fails?" Investing effort capital in anticipating scale can ensure we do not artificially constrict our system's safety boundaries—and that potential thresholds are folded into our mental models of the system.

When we're building components that will run as part of big, distributed systems, part of anticipating scale is anticipating what operators will need during incidents (i.e., what effort investments they need to make). If it takes an on-call engineer hours to discover that the reason for sudden service slowness is a SQLite database no one knew about, it will hurt your performance objectives. We also need to anticipate how the business will grow, like estimating traffic growth based on roadmaps and business plans, to prepare for it. When we estimate which parts of the system we'll need to expand in the future and which are unlikely to need expansion, we can be thrifty with our effort investments while ensuring the business can grow unimpeded by software limitations.

We should be thoughtful about supporting the patterns we discussed in the last chapter. If we design for immutability and ephemerality, this means engineers can't SSH into the system to debug or change something, and that the workload can be killed and restarted at will. How does this change how we build our software? Again, we should capture these *why* points—that we built it this way to support immutability and ephemerality—to capture knowledge (which we'll discuss in a bit). Doing so helps us expand our window of tolerance and solidifies our understanding of the system's thresholds beyond which failure erupts.

Automating Security Checks via CI/CD

One of the more valuable practices to support expansion of safety boundaries is automating security checks by leveraging existing technologies for resilience use cases. The practice of continuous integration and continuous delivery[5] (CI/CD) accelerates the development and delivery of software features without compromising reliability or quality.[6] A CI/CD pipeline consists of sets of (ideally automated) tasks that deliver a new software release. It generally involves compiling the application (known as "building"), testing the code, deploying the application to a repository or staging environment, and delivering the app to production (known as "delivery"). Using automation, CI/CD pipelines ensure these activities occur at regular intervals with minimal interference required by humans. As a result, CI/CD supports the characteristics of speed, reliability, and repeatability that we need in our systems to keep them safe and resilient.

---

5 The "D" sometimes stands for Deployment too.

6 Mojtaba Shahin et al., "Continuous Integration, Delivery and Deployment: A Systematic Review on Approaches, Tools, Challenges and Practices," *IEEE Access* 5 (2017): 3909-3943.

Continuous integration (CI)
> Humans integrate and merge development work (like code) frequently (like multiple times per day). It involves automated software building and testing to achieve shorter, more frequent release cycles, enhanced software quality, and amplified developer productivity.

Continuous delivery (CD)
> Humans introduce software changes (like new features, patches, configuration edits, and more) into production or to end users. It involves automated software publishing and deploying to achieve faster, safer software updates that are more repeatable and sustainable.[7]

We should appreciate CI/CD not just as a mechanism to avoid the toil of manual deploys, but also as a tool to make software delivery more repeatable, predictable, and consistent. We can enforce invariants, allowing us to achieve whatever properties we want every time we build, deploy, and deliver software. Companies that can build and deliver software more quickly can also ameliorate vulnerabilities and security issues more quickly. If you can ship when you want, then you can be confident you can ship security fixes when you need to. For some companies, that may look hourly and for others daily. The point is your organization can deliver on demand and therefore respond to security events on demand.

From a resilience perspective, manual deployments (and other parts of the delivery workflow) not only consume precious time and effort better spent elsewhere, but also tightly couple the human to the process with no hope of linearity. Humans are fabulous at adaptation and responding with variety and absolutely hopeless at doing the same thing the same way over and over. The security and sysadmin status quo of "ClickOps" is, through this lens, frankly dangerous. It increases tight coupling *and* complexity, without the efficiency blessings we'd expect from this Faustian bargain— akin to trading our soul for a life of tedium. The alternative of automated CI/CD pipelines not only loosens coupling and introduces more linearity, but also speeds up software delivery, one of the win-win situations we described in the last chapter. The same goes for many forms of workflow automation when the result is standardized, repeatable patterns.

In an example far more troubling than manual deploys, local indigenous populations on Noepe (Martha's Vineyard) faced the dangers of tight coupling when the single

---

7 Jez Humble, "Continuous Delivery Sounds Great, But Will It Work Here?" *Communications of the ACM* 61, no. 4 (2018): 34-39.

ferry service delivering food was disrupted by the COVID-19 pandemic.[8] If we think of our pipeline as a food pipeline (as part of the broader food supply chain), then we perceive the poignant need for reliability and resilience. It is no different for our build pipelines (which, thankfully, do not imperil lives).

 When you perform chaos experiments on your systems, having repeatable build-and-deploy workflows ensures you have a low-friction way to incorporate insights from those experiments and continuously refine your system. Having versioned and auditable build-and-deploy trails means you can more easily understand why the system is behaving differently after a change. The goal is for software engineers to receive feedback as close to immediate as possible while the context is still fresh. They want to reach the finish line of their code successfully and reliably running in production, so harness that emotional momentum and help them get there.

Faster patching and dependency updates

A subset of automating security checks to expand safety boundaries is the practice of faster patching and dependency updates. CI/CD can help us with patching and, more generally, keeping dependencies up to date—which helps avoid bumping into those safety boundaries. Patching is a problem that plagues cybersecurity. The most famous example of this is the 2017 Equifax breach (*https://oreil.ly/tngk-*) in which an Apache Struts vulnerability was not patched for four months after disclosure. This violated their internal mandate of patching vulnerabilities within 48 hours, highlighting once again why strict policies are insufficient for promoting real-world systems resilience. More recently, the 2021 Log4Shell vulnerability in Log4j, which we discussed in Chapter 3, precipitated a blizzard of activity to both find vulnerable systems across the organization and patch them without breaking anything.

In theory, developers want to be on the latest version of their dependencies. The latest versions have more features, include bug fixes, and often have performance, scalability, and operability improvements.[9] But when engineers are attached to an older version, there is usually a reason. In practice, there are many reasons why they might not be; some are very reasonable, some less so.

Production pressures are probably the largest reason because upgrading is a task that delivers no immediate business value. Another reason is that semantic versioning

---

8 Emerson Mahoney et al., "Resilience-by-Design and Resilience-by-Intervention in Supply Chains for Remote and Indigenous Communities," *Nature Communications* 13, no. 1 (2022): 1-5.

9 New versions can also give you new bugs, but the idea is that now we can fix them more quickly with automated CI/CD.

(SemVer) is an ideal to aspire to, but it's slippery in practice. It's unclear whether the system will behave correctly when you upgrade to a new version of the dependency unless you have amazing tests that fully cover its behaviors, which no one has.

On the less reasonable end of the spectrum is the forced refactor—like when a dependency is written or experiences substantial API changes. This is a symptom of engineers' predilection for selecting shiny and new technologies versus stable and "boring"—that is, picking things that aren't appropriate for real work. A final reason is abandoned dependencies. The dependency's creator no longer maintains it and no direct replacement was made—or the direct replacement is meaningfully different.

This is precisely why automation—including CI/CD pipelines—can help, by removing human effort from keeping dependencies up to date, freeing that effort for more valuable activities, like adaptability. We don't want to burn out their focus with tedium. Automated CI/CD pipelines mean updates and patches can be tested and pushed to production in hours (or sooner!) rather than the days, weeks, or even months that it traditionally takes. It can make update-and-patch cycles an automatic and daily affair, eliminating toil work so other priorities can receive attention.

Automated integration testing means that updates and patches will be evaluated for potential performance or correctness problems before being deployed to production, just like other code. Concerns around updates or patches disrupting production services—which can result in procrastination or protracted evaluations that take days or weeks—can be automated away, at least in part, by investing in testing. We must expend effort in writing tests we can automate, but we salvage considerable effort over time by avoiding manual testing.

Automating Dependency Checking

A worthy example of how higher quality doesn't have to slow down building and delivering software is automated dependency checking, like GitHub's Dependabot. Organizations can integrate Dependabot into their CI/CD pipelines, triggering it when a PR is opened, to automatically update dependencies and save their programmers from having to do so themselves. It makes the process more repeatable (i.e., linear) and scalable (i.e., more loosely coupled to the human).

The more we can dissolve this sort of security toil until it's nearly "invisible" to developers, the more likely we will succeed in our goal of high-quality, resilient software systems. Dependabot is also a reminder that opportunities to more loosely couple and introduce linearity won't always involve a sacrifice of efficiency; if we are curious about local context, we can pioneer clever ways to achieve these goals in tandem. We'll talk more about the process of investigating local context toward delivering internal solutions like this in Chapter 7.

Software engineers should be able to update dependencies "safely"—with confidence that they aren't breaking the software. Automated CI/CD makes this much easier. For example, Dependabot opens a PR, CI reports that none of the tests failed, and updating just involves clicking merge in the PR (if tests do fail, that's another story).

Automating the release phase of software delivery also offers security benefits. Automatically packaging and deploying a software component results in faster time to delivery (*https://oreil.ly/_nykO*), accelerating patching and security changes as we mentioned. Version control is also a security boon because it expedites rollback and recovery in case something goes wrong. We'll discuss the benefits of automated infrastructure provisioning in the next section.

Resilience benefits of continuous delivery

Continuous delivery is a practice you should only adopt after you've already put other practices described in this section—and even in the whole chapter—in place. If you don't have CI and automated testing catching most of your change-induced failures, CD will be hazardous and will gnaw at your ability to maintain resilience. CD requires more rigor than CI; it feels meaningfully different. CI lets you add automation to your existing processes and achieve workflow benefits, but doesn't really impose changes to how you deploy and operationalize software. CD, however, requires that you get your house in order. Any possible mistake that can be made by developers as part of development, after enough time, will be made by developers. (Most of the time, of course, anything that can go right will go right.) All aspects of the testing and validation of the software must be automated to catch those mistakes before they become failures, and it requires more planning around backward and forward compatibility, protocols, and data formats.

With these caveats in mind, how can CD help us uphold resilience? It is impossible to make manual deployments repeatable. It is unfair to expect a human engineer to execute manual deployments flawlessly every time—especially under ambiguous conditions. Many things can go wrong even when deployments are automated, let alone when a human performs each step. Resilience—by way of repeatability, security, and flexibility—is baked into the goal of CD: to deliver changes—whether new features, updated configurations, version upgrades, bug fixes, or experiments—to end users with sustained speed and security.[10]

Releasing more frequently actually *enhances* stability and reliability. Common objections to CD (*https://oreil.ly/q0_Pg*) include the idea that CD doesn't work in highly regulated environments, that it can't be applied to legacy systems, and that it involves

---

10 Humble, "Continuous Delivery Sounds Great, But Will It Work Here?" 34-39.

enormous feats of engineering to achieve. A lot of this is based on the now thoroughly disproven myth that moving quickly inherently increases "risk" (where "risk" remains a murky concept).[11]

While we are loathe to suggest hyperscale companies should be used as exemplars, it is worth considering Amazon as a case study for CD working in regulated environments. Amazon handles thousands of transactions per minute (up to hundreds of thousands during Prime Day), making it subject to PCI DSS (a compliance standard covering credit card data). And, being a publicly traded company, the Sarbanes-Oxley Act regulating accounting practices applies to them too. But, even as of 2011, Amazon was releasing changes to production on average every 11.6 seconds, adding up to 1,079 deployments an hour at peak.[12] SRE and author Jez Humble writes, "This is possible because the practices at the heart of continuous delivery—comprehensive configuration management, continuous testing, and continuous integration—allow the rapid discovery of defects in code, configuration problems in the environment, and issues with the deployment process."[13] When you combine continuous delivery with chaos experimentation, you get rapid feedback cycles that are actionable.

This may sound daunting. Your security culture maybe feels Shakespearean levels of theatrical. Your tech stack feels more like a pile of LEGOs you painfully step on. But, you can start small. The perfect first step to work toward CD is "PasteOps." Document the manual work involved when deploying security changes or performing security-related tasks as part of building, testing, and deploying. A bulleted list in a shared resource can suffice as an MVP for automation, allowing iterative improvement (*https://oreil.ly/nnBFo*) that can eventually turn into real scripts or tools. SCE is all about iterative improvement like this. Think of evolution in natural systems; fish didn't suddenly evolve legs and opposable thumbs and hair all at once to become humans. Each generation offers better adaptations for the environment, just as each iteration of a process is an opportunity for refinement. Resist the temptation to perform a grand, sweeping change or reorg or migration. All you need is just enough to get the flywheel going (*https://oreil.ly/jFj_5*).

Standardization of Patterns and Tools

Similar to the practice of standardizing raw materials to support critical functionality, standardizing tools and patterns is a practice that supports expanding safety boundaries and keeping operating conditions within those boundaries. *Standardization* can

---

11 Michael Power, "The Risk Management of Nothing," *Accounting, Organizations and Society* 34, no. 6-7 (2009): 849-855.

12 Jon Jenkins, "Velocity Culture (The Unmet Challenge in Ops)" (*https://oreil.ly/DULGF*), O'Reilly Velocity Conference (2011).

13 Humble, "Continuous Delivery Sounds Great, But Will It Work Here?" 34-39.

be summarized as ensuring work produced is consistent with preset guidelines. Standardization helps reduce the opportunity for humans to make mistakes by ensuring a task is performed the same way each time (which humans aren't designed to do). In the context of standardized patterns and tools, we mean consistency in what developers use for effective interaction with the ongoing development of the software.

This is an area where security teams and platform engineering teams can collaborate to achieve the shared goal of standardization. In fact, platform engineering teams could even perform this work on their own if that befits their organizational context. As we keep saying, the mantle of "defender" suits anyone regardless of their usual title if they're supporting systems resilience (we'll discuss this in far more depth in Chapter 7).

If you don't have a platform engineering team and all you have are a few eager defenders and a slim budget, you can still help standardize patterns for teams and reduce the temptation of rolling-their-own-thing in a way that stymies security. The simplest tactic is to prioritize patterns for parts of the system with the biggest security implications, like authentication or encryption. If it'd be difficult for your team to build standardized patterns, tools, or frameworks, you can also scout standard libraries to recommend and ensure that list is available as accessible documentation. That way, teams know there's a list of well-vetted libraries they should consult and choose from when needing to implement specific functionality. Anything else they might want to use outside of those libraries may merit a discussion, but otherwise they can progress in their work without disrupting the security or platform engineering team's work.

However you achieve it, constructing a "Paved Road" for other teams is one of the most valuable activities in a security program. Paved roads are well-integrated, supported solutions to common problems that allow humans to focus on their unique value creation (like creating differentiated business logic for an application).[14] While we mostly think about paved roads in the context of product engineering activities, paved roads absolutely apply elsewhere in the organization, like security. Imagine a security program that finds ways to accelerate work! Making it easy for a salesperson to adopt a new SaaS app that helps them close more deals is a paved road. Making it easy for users to audit their account security rather than burying it in nested menus is a paved road too. We'll talk more about enabling paved roads as part of a resilience program in Chapter 7.

Paved roads in action: Examples from the wild

One powerful example of a paved road—standardizing a few patterns for teams in one invaluable framework—comes from Netflix's Wall-E framework (*https://oreil.ly/*

---

14 Thanks to Senior Principal Engineer Mark Teodoro for this fabulous definition.

ICFHV). As anyone who's had to juggle deciding on authentication, logging, observability, and other patterns while trying to build an app on a shoestring budget will recognize, being bequeathed this kind of framework sounds like heaven. Taking a step back, it's a perfect example of how we can pioneer ways for resilience (and security) solutions to fulfill production pressures—the "holy grail" in SCE. Like many working in technology, we cringe at the word *synergies*, but they are real in this case—as with many paved roads—and it may ingratiate you with your CFO to gain buy-in for the SCE transformation.

From the foundation of a curious security program, Netflix started with the observation that software engineering teams had to consider too many security things when building and delivering software: authentication, logging, TLS certificates, and more. They had extensive security checklists for developers that created manual effort and were confusing to perform (as Netflix stated, "There were flowcharts inside checklists. Ouch."). The status quo also created more work for their security engineering team, which had to shepherd developers through the checklist and validate their choices manually anyway.

Thus, Netflix's application security (appsec) team asked themselves how to build a paved road for the process by productizing it. Their team thinks of the paved road as a way to sculpt questions into Boolean propositions. In their example, instead of saying, "Tell me how your app does this important security thing," they verify that the team is using the relevant paved road to handle the security thing.

The paved road Netflix built, called Wall-E, established a pattern of adding security requirements as filters that replaced existing checklists that required web application firewalls (WAFs), DDoS prevention, security header validation, and durable logging. In their own words, "We eventually were able to add so much security leverage into Wall-E that the bulk of the 'going internet-facing' checklist for Studio applications boiled down to one item: Will you use Wall-E?"

They also thought hard about reducing adoption friction (in large part because adoption was a key success metric for them—other security teams, take note). By understanding existing workflow patterns, they asked product engineering teams to integrate with Wall-E by creating a version-controlled YAML file—which, aside from making it easier to package configuration data, also "harvested developer intent." Since they had a "concise, standardized definition of the app they intended to expose," Wall-E could proactively automate much of the toil work developers didn't want to do after only a few minutes of setup. The results benefit both efficiency and resilience—exactly what we seek to satisfy our organizations' thirst for more quickly doing more, and our quest for resilience: "For a typical paved road application with no unusual security complications, a team could go from `git init` to a production-ready, fully authenticated, internet-accessible application in a little less than 10 minutes." The product developers didn't necessarily care about security, but they eagerly adopted it when they realized this standardized patterned helped them ship code to users more quickly and iterate more quickly—and iteration is a key way we can foster flexibility during build and delivery, as we'll discuss toward the end of the chapter.

Dependency Analysis and Prioritizing Vulnerabilities

The final practice we can adopt to expand and preserve our safety boundaries is dependency analysis—and, in particular, prudent prioritization of vulnerabilities. *Dependency analysis*, especially in the context of unearthing bugs (including security vulnerabilities), helps us understand faults in our tools so we can fix or mitigate them—or even consider better tools. We can treat this practice as a hedge against potential stressors and surprises, allowing us to invest our effort capital elsewhere. The security industry hasn't made it easy to understand when a vulnerability is important, however, so we'll start by revealing heuristics for knowing when we should invest effort into fixing them.

Prioritizing vulnerabilities

When should you care about a vulnerability? Let's say a new vulnerability is being hyped on social media. Does it mean you should stop everything to deploy a fix or patch for it? Or will alarm fatigue (*https://oreil.ly/fe0NX*) enervate your motivation? Whether you should care about a vulnerability depends on two primary factors:

- How easy is the attack to automate and scale?
- How many steps away is the attack from the attacker's goal outcome?

The first factor—the ease of automating and scaling the attack (i.e., vulnerability exploit)—is historically described by the term *wormable*.[15] Can an attacker leverage this vulnerability at scale? An attack that requires zero attacker interaction would be easy to automate and scale. Crypto mining is often in this category. The attacker can create an automated service that scans a tool like Shodan for vulnerable instances of applications requiring ample compute, like Kibana (*https://oreil.ly/cXFOK*) or a CI tool. The attacker then runs an automated attack script against the instance, then automatically downloads and executes the crypto mining payload, if successful. The attacker may be notified if something is going wrong (just like your typical Ops team), but can often let this kind of tool run completely on its own while they focus on other criminal activity. Their strategy is to get as many leads as they can to maximize the potential coins mined during any given period of time.

---

15 It's a bit anachronistic today (although Microsoft still uses it for tagging vulnerabilities), but roughly refers to an attack that does not require human interaction to replicate itself across a network. In modern times, that network can be the internet itself. Since we're trying to avoid infosec jargon as part of the SCE transformation, this factor can be referred to as "scalable" rather than "wormable."

The second factor is, in essence, related to the vulnerability's ease of use for attackers. It is arguably an element of whether the attack is automatable and scalable, but is worth mentioning on its own given this is where vulnerabilities described as "devastating" often obviously fall short of such claims. When attackers exploit a vulnerability, it gives them access to something. The question is how close that something is to their goals. Sometimes vulnerability researchers—including bug bounty hunters—will insist that a bug is "trivial" to exploit, despite it requiring a user to perform numerous steps. As one anonymous attacker-type quipped, "I've had operations almost fail because a *volunteer* victim couldn't manage to follow instructions for how to compromise themselves."

Let's elucidate this factor by way of example. In 2021, a proof of concept was released for Log4Shell, a vulnerability in the Apache Log4j library (*https://oreil.ly/VX79q*)—we've discussed this in prior chapters. The vulnerability offered fantastic ease of use for attackers, allowing them to gain code execution on a vulnerable host by passing special "jni:"—referring to the Java Naming and Directory Interface (JNDI)—text into a field logged by the application. If that sounds relatively trivial, it is. There is arguably only one real step in the attack: attackers provide the string (a jndi: insertion in a loggable HTTP header containing a malicious URI), which forces the Log4j instance to make an LDAP query to the attacker-controlled URI, which then leads to a chain of automated events that result in an attacker-provided Java class being loaded into memory and executed by the vulnerable Log4j instance. Only one step (plus some prep work) required for remote code execution? What a value prop! This is precisely why Log4j was so automatable and scalable for attackers, which they did within 24 hours of the proof of concept being released.

As another example, Heartbleed (*https://oreil.ly/thMFO*) is on the borderline of acceptable ease of use for attackers. Heartbleed enables attackers to get arbitrary memory, which *might* include secrets, which attackers could *maybe* use to do something else and then…you can see that the ease of use is quite conditional. This is where the footprint factor comes into play; if few publicly accessible systems used OpenSSL, then performing those steps might not be worth it to attackers. But because the library is popular, some attackers might put in the effort to craft an attack that scales. We say "some," because in the case of Heartbleed, what the access to arbitrary memory gives attackers is essentially the ability to read whatever junk is in the reused OpenSSL memory, which might be encryption keys or other data that was encrypted or decrypted. And we do mean "junk." It's difficult and cumbersome for attackers to obtain the data they might be seeking, and even though the exact same vulnerability was everywhere and remotely accessible, it takes a lot of target-specific attention to turn it into anything useful. The only generic attack you can form with this vulnerability is to steal the private keys of vulnerable servers, and that is only useful as part of an elaborate and complicated meddler-in-the-middle attack (*https://oreil.ly/BylL_*).

At the extreme end of requiring many steps, consider a vulnerability like Rowhammer—a fault in many DRAM modules in which repeated memory row activations can launch bit flips in adjacent rows. It, in theory, has a massive attack footprint because it affects a "whole generation of machines." In practice, there are quite a few requirements (*https://oreil.ly/frZyN*) to exploit Rowhammer for privilege escalation, and that's after the initial limitation of needing local code execution: bypassing the cache and allocating a large chunk of memory; searching for bad rows (locations that are prone to flipping bits); checking if those locations will allow for the exploit; returning that chunk of memory to the OS; forcing the OS to reuse the memory; picking two or more "row-conflict address pairs" and hammering the addresses (i.e., activating the chosen addresses) to force the bitflip, which results in read/write access to, for instance, a page table, which the attacker can abuse to then execute whatever they *really* want to do. And that's before we get into the complications with causing the bits to flip. You can see why we haven't seen this attack in the wild and why we're unlikely to see it at scale like the exploitation of Log4Shell.

So, when you're prioritizing whether to fix a vulnerability immediately—especially if the fix results in performance degradation or broken functionality—or wait until a more viable fix is available, you can use this heuristic: can the attack scale, and how many steps does it require the attackers to perform? As one author has quipped before (*https://oreil.ly/9XztY*), "If there is a vulnerability requiring local access, special configuration settings, and dolphins jumping through ring 0," then it's total hyperbole to treat the affected software as "broken." But, if all it takes is the attacker sending a string to a vulnerable server to gain remote code execution over it, then it's likely a matter of *how quickly* your organization will be affected, not *if*. In essence, this heuristic allows you to categorize vulnerabilities into "technical debt" versus "impending incident." Only once you've eliminated all chances of incidental attacks—which is the majority of them—should you worry about super slick targeted attacks that require attackers to engage in spy movie–level tactics to succeed.

 This is another case where isolation can help us support resilience. If the vulnerable component is in a sandbox, the attacker must surmount another challenge before they can reach their goal.

Remember, vulnerability researchers are *not* attackers. Just because they are hyping their research doesn't mean the attack can scale or present sufficient efficiency for attackers. Your local sysadmin or SRE is closer to the typical attacker than a vulnerability researcher.

The Relationship Between Intentions and Bugs

One theory of "bugs" (whether exploitable or not) is that they reflect a breakdown in intentions from one level of abstraction to the next.[16] In the context of building and delivering, we can think of bugs as when the code does not reflect the design intention. You may design the system to only accept X, but the way it's written actually accepts Y in some circumstances. Then, once you deliver it into production, the Y happens and you feel "baffled."

Remember, when we design a system—whether for the first time or as part of iterating on it—we're creating a mental model of how it works. Hopefully, that mental model is accurately captured in our diagrams and requirements docs. Regardless, when we start writing code to give shape to the design—to implement it—it's unlikely what we build will capture those original mental models perfectly.

To the extent your software doesn't match your intent, that's a bug. Your intention may also be incorrect—sometimes two bugs can even make a right. Organizational memory disappears, but software lasts forever—the intentions lost, but their manifestations persisting as a treasure trove of potential bugs.

Configuration bugs and error messages

We must also consider configuration bugs and error messages as part of fostering thoughtful dependency analysis. Configuration bugs—often referred to as "misconfigurations"—arise because the people who designed and built the system have different mental models than the people who use the system. When we build systems, we need to be open to feedback from users; the user's mental model matters more than our own, since they will feel the impact of any misconfigurations. As we'll discuss more in Chapter 6, we shouldn't rely on "user error" or "human error" as a shallow explanation. When we build something, we need to build it based on realistic use, not the Platonic ideal of a user.

We must track configuration errors and mistakes and treat them just like other bugs.[17] We shouldn't assume users or operators read docs or manuals enough to fully absorb them, nor should we rely on users or operators perusing the source code. We certainly shouldn't assume that the humans configuring the software are infallible or will possess the same rich context we have as builders. What feels basic to us may feel esoteric to users. An iconic reply to exemplify this principle is from 2004, when a user sent an email to the OpenLDAP mailing list (*https://oreil.ly/hXB61*) in response to the

---

16 Nir Fresco and Giuseppe Primiero, "Miscomputation," *Philosophy & Technology* 26 (2013): 253-272.

17 Tianyin Xu and Yuanyuan Zhou, "Systems Approaches to Tackling Configuration Errors: A Survey," *ACM Computing Surveys (CSUR)* 47, no. 4 (2015): 1-41.

developer's comment that "the reference manual already states, near the top…." The response read: "You are assuming that those who read that, understood what the context of 'user' was. I most assuredly did not until now. Unfortunately, many of us don't come from UNIX backgrounds and though pick up on many things, some things which seem basic to you guys elude us for some time."

As we'll discuss more in Chapter 6, we shouldn't blame human behavior when things go wrong, but instead strive to help the human succeed even as things go wrong. We want our software to facilitate graceful adaptation to users' configuration errors. As one study advises: "If a user's misconfiguration causes the system to crash, hang, or fail silently, the user has no choice but [to] report [it] to technical support. Not only do the users suffer from system downtime, but also the developers, who have to spend time and effort troubleshooting the errors and perhaps compensating the users' losses."[18]

How do we help the sociotechnical system adapt in the face of configuration errors? We can encourage explicit error messages that generate a feedback loop (we'll talk more about feedback loops later in this chapter). As Yin et al. found in an empirical study on configuration errors in commercial and open source systems, only 7.2% to 15.5% of misconfiguration errors provided explicit messages to help users pinpoint the error.[19] When there are explicit error messages, diagnosis time is shortened by 3 to 13 times relative to ambiguous messages and 1.2 to 14.5 times with no messages at all.

Despite this empirical evidence, infosec folk wisdom says that descriptive error messages are pestiferous because attackers can learn things from the message that assist their operation. Sure, and using the internet facilitates attacks—should we avoid it too? Our philosophy is that we should not punish legitimate users just because attackers can, on occasion, gain an advantage. This does not mean we provide verbose error messages in all cases. The proper amount of elaboration depends on the system or component in question and the nature of the error. If our part of the system is close to a security boundary, then we likely want to be more cautious in what we reveal. The ad absurdum of expressive error messages at a security boundary would be, for instance, a login page that returns the error: "That was a really close guess to the correct password!"

As a general heuristic, we should trend toward giving more information in error messages until shown how that information could be misused (like how disclosing that a password guess was close to the real thing could easily aid attackers). If it's a foreseen

18 Xu, "Systems Approaches to Tackling Configuration Errors," 1-41.

19 Zuoning Yin et al., "An Empirical Study on Configuration Errors in Commercial and Open Source Systems," *Proceedings of the 23rd ACM Symposium on Operating Systems Principles* (Cascais, Portugal: October 23-26, 2011): 159-172.

error that the user can reasonably do something about, we should present it to them in human-readable text. The system is there so that users and the organization can achieve some goal, and descriptive error messages help users understand what they've done wrong and remedy it.

If the user *can't* do anything about the error, even with details, then there's no point in showing them. For that latter category of error, one pattern we can consider is returning some kind of trace identifier that a support operator can use to query the logs and see the details of the error (or even what else happened in the user's session).[20] With this pattern, if an attacker wants to glean some juicy error details from the logs, they must socially engineer the support operator (i.e., find a way to bamboozle them into revealing their credentials). If there's no ability to talk to a support operator, there's no point in showing the error trace ID since the user can't do anything with it.

 Never should a system dump a stack trace into a user's face unless that user can be expected to build a new version of the software (or take some other tangible action). It's uncivilized to do so.

To recap, during the build and delivery phase, we can pursue four practices to support safety boundaries, the second ingredient of our resilience potion: anticipating scale, automating security checks via CI/CD, standardizing patterns and tools, and performing thoughtful dependency analysis. Now let's proceed to the third ingredient: observing system interactions across space-time.

Observe System Interactions Across Space-Time (or Make More Linear)

The third ingredient in our resilience potion is observing system interactions across space-time. When building and delivering systems, we can support this observation and form more accurate mental models as our systems' behaviors unfold over time and across their topology (because looking at a single component at a single point in time tells us little from a resilience perspective). But we can also help make interactions more linear, augmenting our discussion on designing for linearity in the last chapter. There are practices and patterns we can adopt (or avoid) that can help us introduce more linearity as we build and deliver systems too.

In this section, we'll explore four practices during this phase that help us either observe system interactions across space-time or nurture linearity: Configuration as

---

20 Austin Parker et al., "Chapter 4: Best Practices for Instrumentation", in *Distributed Tracing in Practice: Instrumenting, Analyzing, and Debugging Microservices* (Sebastopol, CA: O'Reilly, 2020).

Code, fault injection, thoughtful testing practices, and careful navigation of abstractions. Each practice supports our overarching goal during this phase of harnessing speed to vitalize the characteristics and behaviors we need to maintain our systems' resilience to attack.

Configuration as Code

The first practice granting us the gift of making interactions across space-time more linear (as well as observing them) is Configuration as Code (CaC). Automating deployment activities reduces the amount of human effort required (which can be allocated elsewhere) and supports repeatable, consistent software delivery. Part of software delivery is also delivering the infrastructure underlying your applications and services. How can we ensure that infrastructure is delivered in a repeatable way too? More generally, how can we verify that our configurations align with our mental models?

The answer is through CaC practices: declaring configurations through markup rather than manual processes. While the SCE movement is aspiring toward a future in which all sorts of configurations are declarative, the practice today mostly consists of Infrastructure as Code (IaC). IaC is the ability to create and manage infrastructure via declarative specifications rather than manual configuration processes. The practice uses the same sort of process as source code, but instead of generating the same application binary each time, it generates the same environment every time. It creates more reliable and predictable services. CaC is the idea of extending this approach to all the configurations that matter, like resilience, compliance, and security. CaC resides in the squishy overlap of delivery and operations, but it should be considered part of what engineering teams deliver.

If you're already familiar with IaC, you might be surprised it's being touted as a security tool. Organizations are already adopting it for the audit trail it generates, which absolutely supports security by making practices more repeatable. Let's look at some of the other benefits of IaC for security programs.

Faster incident response
IaC supports automatic redeployment of infrastructure when incidents happen. Even better, it can automatically respond to leading indicators of incidents too, using signals like thresholding to preempt problems (we'll discuss this more in the next chapter). With automated reprovisioning of infrastructure, we can kill and redeploy compromised workloads as soon as an attack is detected, without impacting the end user experience.

Minimized environmental drift

Environmental drift refers to configurations or other environmental attributes "drifting" into an inconsistent state, like production being inconsistent from staging. IaC supports automatic infrastructure versioning to minimize environmental drift and makes it easier to revert deployments as needed if something goes wrong. You can deploy to fleets of machines flawlessly in ways that humans would struggle to perform without mistakes. IaC allows you to make changes nearly atomically. It encodes your deployment processes in notation that can be passed from human to human, especially as teams change membership—loosening our coupling at layer 8 (i.e., the people layer).

Faster patching and security fixes

IaC supports faster patching and deployment of security changes. As we discussed in the section on CI/CD, the real lesson of the infamous Equifax incident is that patching processes must be usable, else procrastination will be a logical course of action. IaC reduces friction in the way of releasing patches, updates, or fixes and also decentralizes the process, promoting looser organizational coupling. As a more general point, if *any* organizational process is cumbersome or unusable, it will be circumvented. This is not because humans are bad, it's the opposite; humans are pretty great at figuring out efficient ways to achieve their goals.

Minimized misconfigurations

At the time of this writing, misconfigurations are the most common cloud security vulnerability according to the National Security Agency (NSA) (*https://oreil.ly/k_img*); they're both easy for attackers to exploit and highly prevalent. IaC helps correct misconfigurations by users and automated systems alike. Humans and computers are both capable of making mistakes—and those mistakes are inevitable. For instance, IaC can automate the deployment of access control configurations, which are notoriously confusing and easy to mess up.

Catching vulnerable configurations

To catch vulnerable configurations, the status quo is often authenticated scanning in production environments, which introduces new attack paths and hazards. IaC lets us excise that hazard, instead scanning the code files to find vulnerable configurations. IaC also makes it easier to write and enforce rules on a set of configuration files versus writing and enforcing rules across all your cloud service provider's (CSP's) APIs.

Autonomic policy enforcement

IaC helps automate deployment and enforcement of IAM policies, like Principle of Least Privilege (PoLP). IaC patterns simplify adherence to industry standards, like compliance, with an end goal of "continuous compliance" (Figure 4-1).

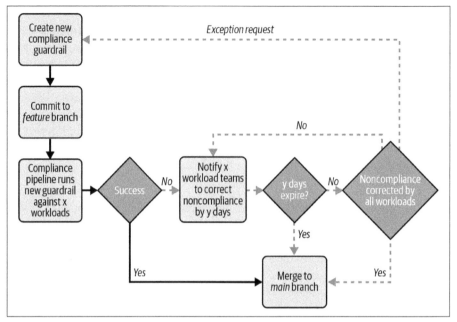

Figure 4-1. An example "continuous compliance workflow for IaC" (https://oreil.ly/ fCFb0) from AWS

Stronger change control
 IaC introduces change control by way of source code management (SCM), enabling peer reviews on configurations and a strong changelog. This also imparts significant compliance benefits.

Because of all these benefits, and the fact that all engineering teams can leverage them to achieve shared goals, IaC supports a more flexible security program and frees up effort capital for other activities. The audit trail it begets and the experimentation environments it enables support curiosity too, which we want for our resilience potion. It strengthens our resilience potion by making interactions across space-time more linear, but also begets flexibility and willingness to change—like a "buy one reagent get one free deal" at the witch apothecary.

Fault Injection During Development

Another practice we can use in this phase to excavate and observe system interactions across space-time is fault injection.[21] In fact, this presents two opportunities for security teams: learning about fault injection to make a case for its value to the

---

21 Peter Alvaro et al., "Lineage-Driven Fault Injection," *Proceedings of the 2015 ACM SIGMOD International Conference on Management of Data* (2015): 331-346.

organization (and trying to pave the road to its adoption), and collaborating with engineering teams to integrate fault injection into existing workflows. If we only test the "happy path" in our software, our mental model of the system will be a delusion and we'll be baffled when our software gets wonky in production. To build resilient software systems, we must conceive and explore the "unhappy paths" too.

When you add a new component in the system, consider what disruption events might be possible and write tests to capture them. These tests are called *fault injection tests*: they stress the system by purposefully introducing a fault, like introducing a voltage spike or oversized input. Given most software systems we build look roughly like a web application connected to a database, an early fault injection test may often take the form of "disconnect and reconnect the database to make sure your database abstraction layer recovers the connection." Unlike chaos experiments, which simulate adverse scenarios, with fault injection we are introducing a purposefully wonky input to see what happens in a particular component.

Many teams don't prioritize fault injection (or fault tolerance) until there's an incident or a near miss. In a reality of finite resources, it's reasonable to wonder whether fault injection is worth it—but, that assumes you have to perform it everywhere to adopt it. Starting with fault injection for your critical functions (like those you defined in the tier 1 assessment from Chapter 2) helps you invest your effort in the places it really matters. Let's say your company provides an auction platform for physical equipment, where serving traffic during an auction must happen continuously without downtime, but it's OK for user analytics to be delayed. Maybe you invest more in fault injection and other testing that informs design improvements in the auction system, but rely on monitoring and observability in the rest of your systems to make recovery from faults more straightforward.

Fault injection tests should be written while the concern is salient—which is during development. Making fault injection a standard practice for critical functions will help developers better understand their dependents before delivering with them, and might discourage introducing components that make the system more difficult to operationalize. This principle holds true for most testing, in fact, which we'll turn to next.

Integration Tests, Load Tests, and Test Theater

Now on to a vital, and controversial, practice that can support observation of system interactions across space-time: testing. As a discipline, software engineering needs to have an uncomfortable conversation around testing (to say nothing of the abysmal status quo of security testing). Are we testing for resilience or correctness over time, or just to say that we did testing? Some forms of testing can serve more as security devices when automated fully, blocking merges or deploys without need for human intervention. Or, we can write up a bunch of unit tests, use code coverage as a specious proxy for a job well done, and claim "we tested it" if something goes wrong. Alternatively, we can invest our effort capital in more constructive ways to observe the resilience properties of the system through integration and load testing—or even to pursue resilience stress testing (chaos experimentation) as part of the experimentation tier we discussed in Chapter 2.

The traditional triangular hierarchy of tests doesn't cut it for resilience; the triangle (and its geometric brethren) look nice and feel intuitive, but they are more aesthetic than true. Different types of tests are better at addressing certain issues, and which tests you might find useful will depend on what is most relevant to your local context—your critical functions and your goals and constraints that define your operating boundaries.

We need to think about testing in terms of the Effort Investment Portfolio. The ideal mix of test types and coverage we invest in might be different by project and by part of the system. A software engineer may not care if their configuration parsing code is slow or wonky as long as the application reliably starts with the right configuration, so integration testing is sufficient. If it's critical to validate incoming user data, however, then fuzz testing might be a candidate for those code paths.

Tests written by engineers are an artifact of their mental models at a certain point in space-time. Because reality evolves—including the systems and workloads within it—tests become outdated. The insights we learn from chaos experiments, real incidents, and even observing healthy systems must be fed back into our testing suites to ensure they are reflective of the production reality. We need to prioritize tests that help us refine our mental models and can adapt as the system context evolves. As the Google SRE handbook (*https://oreil.ly/SmTbv*) says: "Testing is the mechanism you use to demonstrate specific areas of equivalence when changes occur. Each test that passes both before and after a change reduces the uncertainty for which the analysis needs to allow. Thorough testing helps us predict the future reliability of a given site with enough detail to be practically useful."

History has worked against strong testing in software engineering; organizations used to maintain dedicated testing teams, but they are rare to see today. Culturally, there is often the sense among software engineers that tests are "someone else's problem." The issue underlying the excuse is that tests are perceived as too complicated, especially integration tests. This is why *paved roads* for testing of all kinds, not just security, are one of the most valuable solutions security and platform engineering teams can build. To counter performance objections, we could even allow developers to specify the level of overhead with which they're comfortable.[22]

---

22 Jonas Wagner et al., "High System-Code Security with Low Overhead," *2015 IEEE Symposium on Security and Privacy* (May 2015): 866-879.

In this section, we'll explore why, contrary to folk wisdom, the most important test category is arguably the integration test (or "broad integration test" (*https://oreil.ly/1FJd2*)). It checks if the system actually does what it's supposed to do in the most basic sense. We'll talk about load tests and how we can leverage traffic replay to observe how the system behaves across space-time. Despite popular folk wisdom, we'll discuss why unit tests should *not* be considered the necessary foundation before an organization pursues other forms of testing. Some organizations may choose to forgo unit testing at all, for the reasons we'll discuss in this section. We'll close with fuzz testing, a test worth pursuing only once we have our "basics" in place.

What Are the Types of Tests and When Are They Useful?

Unit tests

What are they? Unit tests verify that the smallest units of source code behave as expected, with the tests written using knowledge of the internal structure of the module.

Why use them? You might use them to verify that a unit's behavior produces expected results for specific defined inputs, and to provide developers with immediate feedback when a software change violates a past expectation. Unit tests provide the benefit that, when they fail, they point exactly to the trace through the system that doesn't match the declared expected behavior. The expected outcome is that the engineer adjusts the code or adjusts the expectation.

Integration tests

What are they? Integration tests verify that the numerous modules and components that make up a system integrate and can perform the system's intended function correctly. They are written with knowledge of the application's architecture, but not its internal structure.

Why use them? You might use them to verify that a new version of some part of the system meets prior expectations and is a candidate to deploy. Integration tests provide the benefit that, when they fail, they indicate that the new software would likely fail to run successfully if deployed.

Functional tests

What are they? Functional tests verify that specific functional requirements are met by the resulting system. They are written with the knowledge of the application's architecture and data, but not its internal structure. They can be considered a kind of integration test with the additional requirement that they be attached to some functional requirement.

Why use them? You might use them to ensure that new versions of any of the system's components preserve a specific behavior that is required of the system. Functional tests provide the benefit that, when they fail, they indicate that the new software would not comply with a previously declared requirement. The expected outcome is that the requirement be dropped or the new version of the software will be considered ineligible for deployment.

End-to-end tests

What are they? End-to-end tests verify that an entire flow of user interaction through the system results in an expected end state. They are written with the knowledge of the application's architecture and data, but not its internal structure. They can be considered a kind of integration test or a series of integration tests with the additional requirement that they be attached to some important user interaction flow.

Why use them? You might use them to verify that specific critical user interaction flows are preserved in new versions of the system. End-to-end tests provide the benefit that, when they fail, they indicate that some important interaction flow has changed. The expectation is that documentation on this critical flow will be updated or the new version of the software will be considered ineligible for deployment.

Acceptance tests

What are they? Acceptance tests refer to any set of tests that are used to gauge whether or not a new version of the system satisfies functional and nonfunctional requirements and is a candidate for deployment.

Why use them? You might use them when you want some shared agreement on what validation is required before releasing a new version of the software. These do not describe the nature of the tests themselves, but instead the relation of the software release to software validation.

Performance tests

What are they? Performance tests evaluate how well a system behaves when presented with a particular known workload under particular configurations. They are written with the knowledge of the system's architecture and data, and often with the knowledge of its internal structure and data.

Why use them? You might use them when the performance of your system is a meaningful aspect of how successful a deployment of new versions will be. Performance tests generally do not have an inherent pass/fail condition and require human interpretation to determine whether a proposed version of the software behaves adequately, though sometimes engineers will adopt thresholds or ratcheting as a means of automating this.

Smoke tests

What are they? Smoke tests evaluate whether a newly deployed release functions correctly. They are written with the knowledge of the system's architecture and data, including knowing what sort of operations can be performed on the live system without impacting the real users.

Why use them? You might use them to validate whether newly deployed versions of the system have deployed successfully or whether you may need to roll back. You might use them to have an early indication of when new releases have failed to deploy to production. Smoke tests provide the benefit that, when they fail, they indicate a serious unexpected problem with a release that necessitates roll-back. Some continuous deployment systems will automatically roll back releases that fail smoke tests, but more often it is at the operator's discretion.

Integration tests

Integration testing is typically considered part of "good engineering," but its benefits for resilience are less discussed. Integration tests observe how different components in the system work together, usually with the goal of verifying that they interact as expected, making it a valuable first pass at uncovering "baffling interactions." What we observe is the idealized system, like when we propose a new iteration of the system and test to ensure it all integrates as intended. The only changes integration tests inform are roughly, "you made a mistake and you want to prevent that mistake going live." For more comprehensive feedback on how we can refine system design, we need chaos experiments—the resilience stress tests we covered in Chapter 2.

How does an integration test look in practice? Let's return to our earlier example of a web application connected to a database. An integration test could and should cover that case—"disconnect and reconnect the database to make sure your database abstraction layer recovers the connection"—in most database client libraries.

How Security Teams Can Support Integration Testing

If your organization has a security team that currently performs manual reviews, consider replacing that effort by helping craft integration tests instead. Security teams can declare what is important to them and describe to software engineers what the integration tests should be. Even better, security teams could create integration tests for software engineering teams to use, or partner with engineering leadership to prioritize these tests.

In an ideal world, manual code reviews are an exercise in thinking outside the box—such as assessing confused deputies or over-permissioning—but, in practice and under production pressures, they often amount to going through checklists or OWASP Top 10.

A good rule of thumb is, until you have your integration tests in order—when they are reliable, repeatable, and actually used by developers—investing effort in security tests, which are inherently more niche, is extravagant. Remember, attackers think in systems and thrive in interconnections between components; integration tests could and should find many of the issues they'd love to exploit, like error-handling bugs, misconfigurations, and lack of permissioning.

The AttachMe vulnerability (*https://oreil.ly/g1e1m*)—a cloud isolation vulnerability in Oracle Cloud Infrastructure (OCI)—is an example of what we hope to uncover with an integration test, and another example of how hazardous it is to focus only on "happy paths" when testing and developing in general. The bug allowed users to attach disk volumes for which they lack permissions—assuming they could name the volume by volume ID—onto virtual machines they control to access another tenant's data. If an attacker tried this, they could initiate a compute instance, attach the target volume to the compute instance under their control, and gain read/write privileges over the volume (which could allow them to steal secrets, expand access, or potentially even gain control over the target environment). Aside from the attack scenario, however, this is the sort of interaction we don't want in multitenant environments for reliability reasons too. We could develop multiple integration tests describing a variety of activities in a multitenant environment, whether attaching a disk to a VM in another account, multiple tenants performing the same action simultaneously to a shared database, or spikes in resource consumption in one tenant.

Invariants and Property-Based Testing

If software engineers wrote more linearized systems, it would be easier to build integration tests that validated more invariants. *Invariants* are properties that you expect to remain true at all times. An invariant of an accounting ledger would be that it always balances. No matter what operations you perform on it, it always balances.

Our software and systems produce events, and those events don't always arrive in the same order.[23] Trying to get a sense of reality if you haven't ordered the events is impossible.[24] Deciding the order of things is useful for consistency—and introduces linearity, which we want for resilience. The ordering doesn't even have to be the actual order of events; sometimes an event happened in a different datacenter and you actually can't, with any confidence, say that one thing happened before the other. But you can pick an ordering and say that's the ordering you'll process, and all systems should process it in the same order. This eliminates the complexity of two systems processing data in different sequences and producing inconsistent results.

This relates to property-based testing, where you can declare your invariant—like "the ledger must balance"—and then tell the testing system "here are the operations you can perform on the ledger," like deducting. With these statements in its silicon mind, the testing system will try to find a series of operations that breaks your invariant. It may find a complex series of operations and try to reduce your test case, such as in the form: "Of these 1,000 operations performed, what if we removed some of

---

23 Leslie Lamport, "Time, Clocks, and the Ordering of Events in a Distributed System," *Concurrency: The Works of Leslie Lamport* (2019): 179-196.

24 Justin Sheehy, "There Is No Now," *Communications of the ACM* 58, no. 5 (2015): 36-41.

them? Do you still get the failure?" The general aim is to minimize the set of operations that leads to the failed invariant.

Property-based tests can be cumbersome to set up because most frameworks lack sufficient supporting artifacts and, perhaps worse, they require more effort investments; you must maintain cognitive overhead over your problem domain so you can tell the machine what your invariant is (which relates to the system's critical functions). Unfortunately, invariants can overwhelm our mental models. In Jepsen, for example, the invariant is, "of all the operations that the distributed database claimed it accepted, is the resulting data stored in the database consistent with those operations and potentially the operations that weren't acknowledged?" There are multiple right answers, which is why Jepsen is considered quite fancy technology.

As a general principle, we want to conduct integration tests that allow us to observe system interactions across space-time. This is far more useful to foster resilience than testing individual properties of individual components (like unit tests). One input in one component is insufficient for reproducing catastrophic failures in tests. Multiple inputs are needed, but this need not discombobulate us. A 2014 study found that three or fewer nodes are sufficient to reproduce most failures—but multiple inputs are required and failures only occur on long-running systems, corroborating both the deficiency of unit testing and the necessity of chaos experimentation.[25]

The study also showed that error-handling code is a highly influential factor in the majority of catastrophic failures, with "almost all" (92%) of catastrophic system failures resulting from "incorrect handling of nonfatal errors explicitly signaled in software." Needless to say, as part of our allocation of effort investments, we should prioritize testing error-handling code. The authors of the 2014 study wrote, "In another 23% of the catastrophic failures, the error-handling logic of a nonfatal error was so wrong that any statement coverage testing or more careful code reviews by the developers would have caught the bugs." Caitie McCaffrey, a partner architect at Microsoft, advises (*https://oreil.ly/lKW49*) when verifying distributed systems, "The bare minimum should be employing unit and integration tests that focus on error-handling, unreachable nodes, configuration changes, and cluster membership changes." This testing doesn't need to be costly; it presents an ample ROI for both resilience and reliability.

McCaffrey noted that integration tests are often skipped because of "the commonly held beliefs that failures are difficult to produce offline and that creating a

---

25 Ding Yuan, "Simple Testing Can Prevent Most Critical Failures: An Analysis of Production Failures in Distributed Data-Intensive Systems," *Proceedings of the 11th USENIX Conference on Operating Systems Design and Implementation*, 249-265.

production-like environment for testing is complicated and expensive."[26] The fabulous news is that creating a production-like environment for testing is getting easier and cheaper year after year; we'll talk about some of the modern infrastructure innovations that enable low-cost experimentation environments—a more rigorous form of test environment, and with a larger scope—in Chapter 5. Now that compute is cheaper, traditional "pre-prod" environments where a menagerie of use cases are forced to share the same infrastructure for cost reasons should be considered an anti-pattern. We want to run integration (and functional) tests before release, or on every merge to the trunk branch if practicing CD. If we include deployment metadata in a declarative format (*https://oreil.ly/Cst64*) when writing code, then we can more easily automate integration tests too, wherein our testing infrastructure can leverage a service dependency graph.

Common objections to integration testing include the presence of many external dependencies, the need for reproducibility, and maintainability. If you blend integration tests with chaos experiments, then there's less pressure on the integration tests to test the full spectrum of potential interactions. You can concentrate on the select few that you assume matter most and refine that assumption with chaos experiments over time.

Reluctance to use integration tests goes even deeper, however. Integration tests proactively discern unanticipated failures, but engineers sometimes still despise them. Why? Part of it is that when integration tests fail, it's usually quite an ordeal to figure out why and remedy the failure. A more subjective part is captured in the common engineer refrain, "My integration tests are slow and flaky." "Flaky" (sometimes called "flappy" or "flickering") tests are tests where you run the test one time and it succeeds, then when you run it again, it fails. If integration tests are slow and flaky, the system is slow and flaky. It may be your code or your dependencies—but, as systems thinkers, you own your dependencies.

Engineers are often reticent to update their mental model despite evidence that the implementation is unreliable, usually because their unit tests tell them the code does exactly what they want it to (we'll discuss the downsides of unit testing shortly). If they implemented a more reliable system and wrote better integration tests, there wouldn't be such a need to chase "flaky" integration tests. The true problem—one of software reliability—deludes engineers into thinking that integration tests are a waste of time because they are unreliable. This is an undesirable state of affairs if we want to support resilience when we build software.

---

26 Caitie McCaffrey, "The Verification of a Distributed System," *Communications of the ACM* 59, no. 2 (2016): 52-55.

The 2021 Codecov compromise (*https://oreil.ly/dIdFd*), in which attackers gained unauthorized access to Codecov's Bash Uploader script and modified it, is a good example of the "you own your dependencies" principle.

Codecov's design did not seem to reflect a resilience approach. To use Codecov, users had to add `bash <(curl -s https://code cov.io/bash)` into their build pipelines (the command is now deprecated). Codecov could have designed this script to check code signatures or have a chain of trust, but they didn't. On the server side, they could have implemented measures to limit deployments to that server/path, but they didn't. They could have inserted alerts and logs for deployments to it, but they didn't. There were numerous places where the design did not reflect the confidence users placed in them.

With that said, the developers writing software and implementing Codecov's agent into it chose to use Codecov without fully vetting the design or thinking through its n-order effects. Remember, attackers will happily "vet" these designs for you and surprise you with their findings, but it's better to adopt the "you own your dependencies" mindset and scrutinize what you insert into your systems first.

Countering these biases requires cultivation of a curious culture and a relentless emphasis on the necessity of refining mental models rather than clinging to delusory but convenient narratives. Peer review on tests, as discussed earlier in this chapter, can also help expose when an engineer takes umbrage with the integration test rather than their code.

Load testing

If we want to observe interactions across space-time as part of our resilience potion, we need to observe how the system behaves under load when testing a new version of software. Testing with toy loads is like testing a new recipe in an Easy-Bake Oven rather than a real oven. It is only when we design realistic workloads that simulate how users interact with the system that we can uncover the potential "baffling" functional and nonfunctional problems that would emerge when delivered in production. Needless to say, it isn't ideal from a resilience perspective if we are shocked by a deadlock after the new version runs in production for a while.

An automated approach ensures software engineers aren't forced to constantly rewrite tests, which is counter to the spirit of maintaining flexibility and willingness to change. If we can conduct load tests on demand (or daily), we can keep up as the system evolves. We also must ensure that resulting findings are actionable. When a test takes too much effort to design, run, or analyze, it will be unused. Can we highlight whether a result was part of previous test findings, reflecting a recurring problem? Can we visualize interactions to make it easier to understand what design refinements could improve resilience? We'll discuss user experience and respecting attention more in Chapter 7.

Yet, designing realistic workloads is nontrivial. How users—whether human or machine—interact with software (the load) is constantly changing, and collecting all the data about those interactions requires significant effort.[27] From a resilience perspective, we care much less about capturing aggregate behavior than capturing the variety of behavior. If we only tested with the median behavior, we would likely confirm our mental models, but not challenge them.

One tactic is to perform persona-based load testing, which models how a specific type of user interacts with the system. The researchers behind the tactic give the example (*https://oreil.ly/Cqr5K*) of "the personas for an e-commerce system could include 'shopaholics' (users who make many purchases) and 'window shoppers' (users who view many items without making any purchases)." We could create personas for machine users (APIs) and human users too. From the perspective of refining our mental models about interactions across space-time, discovering unknown personas that influence system behavior (and resilience) is instrumental.

---

27 Tse-Hsun Peter Chen et al., "Analytics-Driven Load Testing: An Industrial Experience Report on Load Testing of Large-Scale Systems," *2017 IEEE/ACM 39th International Conference on Software Engineering: Software Engineering in Practice Track (ICSE-SEIP)* (May 2017): 243-252.

One hazard is writing what you believe are load tests that are actually benchmarks. The goal of a load test is to simulate realistic load that the system might encounter when running in the real world. Benchmarks generally are taken at a fixed point in time and used for all future proposed versions of the software—and those are the better benchmarks based on a real-world corpus. In practice, most of what we witness are synthetic benchmarks that measure a particular workload designed for the test.

The persona-based load-testing researchers even found that, using their approach, "load tests using workloads that were only designed to meet throughput targets are insufficient to confidently claim that the systems will perform well in production." Microbenchmarks (*https://oreil.ly/iLORZ*) veer even further from the reality of the system, exercising only one small part of it to help engineers determine if some change makes that part of the system execute more quickly or more slowly.

Writing an ad hoc benchmark to inform a decision and then throwing it away can be sensible in some circumstances, but as a long-term assessment, they are abysmal. Even so, benchmarking tests are super tricky. It's difficult to know if you're measuring the right thing, it's difficult to know if your test is representative, it's difficult to interpret the results, and it's difficult to know what to do because of the results.[28] Even when the results of some change are super significant, they always need to be weighed against the diversity of factors at play. Many commercial databases prohibit publishing benchmark results for this and other reasons (known as "the DeWitt Clause" (*https://oreil.ly/TdG9m*)).

Traffic replay helps us gain a better sense of how the system behaves with realistic input. If we want to observe system interactions across space-time and incorporate them in our mental models, we need to simulate how our software might behave in the future once running in production. A paucity of realistic flows when testing new environments results in superfluous bafflement when we deploy and run our software in production. Writing scripted requests limits our testing to our mental models, whereas ingesting real production traffic offers healthy surprises to our mental models.

Traffic mirroring (or traffic "shadowing") involves capturing real production traffic that we can replay to test a new version of a workload. The existing version of the service is unaffected; it keeps handling requests as usual. The only difference is traffic

---

28 Bart Smaalders, "Performance Anti-Patterns: Want Your Apps to Run Faster? Here's What Not to Do," *Queue* 4, no. 1 (2006): 44-50.

is copied to the new version, where we can observe how it behaves when handling realistic requests.

Using cloud infrastructure can make traffic replay—and high-fidelity testing in general—more cost-effective. We can provision a complete environment in the cloud for testing, then tear it down once we're done (using the same processes we should have in place for disaster recovery anyway). Traffic replay also works with monolithic, legacy services. Either way, we're getting a more empirical, panoramic view of future behavior when testing than if we attempt to define and divine realistic flows ourselves. The tools can be open source tools like GoReplay (*https://oreil.ly/v7TK0*), service meshes, or native tools in cloud service providers. In fact, many incumbent security solutions—think intrusion detection systems (IDS), data loss prevention (DLP), and extended detection and response (XDR)—use traffic mirroring to analyze network traffic.

 Depending on your compliance regime, replaying legitimate user traffic in a test or experimentation environment may add liability. This problem can be mitigated by anonymizing or scrambling traffic before it is replayed into the environment.

Organizations in highly regulated industries already use the approach of generating synthetic datasets—those that mimic production data but do not include any real user data—to populate preproduction, staging, and other test environments while still complying with privacy regulations (such as HIPAA). Organizations in less privacy-conscious industries may need to adopt a similar approach to avoid unwanted liability.

Unit testing and testing theater

You can think of unit tests as verifying local business logic (within a particular component) and integration tests as checking interactions between the component and a selected group of other components. The benefit of unit tests is that they are granular enough to verify precise outcomes that happen as a result of very specific scenarios. So far so good. The trouble is that they also verify how that outcome is achieved by communicating with the internal structure of a program. If someone were to ever change that internal structure, the tests wouldn't work anymore—either by the tests failing or the tests no longer compiling or type-checking.

Unit testing is often a poor investment of our effort capital; we should likely allocate our efforts elsewhere. Some might call deployment without unit testing reckless, but it can be sensible depending on your objectives and requirements. Unit tests preserve the status quo by adding a level of friction to software development—an example of introducing tight coupling into testing. In fact, a unit test is the most tightly coupled type of test you could write and dwells in the realm of component-level thinking. We can look to a similar critique of formal methods to understand why we need a system-level rather than component-level assessment: "Formal methods can be used to verify that a single component is provably correct, but composition of correct components does not necessarily yield a correct system; additional verification is needed to prove that *the composition* is correct."[29]

This isn't to say unit tests are useless. There is value to adding tests when you don't expect the state of the system to change. When you expect the implementation to be stable, it's probably a good idea to assert what the behavior is. Asserting the intended behavior in a component can expose tight coupling for you—if changes in the rest of the system break this part of it. The unexpected, baffling interaction gets exposed in your development cycle rather than in your deployment and rollback cycle.

Some unit tests even reach into the internal structure of a module to puppeteer it—almost literal test theater. Imagine you have a multistep process that a module implements. Other modules call into it via its exposed interface, triggering each step at the appropriate time and with the appropriate data. Unit tests *should* be calling that exposed interface and affirming that the results are as expected. It does mean that to test any of the steps that have prerequisites, you have to run those previous steps, which can be slow and repetitive. One way around this tedium is to redesign the module in a "functional style" (*https://oreil.ly/O-Om2*) where each step receives its prerequisites explicitly rather than implicitly through the internal state of the module. Callers must then pass prerequisites from the output of one step to the input of subsequent steps. Tests can instead create the prerequisites explicitly with known values and can appropriately validate each step. But instead of refactoring, many engineers will try to "extract" the internal state and then "inject" it via startup code that runs as part of the setup of the test. The interface to the module doesn't have to change, it's only the tests that must contort—which elucidates little knowledge for us.

What happens when you want to add some new behaviors to your system? If you can add them without changing the structure of the code, your unit tests can run as is and may report unintended changes in behavior of the updated program. If you can't add the new behaviors without changing the structure of the code, now you have to change the unit tests alongside the structure of the code. Can you trust the tests that you are changing in tandem with the code they test? Maybe, if the engineer updating them is diligent. Hopefully during code review, the reviewer will examine the test changes to make sure the new assertions match the old assertions...but ask an engineer (or yourself) when you've last seen someone do that. We need a test that verifies the behavior, but doesn't depend on the structure of the code. This is why the common Test Pyramid offers aesthetic appeal more than real guidance or value.

---

29 McCaffrey, "The Verification of a Distributed System," 52-55 (emphasis ours).

Thus, to obtain the benefit of unit testing, you must never change the structure of your code. This stasis is anathema to resilience. Building tools to uphold the status quo and lock the system into its present-day design does not effectuate high-quality software. It takes some brave soul rewriting both the code and the tests that live alongside it in order to push the design forward. Maybe that's perfect for systems that are in maintenance mode, where substantial changes are unlikely to be made, or for teams that experience such churn that no one understands the design of the system—rendering it impossible to redesign anyway. Those systems stifle engineers' creativity and sense of wonder for software—aside from their desiccated brittleness—so we should avoid those anyway lest our curiosity perish.

 The correlation between code coverage and finding more bugs may be weak.[30] Software engineering researchers Laura Inozemtseva and Reid Holmes concluded that "coverage, while useful for identifying under-tested parts of a program, should not be used as a quality target because it is not a good indicator of test suite effectiveness."

We should not conflate high code coverage with good testing. As these researchers advise: "Code coverage merely measures that a statement, block, or branch has been exercised. It gives no measure of whether the exercised code behaved correctly."

Fuzz testing (fuzzing)

A fuzz tester "iteratively and randomly generates inputs with which it tests a target program," usually looking for exceptions to program behavior (like crashes or memory leaks).[31] A fuzz tester (also known as a "fuzzer") runs on a target program, like the one we're developing (attackers also use fuzzers to find vulnerabilities in programs that are potentially exploitable). Every time we run the fuzz tester—a "fuzzing run"—it may "produce different results than the last due to the use of randomness."[32] The same goes for chaos experiments (which we'll explore more in Chapter 8), which are subject to the vagaries of reality.

To set expectations, fuzzers can involve substantial effort to write and integrate with every part of the system that might accept data (and what parts of the system don't accept data?). You *really* want to ensure your other tests are reliable before you attempt it. If engineers are still bypassing integration tests, figure out why and refine

---

30 Laura Inozemtseva and Reid Holmes, "Coverage Is Not Strongly Correlated with Test Suite Effectiveness," *Proceedings of the 36th International Conference on Software Engineering* (May 2014): 435-445.

31 Andrew Ruef, "Tools and Experiments for Software Security" (doctoral diss., University of Maryland, 2018).

32 George Klees et al., "Evaluating Fuzz Testing," *Proceedings of the 2018 ACM SIGSAC Conference on Computer and Communications Security* (October 2018): 2123-2138.

the process before you try something fancier, like fuzzing. Once those "basics" are in place, however, fuzz testing can be a very useful category of test for resilience.

Beware Premature and Improper Abstractions

The final practice we can consider in the context of system interactions across space-time is the art of abstractions. Abstractions are a ferocious example of the Effort Investment Portfolio because abstractions are only convenient when you don't have to maintain them. Consider a noncomputer abstraction: the grocery store. The grocery store ensures plantains are available all year round, despite fluctuations in supply based on seasonality, rain levels, and so forth. The complex interactions between the store and suppliers, between suppliers and farmers, between farmers and the plantain tree, between the plantain tree and its environment—all of that is abstracted away for the consumer. For the consumer, it's as easy as going to the store, picking out plantains with the desired level of ripeness, and purchasing them at checkout. For the store, it is an effortful process of maintaining interaction with multiple plantain suppliers—because tightly coupling to just one supplier would result in brittleness (what if the supplier has an off year and there are no plantains for your consumers now?)—as well as buffering and queueing plantains to smooth out vagaries in supply (while maintaining enough efficiency to turn a profit).

We can even think of *teams* as abstractions over a certain problem or domain that the rest of the organization can use. Most organizations making money have some sort of billing service. In those organizations, not only do software systems use the billing service to bill customers for products, the humans in the system also use the billing team for their billing needs and expect the billing team to know the domain much better than anyone else.

When we create abstractions, we must remember that *someone* must maintain them. Handwaving away all that effort for the consumer comes with a high cost, and someone must design and maintain those illusions. For anything that isn't providing differentiated organizational value, it's worth outsourcing all that illusion-making to humans whose value *is* based on abstracting that complexity. A grocery store doesn't mold their own plastic to make shopping baskets. Likewise, a transportation company with an eCommerce site isn't in the business of creating and maintaining infrastructure abstractions, like, say, handling mutual exclusion and deadlocks.

Each time we create an abstraction, we must remember we are creating an illusion. This is the danger of creating abstractions for our own work; it can result in a self-bamboozle. An abstraction is ultimately tight coupling toward minimized overhead. It hides underlying complexity by design—but it doesn't get rid of it unless we are only consuming, not maintaining. So, if we are the creators and maintainers of the abstraction, we can bristle at the idea of loose coupling because it requires you to account for the truth. It doesn't hide those complex interactions across space-time, which can feel scary. We thought we understood the system and now look at all of this "baffling" interactivity! The abstraction gave us the *illusion* of understanding, but not the truth.

Necessarily, an abstraction hides some detail, and that detail may be important to the resilience of your system. When your software systems are a tangled nest of abstractions and something goes wrong, how do you debug it? You sacrifice a RAM stick at the altar of the eldritch gods, find a different vocation, or silently weep in front of your computer screen for a while before guzzling caffeine and performing the virtual equivalent of slamming your head into a brick wall as you tease the abstractions apart. The abstractions try to conceal baffling interactions and n-order effects of events, but tight coupling cannot eradicate interactive complexity. Smaller faults in components balloon into system-level failures and the immediacy of incident response required by tight coupling is impossible because the information needed is opaque beneath the thick, shiny gloss of abstraction.

Opportunity cost frames the abstraction trade-off well. What benefits do we give up by choosing an abstraction? How does that compare to the streamlining and legibility we receive from the time it is implemented to when it contributes to failure? What we seek is for the *socio* part of the system to get as close to understanding as possible. We will soon talk about the vital importance of sharing knowledge when we explore how we can support the fourth potion ingredient: feedback loops and learning culture. Much like we don't want a single service on which our entire system depends, we don't want a single human on which our entire system depends. Our strength comes from collaboration and communication, that different perspectives not only help, but are explicitly *necessary* to understand the system as it behaves in reality, not just in the static models of our minds or in an architecture diagram or in lines of code.

How to navigate abstractions

With all this said, shared abstractions are critical for ensuring consistency across the system, which is especially important as systems grow larger. It's infeasible (and wasteful) for all teams working on and with the system to independently implement logging, observability, authentication, auditing, TLS termination, tracing, caching, and so forth in a consistent way without providing some level of abstraction over these concepts and common patterns for the teams to follow. And these are just the technical abstractions most organizations maintain; your organization likely has its own domain-specific abstraction that requires even more care and thought. Creating these abstractions and common patterns is what a good platform engineering team will do for engineering-related concerns in their organization (we'll discuss platform security engineering more in Chapter 7).

Abstractions can be really useful. But they also require a bit of fortune-telling: which parts of the codebase should be coupled going forward? On the one hand, a thoughtful abstraction can avoid having to change things in a lot of individual places. On the other hand, abstractions that don't align with the system's real needs can lead to a rigid, tightly coupled mess of code (*https://oreil.ly/7Ldnt*). Remember, our job is to resist the temptation of tighter coupling. We should only create an abstraction after discovering a unifying principle that multiple instantiations of some concept in the system share.

Security chaos experiments can help you discern which abstractions might be necessary. You can repeat yourself in your first iteration, select a hypothesis for an experiment, observe the outcomes of the experiment, and determine which abstractions might make the most sense given the observed system behaviors.

For instance, imagine you are building a service that stores and indexes a user's photos for search (like pictures used for insurance claims). You might start with one system to import and update the index and another to search over the index. These two systems are separate, but they cooperate on the same data format. Now imagine a new user requirement emerges: the ability to tag photos (like with *Dr. Strangelove*) from the search view. This results in two places to update the index.

A dutiful reader of this book, you decide to run a chaos experiment with the hypothesis: when a user adds a tag to a photo from the search view, the photo metadata and index will both be updated and we will receive an alert if this fails. But what you might observe is the weirdness of photos going missing, their metadata updates being lost, or the index becoming corrupted as operations happen simultaneously. You might discover the "baffling interaction" of an update to the index file format in one part of the system resulting in some other part of the system now failing or behaving bizarrely. And you might not receive any alerts at all, which is its own troubling finding.

Through these observations, you can reject your hypothesis and surmise that the two systems modifying the index concurrently results in corrupted or lost data. You've exposed tight coupling that you believed was loose (or loose-ish). This evidence can directly inform new abstractions worth implementing in your code to refine system behavior. You can make the process more linear, ensuring the two systems call into something else that handles the index-updating tasks together. For instance, you could create a logical abstraction in which a reusable part of the code deals with indexing or create a centralized instantiation of that component to avoid conflicts. You could also even separate the two parts of the system, but use a mutex or synchronization primitive to direct how they coordinate together to avoid data corruption.

This example demonstrates how you can use chaos experiments to inform what abstractions might be necessary to improve repeatability and reliability. Experimentation can excavate when you might need to coordinate things in different components in your system, which is an opportunity to leverage reusable code. In fact, trying concurrent operations on data and making sure the result is correct, or at least plausible, is the sort of chaos experiment that could apply to all sorts of systems and expose both design and implementation issues. Attackers will gladly conduct these experiments on their own without informing you of the results to discern where they can coax the system into doing what they want. If you introduce abstractions without first understanding how the components really interact, you can create rigidity that reduces resilience too.

To recap, during the build and delivery phase, we have four opportunities to support observation of system interactions across space-time, the third ingredient of our resilience potion, as well as making them more linear: Configuration as Code, fault injection, thoughtful testing, and careful abstractions. We will now turn to the fourth ingredient of our resilience potion: feedback loops and learning culture.

Fostering Feedback Loops and Learning During Build and Deliver

Our fourth ingredient of the resilience potion is feedback loops and learning culture, the capacity to remember failure and learn from it. When we remember system behavior in response to stressors and surprises, we can learn from it and use it to inform changes that improve system resilience to those events in the future. What can we do to summon, preserve, and learn from these memories to create a feedback loop when building and delivering?

This section covers how to be curious and collaborative about the sociotechnical system to build more effectively, exploring four opportunities to foster feedback loops and learning during this phase: test automation, documenting *why* and *when*, distributed tracing and logging, and refining how humans interact with our development practices.

Test Automation

Our first opportunity to nurture feedback loops and learning during this phase is the practice of test automation. We need to articulate the *why* for tests just as much as we must for other things. When we write a test, can we articulate *why* we are verifying each thing we are verifying? Without knowing *why* each thing is being verified, we'll be flummoxed when our tests fail after changing or adding new code. Did we break something? Or are the tests simply stale, unable to reason about the updated state of the world?

When the *why* behind tests—or anything else—isn't documented and digestible, humans are more likely to assume that they are unnecessary, something that can be ripped out and replaced with ease. This biased reasoning is known as the Chesterton's fence fallacy (*https://oreil.ly/li2xI*), first described in G.K. Chesterton's book *The Thing*:

> In the matter of reforming things, as distinct from deforming them, there is one plain and simple principle; a principle which will probably be called a paradox. There exists in such a case a certain institution or law; let us say, for the sake of simplicity, a fence or gate erected across a road. The more modern type of reformer goes gaily up to it and says, "I don't see the use of this; let us clear it away." To which the more intelligent type of reformer will do well to answer: "If you don't see the use of it, I certainly won't let you clear it away. Go away and think. Then, when you can come back and tell me that you do see the use of it, I may allow you to destroy it."

How can we promote faster feedback loops from our tests? Through test automation. Automation helps us achieve repeatability and standardizes a sequence of tasks (giving us both looser coupling and more linearity). We want to automate the tasks that don't benefit from human creativity and adaptation, like testing, which can also keep code easy to change. If you don't automate your tests, any learning cycle iteration will straggle and will be far more expensive. Test automation speeds up our feedback loops and smooths friction around learning from our tests.

Alas, test automation sometimes spooks cybersecurity people, who lionize heavy change processes for the sake of "risk" coverage (whatever that really means). The traditional cybersecurity team shouldn't be testing software since they should already be involved in the design process (as discussed in the last chapter), and should trust software engineers to implement those designs (we don't want a panopticon (*https://oreil.ly/ecFGx*)). When we interfere with test automation and tightly couple testing to an external entity, like a separate, siloed cybersecurity team, we jeopardize resilience by reducing the *socio* part of the system's capacity to learn.

But, enough about all the ways the cybersecurity industry currently gets it wrong. How do we do test automation correctly? Security test suites can trigger automatically once a PR is submitted, working in tandem with code reviews by other developers to improve efficiency (and satisfy the eldritch production pressure gods). Of course, some traditional security testing tools are not fit for automated workflows; if a static analysis tool takes 10 minutes—or, as is lamentably still common, a few hours—to perform its scan, then it will inevitably clog the pipeline. As of the 2019 Accelerate State of DevOps report (*https://oreil.ly/EJZmw*), only 31% of elite DevOps performers use automated security tests compared with an even more meager 15% of low performers. Security test suites historically are controlled by the security team, but as we will continue stressing throughout the book, this centralization only hurts our ability to maintain resilience—as Figure 4-2 illustrates.

	Low	Medium	High	Elite
Automated build	64%	81%	91%	92%
Automated unit tests	57%	66%	84%	87%
Automated acceptance tests	28%	38%	48%	58%
Automated performance tests	18%	23%	18%	28%
Automated security tests	15%	28%	25%	31%
Automated provisioning and deployment to testing environments	39%	54%	68%	72%
Automated deployment to production	17%	38%	60%	69%
Integration with chatbots/Slack	29%	33%	24%	69%
Integration with production monitoring and observability tools	13%	23%	41%	57%
None of the above	9%	14%	5%	4%

Figure 4-2. Adoption of different forms of automation across DevOps performers (source: Accelerate State of DevOps 2019 report (https://oreil.ly/MVZzm))

We can use static analysis as an example of how test automation can improve quality. Static analysis, aside from the setup cost of writing the test, can be seen as inexpensive when amortized over time as it uncovers bugs in your code automatically. With that said, there is often a substantial meta divide among software engineering teams. When you're on top of your backlog and regularly refining design, you can afford the luxury of caring and doing something about potential security failings. When you're suffocating under a scrapheap of C code and discouraged from refining code, being presented with more security bugs adds insult to injury. The safety net, so to speak, to help the software engineering teams battling with difficult-to-maintain legacy code is woven with tools that can help them iteratively modernize and automate processes. Whether self-serve, delivered by a platform engineering team, or delivered by a security team following a platform engineering model, test automation—among other automation that we've discussed in this chapter—can help struggling teams climb out of the mire bit by bit.

This is why security programs must include software engineering perspectives when selecting tools; there may already be static analysis tools—or more general "code-quality" tools—that are CI/CD-friendly, implemented, or under consideration that could suffice to find bugs with security impacts too. For instance, integrating static analysis tools into IDEs (*https://oreil.ly/Wfg1x*) can reduce time spent by developers fixing vulnerabilities and increase the frequency that developers run the security analysis on their code. Developers are already familiar with tools like these and even rely on them to improve their workflows. You may hear a developer, for instance, raving about TypeScript, a language that exists purely to add type checking to an existing less-safe language, because it makes them more productive. If we can help software engineering teams be more productive while learning more from faster feedback loops, we are well worthy of self–high fives.

Documenting Why and When

Another opportunity for fostering feedback loops and learning when building and delivering systems is the practice of documentation—specifically, documenting *why* and *when*. As we discussed in Chapter 1, resilience relies on memory. We will flail when learning if we cannot recall relevant knowledge. We need this knowledge to remain accessible so that as many humans as possible in the *socio* part of the system can employ it in their feedback loops. Hence, we must elevate documentation as a core practice and higher priority than other "sexier" activities. This section will describe how to develop docs to best facilitate learning.

When we share knowledge, we can't think in terms of static components. Remember, resilience is a verb. We need to share our understanding of the system—not just how the components interact but *why* and *when* they interact—and even why they exist at all. We need to treat it like describing an ecosystem. If you were documenting a beach, you could describe what each thing is and how it works. There is sand. There are waves that move in and out. There are shells. But that doesn't tell us much. More meaningful is how and when these components interact. Low tide is at 13:37 and, when it happens, shrimp and sea stars take refuge in tide pools; tide pools become exposed, as do oysters; crabs scurry along the beach foraging for food—like those tasty oysters and critters in the tide pools; shorebirds also peck for morsels along the shoreline. When the tide comes in six hours later (high tide), oysters and scallops open their shells to feed; shrimp and sea stars wash out into the sea; crabs burrow; shorebirds roost; female sea turtles crawl onto shore to lay their eggs—and high tides will eventually pull the baby turtles into the ocean.

Our software systems are *complex*, made of interacting components. It is those interactions that make systems "baffling" and therefore it's imperative to capture them as builders. We need to think about our systems as a habitat, not a disparate collection of concepts. When encountering a system for the first time, we usually wonder, "Why was it built this way?" or perhaps even more fundamentally, "Why does this exist?" Yet this is what we tend to document the least when building and delivering software.

We mentioned Mozilla's Oxidation project earlier in this chapter in the context of migrating to a memory safe language, but it's also a laudable example of documenting the *why*. For most components they've shipped in Rust, they answer the question

"Why Rust?" For instance, with their integration of the `fluent-rs` localization system they explicitly documented that they compiled it in Rust because: "Performance and memory wins are substantial over previous JS implementation. It brings zero-copy parsing, and memory savvy resolving of localization strings. It also paves the way for migrating the rest of the Fluent APIs away from JS which is required for Fission."

Such a detailed answer indicating the purpose and even the mental model behind the decision deftly avoids Chesterton's fence problem in the future. But even less detailed answers can still support a learning culture, feedback loops, and, crucially, prioritization. For example, one of the proposed components to be "oxidated" into Rust—replacing DOM serializers (XML, HTML for Save As.., plain text)—simply states: "Why Rust? Need a rewrite anyway. Minor history of security vulnerabilities." Migrating to a memory safe language can be an opportunity to tackle long-standing issues that hinder reliability, resilience, or even just maintainability. We should always seek opportunities to maximize our return on effort investments where we can.

Documenting security requirements

Documenting *why* and *when* is a critical part of optimizing effort allocation in our Effort Investment Portfolio. Requirements define expectations around qualities and behaviors, allowing teams to choose how to invest their effort capital to meet those requirements. Documented security requirements support repeatability and maintainability—essential qualities for feedback loops—while reducing effort expended by all stakeholders on crafting specific requirements for each separate project.

For instance, security teams often invest substantial effort into answering software engineering teams' ad hoc questions around how to build a product, feature, or system in a way that won't be vetoed by the security program. In practice, this manual effort causes backlogs and bottlenecks, leaving engineering teams "stuck" and security teams with more limited effort capital to invest elsewhere (like in activities that might fulfill the security program's goals more fruitfully).

> The 2021 Accelerate State of DevOps report (*https://oreil.ly/-lR-2*) found that teams with high quality documentation are 3.8 times more likely to implement security practices (and 2.4 times more likely to meet or exceed their reliability targets).

Defining explicit requirements and granting engineering teams the flexibility to build their projects while adhering to those requirements frees up time and effort for both sides: engineering teams can self-serve and self-start without having to interrupt their work to discuss and negotiate with the security team, and the security team is no longer as inundated with requests and questions, freeing up time and effort for work with more enduring value. If we write documentation around, for instance, "Here is how to implement a password policy in a service," we invest some of our effort capital so other teams have more freedom allocating their own effort capital. They can access the documentation, understand the requirements, and avoid having to ask ad hoc questions about one-off requirements.

As a recent example, Principal Software Architect Greg Poirier applied this approach (*https://oreil.ly/k5mdi*) to CI/CD pipelines, eliminating the need for a centralized CI/CD system while maintaining the ability to attest software changes and determine software provenance. Rather than instituting strict guardrails that apply equally to all engineering teams, we can instead define the desired requirements in CI/CD pipelines (and make them available in a single accessible place). This allows engineering teams to build and evolve their CI/CD pipelines as fits their local needs as long as they meet the requirements.

We can improve how we handle vulnerabilities through knowledge sharing too. When vulnerabilities are discovered in standardized, shared frameworks and patterns, they're easier to fix. If teams drift off the beaten path and build things in a weird way, then we should expect more vulnerabilities. To use SQL injection (SQLi) as an example, it shouldn't take one team suffering an attacker exploiting a SQLi vulnerability in their service for the organization to discover parameterized queries and ORMs (object relational mappers (*https://oreil.ly/tNPVN*)), which make writing SQLi vulnerabilities more difficult. The organization should instead standardize on their database access patterns and make choices that make the secure way the default way. We'll discuss defaults more in Chapter 7. If one engineering team spots a vulnerability in their code, publicizing this to other teams, rather than fixing the single instance and moving on, can lead to brainstorming about how to check for the presence of the vulnerability elsewhere and strategies for mitigating it across systems.

Writing learning-driven docs

No one gets a bonus for writing great docs. Therefore, we need to make it easy for humans to create and maintain docs despite writing them not being their core skill set or their most scintillating challenge. The best resource we can create is a template with a vetted format that everyone agrees to and that requires low effort to fill in. The template should reflect the minimum required for sharing knowledge to other humans; this will make it clear what the minimum is when creating the doc while allowing for flexibility if the human wants to add more to the doc.

Sometimes engineers think that good docs for their feature or service are only relevant if the users are developers. That is not the right mindset if we wish to support repeatability or preserve possibilities. What if our service is consumed by other teams? What if it is useful to our organization if, at some point, our service is sold as an API? In a world that is increasingly API-driven, documentation gives us this flexibility and ensures our software (including firmware or even hardware) is consumable. And through this lens, documentation directly improves our metrics.

When you're building a system, you're interacting with components doing different things with different relationships to each other. Document your assumptions about these interactions. When you conduct a security chaos experiment, you learn even more about those components and relationships. Document those observations. As a thought experiment, imagine a kind stranger gifts you a lottery ticket when you go get your caffeine of choice during a work break; you win the lottery, decide to take a year off work to travel around all the gorgeous islands in the world, and then come back to your desk at day 366 to dive back into your work (assuming relaxing on pristine beaches and frolicking with exotic flora and fauna ever gets boring). Your mind is totally refreshed and thus you've forgotten mostly everything about whatever it was you're doing. Would the documentation you left for yourself be sufficient for you to understand the system again? Would you be cursing Past You for not writing out assumptions about how this component doing one thing relates to another component doing another thing?

Explain to Future You how you built the system, how you think it works, and *why* you think it works that way. Future You may conduct a security chaos experiment that disproves some of those assumptions, but it's at least a basis upon which Future You can hatch hypotheses for experiments. Of course, as you've likely already surmised, we aren't just writing these things for Future You as you develop software; it's also for new team members and existing ones who maybe aren't as familiar with the part of the system you wrote specifically. Documentation can be invaluable for incident response too, which we'll cover more in Chapter 6.

With that said, documents benefit Future You in another way too, by capturing your knowledge in a digestible format that removes the need to contact you directly and interrupt your work. We want to incentivize other humans to use documentation as their go-to source rather than performing the high-cost action of contacting us, which means we need to not only answer the basics in the docs, but also make them accessible and digestible (and if we keep getting asked the same question, it's a call to action to add the answer to the doc). Who among us hasn't looked at a novella-like doc with confusing structure and poor writing and wanted to give up? Or the doc will explain the minutiae about how the component is constructed as a static entity, but completely miss explaining *why* it is constructed that way or how it works across space-time.

If we don't describe how it behaves at runtime, including its common interactions with machines and humans alike, we'll only get a written version of a "still life" portrait of the component. A visual explanation of its interactions across space-time—a movie, rather than a portrait—can make the doc even more digestible to human eyes. Why and when do components interact? When and where does data flow? Why is there a particular temporal order? Ensuring that this visual explanation, whether a diagram or gif or decision tree or other format, is easy to change (and versioned) will keep knowledge fresh as conditions evolve and feedback is collected. For instance, a

README file can be versioned and decoupled from one individual engineer, allowing you to capture a CI/CD process with both a visual and written explanation of why each step unfolds and why interactions exist at each step.

As we will keep stressing, it is far more important to explain *why* the system behaves in a particular way and why we chose to build it this way than *how* it behaves. If our goal is for a brand-new team to be able to get started with a system quickly and understand how to maintain and add to it, then explaining *why* things are the way they are will fill in knowledge gaps much more quickly than the *how*. The *why* is what drives our learning, and continual prodding of those assumptions enlivens our feedback loops.

We want software components that are well-understood and well-documented because when we share our own knowledge about the system, it makes it easier for us to explain *why* we built something using these components and why it works the way it does. Building our own software component might be easier for us to mentally model, but harder for us to share that mental model with others and maintain by incorporating feedback. It also makes components harder to swap out; the endowment effect[33] (a subset of loss aversion)[34] means we never want to discard our "darlings." We don't want to glue things together into a tangled, tightly coupled mess where both the *why* and *how* are difficult to discern. If we declare bankruptcy on having a mental model at all, doing by blind faith, then we will defile our resilience potion; we won't understand the critical functions of the systems, and we will be unaware of safety boundaries (and push closer to them), be baffled by interactions across space-time, and neither learn nor adapt.

Distributed Tracing and Logging

The third practice we'll discuss that can fuel feedback loops and promote learning during this phase is distributed tracing and logging. It's difficult to just look at little breadcrumbs spread by the system that aren't brought together into the story (and humans very much think in stories). Whether triaging an incident or refining your mental model to inform improvements, observing interactions over time is essential. You can't form a feedback loop without being able to see what's going on; the feedback is a core part of the loop.

We should plan for and build this feedback into our services through tracing and logging. Neither one is something you can bolt on post-delivery or apply automatically to all the services you operate. You invest effort during the build and delivery phase,

33 Keith M. Marzilli Ericson and Andreas Fuster, "The Endowment Effect," *Annual Review of Economics* 6 (August 2014): 555-579.

34 Nicholas C. Barberis, "Thirty Years of Prospect Theory in Economics: A Review and Assessment," *Journal of Economic Perspectives* 27, no. 1 (2013): 173-196.

then receive a return on that investment in the observe and operate phase. Alternatively, you can decide not to invest effort capital during this phase and tear your hair out in frustration when you try to debug your complicated microservice system when it fails by guessing which log messages match up to which (which is incredibly cumbersome on services with reasonable volume). We can think of tracing and logging as a hedge against a severe downturn when our software runs in production—the feedback that helps us maintain a productive loop rather than a downward spiral. This section will explore how we can think about each during this phase.

Distributed tracing to track data flows

Distributed tracing is a mechanism to observe the flow of data as it moves through a distributed system.[35] Distributed tracing gives us a timeline of logs and the flow of data between systems, a way to make sense of interactions across space-time. It lets you stitch individual operations back to the original event. By way of analogy, consider a partnership with another organization; every time they make a product or feature request, there is a ticket ID. Any activity internally related to the request gets that ticket ID too, so you know how to bill for it (and can track work dedicated to it). Distributed tracing is the same idea; an incoming request gets tagged with a trace ID, which shows up in the logs of each service as it flows through.

Let's consider a case where an attacker is exfiltrating data from a hospital's patient portal. We can see data is being exfiltrated—but how is it happening? There is a frontend service that's responsible for displaying the dashboard the patient sees when they log in (the Patient Portal service). The Patient Portal service needs to request data from other services maintained by other teams, like recent lab reports from the Labs service, verifying the login token from the Token service, and querying the list of upcoming appointments from the Schedule service. The frontend will make a single request from the Patient Portal service, which makes requests to all those other services. Maybe the lab reports are mixed between in-house and outsourced lab work. The in-house service can read directly from the internal database and properly check user IDs. To ingest the partner lab reports, however, the Labs service must query a partner's lab report integration service. Even in this simple scenario, you're three services deep.

Let's say the team associated with the partner lab results service discovers they made a mistake (like accidentally introducing a vulnerability) and an attacker is exfiltrating data. They might be able to say what data is being sent out, but they wouldn't be able to trace the data flows without understanding all the requests coming from the Labs service—and they'd need to follow it through to all the requests coming from the

---

35 Benjamin H. Sigelman et al., "Dapper, a Large-Scale Distributed Systems Tracing Infrastructure" (Google, Inc., 2010).

Patient Portal service. This is a nightmare, because it's unclear which operations (or events) might even make a request to the partner lab results service, let alone which requests are by the attacker versus a legitimate user. All of the traffic surging into this service is from inside the company, from peer teams, but that traffic is associated with some sort of user operation that is from outside the company (like a patient clicking on their dashboard to view recent lab results).

Distributed tracing dissipates this nightmare by assigning a trace ID at the point of traffic ingress, and that trace ID follows the event as it flows through the system. That way, the partner lab results service can look at where the trace ID appears in logs across other services to determine the event's route through the system.

Distributed tracing not only helps us observe system interactions across space-time, but it also helps us refine system design and design new versions—giving us an elegant feedback loop. At the enterprise scale, you don't have complete visibility into what the teams consuming your data and accessing your service are doing with it. Their incidents can easily become your incidents. When you're refining the design of your system, you want to understand the impact it has on your tree of consumers. The more partners and consumers are braided into the chain, the more difficult it is to understand the chain. You have a mental model of how events flow through the system and how your specific part of the system interacts with other parts—but, how accurate is your mental model?

Distributed tracing helps you refine that mental model by learning about real interactions in your system and between its services. We can use distributed tracing to plan for capacity, to fix bugs, to inform consumers of downtime and API changes, and more. It bears repeating that the value we derive from distributed tracing is when software runs in production; however, we must make our effort investment during the development phase to realize this value. Distributed tracing is, in essence, making the statement that we want to be able to correlate data across systems—that we want that trace ID. It is during development that you must make the decision that you want to have the capability in the system, even if much of the value is derived during the next phase, operating and observing.

If you follow the advice of loosely coupling your systems and splitting them out over logical boundaries, you may end up with visibility problems and it may become more difficult to see the flow—even if that flow is more resilient now. That's exactly what distributed tracing is designed to divulge. It isn't fancy, but it's indisputably useful for powering a feedback loop.

Deciding how and what to log

Logging helps us learn about system behavior; when we insert logging statements into code as it's written, we sow seedlings to stimulate our feedback loops. Logging statements generate a record of system execution behaviors, what we refer to as *logs*.

When we discover that we need some information about the system (or part of the system) to add a new feature, fix a problem (like a bug), or expand capacity, we need logging to furnish that information for the feedback loop. Software engineers sometimes even build a new version of the system with new logging statements in place just to get that information. For instance, during an incident, a software engineering team may expedite deployment of a version that adds a new `logger.log` so they can peer into the system and deduce what is happening with the baffling surprise. Most software engineers know the mechanics of adding logging statements, so we won't cover those details in this section. However, it's worth reminding all stakeholders of what we should log and how we should think about logging.

Blocks are the constructs developers use when adding logging statements. Blocks are the organizational structure of the code. For example, in Python, the indentation levels—like the contents of the function—reflect a block. If you have indentations inside the function, there will be a sub-block for the `true` condition and a sub-block for the `else` part (if there is one). Basically, each of the control flow mechanisms opens a separate block. If you have a `for` loop or a `while` loop, you get a block.

A block is kind of like a paragraph. In compiler and reverse engineering land, a *basic block* is the substructure that always executes from top to bottom. A *statement* is the equivalent of a sentence—one line within a block. *Expression* refers to part of the statement that is evaluated separately. And a *clause* refers to the predicate in an `if` or a `while` statement.

We might not know what we need to log until we start interpreting data generated when our code actually runs. We must be somewhat speculative about what might be useful to recover from a future incident, to inform traffic growth, to know how effective our caches are, or any of the thousand other things that are relevant. When adding logging statements in our code as we write it, we want to preserve possibilities once our code is running in production and fuel a feedback loop. Computing scholars Li et al. describe the trade-off between sparsity and verbosity: "On one hand, logging too little may increase the maintenance difficulty due to missing important system execution information. On the other hand, logging too much may introduce excessive logs that mask the real problems and cause significant performance overhead."[36]

---

36 Zhenhao Li et al., "Where Shall We Log? Studying and Suggesting Logging Locations in Code Blocks," *Proceedings of the 35th IEEE/ACM International Conference on Automated Software Engineering* (December 2020): 361-372.

It should go without saying, but we don't want to include passwords, tokens, keys, secrets, or other sensitive information in our logs. For example, if you are a financial services or fintech company handling multitudes of sensitive PII, that sensitive information—whether names, email addresses, national identifiers (like Social Security numbers), or phone numbers—ending up in your logs constitutes a data leakage that could lead to problematic outcomes.

In general, there is rarely a reason PII must be logged rather than using a database identifier instead. A log describing "There is an issue with Charles Kinbote, *charles@zembia.gov*, database id 999" can be replaced, without loss of utility, with "There is an issue with user database id 999." The investigating engineer can use authenticated systems to scour more information about the impacted user or database record—but without the hazard of revealing sensitive data.

The point of logs is to inform feedback loops—not blast so much noise that it doesn't help anyone, nor be so sparing that it also doesn't help anyone. We log to learn. If the success or failure of something matters to your business, consider logging it. We must think about operations—system functionality—and ensure they're reflected usefully in our logging and observability tools. What you might need to log depends on local context. The closest to generalized logging wisdom is that you need to log faults that occur in your system if you want to preserve the possibility of uncovering them. If your database transaction times out, that may indicate that the data wasn't saved. This kind of event isn't something you want to ignore in an empty catch block, and it should probably be categorized at least at the ERROR level.

Crucially, we want to ensure errors—and their context—are assessed by a human. Often, there is a torrent of logging statements that gush into a bucket (or black hole, depending on whom you ask) for querying later in case you need them. Our mental model might be that errors make it into someone's inbox or notification stream at some point, but that may not be the case—so chaos experiments can verify this expected behavior. In fact, one of the best places to start with chaos experiments is verifying that your logging pipelines (or alerting pipelines) behave the way you expect. We'll talk more about this precise use case for experimentation in "Experience Report: Security Monitoring (OpenDoor)" on page 371.

Log levels indicate the importance of the message; FATAL ("Critical" on Windows) is viscerally dire while INFO ("Informational" on Windows) is less doom-inspiring. When software engineers set log levels, they are based on their mental models of how important this behavior is for understanding the system (whether to troubleshoot or refine). This makes the decision of what level to apply subjective and, therefore, tricky.

We must consider where we should weave local context into log messages too: like the associated user ID requests, trace IDs, whether the user is logged in or not, and more depending on local context. If you're building a transaction processing system, maybe you associate each transaction with an ID so if a specific transaction fails, you can use the ID for troubleshooting and investigation.

As a final note of caution, engineering teams already maintain logging infrastructure, so there's really no need for the security team to create parallel infrastructure. Instead, security teams should insist that their vendors interoperate with that existing infrastructure. There's no reason to invent the wheel—remember, we want to "choose boring"—and, when security teams create this shadow realm of duplicative infrastructure, it disrupts your ability to learn—a crucial ingredient in our resilience potion.

Refining How Humans Interact with Build and Delivery Practices

Finally, we can refine how humans interact with our development practices as another opportunity to strengthen feedback loops and nurture a learning culture. To build and deliver software systems that maintain resilience, our practices in this phase need to be sustainable. We need to be in a constant learning mode of how the humans in our sociotechnical systems interact with the practices, patterns, and tools that allow them to build and deliver systems. We need to be open to trying new IDEs, software design patterns, CLI tools, automation, pairing, issue management practices, and all the other things that are woven throughout this phase.

Part of this learning mode is also being open to the idea that the status quo isn't working—listening to feedback that things could be better. We need to be willing to discard our old practices, patterns, and tools when they no longer serve us or if they make it difficult to build a resilient or reliable system. Remembering local context also helps us refine how work is done in this phase; some projects may demand different practices and we must decide to refine them accordingly.

To recap, we have four opportunities for fostering feedback loops and nourishing learning—the fourth ingredient of our resilience potion recipe—during build and delivery: testing automation, documenting why and when, distributed tracing and logging, and refining how humans interact with development processes. How we change these interactions—and how we change anything during this phase—brings us to the final ingredient of our resilience potion: flexibility and willingness to change.

Flexibility and Willingness to Change

With those four ingredients now stirred into our hot and chocolatey concoction, we can discuss how to plop our final ingredient, the marshmallow—symbolizing flexibility and willingness to change—into our resilience potion that we can brew while building and delivering. This section describes how to build and deliver systems so we can remain flexible in the face of failures and evolving conditions that would otherwise quash success. Distributed systems researcher Martin Kleppmann said, (*https://oreil.ly/wlCsq*) "Agility in product and process means you also need the freedom to change your mind about the structure of your code and your data," and this fits perfectly with the last ingredient of our resilience potion.

For some organizations with lots of "classic" applications, a willingness to change means a willingness to stick with iteration and migration over many quarters, if not years, to transform their applications and services into more adaptable, changeable versions. A seed-stage tech startup is building from scratch and change can happen overnight. A century-old business with mainframes and older languages arguably needs flexibility and willingness to change even more, since they're already starting with a brittle foundation, but that change cannot happen overnight. Nature is a patient architect, allowing evolution to unfold over generational cycles. Migrating from a classic, tightly coupled paradigm to a modern, loosely coupled one requires patience and carefully architected evolution too. There are quick wins along the way, with resilience benefits accumulating with each iteration. None of what we describe in this book is out of reach for even the most mainframey and COBOLy of organizations; what it takes is careful assessment of your Effort Investment Portfolio and prioritization of which resilience ingredients you'll pursue first.

In this section, we will present five practices and opportunities to help flexibility and willingness to change flourish during this phase: iteration, modularity, feature flags, preserving possibilities for refactoring, and the strangler fig pattern. Many of these strategies encourage evolution and interweave willingness to change by design—promoting the speed on which our graceful adaptability depends.

Iteration to Mimic Evolution

The first practice we can adopt to foster flexibility and maintain willingness to change is iteration. As a first approximation of what makes for "good code," it is code that is easy to replace. It helps us foster the flexibility and willingness to change that is essential for systems resilience by allowing us to modify and refactor code as we receive feedback and as conditions change. Code that is easy to replace is easy to patch. Security teams often tell software engineers to mend security issues in code at a more "fundamental" level rather than slapping a bandage on it; code that is easy to replace is also easy to refactor to remedy such problems.

An iterative approach to building and delivering systems enables the evolvability we need to support systems resilience. Minimum viable products (MVPs) and feature experimentation are our best friends during this phase. Not only does it hasten time to market for code—reaching end users more quickly—but also allows us to more quickly determine what works, or doesn't, to escape the trap of rigidity (which erodes resilience). It is a means to achieve not only looser coupling, but the easy substitutions that characterize more linear systems. We need to encourage experimentation, making it easy to quickly innovate, but discard what doesn't work without shame or blame.

We also need to follow through on our MVPs and experiments. For instance, if you develop a new authentication pattern that is better than the status quo, make sure to finish the job—move from MVP to a real product. It's easy to lose steam after getting a prototype to work in part of the system, but follow-through is required for resilience. If we don't follow through or invest in maintaining it, we shrink the slack in the system and let brittleness take hold. This follow-through is necessary even if our experiments don't turn out as we hoped. If evidence suggests the experiment isn't viable, we need follow-through in the form of cleaning up after ourselves and expunging the experiment from the codebase. Remnants of failed experiments will clutter the codebase, causing confusion to anyone who stumbles upon them. (Knight Capital's stunning failure in 2014 (*https://oreil.ly/q-_26*) arguably is an example of this.)

Alas, the incremental approach to building and delivering often fails for social reasons. Humans relish novelty. We often love achieving a big win at one time rather than a bunch of smaller wins over time (*https://oreil.ly/c4L79*). Of course, this penchant for novelty and flashy feature releases means we will sacrifice incremental progress and therefore our ability to maintain resilience. It's far more difficult to evolve software that only gets "big bang" releases once a quarter than software deploying on demand, like every day or every week. When a new high-impact vulnerability strikes like thunder, the incremental approach means a patch can be released quickly, while the big, splashy release model will likely be slower to patch for both technical and social reasons.

How can we keep things feeling fresh in the iterative model? Chaos experiments, whether the security kind or performance kind, can spark adrenaline and offer a novel perspective that can lead engineers to see their code and software through a different lens. For example, we could analyze the architecture and code of a system to try to understand its performance, but a more effective approach is attaching a profiler while simulating load; the tooling will tell us exactly where the system is spending its time. We can also incentivize people to follow through, be curious, and take ownership of code, as in "you own this module personally."

An iterative approach also aligns with modularity in design, which we'll cover next.

Modularity: Humanity's Ancient Tool for Resilience

The second opportunity at our fingertips to cultivate flexibility and maintain adaptability is modularity. According to the U.S. National Park Service (NPS), modularity (*https://oreil.ly/8Ojby*) in complex systems "allows structurally or functionally distinct parts to retain autonomy during a period of stress, and allows for easier recovery from loss." It is a system property reflecting the degree to which system components—usually densely connected in a network[37]—can be decoupled into separate clusters (sometimes referred to as "communities").[38]

We may think of modules in terms of software, but humans have intuitively grasped how modularity supports resilience in sociotechnical systems for thousands of years. In ancient Palestine, modular stone terraces (*https://oreil.ly/IfQcz*) grew olive trees, grapevines, and other produce.[39] The Anglo-Saxons implemented three-field systems (*https://oreil.ly/Mqg_4*), rotating crops from one field to another, a strategy pioneered in China during the first millennium BCE.[40] For this reason, the NPS describes (*https://oreil.ly/sczwb*) modularity as reflecting "a human response to a scarcity of resources or stressors that threaten economic activities." Modularity is enlaced in humanity's history, and with it we can weave a resilient future too.

In the context of cultural landscapes—a natural landscape shaped by a cultural group—possessing modular units (like land use areas) or features (like orchards or fields) improves resilience to stress. During a disturbance, a modular unit or feature can persist or function independently of the rest of the landscape or other modular features. It proffers looser coupling, quelling the contagion effect. The single-purpose nature of the modules also introduces linearity—a way of making the landscape more "legible" without the homogeneity of the tightly coupled Normalbaum we discussed in Chapter 3.

At the John Muir National Historic Site, for instance, there are multiple blocks of multispecies, multivariety trees that foster resilience to frost, as shown in Figure 4-3. This clever design ensures that if late frosts damage some of the blooming trees, there can still be some fruit yield. This resilience did not blossom at the expense of efficiency, either—it actually enhanced efficiency. The NPS writes, "The historic system

---

37 Matheus Palhares Viana et al., "Modularity and Robustness of Bone Networks," *Molecular Biosystems* 5, no. 3 (2009): 255-261.

38 Simon A. Levin, *Fragile Dominion: Complexity and the Commons* (United Kingdom: Basic Books, 2000).

39 Chris Beagan and Susan Dolan, "Integrating Components of Resilient Systems into Cultural Landscape Management Practices," *Change Over Time* 5, no. 2 (2015): 180-199.

40 Shuanglei Wu et al., "The Development of Ancient Chinese Agricultural and Water Technology from 8000 BC to 1911 AD," *Palgrave Communications* 5, no. 77 (2019): 1-16.

of orchards at the John Muir National Historic Site was planted as modular units of species blocks containing mixed varieties, gaining efficiencies in operations but also building resilience into the system."

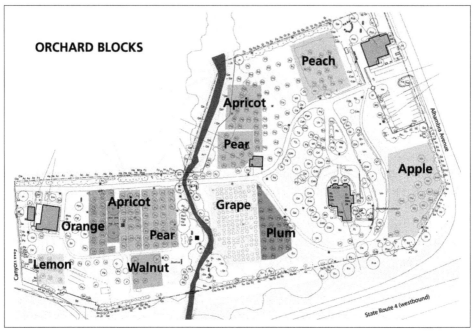

Figure 4-3. An example of modular architecture in a cultural landscape, from the John Muir National Historic Site managed by the NPS (source: National Park Service (https:// oreil.ly/hZRHb))

Whether cultural landscapes or software landscapes, when there is low modularity, failure cascades pervade. Low modularity unfetters contagion effects, where a stressor or surprise in one component can lead to failure in most or all of the system. A system with high modularity, however, can contain or "buffer" those stressors and surprises so they don't spread from one component to the others. It is through this benefit that modularity can be characterized as a "measurement of the strength of dividing a system into groups of communities and is related to the degree of connectivity within a system."[41]

For instance, increased modularity can slow the spread of infectious diseases—precisely the theory behind social distancing and, particularly, "COVID bubbles," where

---

41 Ali Kharrazi et al., "Redundancy, Diversity, and Modularity in Network Resilience: Applications for International Trade and Implications for Public Policy," *Current Research in Environmental Sustainability* 2, no. 100006 (2020).

---

a group of less than 10 humans stay together, but otherwise minimize interaction with other groups (*https://oreil.ly/OqgPW*). Other examples of modularity in our everyday lives include airport quarantine to prevent invasive wildlife or epidemics and firebreaks—gaps in combustible material—that break the spread of wildfire.[42]

While our software "species"—separate services or applications with a unique purpose—rarely perform the same function[43] (like fruit-producing trees), we can still benefit from modularity. To extend the orchard analogy, the common irrigation and maintenance labor applied to all of the trees within the orchard is akin to the common infrastructure in our software "orchards" like logging, monitoring, and orchestration. Modularity can even refine our critical functions. An adtech company could create duplicated services that share 95% of behavior, but with small, critical parts to play user segmentation strategies against each other.

 In the sociotechnical dimension of our software systems, a frenzy of new features are added to a system, then the system stabilizes as we behold the ramifications of our changes. The fact that features are labeled alpha, beta, limited availability, or GA is a reflection of this. We can think of this as a "breathe in, breathe out" cycle for software projects (or a "tick-tock" cycle (*https://oreil.ly/P7xUV*) in the now-defunct Intel architecture metaphor).

Modules often introduce more linearity, allowing for basic encapsulation and separation of concerns. They also create a local boundary upon which we can later introduce isolation. At a more localized level we have modularity for organizational purposes, to make navigating and updating the system easier, and to provide a level of logical linearization (where data flows in one direction, but backpressure and faults disrupt full linearity)—even if the modules aren't isolated.

Modularity, when done right, directly supports looser coupling: keeping things separate and limiting coordination across the codebase. It also supports linearity by allowing us to break things down into smaller components that get us closer to a single purpose. If we try to keep functionality together, we can add complexity. In tef's post on counterintuitive software wisdom, they advise (*https://oreil.ly/SLBlu*), "In trying to avoid duplication and keep code together, we end up entangling things…over time their responsibilities will change and interact in new and unexpected ways." To achieve modularity, the author says we must understand:

---

42 Erik Andersson et al., "Urban Climate Resilience Through Hybrid Infrastructure," *Current Opinion in Environmental Sustainability* 55, no. 101158 (2022).

43 Usually, it's only on the core business services where there is more than one right answer and there are multiple strategies for coming to that answer if there is duplication.

- Which components need to communicate with each other

- Which components need to share resources

- Which components share responsibilities

- What external constraints exist—and which way are they moving

 The most notable downside for loose coupling is transactional consistency. In most natural complex systems, relative time and space suffices, but we want our computers to be in lockstep (or at least appear to be).[44] As any engineer who has built eventually consistent systems knows, eventual consistency is so complicated that it can break your brain trying to mentally model it.[45] So, maybe you allow tighter coupling in a case like this, but only this.

Sometimes tools can't operate in a degraded state; it's a Boolean of working or not working. Phasing is necessary for some activities, but a tool embodying multiple sequences can be brittle and lead to failure cascades. Modularity can keep our options open as we scale, allowing us to maintain more generous boundaries of safe operation and evade such failure cascades. We can piece together phases like LEGO blocks so users can take them apart when they are using the tool, allowing them to adapt, modify, or debug it themselves. It aligns with the reality that, despite our best efforts, our mental models will never 100% anticipate how users will interact with what we build. It's important for some systems to fail quickly rather than attempt to proceed.

Feature Flags and Dark Launches

Another practice to support flexibility and remain poised for rapid change is the art of *dark launches*—like launching a ship from a quiet harbor at midnight under a new moon. The practice of dark launches allows you to deploy code in production without exposing it to production traffic or, if preferred, exposing a new feature or version to a subset of users.

---

44 As one of our technical reviewers noted, "The CALM theorem and related work that seeks to avoid coordination whenever possible is another great way of making eventual consistency easier to understand." Alas, it is not a mainstream idea at the time of this writing.

45 Michael J. Fischer et al., "Impossibility of Distributed Consensus with One Faulty Process," *Journal of the ACM (JACM)* 32, no. 2 (1985): 374-382; M. Pease et al., "Reaching Agreement in the Presence of Faults," *Journal of the ACM (JACM)* 27, no. 2 (1980): 228-234; Cynthia Dwork et al., "Consensus in the Presence of Partial Synchrony," *Journal of the ACM (JACM)* 35, no. 2 (1988): 288-323.

Feature flags allow us to perform dark launches. *Feature flags* (or feature "toggles" (*https://oreil.ly/-slT-*)) are a pattern for choosing between alternate code paths at runtime, like enabling or disabling a feature, without having to make or deploy code changes. They're sometimes considered a neat trick useful to product managers and UX engineers, but this belies their resilience potential. It makes us nimbler, speeding up our ability to deploy new code while offering the flexibility to tweak how accessible it is to users. If something goes wrong, we can "uncheck" the feature flag, giving us time to investigate and refine while keeping all other functionality healthy and operational.

Feature flags also help us decouple code deployments (*https://oreil.ly/kzFNj*) from the big, shiny feature releases we announce to the world. We can observe system interactions on a subpopulation of users, informing any refinements (which are now easier and faster for us to deploy) ahead of making new code available to all users. Of course, there is a cost to feature flagging (like any practice), but product engineering teams should expect the capability as a paved road from their platform teams and use it liberally to improve reliability.

We'll continue emphasizing the importance of inventing clever ways to improve resilience while enticing with "carrots" in other dimensions to incentivize adoption. Dark launching is precisely in that category of delectable medicine. Product Engineering teams can accelerate their feature development and get more experimental—improving coveted product metrics, like conversion rates—while we gain more flexibility, allowing us to quickly change as conditions change (not to mention granting us an opportunity to observe user interactions with the system and cultivate a feedback loop too).

Preserving Possibilities for Refactoring: Typing

Our fourth opportunity for flexibility and willingness to change is preservation of possibilities, specifically with an eye toward the inevitable refactor. When writing code, engineers are swept up in the electrifying anticipation of the release and aren't gazing upon the hazy horizon pondering what matters when the code inevitably needs refactoring (much like movie crews aren't ruminating on the remake when filming the original). Nevertheless, like the destinies allotted by the Moirai of ancient Greece, refactoring is ineluctable and, in the spirit of allocating effort with a wise investment strategy, we should try to preserve possibilities when building software. We must anticipate that the code will need to change and make decisions that support flexibility to do so.

How does this look in practice? At a high level, we need an easy path to safely restructure abstractions, data models, and approaches to the problem domain. Type declarations are a tool we can wield to preserve possibilities—although we acknowledge the subject is contentious. For those uninitiated in the nerd fight, you might be wondering what type declarations and type systems are at all.

Type systems are meant to "prevent the occurrence of execution errors during the running of a program."[46] We won't go into the deep rabbit hole of type systems except to explore how it might help us build more resilient software. A type is a set of requirements declaring what operations can be performed on values that are considered to conform to the type. Types can be concrete, describing a particular representation of values that are permitted, or abstract, describing a set of behaviors that can be performed on them with no restriction on representation.

A type declaration specifies the properties of functions or objects. It is a mechanism to assign a name (like a "numeric" type[47]) to a set of type requirements (like the ability to add, multiply, or divide it), which can then be used later when declaring variables or arguments. For all values stored into the variable, the language compiler or runtime will verify that these values match the expanded set of requirements.

Statically typed languages require a type to be associated with each variable or function argument, with all allowing a named type and some allowing an anonymous, unnamed list of type requirements. For types with a long set of requirements, it is less error-prone and more reusable to define the type requirements once with a name attached to them and then reference the type via the name wherever it is used.

Static typing can make it easier to refactor software since type errors help guide the migration. Your Effort Investment Portfolio may prefer less allocation of effort up front, however, in which case fixing type errors when trying out new structures may be perceived as overly onerous. Table 4-1 explores the differences between static typing and dynamic typing to help you navigate this trade-off.

Table 4-1. Static typing versus dynamic typing

Static typing	Dynamic typing
Requirements are specified and checked ahead of time so that the checks don't have to occur as the program is running	Requirements are declared implicitly, with appropriate requirements checked every time an operation is performed on a value
Checking is performed up front before the program starts	Lots of checking as the program runs

---

46 Luca Cardelli, "Type Systems," *ACM Computing Surveys (CSUR)* 28, no. 1 (1996): 263-264.

47 Computers have multiple types of numbers and it takes complicated type theory to correctly apply mathematical operations to numbers of varying types. What does it mean to multiply an 8-bit integer with an imaginary number? That is complicated. This example glosses over this complication.

Static typing	Dynamic typing
Effort required to ensure all parts of the program (even parts that won't run) are correctly typed with the range of possible values that could be used	No need to expend up-front effort convincing the language that values are compatible with the places they're used
Valid programs that can't be expressed in the type system cannot be written or will need to use the type system's escape hatches, such as type assertions	Invalid programs are allowed, but may fail at runtime when an operation is performed on data of the wrong type

The more we can encode into the type system to help the tools assist us in building safe and correct systems, the easier we can refactor. For instance, if we pass around int64s everywhere to represent a timestamp, then an alternative might be to call them "timestamps" for clarity; that way, we avoid accidentally comparing them to or mistaking them for a loop index or for a day of the month. In general, the more clarity we can provide around the system's functions, down to individual components, the better our ability to adapt the system as necessary. Refactoring code to add useful type declarations can ensure developers' mental models of their code are more aligned to reality.

The Strangler Fig Pattern

Sometimes we may be willing and eager to change our system, but unclear how to do so without contaminating critical functionality. The strangler fig pattern supports our capacity to change—even for the most conservative of organizations—helping us maintain flexibility. Rewriting a feature, a service, or an entire system by discarding the existing code and writing everything anew will suffocate flexibility in an organization, as will a "big bang" release where everything is changed concurrently. Some organizations in more mature industries that are tethered to decades-old systems often worry that modern software engineering practices, patterns, and technologies are inaccessible because how could they possibly rewrite everything without breaking things? They likely would crack like Humpty Dumpty and it would take exorbitant effort to put it back together again if we attempt rewriting or changing everything all at once. Thankfully, we can leverage iteration and modularity to change a subset of a system at a time, keeping the overall system running while we change some of what lies beneath.

The strangler fig pattern (*https://oreil.ly/BhDNV*) allows us to gradually replace parts of our system with new software components rather than attempting a "big bang" rewrite (Figure 4-4). Usually, organizations use this pattern to migrate from a monolithic architecture to a more modular one. Adopting the strangler fig pattern allows us to keep our options open, to understand evolving contexts and feel prepared to evolve our systems accordingly.

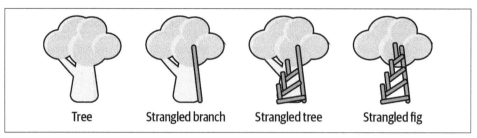

Figure 4-4. The strangler fig pattern for transforming software systems (adapted from https://oreil.ly/KyMO1)

In a browser-delivered service, you could replace one page at a time, starting with your least critical pages, evaluating the evidence once the redesigned component is deployed, then moving to the next page. The evidence collected after each migration informs improvements to the next migration; by the end of the strangler fig pattern, your team will likely be a pro. The same goes for rewriting an on-prem, monolithic mainframe application written in a hazardous raw material like C—a common status quo in older organizations or those in highly regulated industries. The strangler fig pattern allows us to pull out one function and rewrite it in a memory safe language like Go, which has a relatively low learning curve (Figure 4-5). It is, in effect, the conservative approach—but often also the faster one. The "big bang" model is often all "break things" without the "move quickly," since tightly coupled systems are difficult to change.

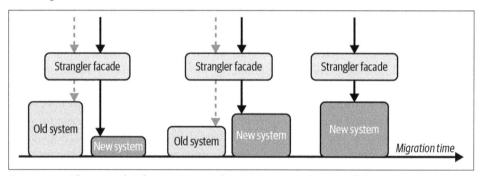

Figure 4-5. The strangler fig pattern involves extracting one part of the system and iteratively migrating more functionality over time

The strangler fig pattern is especially useful for highly regulated organizations or those with legacy, on-prem applications. By drawing on their thoughts presented in the 2021 AWS re:Invent talk "Discover Financial Services: Payments mainframe to cloud platform" (*https://oreil.ly/W4-7G*), we can learn from how they migrated part of their monolithic, legacy payments mainframe application to a public cloud—maintaining PCI compliance—through the strangler fig pattern. This service is a key hub in the payments network, making changes a precarious proposition since disruption in it would disrupt the entire network. Hence, many conservative organizations often stick with their legacy, mainframe applications out of fear of disruption, even if there are tantalizing benefits awaiting them if they modernize those services—like gaining a market advantage, or at least keeping up in an increasingly competitive market.

The global financial services company Discover brainstormed the modernized platform they sought, featuring a few key characteristics: standard interfaces (like REST APIs); edge services tokenizing sensitive data (so core services can only process tokenized, canonical data); loosely coupled microservices (with a service registry for APIs and event bus for messaging); and centralized customer and event data accessed through APIs.

They didn't try to migrate from the mainframe to this modernized platform all at once (a "big bang" approach); they chose to "slowly, slowly shift to the cloud" through the strangler fig pattern, allowing them to incrementally migrate the classic mainframe payments application by gradually replacing functionality. The classic application was tightly coupled, making it difficult to change. It was in fact their conservatism on change that dissuaded them from a "big bang" release to adopt the strangler fig pattern instead, since changing that much code in one fell swoop could spell disaster.

The team identified pieces within modules that they could "reasonably recreate elsewhere" to act in concert with the mainframe until they could be confident in the modern version and switch off the classic version. Discover chose the pricing component as the first one to migrate from the classic settlement system, since it can be "sliced and diced" in a variety of ways (Figure 4-6). Migrating the pricing component allowed them to adopt pricing changes within three weeks versus the status quo six months in the mainframe application—a huge win for the organization, fulfilling the production pressures we'll discuss more in Chapter 7. It allowed them to "open up the possibility of greater flexibility, a lot more consistency, and definitely a lot more speed to market" than they could achieve with the classic mainframe application. It also created the possibility of providing dashboards and analytics about pricing data to their business partners, creating new value propositions.

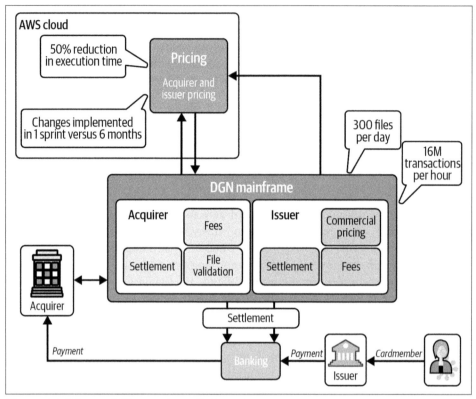

Figure 4-6. Discover's "Strangulation" phase 1

How did they reduce hazards in the migration? They ran the new version of the pricing engine side by side with the mainframe to gain confidence. There were zero incidents in production, and they even reduced the execution time in the settlement process by 50%. To their surprise, they actually uncovered issues in the old system that the business didn't even know were there. As Senior Director of Application Development Ewen McPherson notes, just because a system is "classic" or legacy does not mean it perfectly matches your intentions.

Discover was starting this journey at "ground-zero," with no experience in the cloud. They took a phased approach—aligning with the iterative approach we recommended earlier in this section—starting with a "toe-dipping phase" where the key change was calling Amazon Relational Database Service (RDS) from their internal cloud. The next phase was driven by their data analytics team, which pushed to move their on-prem data warehouse to the cloud because they conceived big data as a potential business differentiator. This push, in particular, forced Discover to "get over" their security and risk fears. A bit over a year later, they entered the next phase where they began migrating core functionality to the cloud.

This first attempt at migrating functionality to the cloud didn't work out as planned; they lacked sufficient effort capital in their Effort Investment Portfolio to allocate to operating microservices. There are two important lessons from this false start. First, only one core change should be made at a time; in Discover's case, they were trying to change both the architecture (transforming to microservices) and migrate functionality (to the cloud). Second, their flexibility and willingness to change—both technically and culturally—allowed them to amend this misstep without severe penalty. Discover implemented this initial attempt in a way that could be extended and changed based on evolving business goals and constraints, so they could pivot based on feedback from the sociotechnical system.

Their refined attempt to migrate pricing functionality was to implement a batch-based model in the cloud, with the resulting calculations sent back to the mainframe (since they only migrated part of the classic application to start). Everything will eventually be migrated from the mainframe, but starting with one part of system functionality is exactly what we want for an iterative, modular, strangler fig approach. We don't have to migrate everything all at once, nor should we. Iteration with small modules sets us up for success and the ability to adapt to evolving conditions in a way that "big bang" releases or attempting multiple sweeping changes at once cannot.

Technology is only one part of this transformation with the strangler fig pattern. We can adopt new tooling and move functionality to a new environment, but the old ways of humans interacting with the technical part of the system likely won't work anymore. Mental models are often sticky. As Discover noted, whoever owns the new process sees it through the lens of their old process—one ritual is being traded for another. The new principles we adopt when changing the system need incremental iteration too. At the core of our principles, however, must be a willingness to change—providing the *socio* part of the system with the psychological safety to make mistakes and try again.

To recap, we have five opportunities for maintaining flexibility and stimulating willingness to change—the final ingredient of our resilience potion when building and delivering systems: iteration, modularity, feature flags, preserving possibilities for refactoring, and the strangler fig pattern. Next in our journey through the SCE transformation is what we must perform once our systems are deployed in production: operating and observing.

Chapter Takeaways

- When we build and deliver software, we are implementing intentions described during design, and our mental models almost certainly differ between the two phases. This is also the phase where we possess many opportunities to adapt as our organization, business model, market, or any other pertinent context changes.

- Who owns application security (and resilience)? The transformation of database administration serves as a template for the shift in security needs; it migrated from a centralized, siloed gatekeeper to a decentralized paradigm where engineering teams adopt more ownership. We can similarly transform security.

- There are four key opportunities to support critical functionality when building and delivering software: defining system goals and guidelines (prioritizing with the "airlock" approach); performing thoughtful code reviews; choosing "boring" technology to implement a design; and standardizing "raw materials" in software.

- We can expand safety boundaries during this phase with a few opportunities: anticipating scale during development; automating security checks via CI/CD; standardizing patterns and tools; and performing dependency analysis and vulnerability prioritization (the latter in a quite contrary approach to status quo cybersecurity).

- There are four opportunities for us to observe system interactions across spacetime and make them more linear when building and delivering software and systems: adopting Configuration as Code; performing fault injection during development; crafting a thoughtful test strategy (prioritizing integration tests over unit tests to avoid "test theater"); and being especially cautious about the abstractions we create.

- To foster feedback loops and learning during this phase, we can implement test automation; treat documentation as an imperative (not a nice-to-have), capturing both *why* and *when*; implement distributed tracing and logging; and refine how humans interact with our processes during this phase (keeping realistic behavioral constraints in mind).

- To sustain resilience, we must adapt. During this phase, we can support this flexibility and willingness to change through five key opportunities: iteration to mimic evolution; modularity, a tool wielded by humanity over millennia for resilience; feature flags and dark launches for flexible change; preserving possibilities for refactoring through (programming language) typing; and pursuing the strangler fig pattern for incremental, elegant transformation.

CHAPTER 5

Operating and Observing

There is nothing staid, nothing settled, in this universe. All is rippling, all is dancing; all is quickness and triumph.

—Virginia Woolf, *The Waves*

The operations phase of software delivery deals with managing and studying the system while it runs in production. Production is where the system interacts with real customers and users. Much like rehearsals of a play, all the other phases build to this one. Once the software we design, build, and deploy is delivered to end users and is prancing in production environments, it can finally deliver value for the organization. For any organization with digitally delivered products and services, this phase is where the money printer is turned on (and goes brrrr! (*https://oreil.ly/5dJnC*)).

The operating and observing phase is where our mental models encounter their challenger: reality. It's tempting to only observe what you expect to encounter; think back to the *Jurassic Park* example from Chapter 1 where they only checked for the number of dinosaurs they expected, not anticipating that there could be more than in their mental models. As we shepherd our systems in the tumultuous pastures of the internet, we must continually refine our mental models—keeping an open mind that our assumptions might be wrong and being curious enough to seek out evidence. That is, we need the last two ingredients in the recipe: feedback loops and flexibility. Operating and observing is the phase where we really start to learn about our systems and where feedback is generated for us to incorporate into our mental models, Effort Investment Portfolios, decision trees, and practices and procedures. The goal in this phase is to refine our mental models with evidence as much as possible.

In this chapter, we'll start by talking about operational goals in a resilience paradigm and the practices that can help us achieve those goals, particularly through the lens of site reliability engineering (SRE). Then we'll talk about scalability as an important systems property and how observability looks in the SCE paradigm, and we'll briefly discuss experimenting with failure (which, after all, ideally happens in production).

What Does Operating and Observing Involve?

When we say this phase includes "managing" the system, we mean performing the ops necessary for the system to behave as intended. To manage the system effectively, you must study its behavior as it runs; this is "observing," and includes activities like logging and monitoring. When we're dealing with "invisible" systems like software—where, unlike in *Jurassic Park*, we cannot perceive it, or its constituent components, physically—the only way to observe them is through logging and monitoring capabilities.[1] If you underinvest in this capability, then it's like flying a plane in unknown conditions with an opaque windshield and no radar. The approaching footsteps of attackers won't cause our servers to rattle in their racks, unlike the Tyrannosaurus rex in *Jurassic Park*. Absent the "blinky light" test and without some kind of instrumented telemetry (or our customers admonishing us on social media), we don't know if our systems are running at all, let alone if they're doing something weird.

Traditionally, engineers who operate and observe software systems are more focused on resilience than product developers for this very reason: their goal is to ensure software can keep delivering value and to minimize the impact of anything that jeopardizes that.

The range of activities in this phase is expansive,[2] but involves three main categories:

Reliability
> CDN, failover, load balancing, orchestration, anti-DDoS, service mesh, blocking attacks, rate limiting, and more

Stateful stuff
> Object storage, file storage, databases—relational, noSQL, cache storage, queues, time series DBs, graph DBs, document storage DBs, wide column stores, and more

Observability
> Logging, tracing, monitoring, metrics, dashboards, security and attack observability

---

1 Thanks to Dr. Nicole Forsgren for this comparison.

2 There are also activities, like business intelligence, that fall under this phase, but those aren't so much under the purview of resilience. They are a topic worthy of a different book.

Observability activities often overlap with incident response, part of the phase covered in the next chapter. The precise point at which an incident begins is usually squishy. But, given it is during this phase that these observability activities are usually managed, we'll cover it here. In general, observability is key to understanding when your systems are running "hot," are in a degraded state, or have been compromised by an attacker who has yet to achieve their goal.

Operational Goals in SCE

In SCE, we want our systems to sustain resilience against attack. We want them to operate sufficiently far from their safety boundary so that when problems or surprises emerge, the system continues operating as we intend. These intentions are where resilience intersects with reliability—a reliable system is one that is consistent; that is, a reliable system is one we can trust to fulfill its duties, which (hopefully) align with our intentions.

These intentions are usually to meet user expectations, whether preconceived or based on interacting with the system previously. Understanding these expectations is usually part of understanding critical functionality, the first ingredient in our resilience potion. No matter what software we are building, we intend for a human to interact with it—whether hobby projects, internal service automation, or a B2B SaaS app. There is always a user, and they always have expectations about how the service will behave. The intentions we create for the service are inherently coupled with those user expectations.

Thus, reliability is made up of three key aspects of intentions, framed as user expectations:

Availability
    Can users access the software when they expect?

Performance
    Is the service doing its thing at the speed users expect?

Correctness
    Does the service perform the functionality users expect?

These categories blur together in practice. If performance degrades to a sufficient degree, it becomes an availability problem. If parts of the system are unavailable, it may not behave with correctness. A system with incorrect or unexpected behavior may even, on occasion, explore untested code paths with terrible performance characteristics, degrading system performance.

Security is woven into all three facets of reliability too. A DoS attack like DDoS or ransomware means users cannot access the service when they want. Data exfiltration or crypto mining can hog system resources, like bandwidth or CPU, slowing down the end user's experience. And injection of malicious scripts into apps or unauthorized access to sensitive user data is certainly not expected service functionality. You can see how security underlies the three key aspects of reliability in practice in Figure 5-1.

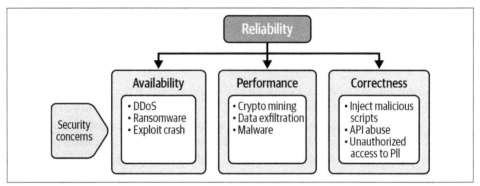

Figure 5-1. The three categories of reliability and examples of how security weaves into them

This means security goals and reliability goals are aligned. Some traditional security professionals might balk at this idea; security is supposed to be special and separate! But the "A" in the classic CIA triad—the three characteristics NIST defined as most important for cybersecurity way back in 1977—stands for availability, the modern business lifeblood and a critical component of reliability. The CIA triad (*https:// oreil.ly/hK8N3*) has nothing to do with the U.S. intelligence agency. It's short for Confidentiality, Integrity, and Availability, and is intended to represent the three "pillars" of information security. In today's reality of business—and organizational activity more generally—being driven by software services, it's perhaps more useful for defenders to think about how security plays into the APC triad: Availability, Performance, and Correctness.

The Overlap of SRE and Security

We can see that this isn't such a crazy idea when we compare the priorities between security and ops teams, especially SRE, which is all about treating infrastructure and operations like software engineering problems. SREs use software as a tool to uphold service reliability: availability, performance, and correctness. In Table 5-1, we list common objectives shared by both security and SRE teams (including some of the security objectives and key results, or OKRs, enumerated in Ryan McGeehan's "Starting Up Security" fundamentals (*https://oreil.ly/gsuCP*)).

Table 5-1. The overlap of SRE and security objectives

Common objective	Key results
Faster incident recovery	Detecting and recovering from outages, bugs, degradations, and unwanted activity; reduce mean time to restore service; reduce estimated incident recovery times; decrease estimated time to coordinate the incident team
Proactive insight into issues	Leading indicators of outages, degradations, and environmental drift help spot problems early before they spiral into crises; discover issues before they become incidents; decrease time it takes for employees to report an incident or exposure; increase probability an employee reports an incident or exposure
Uncover unintended consequences ASAP	Discover second-order events of decisions or activities, security or otherwise, to enable quick mitigation of unintended consequences
Anticipate tech and tool requirements	Anticipate how tech and tools will need to evolve in the future to support business operations; maintainable, reliable, and extendable log pipelines; interview users/stakeholders to capture future goal outcomes and map to the current security program
Minimizing the impact of production issues	Disincentivize developers yeeting around or "going rogue" in production environments, which increases the likelihood of something going wrong; incentivize isolation of production work so outages and damage are limited to only the failing part of the system (or data)
Increase predictability of system operation	Developers will do things to achieve the right outcome that reduce the predictability of the system later (they'll stand it up, but will have changed a bunch of settings, which introduces entropy for the system for later); holding devs accountable for changes
Improve logging and make it accessible	Ensure relevant logs are accessible and searchable in the fewest places possible; shorten incident investigation time; gain confidence in causal factors behind incidents; less coordination required between teams during incidents
Reduce the risks associated with vendors	If your vendor goes down, your service stays up; if your dependency breaks, that doesn't break your service; incentivize isolation of vendor components; verify principle of least privilege for APIs
Lay groundwork for resilient/quality development practices	Security is a subset of quality; feature flags encouraged; nurtures early consideration of observability requirements; fosters constructive retrospectives and incident reviews

As you can see in Table 5-1, this natural kinship between SRE and security teams extends to what they *dislike* too. SREs and operations engineers aren't fans of any developer activity that could disrupt production—and a lot of that activity overlaps with the unwanted behavior from attackers. If a developer can surprise deploy or debug in production, so can an adversary. Developers logging into production and executing privileged commands means attackers could do so without having to elevate privileges too. No one wants to clean up abandoned, broken systems languishing in production, ripe for fomenting downtime. If no one knows how it works or that it's there, it will probably become unavailable or compromised by an attacker without anyone knowing. Such creaky, abandoned systems are best thought of as hazardous waste.

Defenders and SREs are natural allies to tackle these problems. In fact, perhaps you're already seeing how ops, infrastructure, SRE, or platform engineering teams—which often combine infra and ops or SRE—could be the best home for systems defense. Security experts can be sprinkled throughout these teams to assist on particularly thorny security challenges. In the Security Chaos world, the title of "defender" isn't limited to just security professionals; it applies to any stakeholder who is striving to support a system's resilience against attack.

One difference between the traditional security mindset and SRE is around speed. In SCE, as with SRE, moving more quickly is correlated with reducing the cost of failure. Think of it like when you're rollerblading for the first time. One option, the status quo security way, is to wrap yourself in layers of bubble wrap (defense in depth!) to ensure it is impossible for you to experience an injury. When you finally get your rollerblades on, likely with the help of someone else given your cocoon of bubble wrap, you waddle down the street at a snail's pace, barely able to move forward given the intrusive layers of protection around you. But then, something you didn't anticipate happens: a gust of wind tips you over, or perhaps a large dog jumps into the street to bark at this strange Bubble Person and you are moving too slowly to move out of the way. Now you're rolling down the street, pain- and injury-free, but uncertain when you'll finally be able to get up again and make it to your destination.

In contrast, the SCE way embraces the idea that if you're going to be rollerblading, it's likely you'll fall. So, what can you do to protect yourself from serious harm? Knee pads, elbow pads, wrist pads, and a helmet all reduce incident impact while still allowing you to zoom to your destination. By moving quickly, you can dodge obstacles with ease and harness your natural momentum to meet your goals despite the presence of foes like the wind. If you fall, you just get back up again and continue on. (And wearing no protective gear at all would be like running a production system #yolosec style with no logging, no IAM, no isolation, and other obvious omissions.)

SREs care about improving the overall failure isolation of systems—whether that's reducing impact from "surprise" resources, vulnerabilities in code, or overloaded networks (like with a DDoS). Other SRE team objectives often include improving automation, improving monitoring, and improving documentation and procedures—just like we discussed in the last chapter. Another important SRE goal is to flatten and bridge organizational boundaries. If one team gate-keeps knowledge or ownership of a single component, it will be difficult for operators to understand how that component fits into the system as a whole. Done well, SRE teams are made up of engineers who understand what is going on at the system level, understanding how all the pieces fit together, from the physical machine up to clickable buttons on the frontend.

Measuring Operational Success

A *metric* is a quantifiable measurement to figure out whether you're succeeding at a specific thing or not doing so well at it. *Goal metrics*, to state the obvious, measure whether you're hitting your goals, like operational success.

Attackers have an advantage in measuring operational success: they know when they are losing. They come into their office, sit down at their desk, take a sip of coffee, and log in to their machine to check how their attack operation is going. They discover they no longer have a shell on their target—that they have lost access to the victim's system—and sigh, "Well, something has clearly failed." In general, attack organizations maintain upward and downward velocity—across all parts of their activities—and continuously check in to ensure they are learning and making progress toward their goals.

If we want to be worthy opponents against attackers, we must be meticulous about measuring our operational success too. Defenders can leverage DevOps and SRE metrics to measure their operational success, which can serve as a proxy for how well they are supporting systems resilience. What you use to measure success internally may look different from what you report externally to customers to demonstrate accountability. Customers want simple metrics to digest, while more granular measurements will help you better understand your systems. Customers mostly just care (*https://oreil.ly/Otcwb*) about whether you can answer the question, "Is the service working?"

In general, it's best to start out with those simple metrics that can help you communicate service reliability to your customers and then get more advanced as needed. It's also worth noting that measuring *resilience* is an extremely contentious art across disciplines that isn't definitive science yet; we discussed the E&E assessment approach in Chapter 2, but simple reliability metrics remain the subject of ongoing debate. As we'll discuss later in this chapter and in Chapter 8, conducting security chaos experiments can generate evidence that describes your system's resilience to different attack scenarios. This evidence, combined with the measurements and guidance we'll discuss in this section, will get you well on your way to a more resilient operational paradigm.

Crafting Success Metrics like Attackers

Defense is harder than offense, and not because the attacker "just has to be right once," as is proclaimed in infosec myth (and which is false, because they have to be right a bunch of times once they gain initial access, as we discussed in Chapter 2).[3] A more useful model characterizing attackers' asymmetrical advantage is that attackers can measure success—do they have access, how much access do they have, and have they accomplished their goals—and receive immediate feedback on those metrics.

Defenders, in contrast, struggle to create lucid, actionable metrics that offer immediate feedback. There are squishier aspects to security that require thoughtful translation into metrics, like "we were able to quickly understand incident impact" or "we

---

3 Josiah Dykstra, "The Slippery Slope of Cybersecurity Analogies" (*https://oreil.ly/0C9NW*), Talk at USENIX ENIGMA Conference (Santa Clara, CA: January 24-26, 2023).

carefully considered a rule change that would be a big deal." When we implement a new password pattern, for example, how does it impact our metrics? It may take time to reveal the impact and measurements might remain indirect. Metrics also depend heavily on context. If we measure how long it takes to deploy a firewall rule and the answer is a few seconds because it's automated, do we celebrate? If none of the firewall rules are change-controlled, then anyone can have a port party and invite the whole world—not the kind of celebration we want.

 Beware perverse metrics! CISO Lea Kissner warns that perverse metrics delude us; they don't tell you what you think they're telling you.[4] Wrong metrics are worse than no metrics, so we should not collect them for their own sake, but for what they can tell us. There are a few types of metrics perversity, but three especially align with other topics we've discussed:

1. *Measuring efforts, not results.* We shouldn't measure how hard we're working, but instead measure the *outcomes* of our effort investments. For instance, "sending N security notifications to developers this quarter" is most likely a signal of nuisance rather than success.

2. *Just because you can measure something doesn't mean it's important.* Sometimes *not* measuring something leads to better results because the metric was distracting from success. For example, the metric "time to respond to security tickets" can incentivize quick responses to inbound tickets with lengthy or nonexistent follow-up, setting confusing expectations for other teams.

3. *A small number + a big number = a useless number.* Because we are immersed in complex systems, prediction is impossible. Our estimates are rife with uncertainty, rendering them useless. For example, if we dig beneath the common calculation of "risk × impact," there is such a dizzying degree of factors that it is impossible to calculate in a constructive way. As Kissner notes, that number might be bigger than our company's market capitalization, which suggests the appropriate action item is to stop doing work and shut down the company.

---

4 Lea Kissner, "Metric Perversity and Bad Decision-Making" (*https://oreil.ly/jemff*), Talk at USENIX ENIGMA Conference (Santa Clara, CA: January 24-26, 2023).

As step zero of creating metrics, we must pick metrics that allow us to measure success outcomes as quickly as attackers can measure their "do I have access" outcomes. We can conceive metrics for our security activities across the software delivery lifecycle. If we implement two-factor authentication (2FA), we can measure what percent of our user base adopted it—as well as how often the "lost 2FA token" is used or how many endpoints require 2FA. For incident response activities, we can measure how long it takes to get the information we need about something. For a randomly chosen endpoint, how long does it take us to get a process listing? We can think stepwise about each part of incident response and recovery and contemplate how we measure it…then ensure the necessary plumbing is in place to receive those measurements.

Finally, we must remain cautious and curious about the context surrounding each measurement. If the number of vulnerabilities identified pre-deployment increases, is that good or bad? It could be a sign that either code quality is slipping or vulnerabilities are being discovered and remediated more efficiently in developer workflows. Similarly, if more incidents are being reported, is that good or bad? Perhaps your SCE transformation is so successful that software engineering teams proactively and eagerly report security issues. As Kissner notes, with near misses or even false alarms captured, you can gain reasonable confidence that real incidents are being captured, which is great. Or, if the increase is due to real, outage-inducing incidents, then it could be another sign that quality is slipping in a few dimensions. We must inspect what we measure in context and recall that things may look worse because we're doing things better, and vice versa.

The DORA Metrics

We can borrow established metrics from other areas on our transformation journey. In this section, we'll cover the robust, data-driven research into what metrics matter to measure DevOps success (*https://oreil.ly/jiC1A*). The authors of the groundbreaking book *Accelerate*[5] identify four "golden" DevOps metrics, known as the "DORA" metrics (short for DevOps Research and Assessment), which help organizations measure their DevOps prowess. The DORA metrics are meant to measure software delivery performance, not security—but these metrics are rooted in measuring speed and stability, which both security and ops or SRE teams need to reach their goals. These metrics focus on *outcomes* rather than *outputs*—about results rather than busywork (Figure 5-2).

---

5 Dr. Nicole Forsgren et al., *Accelerate: The Science of Lean Software and DevOps: Building and Scaling High Performing Technology Organizations* (Portland, OR: IT Revolution Press, 2018).

Deployment frequency

How often does your organization deploy code to production or release it to end users?

Lead time to changes

How long does it take to go from code committed to code successfully running in production?

Change failure rate

What percentage of changes to production or released to users result in degraded service and subsequently require remediation?[6]

Time to restore service

How long does it generally take to restore service when a service incident or a defect that impacts users occurs?

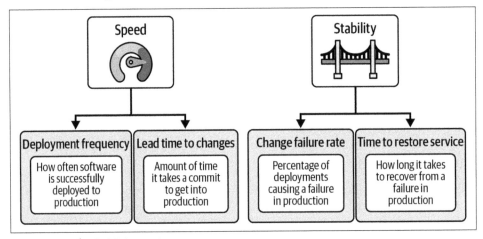

Figure 5-2. The DORA metrics

The organizations that move most quickly are also those that experience the most stability. The more cautious organizations—with heavy change approvals, slower and manual processes—actually experience higher rates of failure and can't respond as quickly when inevitable failure occurs. As researched in the Accelerate State of DevOps 2018 report (*https://oreil.ly/6zk-V*), organizations with "elite" DevOps performance spend half as much time remediating security issues as low performers (5% versus 10% of their time, respectively). Elite performers conduct security reviews as part of their delivery pipeline, completing security changes in just days, while low

---

6 Change failure rate is sometimes an overlooked metric that becomes especially valuable as systems grow larger. At scale, the same change failure rate leads to more disruption. If you can't handle fault isolation or partial availability, you're headed for disaster as you grow.

performers take weeks to conduct security reviews and complete any identified changes (Figure 5-3).

Software delivery performance metric	Elite	High	Medium	Low
Deployment frequency For the primary application or service you work on, how often does your organization deploy code to production or release it to end users?	On demand (multiple deploys per day)	Between once per week and once per month	Between once per month and once every six months	Fewer than once per six months
Lead time for changes For the primary application or service you work on, what is your lead time for changes (i.e., how long does it take to go from code committed to code successfully running in production)?	Less than one hour	Between one day and one week	Between one month and six months	More than six months
Time to restore service For the primary application or service you work on, how long does it generally take to restore service when a service incident or a defect that impacts users occurs (e.g., unplanned outage or service impairment)?	Less than one hour	Less than one day	Between one day and one week	More than six months
Change failure rate For the primary application or service you work on, what percentage of changes to production or released to users result in degraded service (e.g., lead to service impairment or service outage) and subsequently require remediation (e.g., require a hotfix, rollback, fix forward, patch)?	0%-15%	16%-30%	16%-30%	16%-30%

Figure 5-3. Software delivery outcomes across each performance level from the Accelerate State of DevOps 2021 report (https://oreil.ly/MVZzm)

These goal outcomes can manifest as OKRs such as "reduce time-to-restore service (TTR) by 10%" or "reduce lead time to deploy patches by 5%." Don't set objectives like 100% availability (let alone vague, abstract goals like 100% "security"). The idea is to think carefully about the requirements for each service in the context of its users and the broader business and set achievable targets that demonstrate continuous progress.

Of course, as stewards of collecting these metrics, it is our responsibility to provide the necessary context around the metrics we provide. What is the story behind the result of "we reduced time to respond by 10%"? Were we just lucky—looking at the right place at the right time? Perhaps the shape of recent incidents differs from the prior period. Remember, complex systems feature surprises, and sometimes those surprises can work in our favor too. As tempting as it is, we should resist manipulating statistics and dig into the *why* of our metrics, untangling the contributing factors to the best of our ability. That way, when we say "we reduced TTR by 10%," we can be confident that it is at least influenced in part by our teams meaningfully investing effort capital to change. If we provide TTR metrics without providing the necessary context, that is our failure.

SLOs, SLAs, and Principled Performance Analytics

Service-level objectives (SLOs) are popular across organizations spanning every industry as a means to measure service reliability and then, if necessary for its market, communicate these objectives to end users in the form of service-level agreements (SLAs). When we're in the weeds of operating and protecting services, it's easy to lose sight of the fact that resilience and security matter *because* end users interact with our services. If they didn't, we could just airgap the service, restrict all permissions to "deny," and call security "solved." Our end users expect a certain level of reliability in the services we provide them, and we must inspire confidence that we can and do meet their expectations.

 Common wisdom is to set SLOs that target higher performance than the targets specified in SLAs. That way, failing to meet your objectives means you don't lose money.

We can draw on our Effort Investment Portfolio in thinking through SLOs, and particularly SLAs too. It can be trivial to propose a bunch of SLAs that will delight customers or "sophisticated" SLOs that flatter our prowess, but the work required to measure those SLAs and SLOs—data collection, pipelines, analysis—can balloon into a daunting undertaking. As a heuristic, any SLO (and its corresponding SLA if applicable) that takes more effort to measure than to achieve is a suboptimal SLO. If you think of each SLO as an incentive, then SLOs should *also* be seen as components in the system, and therefore the interactions between SLOs, and between SLOs and humans, can lead to "surprises" too.

SLOs are useful in all the other phases leading up to software running in production. If your team only needs 99% uptime for a particular service and can schedule maintenance, it's likely that a simple leader/follower setup with manual failover is all right. But if you need more availability, then it might be worth the effort investment during the design phase of brainstorming a fancy distributed database and hiring additional headcount to operationalize it.

As SLAs become more stringent, it becomes less possible for humans to even acknowledge an incident in time, let alone respond to it. The reality of 99.99% availability ("four nines") is that it's barely enough time—only 52 minutes, 36 seconds—for a human to respond to a single incident in a year. Realistically, automated failover and other forms of remediation are essential to hit availability requirements that are at least 99.99%. The coveted "five nines" only allows 5 minutes, 15 seconds of downtime per year, making automation a strict requirement barring the invention of a time-traveling device for human operators.

Which SLOs are commonly defined to measure reliability? There are rumors of some services having hundreds of thousands of SLOs for extremely granular reliability characteristics that are unique to the service, but usually SLOs are inspired by four specific signals:

Latency
    The time it takes to serve a request

Traffic
    The total number of requests across the network

Errors
    The number of requests that fail

Saturation
    The load on the network and servers

Combining SLOs with security chaos experiments can make reliability proof points even more credible. When conducting an experiment related to a particular attack scenario (with a hypothesis about how the system will behave in that scenario), we gain evidence about how our system is or isn't still meeting our SLOs. If an attacker is exfiltrating data, maybe latency is too high. If an attacker steers a DDoS attack in our direction, traffic will likely balloon. During a ransomware event, we might see errors spike to an unacceptable level. Crypto miners might saturate the servers, crushing them under increased load (mining all that Monero takes a lot of work).

SLOs are useful for particular problems, but they shouldn't be wielded as a panacea. They are extremely useful tools to communicate information about the reliability of our systems in a digestible way, but that shouldn't be mistaken for them being omniscient palantíri. They can help us define shared goals that clarify where teams should invest their time, money, and effort.

However, SLOs don't necessarily grant us the level of granularity we need to understand if our systems are behaving as expected, or to catch problems early. You can use security chaos experiments to learn how unfolding problems look from the perspective of your SLOs, allowing you to pattern-match and define new alerts based on the evidence that seems to emerge early. Experiments help you get a feel for how system signals look when something's starting to go wrong.

SLOs are best at showing when something is *really* wrong rather than when it's just starting to become problematic. It's quite possible that you *can't* seem to find a strong signal even when something was quite obviously going wrong during the security chaos experiment. This suggests there is a chance to think through which signals might be better, but simply adding more SLOs isn't necessarily the right solution—as much as it's tempting to define new SLOs after each incident review to feel like you're "solving" the issue.

The Principled Performance Analytic (PPA) method (*https://oreil.ly/ok0GB*) is an alternative to SLOs that offers more granularity to sense those emerging problems. These analytics still seek to understand systems through the lens of user expectations about reliability, but offer a closer look at deviations from those expectations. The trade-off is they're also trickier to communicate to customers or define in contracts. Thus, you probably want a mix of both SLOs and PPAs in your reliability measurement strategy.

Embracing Confidence-Based Security

Success in SCE should be seen as an active process, not a static achievement. That isn't to say we should live in fear. But much like for professional athletes or musicians, practice is an essential part of staying performant. If you conduct a security chaos experiment and all your metrics look healthy given their context, you should absolutely celebrate…and then get excited about continuing to practice it and challenging your teams and your systems in new ways.

At the risk of getting philosophical (too late), an important element of self-esteem is feeling competent—that you can surmount any challenges that ambush you. Comfort—despite feeling, well, comfortable—can erode that sense of agency and capability. With SCE, we're encouraging that same healthy level of discomfort that comes from completing a tough workout, a challenging musical score, a harder video game boss, or a complicated knitting pattern. We're pushing ourselves to continually exceed our expectations of our own capability. And, by documenting the journey and outcomes along the way, we can bask in that fantastic feeling of fulfillment that flows from seeing how far we've progressed over time.

The cybersecurity industry traditionally thinks of adaptation during operation as a dangerous thing. That's when their dreaded "human error" is likely to strike, jumpscare style! But SCE recognizes that adaptation can also lead to success, not just reduced capacity or unwanted surprises. Often, the best action you can take during an incident is to find the part of the system that is failing or unhealthy, add additional logging statements, redeploy the service, and then learn from the new data. You and your team may throw this insight-driven build away after the incident, but it can be a valuable tool for understanding unexpected behavior causing damage.

In general, if a system is running near its boundaries of safe operation—such as trying to handle seasonal traffic spikes after a round of layoffs on the engineering team—then clever humans are often the best line of defense against flopping into failure. This supports *graceful extensibility*: the capability to anticipate bottlenecks and "crunches," learn about evolving conditions, and adapt responses to stressors and surprises as they change.[7] One way for engineers to embrace graceful extensibility is by injecting failure scenarios via chaos experiments. Experiments facilitate adaptation at the boundary, working operators' creative muscles and getting them more acquainted with the system, much like a masterful painter or pianist begins treating the canvas or instrument as their home after many years of practice.

Security chaos experiments also serve as healthy challenges to your assumptions about system operation and observability (we'll dig into this more later in the chapter). Staff Security Engineer Prima Virani has described (*https://oreil.ly/hm4b8*) how it is vital to verify your log pipelines—the foundation of any observability or security detection workflow—are working as you expect. Experiments can grant you confidence that this, and other, foundational elements can be relied upon when things go wrong; and if experiments generate evidence that these foundations are *not* trustworthy, then you now have constructive feedback that you would otherwise discover in the midst of a real incident—the absolute worst time for such discoveries.

We're now closer to understanding how to measure success when operating resilient systems. But a crucial ingredient in our resilience potion is learning, a thirst for knowledge—maintaining an intense curiosity about our systems. In the next section, we'll explore security observability and how it helps us better understand our systems and the attackers who seek to destabilize them.

Observability for Resilience and Security

When we think about observability in our systems, we want to imitate the interacting sensitivities of biological systems where there are responses to responses.[8] In essence, we want our sensing abilities to be decentralized, and to engage each other across a variety of realms. Instead of the visible, auditory, olfactory, and invisible radiative realms of living environments, we instead want interactive sensitivities in the memory, disk, network, and social realms.

---

7 David D. Woods, "The Theory of Graceful Extensibility: Basic Rules That Govern Adaptive Systems," *Environment Systems and Decisions* 38, no. 5 (2018): 433-457.

8 Lynn Margulis and Dorion Sagan, *What Is Life?* (Berkeley and Los Angeles, CA: University of California Press, 2000).

Observability itself is ultimately about system interactions, which, as we've discussed extensively, is vital when seeking to understand complex systems. If we are to manage complex systems and ensure they do not topple over their boundaries of safe operation, we must maintain the ability to reflect on three key questions:[9]

- How well is the system adapted to its environment?
- What is the system adapted to?
- What is changing in the system's environment?

Observability capabilities can help us answer these questions. *Observability* can be defined as "a measure of how well components' internal states can be inferred from their external interactions."[10] Despite its obvious applicability to systems security, why hasn't cybersecurity focused on observability? The old world of security theater does not prioritize understanding the system; it's just about hunting "badness."[11] And it focuses more on flimsy measurements like "time to detect" rather than more organization-aligned measures of how effectively and quickly we restore critical functions.

Because resilience is about the system's adaptation to a disturbance, part of assessing it is the completeness of recovery. This means that we can really only assess resilience after the adverse scenario is over.[12] Luckily for us, we can combine observability with chaos experiments to simulate those adverse scenarios and determine how the system responds and recovers from them. To do so, observation must happen beyond the temporal frame of an acute stressor; we must evaluate how the system behaves over time after a surprise to see how "complete" its recovery is. Maybe it bounces back to seemingly healthy behavior after a fix is pushed but, as measured over time, seems to be more sensitive to smaller disturbances than before. For chronic stressors, as we discussed in Chapter 1, we can assess how the system behaves as the stressor's severity increases and again how it recovers (or doesn't) when the stressor abates.

The term *observability*, at the time of writing this book, is uncommon in cybersecurity discourse. Detection and prevention are the most prevalent functions in security tooling related to unwanted activity (and are separate from the tooling related to evaluating the security "status" or "readiness" of an organization's systems—which is just

---

9 David D. Woods and Matthieu Branlat, "Basic Patterns in How Adaptive Systems Fail," *Resilience Engineering in Practice* (2011): 127-143.

10 Peng Huang et al., "Capturing and Enhancing In Situ System Observability for Failure Detection," *13th USENIX Symposium on Operating Systems Design and Implementation (OSDI)* 18 (2018): 1-16.

11 Threat hunting is the more "advanced" monitoring and it's totally different from observability too (and often a vanity function or distraction).

12 Philip S. Lake, "Resistance, Resilience and Restoration," *Ecological Management & Restoration* 14, no. 1 (2012): 20-24.

as nebulous in practice as it sounds). While software engineering teams and security teams could both benefit from observability today, in practice, each organization uses separate tooling to pursue their goals of understanding when something is amiss. But this book is about how modern security should and can look, which means organizations should embrace security observability.

What kind of signals do we want to observe to ensure we have what we need to understand when things are going right and wrong? The signals we want in order to understand our systems better (in the context of reliability) also benefit us for understanding systems security:

- Who deployed what and when (like orchestrator and deployment logs)
- Who accessed what and when (like cloud audit data)
- Database logs
- Billing records
- Netflow
- Production crash dumps
- Error messages

From an ops standpoint, it's well understood that if you care about the availability of a system you should be collecting its logs and monitoring it. "Is it still alive?" is the bare minimum. Given availability is the "A" in the CIA triad, it should be a no-brainer for security too. "Best practice" from the ops standpoint is generally seen as alerting on logging failures, alerting on metrics going outside known bounds, and alerting on well-understood error messages that represent future or present downtime. Being able to examine or search logs later has substantial value, especially when triaging an incident. This is true regardless of your architecture; logs are an essential mechanism for understanding problems as they're happening.

A detailed report by the Office of Inspector General (OIG) titled "The U.S. Census Bureau's Mishandling of a January 2020 Cybersecurity Incident" (*https://oreil.ly/ bOeX9*) highlights lack of functional logs as a critical issue contributing to the failure. Specifically, the Census Bureau's remote access system logs were not being fed into the security information and event management (SIEM) tool because they forgot to update where logs were sent for approximately two years. As this example demonstrates, log pipelines are our lifeblood whether our background is security, software engineering, or SRE. Ensuring we configure logs correctly is much higher up the priority list than trying to stop fancy kernel exploits by nation-states. Experiments—and real incidents, of course—can highlight when logs are insufficient or overkill, which we can dispense to developers in our continuous learning loop to ensure they refine their log levels accordingly (like we discussed in Chapter 4). When monitoring data is unavailable, it impairs the ability for on-call operators and engineers to resolve issues (*https://oreil.ly/1YkZr*), potentially exacerbating incident impact.

 Metrics and monitoring data are trickier than they seem. Monitoring requires not just more thought in crafting specific metrics, but also sufficient understanding of how to translate them into actions that can uphold, improve, or fix your systems. If we aren't extracting value from the data we collect, why are we collecting it at all?

Cybersecurity programs are littered with superfluous data collection. Security leadership is often enthralled by the MITRE ATT&CK framework and clamors for more "coverage" of it. Detection engineers dutifully set off to create alerts for everything in the framework. The only problem? No one bothered to understand what remediation for 99% of the alerts looks like, so security operations analysts ignore most alerts as no-ops (null operations): "Might be legit, might not, but we don't know." Similarly, a deluge of real alerts produces prioritization problems, which then means that alerts deemed lower quality are deprioritized in favor of the ones that are deemed more important—usually without standard guidance or process in place. The Effort Investment Portfolio can temper leadership expectations and hopefully lead to prioritization of outcomes rather than "coverage."

Automation and workload awareness can help us optimize the return on our monitoring data. Humans performing manual processes can't report metrics or fire monitoring alerts with speed or scale. But automation can allow you to implement automated responses to system signals to support resilience at scale. Machines can react more quickly than humans, so a lot of obvious, commonly seen issues can be fixed more quickly. Thus, automation can help you measure and uphold stability and speed.

 It isn't expensive to collect system signals. But alerting on those signals bears an extortionate price, especially in terms of cognitive attention. We must be extra careful about what alerts are sent to a human (especially at 03:00 on Saturday; no one wants to be rudely awakened by a false-positive alert).

Remember, humans are a part of the sociotechnical system. If you burn out all your operators, the system will eventually fail. We want to avoid overload in our human components, not just our silicon ones. And we should make sure to consider the expense involved in the processing of signals to cultivate alerts because those resources might be better expended elsewhere. We'll talk more about the caveats of warning systems and better mechanisms to consider in Chapter 7; as David D. Woods observes, "alerts are not a panacea."

Thresholding to Uncover Safety Boundaries

In Chapter 1, we talked about the importance of understanding the system's safety boundaries as an ingredient in our resilience potion. These safety boundaries reflect the thresholds beyond which the system is no longer resilient to stress; the system can only stay healthy up to a certain point of changing conditions. The operate and observe phase is where we can uncover and monitor those thresholds toward the goal of taking action when a system crosses its boundary of safe operation.

At first glance, this may feel unrelated to security; aren't we supposed to look for "threats?" We are. And that is precisely why thresholding is vital to security and ops alike. It seeks to uncover new failures as they are emerging rather than after they've stampeded through your system.

Computer systems are extremely elastic, but are uncreative in their adaptive behavior. In contrast, humans are comparatively inelastic, but highly creative and adaptive. Autoscaling can easily burst to 100x capacity (if the configuration allows it), but good luck doing the same with humans. Similarly, humans can often determine what to do in the presence of an unforeseen circumstance, but machines are unlikely to. Hence, we need to help our software systems adapt and to ensure we are preserving the humans' ability to adapt too.

For example, if available disk space falls below 10% of total disk space, an action is performed when it reaches a specific threshold so that limited disk space doesn't cascade into a failure. Or, if we opt for a warning system rather than a more effective design-based change, we can generate an alert so operators can investigate and respond. Disk space is not just an ops problem. Disk space limitations could result from an attacker staging data for exfiltration too. We'll explore more of these system signals later in the chapter.

Ideally, thresholding tracks when a system is repeatedly stretching toward its limit. We want to observe when delays in system recovery to a stressor appear to be lengthening—or when its performance level post-recovery atrophies—a dynamic referred to as a "critical slowing down."[13] Compensating for constraints in the face of stressors is inevitable. We make use of creative workarounds, opportunistic adjustments, and spare resources to adapt to stressful scenarios. But those adaptive mechanisms get worn out and depleted. Eventually, they break down. This state of system exhaustion is called decompensation. *Decompensation* refers to the general pattern of a socio-technical system exhausting its capacity to deploy responses to stressors as they grow and concatenate[14] (the contagion and domino effect we discussed in Chapters 1 and

---

13 David D. Woods, "Four Concepts for Resilience and the Implications for the Future of Resilience Engineering," *Reliability Engineering & System Safety*, 141 (2015): 5-9.

14 Woods, "The Theory of Graceful Extensibility," 433-457.

3). In essence, it means that the system can no longer compensate for growing or repeated stressful surprises (hence *de*compensation). Its potential for adaptive behavior weakens. Its options grow thinner. This can manifest as human burnout,[15] overloaded microservices, or monoliths that throw errors every time you make a change.

Thus, an increasingly laggy recovery from disturbances is potentially an indicator of an impending breakdown, that the system might tip over its safety boundaries soon. As a simple analogy, think of when you're doing a tough workout, like boxing or high-intensity interval training (HIIT). At the start, you can take a short break and feel ready to go at it again, but as the workout goes on, that short break doesn't cut it and you feel like you're going to collapse. We don't want our systems to grow so exhausted that they can't adapt their behaviors to new challenges. Thresholding helps us preempt that collapse.

Attack Observability

Attack observability refers to collecting information about the interaction between attackers and systems. The benefits of observing how attackers make decisions in real operations resemble those of observability and tracing to understand how a system *actually* performs rather than how it is *believed* to perform. We can try to predict how a system will perform in production, but its actual performance is quite likely to deviate from expectations. Similarly, we may believe attackers will behave one way or another, but observing and tracing *actual* attacker behavior will generate the evidence we need to improve system design against adverse activity.

Deception environments

Advancements in modern computing enable the possibility of creating deception environments (*https://oreil.ly/qR0_E*) we can use for attack observability, allowing us to refine our mental models. A *deception environment* is "an isolated replica environment containing complete, active systems that exist to attract, mislead, and observe attackers."[16] Deception environments are a means for observing how your mental models hold up in real-world conditions, which has the added benefit of beguiling attackers. If decision trees are like a form of static analysis for your mental models, deception environments are a form of dynamic analysis for them. They enable two primary activities:

---

15 As an example, see key findings in Jonathan Rende, "Unplanned Work Contributing to Increased Anxiety," (PagerDuty, March 10, 2020): *https://oreil.ly/jKewe*. See also Sathya Chandran Sundaramurthy et al., "A Human Capital Model for Mitigating Security Analyst Burnout," *Eleventh Symposium on Usable Privacy and Security (SOUPS 2015)* (Ottawa, Canada: USENIX Association, July 22-24, 2015): 347-359.

16 Kelly Shortridge and Ryan Petrich, "Lamboozling Attackers: A New Generation of Deception," *Communications of the ACM* 65, no. 6 (2022): 44-53.

- Building the capability to collect relevant information about attackers
- Implementing anticipatory mechanisms that impede the success of attackers' operations

Deception environments allow software engineering teams to continuously achieve both outcomes (perhaps the new "CD" will be Continuous Deception). There are three powerful use cases for deploying a deception environment, all of which beget resilience benefits: resilient system design, attacker tracing, and an experimentation platform. We'll cover each of these next.

SMBs and Deception Environments

Smaller organizations can absolutely leverage deception environments for the benefits we'll discuss. In fact, it might serve as one of the thriftier investments they can make. The code pipelines we need to define and provision deception environments with ease also help you release patches (or configuration changes like firewall rules) more quickly. You likely already want to use cloud resources because they help you offload toil—security, maintenance, and more—to the cloud providers. Cloud resources also help avoid more classic attack patterns like compromising a VPN or seizing your domain controller. And, if you do want to evaluate security vendors, the deception environment can serve as a great place to run a proof of concept.

Resilient system design.   A dedicated sandbox for exploring how attacks impact systems is an invaluable tool for anticipating how production systems will behave when failure occurs and preempting failure through design improvements. Attackers will interact with monitoring, logging, alerting, failover, and service components in ways that stress their overall reliability. A resilient system must be aware of and recover from failures in any of these components to preserve availability. Deception environments can corroborate any measures implemented to support visibility into and recovery from component failure.

Deception environments can also expose opportunities for architectural improvement in operability and simplicity. For example, if spawning remote interactive shells (so attackers can write their tools to disk) is a consistent attacker behavior seen across deception environments, this evidence could motivate a design specification of host immutability to eliminate this option for attackers.

Thus, you can leverage a feedback loop fueled by real-world evidence (from the deception environment) to inform improvements across the software delivery lifecycle. These improvements need not be limited to security or even resilience. Deception environments can teach you many things about your system, and you can reify them just to conduct "regular" chaos experiments too.

Attacker tracing. Deception environments equip you to "trace" the actions of attackers. Since attacker behavior is traced in detail on a system with the same shape as a real system, the resulting insight is perfect for modeling likely decision patterns via frameworks such as decision trees.

In-the-wild evidence collected from deception environments can validate or update existing hypotheses—like those documented in our decision trees from Chapter 2—about how attackers learn and make decisions in specific systems. For example, attacker tracing can establish which tactics (or combinations of them) nudge attackers toward certain choices. Deception environments can also excavate the hidden flows within systems that are ordinarily discovered only upon failure and system instability. Attackers are adept at ferreting out unaccounted flows to achieve their objectives, so tracing their traversal paints a more precise picture of the system.

Experimentation platform. A lifelike environment indistinguishable from a production environment maximizes success in deceiving attackers across all levels of capability. A deception environment can therefore serve as a platform for conducting experiments to test hypotheses (like those on your decision tree) on how attackers will behave in various circumstances. When you're conducting an E&E resilience assessment, as described in Chapter 2, you can use deception environments as an experimentation platform, making it easier to conduct the tier 2 assessment.

Experimentation can test the efficacy of monitoring or resilience measures and whether they can be subverted without the operator's knowledge. How much do you actually trust your fancy endpoint detection and response (EDR) tool is meeting your expectations?[17] Experiments can verify or deny your trust.[18]

Chaos experimentation and observability

As we've discussed so far in this chapter, chaos experiments can expose where our metrics are on point or missing, which SLAs are reasonable to promise to customers, and how our thresholds look and how to identify when we're approaching them, as well as help us better understand and anticipate attacker behavior.

You can inject a few different adverse scenarios and see how your system fares. Looking at historical metrics and the hazards uncovered by experimentation should suggest whether you're likely to meet, exceed, or fail to meet your currently defined SLAs. If you provide payroll software, people expect to be paid twice a month; if you fail, then people may not be able to eat or pay rent. To avoid causing such hardship,

---

17 George Karantzas and Constantinos Patsakis, "An Empirical Assessment of Endpoint Detection and Response Systems against Advanced Persistent Threats Attack Vectors," *Journal of Cybersecurity and Privacy* 1, no. 3 (2021): 387-421.

18 Ken Thompson, "Reflections on Trusting Trust," *Communications of the ACM* 27, no. 8 (1984): 761-763.

you likely want to conduct a variety of chaos experiments to assess your system's ability to perform its critical functions despite adverse conditions. You could inject a denial of service on your most critical API; inject improper data entry (like incorrect bank information for one user to ensure it doesn't affect peers); or simulate temporary downtime of a partner bank (if it's down for an hour, people should still get paid, just an hour late). Indigenous communities have understood for centuries, through controlled burns to manage forests, that injecting adverse scenarios nurtures system health.[19]

Experiments can also be used as an ops tool to communicate feedback and findings. Humans learn through stories, so communicating how designs and implementations are not working when operationalized through a narrative can make it more salient and actionable. In essence, the goal during the ops phase is to enrich our mental models as much as we can, and experiments can help us do so in a collaborative way.

Scalable Is Safer

A more scalable sociotechnical system is a safer system. What do we mean by "scalable?" To borrow from distributed systems researcher and author Martin Kleppmann, scalable means that "as the system grows, there should be reasonable ways of dealing with that growth."[20]

In the context of systems resilience, a scalable system will usually offer more buffering capacity in the face of surprises than a system that struggles to scale (regardless of whether that friction is intentional or accidental). The idea that scalability benefits systems resilience (and security) may seem counterintuitive; the traditional infosec industry folk wisdom is often that the bigger the scale, the bigger the fail. If you operate a massive and global distributed system, so the wisdom goes, then the risk of contagion and catastrophe is monumental. But, per Kleppmann, a truly scalable system is one that can gracefully handle growth, regardless of whether it is sudden or planned. With scale comes the ability to invest in isolation and resilience engineering in ways you couldn't at a smaller scale. In a sense, you can say that scalability is about the system's ability to handle *growth* surprises—the system's resilience to growth in usage.

---

19 Jayalaxshmi Mistry et al., "Community Owned Solutions for Fire Management in Tropical Ecosystems: Case Studies from Indigenous Communities of South America," *Philosophical Transactions of the Royal Society B: Biological Sciences* 371, no. 1696 (2016): 20150174.

20 Martin Kleppmann, *Designing Data-Intensive Applications: The Big Ideas behind Reliable, Scalable, and Maintainable Systems* (Sebastopol, CA: O'Reilly, 2017).

Traditional cybersecurity programs usually don't measure system behavior like load, latency, performance, and throughput, but they are valuable signals for changing conditions—like stressors and surprises—and can even indicate the presence of attackers. For instance, high CPU usage and memory shortages are signals about system security. They could be signals of an attacker rummaging around a system, the presence of a misconfiguration, or more generally, nonoptimal status of services and systems. In fact, well-resourced attackers will monitor the host or system they're attacking to avoid hitting any defined limitations (like configured thresholds) or avoid making too much noise to tip off defenders.

Table 5-2 highlights examples of system signals and what kinds of attack activity might be associated with them. Security leaders take note: there are ample opportunities to combine forces with software engineering and SRE teams to collect valuable system signals. The Utilization Saturation and Errors (USE) Method (*https://oreil.ly/bt8QH*)—a checklist for analyzing system performance—can reap benefits for resilience to attack too.

Table 5-2. System signals that could indicate attacks

System signal	Relevant attack(s)
Accept queue depth and how quickly an accept queue is growing	Impending service failure, like an attacker hijacking system execution or process hollowing (MITRE ATT&CK T1055 (*https://oreil.ly/rfR0T*))
Autoscaling replica count[a]	Lateral movement by forcing service deployments on new nodes (MITRE ATT&CK T1072 (*https://oreil.ly/Nh60Y*)); DoS; crypto mining; brute forcing (MITRE ATT&CK T1110 (*https://oreil.ly/KOHT4*)); data exfiltration via elaborate methods
Billing alerts	Crypto miners (MITRE ATT&CK T610 (*https://oreil.ly/eor3U*)), cloud privilege escalation, querying data as part of reconnaissance
Cache hit rate	DoS, data exfiltration (MITRE ATT&CK T1567 (*https://oreil.ly/yeBN8*)), brute force
Disk usage, throughput, and IOPS	Ransomware, staging data for exfiltration (MITRE ATT&CK T1074 (*https://oreil.ly/emTth*))
DNS lookup errors	Lateral movement; data exfiltration or command and control for locked-down environments (MITRE ATT&CK T1071.004 (*https://oreil.ly/CKLDX*)); DoS for ransom
Error rate	Brute forcing with stolen credentials, like credential stuffing (MITRE ATT&CK T1110 (*https://oreil.ly/KOHT4*)); DoS
Heartbeat response time (latency) or failing	DoS attacks on endpoints (MITRE ATT&CK T1499 (*https://oreil.ly/jv9Dm*)); purposefully restricting connections out to evade detection
Replication lag (database)	Unauthorized access or modification (MITRE ATT&CK T1565 (*https://oreil.ly/gJxOW*)); exploitable inconsistencies
Response time	DoS; inconsistent exploit (MITRE ATT&CK T1190 (*https://oreil.ly/mXHLH*))
System log lag	Stopping or deleting logs to conceal attack operations (MITRE ATT&CK T1070 (*https://oreil.ly/6yGzC*))
Rate limit availability	DoS; Server-side request forgery (SSRF); brute force logins (MITRE ATT&CK T1110 (*https://oreil.ly/KOHT4*))

System signal	Relevant attack(s)
Resource consumption creeping toward maximum levels—CPU, memory	Crypto miners and a variety of attacker activity that hijacks resources (MITRE ATT&CK T1496 (*https://oreil.ly/1jSZN*)); in-memory attacks; many forms of exploitation
Swap usage	Data exfiltration (MITRE ATT&CK T1074.001 (*https://oreil.ly/rvDi-*))

ª When you set up autoscaling, the orchestrator will decide how many replicas to instantiate based on policy and then adjust the number continuously based on the current load on the system. When there's a high load and the policy indicates that more replicas can be added, the orchestrator will add them. When there's low load and the policy indicates that fewer replicas are allowed, the orchestrator will retire one of them. An out-of-control replica count indicates not just cost increases, but potential downtime in the future.

Navigating Scalability

There are sometimes social reasons why organizations, leaders, or engineers resist scalability. There can be power in being the gatekeeper to growth; when there are manual processes in place for every change, there's undue influence—we become the gatekeeper. In essence, gatekeeping reflects tight coupling of a human to a process or resource. It will be difficult, if not impossible, to achieve the growth your business desires while preserving the tight coupling that entrenches existing power structures. Scalability checks against this friction. It forces those manual processes to evolve and adapt to have reasonable ways of dealing with system growth.

Standardization of tooling is vital for scalability during the operations phase of software delivery (perhaps even more than it is important for repeatability during the build and deploy phases). Organizations often have under-resourced ops, which makes automation a must-have rather than a nice-to-have. Having to translate data formats across many vendor tools is tight coupling that encourages interactive complexity. Nonstandard ways to debug issues decimate linearity, including workarounds created because prescribed ways are laughable (*https://oreil.ly/aAGSO*) in the face of pragmatism and reality.

If it feels like your teams never have enough time for more strategic work or cannot take vacations without things falling apart, it's worth scrutinizing the teams' interactions with your sociotechnical systems to spot any tight coupling. Do the humans in your teams have to follow a bespoke security check for every release? Must they use different vulnerability scanning tools for each language? Is the information presented to them (including things like "threat intelligence") actionable? And, if so, is that action repeatable? Are teams expected to manually wade through false positives to find the proverbial diamond in the rough? How much time do humans spend tuning different tools? Answering these questions can identify a lack of slack, which is often evidence of tight coupling.

One caveat to scalability-as-a-requirement is to avoid "pre-scaling." If you're a smaller company or building a grassroots SCE program, don't "pre-scale"—that is, don't shoot down ideas that would work well today and in the near-term future just because years from now they might not support the speculative scale. While it's important to anticipate future growth—to preserve possibilities—it shouldn't be at the expense of solving problems today. Incremental improvement can help get flywheels moving (*https://oreil.ly/jFj_5*), and huge, sweeping changes may be impressive on resumes but are less likely to solve ruts.

Automating Away Toil

Toil is a valuable concept out of SRE that we can readily apply to cybersecurity and our broader purview of resilience. *Toil* reflects work that is tactical, manual, tedious, and only offers ephemeral value—the stuff that demoralizes people, burns them out, and sops up time like a dirty sponge.

Here are some common examples of toil in security programs:

- Ticket-driven processes, like securing machines when new employees are onboarded or manually applying patches
- Manually updating access control lists, like provisioning or deprovisioning users (also ticket-driven)
- Conducting manual security reviews, emergency patches, configuration changes, and release approvals (known as "release shepherding" (*https://oreil.ly/4Mzwi*))
- One-off or ad hoc events, like a newly announced vulnerability
- Troubleshooting security or monitoring tools
- Triaging thousands of alerts across dozens of security tools
- Copying and pasting commands from incident runbooks
- Triaging noncritical findings from vulnerability scanners and fixing or dismissing them one by one
- Manually updating firewall rules or pushing new signatures to security tools

For systems to scale, toil cannot prevail. While sometimes you may hear the heuristic "automate anything that can be automated," it offers salience more than value.[21] A better heuristic is "automate anything that a computer can do much better than a human." Humans are adroit at inventing novel strategies to adapt to unfamiliar situations. Humans are terrible at performing the same task the same way every time. This

---

21 Lisanne Bainbridge, "Ironies of Automation," *Automatica* 19, no. 6 (1983): 775-779.

means that tasks that benefit from repeatability are worthy candidates for automation. Tasks that require decision making in ambiguous situations are better left to humans. This is why you commonly see a goal of reducing *tactical* work to free up time for *strategic* work.

Think about the various types of security testing we discussed in the last chapter. For changes estimated to have minimal impact, automated security tests might be sufficient; it covers the basic known issues and can do so much more quickly than a human. But for changes to, for instance, payment flows, manual reviews—and manual testing more broadly—may still be warranted (with enough lead time before the target release date) to uncover unknown issues and explore the code with curiosity rather than through a checklist. We see similar delineation in quality assurance (QA), in which many changes are left to automation, but changes to UI—which impact the human experience rather than technical functionality—are probably best reviewed by human eyeballs and brains.

Chapter Takeaways

- Operating and observing the system is the phase where we can witness system behavior as it runs in production, which can reveal where our mental models are inaccurate. It is when we can glean valuable insights about our systems and incorporate this data into our feedback loops.

- Security is woven into all three key aspects of reliability that reflect user expectations: availability, performance, and correctness.

- Site reliability engineering (SRE) goals and security goals overlap to a significant degree, making those teams natural allies in solving reliability and resilience challenges. A key difference is that SRE understands that moving quickly is correlated with reducing the impact of failure; security must adopt this mindset too.

- Attackers can directly measure success and immediately receive feedback, giving them an asymmetric advantage. We must strive to replicate this for our goals too.

- To measure operational success, we can borrow established metrics like the DORA metrics and craft thoughtful SLOs that help us learn more about the system.

- Success is an active process, not a one-time achievement. We must support *graceful extensibility*: the capability to anticipate bottlenecks and "crunches," learn about evolving conditions, and adapt responses to stressors and surprises as they change.

- We want to mimic the interactive, overlapping, and decentralized sensitivities of biological systems in our observability strategy. In particular, we want to observe system interactions across space and time. We must maintain the ability to reflect on three key questions: How well is the system adapted to its environment? What is the system adapted to? What is changing in the system's environment?

- Tracking when a system is repeatedly stretching toward its limit ("thresholding") helps us uncover the system's boundaries of safe operation. Increasingly "laggy" recovery from disturbances in both the *socio* and *technical* parts of the system can indicate erosion of adaptive capacity.

- *Attack observability* refers to collecting information about the interaction between attackers and systems. It involves tracing attacker behavior to reveal how it looks in reality versus our mental models. *Deception environments* can facilitate attacker tracing, fuel a feedback loop for resilient design, and serve as an experimentation platform.

- A scalable system is a safer system. System signals used to measure scalability can be used as indicators of attack too; we discussed many, including autoscaling replica count, heartbeat response time, and resource consumption.

- Being a gatekeeper to growth is not an effective way to achieve security outcomes. Scalability forces high-friction processes and procedures to adapt to growth, which is healthy for sustaining resilience.

- We should apply the concept of *toil*, from SRE, to security. For any task that a computer can perform better than a human—like those requiring accurate repetition—we should automate it. Doing so frees up effort capital that we can expend on higher-value activities that leverage human strengths like creativity and adaptability.

CHAPTER 6

Responding and Recovering

truth is a seed
planted deep
if you want to get it
you have to dig
　　—Katherena Vermette, "river woman"

As is true for any complex system, stressors and surprises are inevitable. Resilience entails the ability to gracefully recover from these adverse scenarios. Therefore, responding to and recovering from incidents reflects a critical phase in software delivery for systems resilience and its subset of systems security. Incidents astound us into seeing the differences between reality and our mental models in vivid, visceral relief. Incidents are a call to action for us to learn and revise our mental models, a signal that the system's normal functioning may not be sufficient to maintain resilience against attack. Every incident may feel "irregular," but if we dig deeper, we may distinguish patterns that challenge our assumptions and beliefs about system design.

In this chapter, we will explore how we can learn from those incidents and ensure we digest insights in all the other phases of software delivery to inform change, which is crucial for completing the resilience potion. There are tactics we can employ to make incident response efforts more decentralized too, sharpening our sensing abilities. And, as we'll cover in depth, fostering a blameless culture promotes the final ingredients of our resilience potion: learning and willingness to change—resulting in a security program that is open to challenging assumptions and is enthused to continuously improve system design and operation.

SRE teams arguably possess all the ingredients necessary to implement a strong incident response function within an SCE program. The future could evolve so that SREs are the operators who respond to *any* sort of incident, including those involving attackers, and the SRE team weaves curious security engineers into the fold. Why this way? Because the number of hiccups, snafus, speed bumps, and big oofs begotten by attackers is simply less frequent than those begotten by nonattack events. Security is a subset of resilience. Attacks are a type of unhealthy behavior in our systems, but not the only kind.

Likewise, current security operations (SecOps) professionals could skill-up their computer systems knowledge to extend their response expertise to performance-related incidents too. But this is getting into a piezoelectric crystal ball, and, as we admonished in Chapter 1, prediction is folly in any complex system. The goal of this chapter is to outline how incident response and recovery looks through the lens of resilience with suggestions for how to implement it in your organization along the way.

Responding to Surprises in Complex Systems

Responding to a surprise is kind of like a pop quiz; are you comfortable enough with the material to pass? Much like a pop quiz, your ability to pass a security event depends heavily on the context. The guidance you need to pass a quiz on world history is quite different from that for a quiz on Russian literature. Likewise, the guidance you need to pass the quiz on ransomware is very different from that for a new exploit dropping for a vulnerability in a widely used software library.

Therefore, in this section on incident response, we'll focus on the benefits of practicing response activities using chaos experiments rather than prescribing specific response activities. If you are gradually easing into chaos experimentation, you can start assessing the technical response to surprises with fault injection (as we discussed in Chapter 4). It can allow you to observe the machinery's response to a surprise without spinning up a full incident response process.

But to *practice* response activities, you need to engage the sociotechnical system as a whole—which is precisely what will be involved when responding to a real attack. To do so, you want to inject adverse scenarios (what we refer to as chaos experiments). Your response success depends on your preparation; as crisis management researcher Pat Lagadec (*https://oreil.ly/LZuDZ*) observes: "The ability to deal with a crisis situation is largely dependent on the structures that have been developed before chaos arrives. The event can in some ways be considered a brutal and abrupt audit: at a moment's notice, everything that was left unprepared becomes a complex problem, and every weakness comes rushing to the forefront."

Incident Response and the Effort Investment Portfolio

Incident response is stressful work. In fact, you can think of it in terms of the Effort Investment Portfolio. If you spend tons of time thinking up and crafting detailed response plans before an incident occurs, then you've spared on-call engineers a lot of effort when responding to an incident. They can reduce cognitive load by following the guidance, sparing their thinking for adaptation as needed. This also highlights why establishing foundations like logging and observability (as discussed in Chapter 5) is usually worth the effort. If downtime hurts your bottom line (as it does for most organizations), you don't want on-call engineers scrambling to find the data they need to restore service. You want them to use their brainpower to solve the hard problems, like investigating what went wrong and brainstorming the best way to get things back to a healthy status—not tracking down the right person to contact to get basic data.

This also demonstrates the importance of thoughtful architecture and design (as we discussed in Chapter 3). If availability is a product requirement, then you should design the system to automatically recover from common faults. Architects and designers should also pay more attention to the sorts of tools available to on-call engineers. For instance, are there opportunities to reduce friction for engineers in failing over to a second site, rolling back to a database snapshot, putting the system in read-only mode, or scaling the service to the moon? If you design your system in a naive way, there's a whole category of failures that would take it offline—you should design for mitigating that set of failures. This also ties into our decision trees from Chapter 2: if the database goes offline, you can fail over to the secondary (and you could add branches to your decision tree for other mechanisms as well). In essence, design for the incidents that would otherwise crush you.

It's impossible to provide mechanisms to ease response and recovery activities for *every* type of failure, especially security failures—which can be particularly nefarious and contagious—but many mechanisms can at least allow operators to keep the system limping along and fulfilling its function during an incident, giving more breathing room to investigate the optimal fix (and avoid action bias, which we'll discuss later in this section).

You can also zoom out and consider the Effort Investment Portfolio across the entire software lifecycle. If lessons learned from incidents never inform improvements in design or operation, then effort investments will stay anchored to responders. But if you can recover from incidents gracefully and actively learn from them, you shift some effort off of incident response and onto the up-front work involved in incorporating insights into a feedback loop and then onward across design, build, and operate.

The same goes for conducting security chaos experiments. You're shifting effort into crafting hypotheses, conducting experiments, and practicing response and recovery activities. But because you're building muscle memory around those activities and leveraging experimental evidence to improve system design and operation, you're reducing the effort involved in responding to real incidents—and that's precisely where you want to minimize effort however you can.

Action Bias in Incident Response

As we've reinforced throughout the book, humans really don't like uncertainty. When humans are thrust into chaotic scenarios (like a surprise attack), they want to regain a sense of control and therefore feel an impulse toward action. Behavioral scientists refer to this quirk of human judgment as action bias.[1] This quirk is compounded by the traditional security community's relentless obsession with prevention, which inherently (due to the finitude of resources) comes at the expense of preparation.[2] When encountering surprises, organizations that prevent rather than prepare therefore succumb to the gravitational pull of action bias to relieve their discomfort.

Prevention seeks to stop an attack from happening at all—like blocking specific IPs on a network or executables with specific strings on a laptop. Preparation poises us to recover gracefully from an attack. That could be automatically terminating and restarting an application when it's compromised or letting it run isolated from the rest of the network while an operator investigates.

When we lean into action bias by snapping into action, we fail to consider alternatives and thereby can make suboptimal decisions. Action bias bears considerable opportunity cost (which we covered briefly in Chapter 3).[3] For example, if you allocate resources to rebuild a server after an attack without analyzing or otherwise preserving its logs, you can no longer use those resources to figure out how the attacker(s) gained access (which could be useful to inform design improvements). The main problem is that opportunity cost isn't natural to our decision making, even when we're feeling calm. When we're in the pressure cooker that is an active incident, our critical thinking can easily derail and we won't remember to consider alternatives in our stress-fueled tunnel vision.[4]

Unfortunately, instructive public examples around incident response to attacks are virtually nonexistent, which doesn't help us in our quest to understand healthy and unhealthy incident response patterns—like resisting versus succumbing to action

1 Anthony Patt and Richard Zeckhauser, "Action Bias and Environmental Decisions," *Journal of Risk and Uncertainty* 21, no. 1 (2000): 45-72.

2 Rock Stevens et al., "How Ready Is Your Ready? Assessing the Usability of Incident Response Playbook Frameworks," *CHI Conference on Human Factors in Computing Systems* (New Orleans, LA: April 29-May 5, 2022): 1-18.

3 N. Gregory Mankiw, *Principles of Economics,* 9th Edition (Boston: Cengage Learning, 2020).

4 Johannes Martinus Cornelis Schraagen and Josine G.M. van de Ven, "Improving Decision Making in Crisis Response Through Critical Thinking Support," *Journal of Cognitive Engineering and Decision Making* 2, no. 4 (2008): 311-327.

bias. We know that companies experience incidents all the time, but how response decisions are made—and what plays out based on those decisions—remains obscure, confined to invite-only community groups.

A recent paper on opportunity cost in incident response activities analyzed the Sony breach (*https://oreil.ly/m4ptB*) through the lens of action bias.[5] On November 24, 2014, attackers publicly leaked PII, internal communications, IP (like unreleased films and scripts), and other proprietary information from Sony Pictures Entertainment (SPE), then erased it from SPE's systems using a variant of Shamoon wiper malware (*https://oreil.ly/WJtms*). In less than 24 hours after discovering the first (extremely) visible signals of an attack, SPE shut down its entire network. This affected more than 9,000 employees, who were instructed not to connect to corporate networks nor access email, and, perhaps even more extreme, to turn off their computers and disable WiFi on all mobile devices. While this alone can be characterized as a knee-jerk reaction and evidence of a lack of planning or practice, it is especially so when considering that attackers had been exfiltrating data from Sony's systems for about a year. The actions were also costly; it is difficult from the outside to quantify how much the downtime cost Sony from either a financial or productivity perspective, but the total cost of investigation and remediation reached $35 million for the fiscal year through March 31, 2015.

Overall, from the outside, Sony's response to the incident appears to exemplify action bias, the temptation to "do something—anything—to gain control" (*https://oreil.ly/2u_i3*). It's likely most of you have experienced or witnessed action bias during your career. Action bias is a common pattern in incident response, but it results in suboptimal actions and forfeited benefits of alternative choices, including wasted time, wasted money, a false sense of security, or even reduced innovation and productivity (like shutting down networks or instituting high-friction hurdles meant to prevent future incidents). Many of these ills are negative externalities, not shouldered by the team performing the actions (like the security team), but instead foisted upon other stakeholders.

A Handy Heuristic: The Null Baseline

One mental shortcut to counter action bias and prompt yourself (or others) to consider the opportunity costs of an action is the null baseline.[6] The *null baseline* is simple: what would we gain by *not* taking this action? In the context of incident response, the null baseline likely takes the form of: What would be gained by *waiting* to act (or take this particular action)?

---

5 Josiah Dykstra et al., "Opportunity Cost of Action Bias in Cybersecurity Incident Response," *Proceedings of the Human Factors and Ergonomics Society Annual Meeting* 66, no. 1 (September 2022): 1116-1120.

6 Kelly Shortridge and Josiah Dykstra, "Opportunity Cost and Missed Chances in Optimizing Cybersecurity," *Queue* 21, no. 1 (2023), 30-56.

This, of course, doesn't incorporate all opportunity costs of the decision, but it's easy to remember and "good enough" to trigger a reminder to explore alternatives—and that kind of streamlined thinky thinky is exactly what you need when in the midst of responding to a surprise.

That isn't to say you should sit back and admire an attacker as they binge on your systems. There are also costs of waiting too long during a crisis, especially the potential gains forfeited by not acting, like extended downtime, stress, contagion, or cognitive effort from ruminating (Figure 6-1). But it's always worth considering alternative courses of action and practicing "watchful waiting" rather than impulsively springing into action to gain a sense of control. For example, do we rebuild compromised infrastructure immediately? Or do we preserve it to evaluate and analyze it?

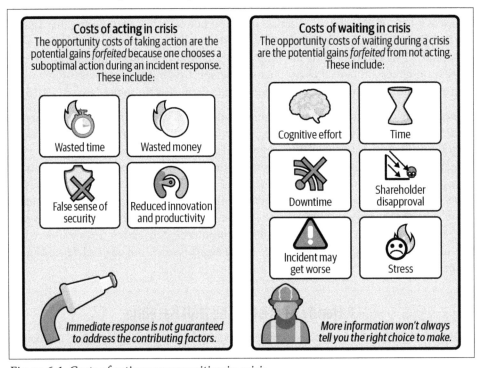

Figure 6-1. Costs of acting versus waiting in crisis

Practicing Response Activities

Many teams, both security and ops alike, document best practices and plans for responding to incidents in what are often called "runbooks" or "playbooks." But these plans are better for creating a sense of comfort rather than a sense of confidence during real response activities. Incidents rarely unfold exactly as people imagine. The problem with playbooks is that they pretend like there are "best practice" ways to respond to incidents of various types and, even if they're released just as "guidance" rather than prescriptive, human operators will likely feel obligated to follow the steps within. This represses adaptation and is the opposite of the decentralized management we need in complex systems.

Even worse, these "best practices" can hurt incident response. For example, "Never, ever log in as admin for this tool" is wise until all other accounts are locked out—which then lurches operators into the uncomfortable position of either disobeying the rules or allowing an incident to worsen.

What Makes a Good Playbook?

In general, playbooks should be super general and focus more on providing information, like architectural diagrams for the affected service, during an incident than prescribing detailed steps. Whenever you, or another well-meaning individual, are tempted to add detail to a playbook, it's a sign of opportunity. Instead of writing down detail as a reference, could you implement it into a warning system? Even better, is there a possible design change, like implementing automation? For instance, if there's a step required to query the service's region, could you expose that as metadata in the incident alert itself so the on-call engineer doesn't have to hunt for it? Or, if the detail pertains to a series of steps or commands the on-call engineer must perform in response to a specific type of event, can you automate it?

As we discussed in Chapter 1, complex systems inherently involve evolution. Playbooks are a reflection of the right guidance for a particular slice of space-time,[7] usually one quite stale by the time an on-call engineer must consult it for the latest incident. It will save your teams time and frustration to keep playbooks general and focused on less mutable reference information, like architecture diagrams, rather than specific actions to take. It's also valuable to practice your playbooks to surface knowledge that responders are missing about the service. In essence, playbooks should not include answers; instead, they should provide the context responders need to take faster, smarter actions during an incident.

Drawing again on our favorite complex system, *Jurassic Park*, the blueprint of the power station is helpful for the on-call operator (in the movie's case, Dr. Ellie Sattler) to know the location of the target equipment toward her goal of restoring service (electricity). But when she battled the velociraptors that were intervening with her goal, it is difficult to imagine a playbook that would have helped more than her own ingenuity and adaptation in the moment.

---

7 Raphael Bousso, "The Holographic Principle," *Review of Modern Physics* 74, no. 3 (2002): 825.

The most important skill in an operator when responding to an active incident in a complex system is *adaptation*, as we discussed in Chapter 1. It's really difficult to write a manual on how a human can be adaptive. No one learns how to do improvisational acting just by reading a guide on it; you learn improv by taking a class, by experimenting, by actively performing unplanned, spontaneous steps. We need the same for incident response—and we're in luck. We can teach adaptation skills by conducting chaos experiments.

Let's say you conduct our original experiment from Chapter 2, injecting a misconfigured port. The incident playbook might tell the on-call engineer that when they receive an alert about a network security violation, they should immediately check the logs to investigate and learn more about the violation to determine the appropriate fix. But when you run the chaos experiment, you disprove the hypothesis that the firewall would detect or block the change in all instances. The port change doesn't trigger an alert and the log data shows a successful change audit. The playbook has only created confusion for the on-call engineer. Unexpectedly, the configuration management tool catches the change and alerts the on-call engineer. This teaches the engineer flexibility, that there can be multiple sources of valuable insight into an incident that are worth checking to clarify an adverse situation.

The more you conduct experiments reflecting the potential security failure scenarios in your decision trees, the more your teams can build new muscle memory for responding to incidents. Repeated practice of these experiments can make incidents feel boring instead of scary and stressful—and burnout and stress is a notorious problem for incident responders in infosec (and other industries with similar functions).[8] Security chaos experimentation can transform incidents into problems with known processes for solving them, which directly leads to faster and higher-quality security outcomes.

Defenders, somewhat ironically, often feel insecure about their ability to handle incidents, both in terms of human and systems resilience. The repeated experimentation borne from security chaos experiments helps us grow confidence in our system's resilience in the face of failure, and in the resilience of our teams. This cool, collected confidence also comes from using our experimental evidence to inform refinements in our system design—whether architecture, mitigations, processes, policies, and so forth. We'll talk more about the full experimental process in Chapter 8.

The misconfigured port example also elucidates the value of experiments in teaching software engineers who design and architect systems how to better support adaptation, namely by designing to preserve possibilities. In this case, preserving

---

8 Josiah Dykstra and Celeste Lyn Paul, "Cyber Operations Stress Survey (COSS): Studying Fatigue, Frustration, and Cognitive Workload in Cybersecurity Operations," *11th {USENIX} Workshop on Cyber Security Experimentation and Test ({CSET} 18)* (Baltimore, MD: August 13, 2018).

possibilities can take the form of providing a variety of vantage points on system behavior (as discussed in the last chapter). It could also mean designing to prune on-call engineer workflows so they don't have to navigate to disparate tools to query data or make changes, such as allowing them to perform most of their work via the command line (a type of platform engineering we'll discuss in the next chapter).

You don't even have to conduct chaos experiments to discover these developer experience (DX) opportunities. As part of their on-call onboarding, Google engineers practice (*https://oreil.ly/E2RBj*) two dozen "focus areas" before handling real incidents, including activities like administering production jobs, understanding debugging info, "draining" traffic away from a cluster, rolling back a bad software push, blocking or rate-limiting unwanted traffic, bringing up additional serving capacity, using the monitoring systems (for alerting and dashboards), and more. Interviewing engineers as they onboard and try out these activities can be an insightful source of user research on how to improve usability and support fast, safe decisions during incident response (we'll talk more about conducting user research in the next chapter). This also takes us back to Effort Investment Portfolios; if, during onboarding, your engineers are straining to become reasonably familiar with the services they'll need to deal with during incident response—that is, they struggle to conceive mental models of it at all, let alone relatively accurate ones—then it suggests a design issue.

As a final note, sometimes your response activities won't unfold at all the way you hope—and that's OK! If you don't have enough data to make a decision safely, you're in luck because you're responding to a chaos experiment and not a real incident. You can channel this failure to inform what design revisions and additional data, features, or tools you need to make safer decisions during response. And once you implement an MVP—in the spirit of iterative, continuous improvement—you can try the chaos experiment again and procure both qualitative and quantitative feedback on resulting improvements to your response decisions.

How do we learn from chaos experiments or real incidents, anyway? This brings us to the topic of incident recovery.

Recovering from Surprises

Incident recovery usually refers to getting a system's critical functionality back to performing as expected. But real recovery only ensues when you learn from the incident—when you review it, digest any findings, and funnel those insights back into earlier phases of the lifecycle. That is, recovery involves *adaptation*. Sometimes that's as simple as tweaking what metadata you collect in your monitoring pipelines. Other times it might involve carefully considering a re-architecture of your systems to reduce the potential for contagion. It might even take the form of changing who is on call to respond to incidents, like rotating one software engineer from each product team to ensure there's sufficient systems knowledge during the incident as well as dissemination of knowledge after it too.

We won't cover the technical and tactical bits of recovering from an incident (which, like the pop quiz analogy earlier, can take infinite forms). Instead, we'll focus on how to learn from an attack or other nasty surprises—how the sociotechnical system can recover and, in a sense, how your organization can recover. This section is all about revamping our mental models after an incident and resisting the temptation of sticking with inaccurate models by accepting shallow explanations for why an attack happened. So, we will focus primarily on incident review and analysis.

Incident review helps you tease out mental models and probe the difference between expectation and reality. As David D. Woods noted in his testimony to the Columbia Accident Investigation Board (*https://oreil.ly/J0PZa*), "The past seems incredible, the future implausible." This sense of wonder (even if negative) is because our mental models have been violated and we know they will be violated again in the future too.

Mental model violation elucidates the importance of cultivating community memory, like our example of Constantinople from Chapter 1. Learning from incidents really is about *community*. Communities can't thrive when its members are blamed and punished, especially for performing allegedly "unsafe" actions in the course of pursuing goals benefiting the community (like increasing revenue, profit, or intangibles like inclusion, productivity, or morale).

As much as counterfactuals are fun and arguably how cybersecurity has cultivated power as an industry, they aren't useful during incidents and distract from what *is* useful. In fact, counterfactuals are a red flag (*https://oreil.ly/czTBW*) for blame*ful* incident reviews. Dreaming up what *should* have existed or what *should* have been done is a coping mechanism disguised as inquiry, but it's curiosity's nemesis. As we'll explore, there's a wealth of teachings to be extracted from exploring why something happened—including why something went *right*—and none of it involves finger-pointing or settling for a convenient, shallow answer.

Blameless incident reviews can serve as a sort of healthy, cathartic ritual for "letting go." Think of the stirring scene from *The Northman* where the Viking squad are in furs and on all fours around a firepit, howling and snarling at the moon. That's probably not the right fit in a reality of remote work during daylight hours, but feel free to be playful and have fun brainstorming what rituals you can implement as part of this "letting go" process.

Magic Ritual to Restore and Recover

- Light a candle and embrace change through fire while respecting the value of memory through scent. (Smell)

- Chime a bell and hum in tune with it until it fades away—just as the impact of the incident shall eventually. (Sound)

- Rub vanilla-infused oil to nourish your hands and keep them distracted from finger-pointing. (Touch)

- Clutch a quartz crystal near light to watch it dazzle and refract through its facets, just as each incident bears many facets worth exploring. (Sight)

- Munch on edible pansies, which embody thoughtfulness and compassion; their soft petals will encourage neutral practitioner questions and empathy for operator constraints. (Taste)

Practicing how to unwind your organization's collective nervous system after responding to an incident can increase your collective capacity to respond and adapt to real, large-scale incidents in the future. Maybe you send out hot cocoa kits in advance, encouraging everyone at the beginning of the call to join in practicing mindfulness by watching the marshmallow melt into the rich, redolent chocolate. Maybe you encourage everyone to take five minutes to draw, watercolor, or interpretive dance their feelings about the incident. The point is that rituals are common throughout human history for a reason: they're an incredibly healthy way not only to release stress, but also to bond with others, to gain a sense of trust and community.[9] And that vibe is essential when the inevitable happens and you all must link arms to respond to an attack.

How do you implement a blameless culture? What cognitive biases can impede constructive incident reviews? What new heuristics and tricks can you leverage to learn as much as you can from incidents—whether of the natural or controlled chaos variety? The rest of the chapter will explore how we can cultivate this kind of blameless culture in our security programs and the impediments to doing so—which are mostly due to our cognitive processes rather than our technological ones.

---

9 Rachel E. Watson-Jones and Cristine H. Legare, "The Social Functions of Group Rituals," *Current Directions in Psychological Science* 25, no. 1 (2016): 42-46.

Blameless Culture

It is relatively impossible to learn from failure when pointing fingers at a particular human or group of humans. If you settle for "the human did a big oof" as an explanation for an incident, you will miss all the other factors that contributed to an incident. Was the system design confusing? Was there a high-stress environment requiring attention to be split in many directions at once? You can't answer those questions if you've already accepted the simplistic, scapegoating answer—which means similar failures are more likely to occur in the future, without other lessons learned. Poetically framed by safety science scholars, "We can blame and punish under whatever labels are in fashion but that will not change the lawful factors that govern human performance nor will it make the sun go round the earth."[10]

If you play—or even win—the "blame game," you will lose the "actually improving security outcomes" game. A blameless culture can create structure that prevents slipping into the Land of Pointing Fingers. Some people bristle when they hear about a blameless culture for the first time. Won't people become reckless if blame is banned? A blameless culture is not one in which you are absolving people from any responsibility for their actions. A blameless culture (*https://oreil.ly/m4HDn*) seeks to balance accountability and safety. It encourages people to speak up about issues without fear of being punished for doing so, which helps the organization discover problems early and gain clarity around incidents that occur. This helps the organization adopt a perpetual state of learning, ensuring that critical information is not suppressed that can help establish the full context around incidents.[11]

To begin down the blameless culture path, you must change the questions you ask. There are answers, such as "it is the accountant's fault for wiring the money to the attacker," which feel satisfying but clarify little. Asking the right questions helps guide investigations (*https://oreil.ly/gt1si*) toward understanding multiple perspectives around the event, which can uncover the full picture of relationships between components in a system that sets the context for the event.

A Blameful Analysis of the Death Star Explosion

Let's explore an example line of inquiry illustrating the problems with a blame*ful* culture from the Star Wars Universe. Why did the Death Star blow up? Well, Darth Vader failed to stop Luke Skywalker. OK, well, we can't blame him—is there an intern or something we can blame? Well, the people piloting the defensive artillery also failed. Better. But also, Galen Erso designed it badly. Yeah, but Orson Krennic

---

10 David D. Woods et al., *Behind Human Error*, 2nd Edition (Boca Raton, FL: CRC Press, 2010).

11 For a fun example of a blameless incident review, we highly recommend Matt Stratton's talk: "Avengers Assemble: the Thanos Incident" (*https://oreil.ly/lZYAw*).

recruited him, so isn't he to blame? Tarkin already blew him up. What about the prisoners constructing it? Which ones, on which planet? They're all dead anyway, so we can't execute them again. Wait a minute, wasn't Krennic forced to recruit Erso because the scientists couldn't figure out the kyber crystal technology? Yeah, you're right! Are any of them still around? I think Bevel Lemelisk is! Excellent, let's get on a Zoom meeting with Emperor Palpatine.

As crisis management and human-centered design scholars Rankin et al. advise, "Interpreting people's actions in the light of what 'should have happened' and what they 'could have done' to avoid the incident allows a convenient explanation of the situation, but it does not necessarily provide a deeper understanding of underlying factors contributing to the outcome, such as context, pressures from the organization, and conflicting goals."[12] We can summarize two contributing factors always worth discussing in each incident, because they are inevitably there, lurking beneath the shallow explanation of errors (whether of the human or machine variety):

- Relevant production pressures
- System properties

Production pressures, over time, push complex systems toward the boundaries of safe operation. Production pressures consume buffer capacity and reserve resources that contribute to resilience against surprises. As the system trends toward brittleness, it gives off signals—but they may not be the ones we were collecting. For instance, employee turnover can be a signal that the *socio* part of the sociotechnical system is nearing its tipping point, after which it will crumble in the face of an attack. Therefore, during incident recovery and analysis, we must consider what signals might have captured those production pressures and how they were eroding the properties relevant to system resilience.[13] We'll discuss production pressures in more depth in the next chapter.

These system properties are important to analyze too. It's tempting to focus on the obvious errors that emerged prior to and during the incident, but doing so creates comfort rather than knowledge. Has the system been difficult to update or change? Have operators been devising alternative work patterns to get their job done? Is there evidence of tight coupling somewhere in the system, especially a trend toward tighter

---

12 Amy Rankin et al., "Resilience in Everyday Operations: A Framework for Analyzing Adaptations in High-Risk Work," *Journal of Cognitive Engineering and Decision Making* 8, no. 1 (2014): 78-97.

13 David D. Woods, "Engineering Organizational Resilience to Enhance Safety: A Progress Report on the Emerging Field of Resilience Engineering," *Proceedings of the Human Factors and Ergonomics Society Annual Meeting* 50, no. 19 (October 2006): 2237-2241.

coupling prior to the incident? If the answer to any of these questions is yes, we need to dig deeper into the context created by these properties.

Answering these questions goes a long way to uncovering the most valuable takeaways from an incident to support learning and continuous improvement. While we'll talk more about delivering solutions based on feedback in the next chapter, it's worth digging more into why we, as humans, love to blame each other for failure as well as what we can do to counter that tendency.

Blunt end versus sharp end

Because security is something a system *does* rather than something a system *has*, having one centralized arbiter of security makes no sense. Whether your organization's business is conducted primarily in software from day one, or it's in the process of shifting more operations to software, the more your software systems grow in size and complexity, the harder it will be for a centralized security team to keep up with the rest of the business. The biggest cost in systems security will be ongoing maintenance of that security, and a centralized, siloed team cannot scale to meet that demand.

A disconnect between the humans performing the work and the humans defining how the work should be done exacerbates this cost. This can be described as the delta between work-as-imagined (humans at the "blunt end") and work-as-practiced (humans at the "sharp end"). Humans at the "blunt end" of systems are the policy makers, administrators, regulators, or tech creators and suppliers who are not the users of systems, but are generally responsible for imagining how work should be done. For the most part, security professionals rest at the "blunt end" of systems.

The "sharp end," in contrast, is made up of the individual operators of systems—the users who actually interact with the systems—like the pilot flying the plane, the surgeon operating on patients, the executive assistant scheduling events, or, in our computer world, the developer writing software. These operators are usually blamed when something goes wrong, but they are never solely responsible for a failure and "tend to be the inheritors of system defects."[14] These defects are created by factors well outside the operator's control, such as bad implementation, unsatisfactory design, poor maintenance, and undesirable management decisions. As safety researcher and psychologist James Reason puts it, the human error by operators "adds a final garnish to a lethal brew whose ingredients have already been long in the cooking."

In an ideal world, there is ample communication between the blunt end and the sharp end to ensure continuous refinement to the blunt end's "work-as-imagined" so it better reflects the sharp end's "work-as-practiced." When the blunt end works best, it can define values and goals that inform overarching requirements for the work, like

---

14 James Reason, *Human Error* (Cambridge, UK: Cambridge University Press, 1990).

quality, cost, efficiency, or security requirements. In tandem, when the sharp end works best, it "adapts its work accordingly…modifications of performance are continuously made at the sharp end, even in highly controlled task situations."[15] Whether looking at resilience in aerospace, healthcare, or software, what never emerges is that a centralized, siloed group of professionals at the blunt end can anticipate future conditions enough to define how work should be done with 100% accuracy.

Regrettably, the disconnect between the blunt end and the sharp end often devolves into the "blame game" we know too well—the blunt end points fingers and invokes "human error" when an operator tries to adapt to evolving conditions. That is, the blunt end gets defensive when work-as-practiced violates their work-as-imagined, and this defensiveness quickly shuts down a learning culture. Cybersecurity suffers from this lack of communication and cohesion—recall the industry statistics purporting that 85% to 88% of all breaches are due to "human error." Policies and procedures are declared by practitioners at the blunt end, divorced from the work affected by the policy, which means that the people doing the work (at the sharp end) can find themselves confused and frustrated when expected to adhere to policies that don't align with their reality. "Don't click on links," says the blunt end; marketers, recruiters, and sales professionals now are vexed in how to do their work-as-practiced.

Whether designing secure systems or responding to incidents in systems, knowledge about the systems matters most. The security part is arguably easier to learn than the systems part. The biggest pain is in maintaining secure systems—to ensure their ongoing resilience to unwanted events, like attacks. This maintenance is core to the continuous adaptability we seek. How can we make this less painful?

If we seek a security program that can scale, security cannot skulk in a secluded ivory tower (*https://oreil.ly/ohL4P*). We can look to examples from other technical disciplines, like DBA (as covered in Chapter 4), to see why one viable organizational model is for security programs to rest under software engineering or ops and SRE teams—so the people who actually understand the systems that we're trying to protect own the security program.

Blaming Human Error

One of traditional infosec's favorite pastimes seems to be invoking "PICNIC" or "PEBKAC"—"problem in chair, not in computer" and "problem exists between keyboard and chair," respectively. Blaming failure on humans is convenient, but folly. The better acronym is PEBRAMM—"problem exists between reality and mental model."[16] This does not mean we absolve humans of accountability, since there can

---

15 Rankin, "Resilience in Everyday Operations," 78-97.

16 Thank you to technical reviewer Jason Strange for suggesting this delightful acronym.

indeed be malicious individuals who plot to inflict harm. What it means is that you cannot settle for blaming the individual closest to the event. You must examine all contributing factors if you are to productively investigate.

The Fundamental Attribution Error

Another bias commonly seen in status quo security is the fundamental attribution error.[17] The *fundamental attribution error* is the tendency for people to assume others' actions are a result of their innate character traits, while holding themselves to a different standard—that one's own actions are situational. For example, if we are a cybersecurity professional and fall victim to a phishing test, we will perhaps chuckle, blaming a lack of coffee or being distracted by the million other things on our plate. However, there are those in cybersecurity who slander other humans who click links as inattentive, lazy, stupid, naive, or sloppy. Believing that someone deliberately made the choice to go on an error-prone path ferries us toward the strategy of blaming humans as a "root cause."

An error or mistake occurring represents a starting point for investigation, rather than a conclusion. Errors are a symptom of failure, not a cause, because they arise from the relationships between components of complex systems. When someone clicks on a link they should not, the first question should be "Why did they click on the link?" Another relevant question is "Why did clicking on a link lead to an incident?"

These questions go unanswered if we are satisfied that the incident is explained by "human error," followed by a proposed mitigation, like user education, that has no chance of succeeding. A focus on "human error" as a root cause leads to solutions that fail to understand the real priorities for the users in question. For instance, expecting a software engineering team to care more about security problems after a training module is unrealistic and unlikely to impact how they behave across the software development lifecycle.

Beware security programs that rationalize issues of design or policy by blaming people who wrestle with the rules to perform their function. It's comforting to blame rule breakers rather than system design because it's much easier to wrist-slap someone than to redesign the system or find a way to reduce hazards. Some savvier security teams use the "5 whys" approach to investigation, seeking to understand the underlying factors that contributed to events to determine whether other systems might have

---

17 Gilbert Harman, "Moral Philosophy Meets Social Psychology: Virtue Ethics and the Fundamental Attribution Error," *Proceedings of the Aristotelian Society* (1999): 315-331.

the same issue. However, there are still too many instances of blaming a human and firing them to "solve" the problem across the industry.

For example, the ex-CEO of Equifax (*https://oreil.ly/F3hTk*) blamed "human error" for the infamous breach. Specifically, the ex-CEO identified a single individual as "not ensuring communication got to the right person to manually patch the application." There did not appear to be an exploration of the friction-filled workflow for patching, the organizational pressures to minimize downtime, the reliance on legacy systems, or the inappropriate workflow placement of their vulnerability scanner.

This is not limited to cybersecurity. In the investigation of 27 major aviation accidents by the National Transportation Safety Board (NTSB), 96% cited humans as the probable cause of the accident.[18] In 81% of accidents, humans were the sole cause reported—and similar statistics are found in cybersecurity, as we discussed in Chapter 1.

When we blame human error, we are tacitly absolving technology from culpability, which sneakily coaxes us toward behavioral control, unnecessary technological accumulation, and misguided automation. The underlying theory is that we can reprimand and restrict humans into behaving exactly the way we want. Or, it's supposed, if the human is removed from the process—or at least has their role heavily demoted—then error does not have the chance to occur. Our eternal hope is that there is a tool just around the corner that will completely solve our problems.

In the rest of this section, we'll cover the biases that distort our perception of causal factors and inhibit our learning during incident recovery and analysis. We'll start by exploring the pernicious problems with root cause analysis and blaming human error in healthcare, so we can learn from another domain's struggles (and hopefully avoid stagnation of success in our own domain). We'll then discuss hindsight bias, outcome bias, and the just-world hypothesis, and finally turn to neutral practitioner questions as an antidote to these learning impediments.

---

18 Richard J. Holden, "People or Systems? To Blame Is Human. The Fix Is to Engineer," *Professional Safety* 54, no. 12 (2009): 34.

One thought experiment to run during incident review is the "Humanless Error" heuristic. Imagine it's impossible to blame humans. What else would we blame instead? This can be a useful forcing function to consider other influencing factors of failure.

For example, rather than proclaiming that "Orlando pressed the wrong button," we might instead muse that "Hmm, Orlando had been asking for new labels for all the buttons for a while, but the company wouldn't allocate funds to it because it would require slashing our corporate swag budget." When we zoom out, both are mistakes by humans; one influences the failure more than the other and addressing it would better prepare us for failure, but blaming the human is easier and more localized—as well as utterly useless in preventing *or* preparing for future incidents.

Case study: Healthcare and root cause analysis

"Root cause analysis" (RCA) often promulgates the blame game and "human error" slander. If that sounds like cybersecurity, you're right, but there's another industry wrestling with the insidiousness of RCA: healthcare.

Healthcare professionals must conduct reviews of incidents in their domain too. Despite the focus on RCA and blaming human error (*https://oreil.ly/f44v-*), "adverse event rates" are stagnating rather than improving—strongly suggesting that the current approach to RCA in healthcare is a contributing factor to the industry's metafailure of not improving patient safety.[19]

Why might this be? Well, fewer than half of healthcare RCAs resulted in recommendations for improving system-level properties or implementing system-level solutions, such as through a redesign of product or procedures.[20] Instead, they typically recommend action plans involving education, like awareness training, or changes to policy, both of which attempt to "fix individuals" and neither of which results in sustained, effective improvements in the system. (Sound familiar?) The picture one study paints of healthcare RCAs bears a striking resemblance to the RCAs in our own realm, which prioritizes blame over outcomes:

> Many times, the RCA does not identify meaningful aspects of the event but simply observes that humans are imperfect. For example, failures involving people forgetting something previously known or taught to them simply observes that human memory is imperfect... Just as our parents taught us when we were toddlers, human error is

19 Kathryn M. Kellogg et al., "Our Current Approach to Root Cause Analysis: Is It Contributing to Our Failure to Improve Patient Safety?" *BMJ Quality & Safety* 26, no. 5 (2017): 381-387.

20 Peter D. Mills et al., "Actions and Implementation Strategies to Reduce Suicidal Events in the Veterans Health Administration," *The Joint Commission Journal on Quality and Patient Safety* 32, no. 3 (2006): 130-141.

inevitable, thereby proposing a solution for safety mitigation that focuses on reminding people not to make mistakes is an indictment of our approach to safety.[21]

One elegant analogy for RCA as currently practiced is "swatting at mosquitoes versus draining the swamp."[22] It's worth reading the elaboration on this analogy from scholars in healthcare as it is just as applicable to cybersecurity:

> We do not want to spend our time and expend our resources swatting at the mosquitos of "not double checking." Rather, we want to drain the swamp of the many latent conditions that make not double checking more likely to occur. Too often, RCA teams focus on the first causal factor identified (eg, staff violation of the allergy-checking policy) rather than considering such factors holistically as parts of a sociotechnical system (ie, interactions between people and technology embedded in an organizational structure).

The incentives and influencing factors that shape behavior—like task complexity, cumbersome workflows, or confusing tool design—are never surfaced. Traditional healthcare and cybersecurity RCAs focus on "active failures," like not double-checking a patient's allergies before administering medication, rather than "latent conditions," like the nurse's workload and a critical safety mechanism relying on human memory (interfaces with built-in reminders are an alternative).

The new call to action in healthcare—toward draining swamps, not swatting mosquitoes—with RCA is twofold:

1. Treat any proposed interventions as hypotheses that require testing.
2. Leverage simulation[23] to identify "system-based causes of events or organizational structures" that influence unintended human behavior.

This mirrors our imperative in SCE: to conduct experiments and analyze evidence to drive empirical security decision making.

Hindsight Bias and Outcome Bias

Cognitive biases represent mental shortcuts that are optimal for evolution, but not necessarily for the demanding mental environments that pervade modern life.[24] We

---

21 Kellogg, "Our Current Approach to Root Cause Analysis," 381-387.

22 Patricia Trbovich and Kaveh G. Shojania, "Root-Cause Analysis: Swatting at Mosquitoes Versus Draining the Swamp," *BMJ Quality & Safety* 26, no. 5 (2017): 350-353.

23 Eric R. Simms et al., "Can Simulation Improve the Traditional Method of Root Cause Analysis: A Preliminary Investigation," *Surgery* 152, no. 3 (2012): 489-497.

24 Dominic D. P. Johnson et al., "The Evolution of Error: Error Management, Cognitive Constraints, and Adaptive Decision-Making Biases," *Trends in Ecology & Evolution* 28, no. 8 (2013): 474-481.

must learn from the past in order to progress, but our "lizard brains" can take things too far and trespass into the territory of hindsight bias and outcome bias.

Hindsight bias involves our present knowledge influencing our consideration of past events—the "I knew it all along" effect, or, more sinisterly, the "curse of knowledge."[25] For example, think of all the armchair experts on social media who burst forth after every breach bragging about how obvious it was that the breach would occur.

Repeated experiments show that humans overestimate their predictive abilities and struggle to predict whether a decision will be successful or not without the benefit of future knowledge.[26] As a practical example, the general public condemned financial analysts who did not see the 2008 financial crisis coming, now deeming it as inevitable. In cybersecurity, when the Sony Pictures leak first happened, many people did not believe (*https://oreil.ly/JFp23*) it was North Korea, believing the now-defunct startup Norse over the word of U.S. officials. Now, of course, it is "obvious" it was North Korea.

Outcome bias is when we judge the quality of a decision based on its eventual outcome.[27] We tend to judge a decision far more harshly if a negative outcome results than if the potential for a negative outcome still existed but never materialized. Outcome bias weighs the ultimate outcome as the most important factor in evaluating correctness of decisions.

In both cases of bias, we should evaluate whether it was the best decision at the time given what was known at the time—without the benefit of hindsight (knowing more information than in the past) or outcome (knowing what would result). As the philosopher David Hume mused, "If that object be entirely new to [someone], [they] will not be able, by the most accurate examination of its sensible qualities, to discover any of its causes or effects."[28]

When we succumb to outcome bias, we are unfairly holding humans accountable for events beyond their control. The classic example of outcome bias is that humans rate the decision to operate on a patient far worse if the patient died than if the patient lived.[29] Logically, however, the decision to operate should be correct regardless of

25 Shaudi Mahdavi and M. Amin Rahimian, "Hindsight Bias Impedes Learning," *Imperfect Decision Makers: Admitting Real-World Rationality* (August 2017): 111-127.

26 Hal R. Arkes et al., "Hindsight Bias Among Physicians Weighing the Likelihood of Diagnoses," *Journal of Applied Psychology* 66, no. 2 (1981): 252.

27 Andy Brownback and Michael A. Kuhn, "Understanding Outcome Bias," *Games and Economic Behavior* 117 (2019): 342-360.

28 David Hume, "An Enquiry Concerning Human Understanding," in *Seven Masterpieces of Philosophy* (Oxfordshire, UK: Routledge, 2007): 191-284.

29 Jonathan Baron and John C. Hershey, "Outcome Bias in Decision Evaluation," *Journal of Personality and Social Psychology* 54, no. 4 (1988): 569.

outcome, as the decision in both cases bears the same probability of success. Such evaluation punishes practitioners for only holding knowledge of the present, not the future. For instance, when CapitalOne was compromised in 2019 (*https://oreil.ly/ 3p3_9*), there was talk of how CapitalOne's more modern cloud- and DevOps-driven strategy had failed. They experienced a security failure, for sure, but it is impossible for outsiders to truly evaluate whether the strategy itself represented a failure.

These biases change how we cope with failure and beguile us into believing humans are the "root cause"—a misguided notion about how systems work. Let us now turn to examining a key factor at play when status quo security blames "human error": the just-world hypothesis.

The Just-World Hypothesis

Attempting to unearth the ultimate seed that sowed failure—whether the seed is an errant human or a policy violation—is a mechanism for coping with fear. If we accept that all hangs in a delicate balance and tips into failure not due to a single event, but an unfortunate fusion of interrelated factors, then the world feels like a more "disordered and dangerous place."[30]

This concept naturally fuels fear. Humans prefer believing the world is an orderly, just, and consequential place, which is known as the *just-world hypothesis*. Believing that the same components and procedures can just as easily produce success and failure, that there is not a single event that sets destiny, contradicts the just-world hypothesis. Unfortunately, this is precisely how the just-world hypothesis poisons incident review, snuffing curiosity and goading unconstructive takeaways.

If you've seen the 2019 HBO miniseries regarding the Chernobyl disaster, you'll likely be familiar with this dynamic. As the show highlights, the contributors to failure existed well before the days or even weeks leading up to the meltdown—and it was far from a linear process. As human factors engineering professor Kim Vincente points out, reduced operating power, a disabled safety system, a lack of information on system state, missing feedback for operator actions, unfamiliarity among operators for such an anomalous situation, and the complexity of the nuclear reactor itself all concurrently led to failure. Any one of those factors in isolation may not lead to a meltdown.[31] It was the alignment of unfortunate stars that led to the disaster.

---

30 Peter Galison, "An Accident of History," in *Atmospheric Flight in the Twentieth Century* (Berlin/Heidelberg, Germany: Springer Science & Business Media, 2013): 3-43.

31 Kim Vicente, *The Human Factor: Revolutionizing the Way People Live with Technology* (Oxfordshire, UK: Routledge, 2004).

We must view errors as the "to-be-expected byproduct or side effect of the pursuit of success under the constraints of limited resources."[32] The routes to failure are generally longer and more circuitous than we conceive, requiring us to zoom way out to a systems level.

A sneaky way to fool yourself that you are not solely blaming individual humans is to frame the blame as a protocol or policy violation; it may feel like a more neutral statement but it's still an unproductive reaction. If we believe the source of failure is by someone violating a single policy, then the typical conclusion is to resort to disciplinary measures, training programs, and writing new procedures that specify even narrower bands of behavior.

Formal policies and procedures are rarely written by those who sail the rivers of work being policed. Seldom do you see security professionals shadowing the workers whose behavior they are regulating to understand their priorities and challenges, their goals and constraints. As described earlier, we tend to denounce whoever lies closest to the error, even if the contributing circumstances are beyond their control.

Returning to the Equifax example, their security department maintained a 48-hour patching policy, which was obviously not followed for the Apache Struts vulnerability (as noted in the ex-CEO's testimony). There appeared to be no enforcement mechanism for the policy, nor a reminder within work streams. Creating words on a piece of paper and expecting them to be followed seems like an overconfident tactic. For example, requesting engineers perform integration testing on their own, and manually, is unlikely to produce meaningful outcomes—no matter how fervently you plead your case about its importance for reliability and security. But automating integration testing and incorporating it as a step in CI/CD pipelines—a practice we covered in Chapter 4—both reduces friction for engineers and ensures it's actually performed.

In 2016, a lawsuit was filed (*https://oreil.ly/rj_Ab*) against SS&C, a fintech company, alleging that a failure to follow their own policies led to millions lost in a business email compromise (BEC) scam. SS&C maintained plenty of written policies regarding the need for four people to verify transfers and to check email fields for signs of fraud, but those policies failed to prevent the incident. "Policy violations" was deemed the root cause, but a closer examination shows that there was little process or technology in place to deter the BEC. Solely implementing controls to regulate human behavior does not magically beget resilience.

A classic example outside of cybersecurity teleports us to right after World War II. Experimental psychologists Paul Fitts and Richard Jones studied how the features of

---

32 Sidney W. A. Dekker, "Accidents Are Normal and Human Error Does Not Exist: A New Look at the Creation of Occupational Safety," *International Journal of Occupational Safety and Ergonomics* 9, no. 2 (2003): 211-218.

cockpits influenced how fighter pilots made decisions, particularly errors (*https://oreil.ly/VIJFo*). The location of controls would change between cockpits, leading to confusion and use of the wrong control. Fitts and Jones chose to dig deeper, focusing on improving the design of displays and controls in cockpits rather than trying to train away the "human error." This design overhaul helped pilots process information more quickly, which supported smarter action.

Guidance will serve us better than prescribing policies and procedures, as will investing effort in helping teams—or ourselves—follow this guidance. This guidance must stay tethered to reality, not ignoring the demands, dilemmas, and workflows of those who fall under the policy's purview. For example, checklists can be a valuable aid to help practitioners remember important safety steps. However, as we'll discuss more in the next chapter, checklists are only productive if they are built on an understanding of each step in the workflow and insert security at the right point.

Guidance must encourage safer contexts, not lord over human behavior with an iron fist. Across other disciplines that have grappled with the problem of systems safety, engineering controls—sustaining safety via design—are the preferred method of reducing failure. We'll discuss the priority of security-by-design, the right way to craft security guidance, and how to avoid the trap of behavioral control more in the next chapter.

This brings us to an approach for more productively dealing with security failures, discarding "human error," the blame game, behavioral control, and the just-world hypothesis during this phase. That approach is to ask neutral practitioner questions.

Neutral Practitioner Questions

Unfortunately, simply being aware of hindsight bias, outcome bias, and the just-world hypothesis does not curtail their occurrence. What does help reduce these unproductive biases that ooze into our incident review is asking *neutral practitioner questions*. These questions re-create the context surrounding an event and ask practitioners what actions they would take given this context. The answers give us insight into what most practitioners would consider a reasonable course of action, which we can compare against what transpired. It can also help us identify additional points of confusion or potential for error beyond what the case in question surfaced.

For instance, imagine you are an accountant receiving a new request to transfer money for one of your premier clients. You deal with hundreds of transfers per day, in addition to your job's other demands, and your clients get upset when their transfers do not happen quickly enough. You skim the request, initiate the transfer, and then one of your colleagues approves it. Would you proceed with sending the request at that point? Would you catch that it is the first instance of the client sending money abroad? As an accountant in a client-facing role, would you assume that it is fraud, rather than a new employee at the client who is less familiar with the transfer process?

Through this sort of process, "human error" instead becomes a reasonable action given the human's current circumstances. It is natural that attention will be divided, that knowledge will be imperfect, and that goals will be in conflict. If your system relies on superhumans who do not have these constraints, then failure is ingrained in your system. If your security program blames humans for making reasonable decisions given the situation's context, your security program is set up to fail.

In a sense, neutral practitioner questions sketch a portrait of local rationality. *Local rationality*, which we briefly covered in Chapter 2, deserves its own discourse, but it suggests that what we perceive as irrational behavior is only irrational when viewed without context. In the moment, given the constraints, knowledge, goals, and other aspects of a particular space and time, humans make the most rational decision available.

Local Rationality

Local rationality, more commonly referred to as "bounded rationality"[33] in behavioral science, is the theory that an actor (i.e., a human) makes the most rational decision they can in the presence of trade-offs and constrained information-processing abilities (like having incomplete information about alternative choices or finite attention). In essence, it acknowledges that it is impossible to calculate "the best" course of action in any given scenario if one lacks omniscience (which all humans, to our knowledge, do). It is a fact of humans' "cognitive and emotional architecture" (*https://oreil.ly/3FLRJ*) that they sometimes fail to achieve their goals when making decisions.

What we usually deem "rational" is a global notion of the optimal choice or behavior given a goal. Or, if we consider a specific context—such as after an incident—we'll describe "rational behavior" based on our benefit of hindsight, to which the human in the situation was not privy. This is a frequent phenomenon in status quo security. An employee clicks on a link and we say, "What were they thinking?" or "How could they be so negligent?" But if we consider their local context and constraints, we realize that this was one of maybe a hundred emails they opened that day—without consequence—and, given their goal of processing important emails before the end of the workday, clicking the link was rational. It is only in hindsight, where we can ascribe the goal of preventing phishing compromise and know the outcome, that we can deem it irrational.

If we start from the assumption that someone's behavior was rational, we cannot rely on the answer of "human error." It forces us to consider the local context that led to the behavior. From there, we can parse how we can improve our environments and

---

33 Herbert A. Simon, "Bounded Rationality," in *Utility and Probability* (London: Palgrave Macmillan, 1990): 15-18.

our systems—the context of decision making—so that this context encourages safer behavior.

This framing also makes it easier to reveal and explore what went right. What steps did the operator take that were wise, even in hindsight? What actions should operators continue? What beneficial adaptation to their local context did they perform? Were there adaptive actions they took that perhaps prevented the incident from becoming worse? Were there system properties that either reduced impact or sped up recovery? Basically, when did system adaptation and variability go well before and after the incident?

Gleaning and disseminating knowledge about what is going right in the sociotechnical system not only helps build confidence among the humans interacting with the system, but is also invaluable feedback to inform what not to change when rethinking design or operation. Similarly, if an incident does not impart adverse effects on the organization—perhaps through well-practiced incident response activities that ensured relevant signals were readily available for on-call responders—then you can make the case that the incident is an example of success, not failure. If we treat failures, like attacks, as inevitable, then when the inevitable occurs and leaves no damage we see a strong signal of resilience. And, as always, even if there is a bruise or more left by an attack, investing in preventing future incidents will do nothing more than erode resilience in some dimension by flushing precious resources down the drain of false hopes.

Chapter Takeaways

- Incidents are like a pop quiz. To prepare for them and ensure we can respond with grace, we must practice incident response activities—and can do so through chaos experimentation.

- The Effort Investment Portfolio applies to incident response too. Effort expended earlier in the software delivery lifecycle will reduce the effort required when responding to incidents (this does not mean "shift left").

- Humans often feel an impulse toward action (action bias), which can reduce effectiveness during incident response. Practicing "watchful waiting" can curtail knee-jerk reactions.

- There is no "best practice" for all incidents. The best we can do is practice incident response activities to nurture human responders' adaptive capabilities. Repeated practice of response activities through chaos experimentation can turn incidents from stressful, scary situations into confidence-building, problem-solving scenarios.

- Recovering from incidents requires adaptation, and learning is a prerequisite for this adaptation. Learning from incidents to develop memory of failure is about community, so if we blame community members for the incident, we will struggle to learn.

- A blameless culture helps organizations stay in a learning mindset—uncovering problems early and gaining clarity around incidents—rather than play the "blame game." It encourages people to speak up about issues without fear of being punished for doing so.

- There are two contributing factors always worth discussing during incident review: relevant production pressures and system properties.

- Humans at the "sharp end," who interact directly with the system, are often blamed for incidents by humans at the "blunt end," who influence the system but interact indirectly (like administrators, policy prescribers, or system designers). The disconnect between the two can be summarized as the delta between "work-as-practiced" and "work-as-imagined."

- The cybersecurity industry often (unproductively) blames users for causing failures, as evidenced by the acronym PEBKAC: problem exists between keyboard and chair. A more useful heuristic is PEBRAMM: problem exists between reality and mental model. An error represents a starting point for investigation; it is a symptom that indicates we should reevaluate design, policy, incentives, constraints, or other system properties.

- There are numerous biases that tempt us to blame human error during incidents, which hinders our capacity to constructively learn from and adapt to failure. With hindsight bias, we allow our present knowledge to taint our perception of past events (the "I knew it all along" effect). With outcome bias, we judge the quality of a decision based on its eventual outcomes. The just-world hypothesis refers to our preference for believing the world is an orderly, just, and consequential place. All of these biases warp our perception of reality.

- During incident review, use neutral practitioner questions to stay curious and intellectually honest. Neutral practitioner questions re-create the context surrounding an event and ask practitioners what actions they would take given this context. It helps sketch a portrait of local rationality: the reasonable course of action in the presence of contextual trade-offs and constrained information-processing capabilities.

CHAPTER 7

Platform Resilience Engineering

You never change things by fighting the existing reality. To change something, build a new model that makes the existing model obsolete.

—Buckminster Fuller

This chapter is where the revolution of security transforming into resilience takes shape as an organizational metamorphosis. Here, we can reimagine how a security program is crafted, dismantling the social, organizational, and process dynamics of the worn-out status quo. By necessity, it becomes a resilience program to resist the persistent "production pressures" that push our sociotechnical systems toward brittleness. In SCE, we transform the security program from a siloed group prescribing policies and procedures, totally divorced from the work being done, into a platform engineering effort that treats resilience as a product, prizing design-based security solutions grounded in systems thinking.

In this chapter, we'll talk about "meta design"—how software is designed, built, used, and refined through your organizational structure—and how we can support resilience through organizational structure and practices. We'll delve deeper into production pressures, discover why Platform Engineering teams are the right organizational structure to apply resilience pressures, and learn how these teams can design, build, use, and refine software that supports resilience as a product.

Production Pressures and How They Influence System Behavior

We've talked about boundaries of safe operation and how, when a system nears them, it becomes brittle and trembles precariously on the boundary of failure conditions. What forces incite the system to push toward those boundaries in a sociotechnical system? In most sociotechnical systems, this merciless compulsion is driven by production pressures: incentivization of less expensive and more efficient work. Managers often focus on short-term financial success and market survival, rather than on long-term success (including security or sustainable workload), to perform work faster and cheaper. Workers, in response, optimize for efficiency to reduce their workload and level of effort (especially when incentivized to perform work faster and cheaper). Combined, these pressures propel the system toward its boundary of safe operation, beyond which failure lurches out of the void to snatch our system in its maw, as shown in Figure 7-1.

Leanness and efficiency can compound complexity and molder the system into brittleness. As human factors researchers explain, "Economic pressures to make a system leaner can increase the complexity of interactions among its elements, tighten their coupling, and lead to a system that the slightest disruption can render dysfunctional."[1]

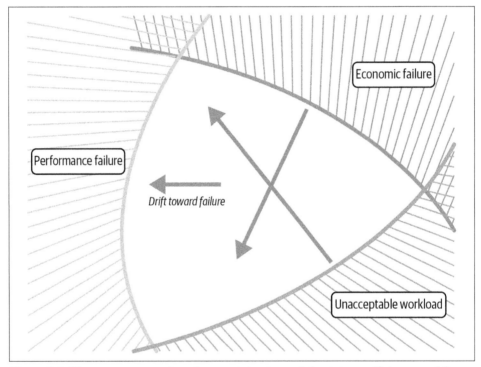

Figure 7-1. How managers and workers, striving toward short-term efficiency and financial success, push the system toward unsafe conditions (adapted from https://oreil.ly/joTlg)

1 Christopher Nemeth et al., "Minding the Gaps: Creating Resilience in Health Care," in *Advances in Patient Safety: New Directions and Alternative Approaches*, Vol. 3: Performance and Tools (Rockville, MD: Agency for Healthcare Research and Quality, August 2008).

In an imaginary world where humans value future benefits more than present benefits, we might see the opposite dynamic in our sociotechnical systems: the pressure
for quality and security would push the system toward economic failure or unacceptable workload. In reality, however, production pressures are omnipresent and it is
usually the incentives for safer and higher-quality systems that fail to apply sufficient
counter-pressure. Ideally, these three forces—management pressure toward efficiency, gradient toward least effort, and pressure for improved safety and quality—
would balance each other on a continual basis for a safe, efficient, and acceptable
(from a workload perspective) operating state, as shown in Figure 7-2.

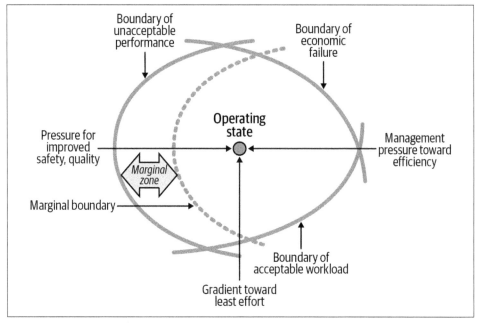

*Figure 7-2. Systems safety researcher Jens Rasmussen's modified safe operating envelope,
which shows how these three pressures result in a particular operating state[2]*

Production pressures are woven into the immemorial tapestry of life. Shortages
and pollution are not exclusive to humanity nor the Anthropocene age, and are the
result of life's "tendency to reproduce to the limit"[3] of its environment. In the case of
bacteria, life's earliest and enduring experiment, there is a perpetual cycle of responding to adverse scenarios, evolving new metabolic pathways, pushing reproduction to

2 Jens Rasmussen, "Risk Management in a Dynamic Society: A Modelling Problem," *Safety Science* 27, no. 2-3
  (1997): 183-213.

3 Lynn Margulis and Dorion Sagan, *What Is Life?* (Berkeley and Los Angeles, CA: University of California
  Press, 2000).

the limit with new shortages and pollution, and then evolving new metabolic pathways in response.

Given their sociotechnical nature, it's no different in computer systems. When facing limitation or waste, humans innovate to overcome it. Innovation incubates more production, more scale, and more possibilities, which are exploited over time; new limits and waste intrude as humans, in their indefatigable drive to produce, and push the new status quo to its limits; then humans innovate in response to these impediments. The ascendancy of cloud computing adheres to this pattern: it arose from humans innovating in response to limitations on growth, enabling new opportunities for growth, eventually leading to new forms of limitations that require new innovations.

 By conducting security chaos experiments, we can proactively evolve by introducing "mess" rather than only evolving when we face a real crisis scenario. This aligns with the continual evolution of life, as eloquently stated by evolutionary biologist and author Lynn Margulis: "A thermodynamic truth is that as heat dissipates, life organizes and its surroundings degrade. There is no life without waste, exudate, pollution. In the prodigality of its spreading, life inevitably threatens itself with potentially fatal messes that prompt further evolution. But sometimes waste can be fashioned into something useful."[4]

When we are designing security programs—what we hope evolves into resilience programs—we may feel tempted to cement guidelines and policies that are static. But doing so will accomplish little more than muzzle how humans respond in our naturally capricious systems. When we see innovation, we may think it's inherently insecure or unsafe, and try to resist it—like CISOs resisting cloud migration because it would mean IT resources were no longer under their control.[5]

Change implies new *opportunities*, not just new dangers. If we take the time to understand production pressures in the systems under our purview, we can be the ones to innovate, to enable a safer, higher-quality way to fulfill those pressures. Innovation springs forth and we panic. Our primary fears take hold—what if the new is inherently insecure or unsafe? Then we decompose into fear, uncertainty, and doubt, trying to resist innovation. Such nightmares easily evanesce in the illuminating light of resilience, however. We can be the "clever girls," like the raptors in *Jurassic Park*, who introduce looser coupling or more linearity that also beget speed boosts (as we discussed in Chapter 3).

---

4 Lynn Margulis and Dorion Sagan, *What Is Life?* (Berkeley and Los Angeles, CA: University of California Press, 2000).

5 Intel IT Center Peer Research, "What's Holding Back the Cloud?" (2012) (*https://oreil.ly/-VOYH*).

Plenty of people promulgate production pressures in organizations. We need to encourage stakeholders to apply quality and security pressures as a check against production pressures. The sharp end can help brew the resilience potion recipe while the blunt end can help the sharp end succeed in doing so via a wider viewpoint. We need leaders who can not only propagate resilience, but pave the road for the organization to actively pursue it—to pave the path to resilience, as a verb. We'll discuss how to achieve this on a continual basis throughout the chapter.

Of all the persistent threats, production pressures might be the most formidable foe to a system's resilience. Production pressures are pervasive and perpetual. Platform engineering teams, which we will discuss next, can harness this timeless tension by building solutions that support safer and higher-quality work that is also faster or cheaper to deliver—a value proposition sure to tantalize internal customers. Resilience characteristics we seek to cultivate, like easier change paths or more linear releases, can also beget the speed boosts production pressures covet, which thereby incentivizes swift adoption.

As is clear, a team that prescribes and enforces rules, guidelines, training, and other forms of behavioral-based control will be intrinsically incapable of achieving this aim. We need a dedicated team that does the hard work of designing, delivering, and maintaining design-based solutions that support resilience to attack (and to other forms of stressors and surprises). The uncomfortable truth is that we have failed in our mission if our program's success relies on behavioral enforcement. Reality does not care about how we say things "should" be. Production pressures will pat us on the head and say, "That's nice, dear" while continuing to chase thriftiness and efficiency. It is only when we are curious about reality—and in particular the local context of the humans interacting with our systems—that we can build effective resilience and security solutions that stick.

What we want in this modern security era—the *resilience* era—is for the people guiding resilience to be experts in the sociotechnical dynamics that influence the people *doing* the work. We must be systems thinkers and make it seamless for engineering teams within our organization to be so too. We must be aware of how these dynamics either help or hurt humans in realizing the goal of building high-quality, resilient systems. Software engineering expertise is necessary to understand the systems we're protecting and to build tooling that can make the easy, fast way the more resilient, secure way. But an equally important skill is a relentless focus on solving problems *for the real humans* interacting with your systems. We cannot oversee or evangelize resilient system design if we pretend that the relevant humans are either infallible or stupid. We cannot achieve systems resilience if we do not understand *who* will be interacting in and with our systems.

In the rest of this chapter, we'll describe this dedicated team—which we call a Platform Resilience Engineering team—as well as the process by which we can define real problems worth solving and deliver solutions that solve these problems with real efficacy.

What Is Platform Engineering?

When we look across the existing disciplines of IT, cybersecurity, and infrastructure engineering, they often create tools and procedures for internal users that follow "best practices" or "textbook" ideas of how those activities should look. Employees may be subjected to multistep processes (like requesting access to a new application and then facing a multiday or multiweek waiting time for access), the inability to use technologies that would help them accomplish their work (like disabling Bluetooth or internet connectivity on engineers' devices), or a daunting list of requirements that jeopardizes deadlines. It's no wonder the salesperson downloads their own meeting software, the software engineer creates hacky workarounds to use their Bluetooth keyboards, or the product manager ignores security requirements to ship code by the date promised to customers—all of which could be an influencing factor in an incident.

What these disciplines traditionally have in common is a lack of curiosity about their users. IT, cybersecurity, or infrastructure is not seen as a product used by humans, but as a project optimizing for what "best" means in a vacuum. They try to mold humans to the solution rather than molding the solution to the humans.

Platform engineering (*https://oreil.ly/Sj6xU*) (sometimes referred to as PIE: platform infrastructure engineering) is an emerging discipline that treats the delivery of employee-enabling technology like a product. Platform engineering teams create tools, libraries, components, and standard practices that other engineering teams can use to deliver systems for greater productivity and reliability. In an SCE transformation, platform engineering also includes resilience under its purview. A platform engineering approach to resilience treats security as a product, as something created through a process that provides benefits to a market. Platform engineering teams treat their internal customers' outages as their own outages, as a call to action to build a better product for them.

What is the "market?" The answer is our eternal refrain: it depends on your context. In classic platform engineering, the market is software engineering teams within your organization. It might be the organization's entire employee base, as is common with authentication schemes to internal resources. It could even be a product ultimately interacting with an organization's customers, like requiring external users to authenticate to access their accounts.

A Platform Resilience Engineering team prioritizes work that enables resilience by design rather than relying on behavior-based solutions (we'll discuss the Ice Cream

Cone Hierarchy of Security Solutions later in this chapter to navigate this problem). Rather than enforcing requirements or recommendations through policy, platform resilience engineering endeavors to build and maintain tools, libraries, frameworks, and other design-based solutions that make the more resilient way the easier and faster way.

If the Platform Engineering organization is treated like its own business unit, then the Platform Resilience Engineering suborganization is like a product line. It likely includes a suite of products supported by teams dedicated to solving a particular facet of resilience in a particular context. This is an important distinction from the traditional, siloed ivory tower model of cybersecurity. In a Platform Engineering team (whether covering resilience or another focus area), we are not dictating how work should be performed as sanctimonious authorities. We are explicitly not centralizing management of resilience or security. Our goal is to enable resilience, including security, for other teams—to decentralize management—by building supporting technology. Our goal is to make it easy for the *socio* parts of our organization's systems to promote resilience in their activities. We want to support resilience and security by design with such elegance and discretion that it slips into invisibility—software engineers need not be troubled (*https://oreil.ly/XCTYi*) by it at all. There are a few ideals we seek in a Platform Resilience Engineering team:

- We want to minimize how much the humans in our organizations must consciously think about resilience or security.

- We are mortified if these humans are hypervigilant—constantly "security aware"—because that is a path to resentment, burnout, and disappointing outcomes.

- We believe it is disgraceful and fruitless to attempt control of humans; we take pride in performing the hard work of finding ways to help them succeed, of helping the sociotechnical system *resilience* (as a verb) better.

Because of these goals, any Platform Engineering team must include software engineers who can design, build, and deliver products to end users. In fact, Platform Engineering teams often resemble Product Engineering teams for this reason, including product managers and UX experts who are (ideally) specialized in understanding a market and relevant problems. For a Platform Resilience Engineering team specifically, it will be more important to have strong engineers than resilience experts. Just like any problem domain, a good engineer (or product manager) is one who is curious about the problem and relevant context, learning quickly and continuously about it to inform the right solution to build. We'll discuss how to define user problems and solutions later in this chapter.

A Security team could adopt this platform engineering approach to resilience. In other cases, a dedicated Security team may not be needed at all; a Platform

Engineering organization could adopt resilience as a focus area and promote high-quality software to beget resilience, security, quality, and reliability benefits. A title of "VP of Resilience, CISO," reporting to the SVP of Platform Engineering or CTO, might even be on the horizon.[6] The strangler fig pattern (*https://oreil.ly/ BhDNV*) could help get us there. We can start extracting relevant responsibilities from the existing security program and migrate them to a parallel resilience team one by one. Or the Security and Platform Engineering teams could begin to combine forces and eventually merge (with IT management and compliance, like provisioning laptops or maintaining compliance reporting, kept separate).

Platform resilience engineering allows developers to ingest toolchains as a service that sustains resilience and security (even if touted as solving other goals, like speed). *Resilience engineers* will work with underlying infrastructure (like the Configuration as Code tools we discussed in Chapter 4), refining it so it better supports resilience against attack (or other adverse surprises). By doing so, developers don't have to worry about the pipelines, frameworks, libraries, or other supporting technologies; they just focus on their work, which is usually building experiences for external end users. In essence, resilience engineers are building experiences for internal end users.

Platform Engineering for Smaller Organizations

Platform engineering applies to midsize and smaller organizations too, even if it won't look quite the same as in large organizations. Many smaller organizations don't have dedicated Security teams or Infrastructure Engineering teams; everything is lumped under "IT" and they're supposed to solve all the challenges related to the technology that powers the organization. That isn't quite so different conceptually than how we described platform engineering above—just without the dedicated Product Engineering teams for different focus areas.

As a small organization, you can still follow the principles we'll describe in this chapter, adapting them to fit your resource constraints and Effort Investment Portfolio. You will still want to craft a vision, to define user problems, to design thoughtful solutions, and to implement those solutions successfully. Following these principles will ensure your resource expenditure is optimizing for ROI. It's difficult to waste money with an evidence-driven approach. It also means you can more concretely evaluate vendors based on which of your user problems they can solve, rather than relying on their promises.

---

6 Some regulations now require someone in the organization to be called the "CISO," which we envision might become a bolt-on title to whoever leads the broader resilience effort as part of platform or infrastructure engineering.

Framing security as a product elucidates the problem with status quo security. If you create a product that doesn't benefit your relevant user personas or is difficult for them to adopt, then you are trying to sell a product into a market that doesn't want it. It also means you've squandered precious resources. Imagine a company that forces their undesirable product onto the market, banning all competitive products and punishing the consumers if they do not use the product. Such a travesty is difficult to imagine because of how preposterous it would be in most modern economies. The inevitable inflexibility and inefficiency is obvious—and that is precisely what we observe with traditional cybersecurity programs that pursue this UX-negligent strategy.

We can do better. The remaining sections describe how to get to that better, more resilient world. We'll explore the lifecycle of platform engineering and how we can deliver resilience solutions for our organizations through it. We start by defining a vision for our product (whether resilience or its subset, security), defining a user problem, designing a solution for that problem, and implementing the solution.

The Blunt End Versus the Sharp End: Redux

Now that we've journeyed through each phase of software delivery and explored what activities can support system resilience, our focus returns to the blunt end: the humans who prescribe and imagine how work *should* happen, but who do not directly perform the work. They indirectly influence by shaping, through a variety of means, how work is performed by the sharp end. All the humans we discussed in previous chapters—the architects, developers, ops engineers, SREs, and more—are at the sharp end, directly engaging with software and machines and making active choices that we sometimes denigrate as "human error."

The blunt end can make mistakes too, but they are *latent*. Software architect James Hamilton estimates that as many as "80% of operations issues originate in design and development."[7] It is far easier to trace an incident to an engineer accidentally adding a vulnerability to an application than to trace it to the blunt end—whether the high-friction security policies set by the security leader that are bypassed by necessity to achieve business goals, the vulnerability scanners chosen by an executive without empathy for deployment workflows, the choice to invest in application security awareness training rather than crafting patterns or automation to make the secure way the easy way…you get the drift. Alas, the effects of these blunt end choices are only revealed over time.

If we reside at this blunt end, we must take our delivery of mitigation, management, policy, and other supervisory or advisory activities just as seriously—if not more so—than the humans at the sharp end. When we prescribe something to humans at the

---

7 James R. Hamilton, "On Designing and Deploying Internet-Scale Services," *LISA* 18 (2007): 1-18.

sharp end, we are, in effect, telling them to follow our mental model of the system (which includes their behavior). Any procedures and policies we create are based on the world we imagine. Such programmatic approaches *feel* comforting because they are simple and seem successful at a superficial level, but they are nothing more than comfort-based security. The policies and procedures based on this imaginary world are "ineffective, unsustainable, and badly suited to real work" (*https://oreil.ly/mhvf1*).

How do we ensure we guide the organization toward systems resilience with a program that is aligned with reality? *We must treat resilience as a product that we are creating and shipping to target end users.* Thus, in an SCE world, resilience—and its subfocus area, security—looks like platform engineering, and we'll explore how we can implement it in practice next.

Defining a Vision

Any product requires a long-term vision. Without an unequivocal statement on what the product must become and why, the people building the product struggle to prioritize work or choose the right trade-off when faced with uncertainty. Likewise, a Platform Resilience Engineering team must articulate a vision for resilience. They must define a perspicuous vision for how security can support the organization's survival in a world where internet-connected computers are necessary to make money, but can be accessed by attackers to make money as well.

A product vision is more than a stated direction for a particular project. It is the unifying theme for all your projects toward a defined end. An ambitious resilience vision for a Platform Engineering team might be: "Security becomes invisible to developers, while security successes become visible." Another might be: "Security becomes the organizational antidote to anxiety (*https://oreil.ly/XCTYi*), alleviating fears about attackers disrupting our growth." These are not ill-defined epics focused on functional areas, as sometimes plagues mediocre product management. These statements are at a higher level, guiding how resources are directed toward each effort and what decisions matter. In a sense, it is the thesis for your Effort Investment Portfolio.

A vision is a story. It tells people what is being built and why. In the context of improving systems resilience, the vision tells the story of why the platform team's work elevates the overall engineering team—or overall organization—to achieve superior resilience outcomes. The vision—like the Platform Engineering team that defines it—doesn't exist in a vacuum. The vision is about value: what tangible impact you will have on the engineering organization, the overall organization, or end users. It inspires us to solve real, thorny problems, not to adopt new, shiny technology. Platform engineering pioneer and engineering executive Camille Fournier elegantly captured how great platform teams succeed (*https://oreil.ly/fqR3y*):

Great platform teams can tell a story about what they have built, what they are building, and why these products make the overall engineering team more effective. They have strong partner relationships that drive the evolution of the platform with focused offerings that meet and anticipate future needs of the rest of the company. They are admired as strong engineers who build what is needed, to high standards, and they are able to invest the time to do that because they don't overbuild.

Whether you are a platform engineer, engineering manager, product manager—or executive responsible for those stakeholders—you need to be customer-focused and strategic about your platform offerings. It is a principle we cannot forget or dismiss just because the work is hard or because we want to build something "cool." As Fournier observes, "Without a clear strategy for showing impact and value, you end up overlooked and understaffed, and no amount of cool new technology will solve that problem."

Defining a User Problem

Resilience—including security—as a product starts with identifying the right user problems to tackle. We need to understand the problem—and, critically, be aligned on it—in the relevant context before we can even dream of a solution. An investment in solving one problem in a particular way means you cannot invest those resources in an alternative way or to solve another problem. If you recall how opportunity cost applies to your Effort Investment Portfolio, it is equally relevant here too.

Whether you are a Platform Engineering team, a Security team, or even a Software Engineering team looking to undergo the SCE transformation, you are assuredly resource-constrained. There's always more work that could be done, and headcount rarely grows as quickly as you'd like it to. By necessity, we must be picky about what security products we choose to build (again, a product in this case could be a tool or a practice). While we do cite numerous examples of amazing feats of platform engineering to achieve spectacular security outcomes throughout the book, building the same thing in your organization may not make sense and will instead lead you on an Icarus-style journey to the sun. As Fournier cautions (*https://oreil.ly/A61iZ*), "When platform teams build to be building, especially when they have grand visions of complex end goals with few intermediary states, you end up with products that are confusing, overengineered, and far from beloved."

Your human users might say, "We need [insert technical solution here]." But when you dig deeper into understanding *why* they want that solution, you realize it's worth trying a simpler fix first. A classic example of this is when customers ask for fancy, elaborate reporting mechanisms. They want to export high-fidelity PowerPoint charts—in their brand's color palette, no less—and that's what they ask us to create. What *really* satisfies them, however, is a simple "Download CSV" button. They get the data into their spreadsheet of choice (usually Excel), allowing them to create charts how they prefer. If we listened only to what they asked for, we'd miss the *why* and thereby an opportunity to more quickly deliver on a simpler solution.

Our job is to infer the *why* behind the complaints and challenges of our internal customers. Perhaps the solution is as simple as a configuration change. As Fournier advises, "Only build when you have exhausted the alternatives."

Local Context Is Critical

We must understand the *local* context of our users. When it comes to identifying problems, they will arise from the perspective of users who are *not* exclusively focused on security or resilience. Considering the user perspective of the tools, workflows, policies, procedures, and training (or whatever else you cook up) is nonnegotiable. Unless we research the context of our end users, we will struggle to build security solutions that are consumable and accessible. We will introduce friction and curtail adoption, the opposite of our goal. This lack of user research and user experience (UX) consideration is a fast path for saying no to projects in the name of security (the dreaded "Department of No") rather than proposing an alternative way (*https://oreil.ly/SMvmF*) to still achieve the objective while nurturing systems resilience (or at least not degrading it).

 We need to empathize with the reality "on the ground"—the reality as humans interacting with the system experience it. Systems safety and cognitive systems engineering researcher Richard Cook's iconic observations (*https://oreil.ly/I65yR*) about reality can guide us:

- World is not nice
- Constant change
- Flaws are so common
- Maintenance is continuous
- Procedures don't match conditions
- Production pressures unbalanced
- New hazards appearing

We can't discern reality from an ivory tower where we gaze upon mortals doing their work and sneer at how they deviate from how we pontificate that work should be done. If we are to support systems resilience, we need to be curious about users' experiences and listen to their perspectives to develop sufficient mental models of the problem(s) worth solving.

User Personas, Stories, and Journeys

Of course, if we want to understand the local context of our users, we should understand who those users are. *User personas* describe a prototypical user of the system, including their functional purpose in their organization and what they care about—their goals, challenges, and adoption criteria—sometimes with a little bit about their background and experience for flavor. Defining clear user personas can help to align everyone on the type of person you're seeking to satisfy. User personas help us decide why we should build certain products and not others and why we should build them one way or another. You can even develop *buyer personas* to characterize the internal leaders who influence adoption. Internal buyers may not purchase your product with money, but they can certainly opt out of using the product based on variegated grievances. Whether dissatisfied or satisfied, these buyer personas will influence your ability to budget for maintaining the service and building future services—so planning to appease them is prudent.

Drawing on an example given by Betterment Staff Security Engineer Omar Biggle (*https://oreil.ly/-EfU4*), let's say you want to deploy a web application firewall (WAF). Your user persona is likely an infrastructure engineer, or whoever handles the tech stack underlying your application, while the buyer persona is perhaps their boss's boss. You'd want to ensure their goals are clear—like deploying reliable infrastructure, ensuring applications can scale, and demonstrating a tangible contribution to business growth—as well as their challenges—like having way too many projects going on at the same time, the push-pull of being both strategic *and* tactical, and not wanting to be blamed when things go wrong. From there, you want to talk to and, more importantly, listen to any infrastructure engineers who are willing to chat to understand how their context would be impacted by a WAF. Would it change the way HTTP errors are handled? If so, then documentation or other mitigations might be necessary so they aren't lost when encountering errors or looking at confusing error monitoring output. The team lead—the buyer—is perhaps focused on latency at all costs. Listening to their perspectives and context can help us understand how implementing this kind of mitigation would impact their work and therefore informs both what problem to solve and how best to solve it (as we'll discuss more in the next section).

While there is no end to the questions you can ask to get curious about engineers' perspectives and identify problem areas, here are some thoughtful ones to start:

- What is the thing you spend the most time on that doesn't deliver value? What do you swear at every day? (Common answers might include their IDE setup or "flaky" tests.)

- How well do you think you understand the various components of the system? How would you stack-rank your understanding? (Cross-referenced against which components they work on.)

- What would you be embarrassed about having someone discover if they took over your role that you haven't figured out a way to solve?

- What is the biggest technical risk you believe you have?

- How many steps does it take for you to accomplish your most important work? Are there any steps where you think, "Why can't someone else handle this?"

- If someone new joined, where would you have to hold their hand the most?

- What takes you the longest to find? (This could be information, a tool, a feature.)

- If someone asked, "Why is this not working *again*?" which thing would you immediately think they were referencing? What if they said, "Why is this such garbage?"

- What do you wish you used more? What is keeping you from using it more?

- What is the thing that makes you question your skills or knowledge?

- Are there any components you think are adopted because management/leadership wants them in place? If engineers suddenly had full purchasing authority, what would they rip out and what would they add?

These questions can shape the user stories—or, even better, user journeys—we create that document our understanding of the problem and the local context of the user. A *user story* is a description of the outcome the user seeks from a feature. It isn't supposed to be a description of how the feature works or why it's cool from a technical perspective, but instead is presented from the perspective of the human using the feature to accomplish some sort of goal.

 A *user journey* (*https://oreil.ly/oFdI5*) is a "visualization of the major interactions shaping a user's experience," whether solving a particular problem or interacting with a particular product or service. It helps us understand why and when interactions unfold, revealing the emotional and cognitive highs and lows a human experiences. It provides a visual way of empathizing with our user's internal and external context, and helps us define where there are opportunities to make their experience better.

Table 7-1 explores some basic user stories you might define as a Platform Resilience Engineering team to understand and prioritize the problems worth solving.

Table 7-1. Example user stories for a Platform Resilience Engineering team

User persona	User story
Software developer	I want to release code that works and is safe so that I can move on to my next assigned task. Coming back to old features and the code that powers them to fix a bug or make them compliant is super tedious.
Infrastructure engineer	I want service infrastructure provisioned automatically, even as service requirements change from release to release and as traffic fluctuates.
Product manager	The last thing I want to worry about is how to incorporate resilience or security features. I'm already swamped trying to prioritize and define what features we need to build to satisfy our end users. I don't want my engineers distracted by building things to meet security requirements.
Software architect	I want to architect a system that scales and facilitates resilience to traffic spikes (including DoS), but I don't have enough time to get in the weeds on what kinds of platforms will help us more loosely couple, like which type of isolation is best.
Lead engineer	I'm expected to get my team to ship stuff by the date we promised. If my release is slowed down because of a security review or needing to tune a security tool, my neck is on the line and I'll just go around the process to meet the deadline.

Revealed Versus Stated Preferences

Humans are curious creatures. Sometimes we answer questions in the way we *wish* were true rather than the way they're actually true. When conducting user research, remember that what people *say* is their preference is not always accurate. In economics, this dichotomy is referred to as "stated" versus "revealed" preferences.[8] *Stated preferences* are the ones we state when answering questions like "Do you prefer X or Y?" Revealed preferences are the ones we demonstrate in practice—that we choose Y rather than X.

For instance, most people, if asked, "Would you rather donate $100 to charity or spend $100 on your favorite vice?" would answer "donate to charity." That is our earnest intention in the hypothetical scenario and most of us like to feel like generous people. But if $100 fell from the sky into your hand—and assuming your basic living expenses were already met at present—you might not be as decisive (but, as you read this, you might bristle at this assumption because beliefs about ourselves are highly sensitive!).[9]

As part of defining user stories, we must understand how humans make trade-offs under pressure in practice—because, as we keep stressing, pressure is persistent and omnipresent.

---

8 Kaat De Corte et al., "Stated Versus Revealed Preferences: An Approach to Reduce Bias," *Health Economics* 30, no. 5 (2021): 1095-1123.

9 J. A. Bouma and M. J. Koetse, "Mind the Gap: Stated Versus Revealed Donations and the Differential Role of Behavioral Factors," *Land Economics* 95, no. 2 (2019): 225-245.

Understanding How Humans Make Trade-Offs Under Pressure

One theory of human decision making is that humans calculate the probabilistic outcomes of different choices, choosing the option that maximizes their utility. This is the "rational" account describing how *Homo economicus* behaves. Probability theory is a fantasy of human decision making.[10] The scientific discipline of risk management, true to the strange vagaries of history, pushed a probabilistic definition of risk onto society, despite society not interacting with uncertainty in probabilistic terms.[11] In contrast, another theory is that humans optimize for cognitive efficiency, using speedy shortcuts and other tricks to make quick decisions with "good enough" accuracy.[12] These shortcuts are referred to as "bias" and have served our species well for survival across a variety of environmental contexts.

The problem is that much of our technology—and especially our security—is designed under the assumption of bias-free decision making. Even worse, technology is typically designed with the assumption that the designer's priority matches the user's priority. Assuming that we have a perfectly rational human being, they will still manage to click on phishing links in emails because being able to archive it as "complete" outweighs the risk of compromise.

At the root of this issue—in cybersecurity, as in other industries—is that policies target the slower, rational part of our brain rather than the fast and automatic part, "despite the evidence demonstrating the importance of automatic processing in decision making."[13] If we can't just tell humans what to do, is the answer some sort of nihilism—that whatever security strategy we architect is meaningless due to human nature? Of course not.[14]

Humans make mistakes, but they also make the right choices given constraints that only later seem like bad choices because of the resulting outcome (outcome bias). The sharp end—the human users interacting with our systems—will adapt their work based on the priorities and incentives presented to them. Work, then, involves constant navigation of trade-offs under competing pressures.

---

10 Any introductory behavioral economics material suffices here, but we recommend: Richard H. Thaler's *Misbehaving: The Making of Behavioral Economics* (New York: W.W. Norton & Company, 2016).

11 Preston Cline, "The Etymology of Risk," working paper (Cambridge, MA: Harvard Education Graduate School of Education, 2004).

12 It's worth noting that individuals with autism spectrum disorder (ASD) exhibit less of the tendency toward cognitive efficiency during decision making, leading to "enhanced rationality." Liron Rozenkrantz et al., "Enhanced Rationality in Autism Spectrum Disorder," *Trends in Cognitive Sciences* 25, no. 8 (2021): 685-696.

13 Dominic King et al., "Approaches Based on Behavioral Economics Could Help Nudge Patients and Providers Toward Lower Health Spending Growth," *Health Affairs* 32, no. 4 (2013): 661-668.

14 Nihilism is never the answer. See, among others, Nietzsche and Camus.

In the presence of goal confusion and conflict, no amount of specified process will help us resolve it. The blunt end determines our goals and values around effectiveness, efficiency, cost, safety, security, and quality, and then the sharp end adapts work accordingly.[15] Humans performing the work (versus managing the work) are constantly tweaking how they perform work based on these influences, no matter how rigidly defined the work is.

We talked about local rationality in Chapter 6: what is rational given a specific, local context may be seen as "irrational" at the global level. In aggregate, when you have humans making lots of locally rational decisions, what emerges is even less likely to match what is perceived as globally rational or even intended.[16]

The first crucial aspect of human behavior important for resilience and security UX is that decision making—especially in enterprise contexts—is informed by competing goals and the harrowing pressure required to meet those goals. This emphasizes the urgency of understanding production pressures. The accountant who wires money out to attackers because of a business email compromise does so for a reason (and spoiler alert: it isn't stupidity). What drives the accountant's opportunities for promotion? What kind of performance or actions would lead to the accountant being fired? Does the Accounting team base their success metrics on minimizing transaction processing time? Many, but certainly not all, performance goals held by an organization will conflict with security. Gatekeeping rejects this reality, while a resilience program accepts this reality and finds a way to work around it.

Being curious about workarounds

It's valuable for us to also investigate how humans are solving problems successfully. What workarounds have our customers invented to adapt to certain conditions or scenarios? Where are problems already being solved via clever adaptation? What can we learn from them? As Rankin et al. advise: "Adaptations or work-arounds are pointers to identify a poor fit between technology and procedures and the actual conditions of work. From a resilience perspective, the focus is on the system's ability to cope with increasing demands and compensate for the increased demand by adapting its performance."[17]

These new ways of working are *not* a call to action to "solve" them away. The best solution might be to design explicit support for this invented functionality, making these alternate courses of action easier to complete. Remember, "workarounds" may compensate for inadequate or improper design, or for issues emerging from

---

15 Rankin, "Resilience in Everyday Operations," 78-97.

16 Ibid.

17 Ibid.

components. Production pressures are like a pressure cooker, forcing people to find ways of coping with heavier workloads and demands for efficiency—doing more with less.

 Roman concrete is a fun example of this in action. For many years, scholars wondered why Roman concrete fared better than our modern version (especially in terms of durability when exposed to water). What was the secret ingredient? It was in front of them the whole time—a workaround disregarded as sloppy, low-quality work, but that, in fact, granted Roman concrete the self-healing properties that our modern concrete lacks: lime casts (*https:// oreil.ly/m3pI6*).

The law of the land is constant compensation, whether for design flaws or unrealistic production demands. We don't want to strip those compensatory mechanisms away without knowing how they influence resilience.

Respecting cognitive load

The connection between cognitive load, a concept from behavioral science, and SCE may not be readily apparent. However, just as we must embrace the reality of failure as a philosophical underpinning of SCE, we must also embrace the reality of how humans behave. Humans, like computers, possess finite levels of computational resources. When those resources are burdened by heavy overhead, errors or disruption are more likely to occur in both software and wetware (our brains).

Cognitive load represents the level of resource overhead occurring in wetware, typically considered through the lens of humans learning or solving problems.[18] Because of the brain's processing constraints, it is essential to assess cognitive load when designing systems for use by humans—that "working memory architecture and its limitations should be a major consideration."[19] Just like the variety we encounter in computer systems, there are some brains capable of high levels of performance and some possessing less performant processing capabilities.[20] Each brain is optimally efficient at different levels of working memory, described as "a limited amount of information that can be temporarily maintained in an accessible state" in support of

18 Paul A. Kirschner et al., "From Cognitive Load Theory to Collaborative Cognitive Load Theory," *International Journal of Computer-Supported Collaborative Learning* 13 (2018): 213-233.

19 Fred Paas et al., "Cognitive Load Measurement as a Means to Advance Cognitive Load Theory," *Educational Psychologist* 38, no. 1 (2003): 63-71.

20 Susanne M. Jaeggi et al., "On How High Performers Keep Cool Brains in Situations of Cognitive Overload," *Cognitive, Affective, & Behavioral Neuroscience* 7, no. 2 (2007): 75-89.

cognitive processing.[21] Just as you want to ensure your code can successfully run on any relevant computers within your system, you want to ensure that any tools, policies, programs, procedures, and other system components that you design can successfully run on the relevant brains within your overall system.

> ## Coding with Your Prototype to Assess Usability
>
> Fournier espouses the importance of figuring out usability and getting a "feel" for the problem, especially by trying out the prototypes we build in our own software engineering workflows:
>
> "In fitting with the goal of really understanding the feel of a problem, having platform engineers build an application with a prototype idea for a platform within it, then using the lessons from that project to extract a more general system, is a productive way to quickly iterate an idea into something that is usable. After all, the hardest part of the product side of platform engineering is figuring out usability. Want to know how people will actually write code around this offering? Well, writing code around the offering yourself is a good way to figure that out."

Recognizing cognitive load when spelunking through user problems means we appreciate that human attention is a finite and precious resource. UX is more than just figuring out the right button placement to drive clicks; it explores how information should be presented and how to help practitioners better perform their work. Security gatekeepers are often stereotyped as believing security should be the top priority in any situation—but this doesn't mean it will be when so many other things are competing for limited cognitive bandwidth. When starting on the path of conducting user research for your resilience or security program, you should be in question-asking mode. What sorts of events attract user attention? How can you draw their attention toward potential security concerns instead? While it may be tempting to brainstorm answers on your own, you can't answer these questions without user research; otherwise, it simply amounts to guesswork.

---

21 Eryn J. Adams et al., "Theories of Working Memory: Differences in Definition, Degree of Modularity, Role of Attention, and Purpose," *Language, Speech, and Hearing Services in Schools* 49, no. 3 (2018): 340-355.

It's difficult to figure out how to stop being a gatekeeper if you don't understand how you're gatekeeping in the first place. What goals are you hindering when you implement a security policy? What cognitive load exists when a user encounters a security tool in their workflow? Understanding how the human brain works, in all its messy glory, will help you craft smarter security strategies, because you can design your security program to work *with* brains, rather than against them.

Designing a Solution

We've defined a vision, relevant problems, and the user personas subject to those pains. Now it's time to design a solution that will help solve one of those problems and fulfill our vision. This section will cover how we can design successful solutions and what we must prioritize when doing so.

The Ice Cream Cone Hierarchy of Security Solutions

How should we prioritize the types of solutions we design? Are certain solutions better than others if our goal is to support system resilience to attack (and other types of failure)? Yes, they are—and the most successful options are the ones pursued *least* in traditional cybersecurity. We want to design solutions that empower, rather than impede, humans at the sharp end. We want to design solutions that help our socio-technical systems operate with high quality and security rather than to be "secure" at a single point in time. We want to design solutions that demonstrate tangible value (like during chaos experiments). And we want to design solutions that encourage the resilience potion recipe we introduced in Chapter 1.

We will draw on Manuele's "Safety Decision Hierarchy,"[22] but tailor it for computer systems rather than industrial ones, resulting in the Ice Cream Cone Hierarchy of Security Solutions, depicted in Figure 7-3, which can guide our prioritization of effort when solving a problem.

---

22 Fred A. Manuele, "Risk Assessment & Hierarchies of Control," *Professional Safety* 50, no. 5 (2005): 33-39.

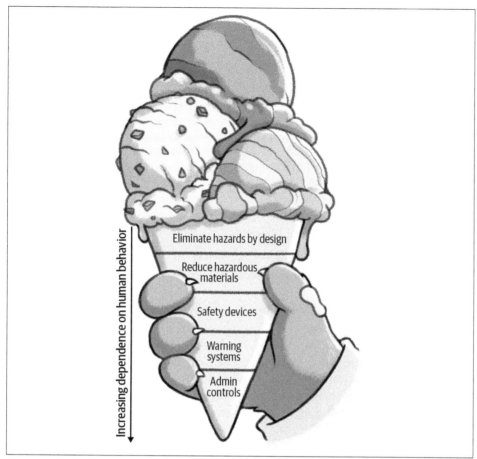

Figure 7-3. *The Ice Cream Cone Hierarchy of Security Solutions*

The Ice Cream Cone Hierarchy of Security Solutions visualizes how we should prioritize resilience and security mitigations. A handy heuristic is that the *less* the solution relies on human behavior to succeed, the better it is; if it is entirely dependent on human behavior to succeed (like a policy), it is our least preferred option. As psychology professor and author James Reason opined, "Human fallibility is like gravity, weather, and terrain, just another foreseeable hazard."[23] So, measures that rely on human behavior—from warning systems down to control measures, like training— are inferior to solutions that eliminate hazards. Once we get closer to the bottom of the cone, we can't scoop as much resilience ice cream into it. In between these ends are solutions that somewhat rely on human behavior, like any safety devices that can

---

23 James Reason, *Managing the Risks of Organizational Accidents* (Oxfordshire, UK: Routledge, 2016).

be forgotten or bypassed. Relying on human behavior makes the security solution unreliable for all the reasons we discussed in the last section: our cognitive resources are finite, we face competing pressures, we can be tired, stressed, distracted—an astonishing kaleidoscope of physiological and psychological experiences that naturally influence how we make choices. Plus, most humans have better things to be doing with their time and energy than expending effort on security.

 From a high-level goal perspective, we want to craft solutions that support the ingredients of the resilience potion recipe from Chapter 1:

1. Critical functions
2. Safety boundaries (thresholds)
3. Space-time interactions
4. Learning culture and feedback loops
5. Flexibility and openness to change

When we hear something failed due to "user error" or a problem persists because "humans keep doing X wrong," we can recharacterize it through the Ice Cream Cone Hierarchy of Security Solutions. If the "error" is due to human perception, it's a red flag that a "poorly-designed system, product, or environment"[24] is adulterating human interactions in our system. It's a call to action to brainstorm better solutions, and we can use the hierarchy to inform our priorities, starting at the top of the cone with the most successful solutions for supporting resilience down to the least successful:

1. System design and redesign to eliminate hazards.
2. Substitute less hazardous methods or materials.
3. Incorporate safety devices and guards.
4. Provide warning and awareness systems.
5. Apply administrative controls (guidelines, training, etc.).

The next section will go through each solution category and discuss why we either want to prioritize or deprioritize it.

---

24 Marc Green, "Perception & Human Factors" (*https://oreil.ly/RSk3D*).

Hazards are the potential for harm. Hazards include the characteristics of technology (things) and the actions or inactions of people (activities) that can produce harm.[25]

System Design and Redesign to Eliminate Hazards

When designing solutions to solve resilience challenges in our organizations, we should first consider how they could be solved through system design or redesign. Design-based solutions that eliminate hazards feature two key traits:

- They do not depend on human behavior.
- They provide complete separation of the user from the hazard.

Both features engender more reliable success outcomes. Let's make this more concrete through some software examples.

Let's say that your organization is reeling from a breach of customers' payment data. Someone proposes another 20 hours of "secure development" training so software engineers "stop writing exploitable bugs." You, now wise in the ways of resilience, shake your head and explain how that will never work (because mistakes are inevitable, among all the other lessons we've learned about complex sociotechnical systems in the book thus far). Instead, you propose breaking apart your application's monolith into smaller services with isolated access to data. The billing service will have access to payment data, as it must, but now the rest of the application—all the other services that make up its functionality—will not have access to that data. If your order volume is proprietary, then this also gives you the benefit of being able to partition and slice up data to keep it private (as a form of classification or compartmentalization).

An alternative you could also propose is to outsource payment data handling to a third party—you've eliminated the hazard by design by not even storing or handling payment data in your systems. Many Software Engineering teams already do this for tricky engineering problems, like content delivery (to handle scale, regionality, and caching) or mutual exclusion, which will let your database handle the hazard instead.

We discussed a number of design-based solutions in Chapter 3 in the context of introducing looser coupling and linearity in our systems to support resilience from the earliest phases of a project. Those design choices apply here too. Isolation, for instance, usually does not rely on human behavior and can completely separate the user from the hazard (including machine users, like other services interacting with another service). Table 7-2 lists the ideas from Chapter 3 for looser coupling and

---

25 Manuele, "Risk Assessment & Hierarchies of Control," 33-39.

linearity, whittled to just the mechanisms that either eliminate hazards by design or substitute less hazardous methods or materials by design (which we'll explore next).

Table 7-2. Potential design-based solutions to sustain resilience (via looser coupling and linearity)

Goal outcome	Potential mechanisms
Can absorb the impact of surprises with spare capacity	Buffers, failover, autoscaling, queueing, backpressure, job systems, background/batch processing
Independent, or flexible dependencies	Isolation, declarative dependencies (like Infrastructure as Code)
Easier to untangle interactions after incidents	Isolation, standardization, design documentation
Easier to debug and troubleshoot at runtime	Standardization, iterative design, break-glass debugging mechanism with audit
Cost-effective over the long term	Standardization
Issues arising from interactions are more visible	Failover, isolation
Supports reusability	Standardization, design documentation, libraries, component model, specifications
New changes can be implemented independently	Isolation, iterative design, design documentation
Adding new components increases system resilience	Failover, buffers
Processing delays are tolerable	Isolation, failover, autoscaling, queues, job systems, background/ batch processing, asynchronous processing
Order of sequences can be changed	Message passing, queues, background/batch processing
Alternate methods available to achieve the goal	Design documentation, standardization, specifications, common protocols
Slack in resources possible	Autoscaling, spare capacity/failover
Buffers and redundancies are natural; emergent from the design	Message buses, queueing, log-oriented designs, resource pools
Substitutions are natural, available, and extensive; emergent from the design	Failover, standardization, specifications, common protocols
Logical isolation	Sandboxing/virtualization, physical isolation
Dedicated resources	Virtualization, resource limits/allocation, physical isolation, functional diversity
Isolated subsystems	Sandboxing/virtualization
Easy substitutions	Fast, easy change paths; standardization; machine-verifiable schemas and protocol definitions, functional diversity
Few surprising causal chains	Standardization, choose "boring" technology
Single-purpose, isolated controls	Virtualization; modularity, functional diversity
Direct, documented information	Design documentation
Extensive understanding	Standardization, choose "boring" technology, common "raw" software materials (languages, libraries, tooling, protocols, data formats), design documentation

Substitute Less Hazardous Methods or Materials

Substituting less hazardous methods or materials is the second-to-the-top level of the Ice Cream Cone Hierarchy of Security Solutions because it also doesn't depend on user behavior. Implicit in this solution type is the ability to substitute or swap components—to preserve possibilities, as we've discussed throughout the previous chapters. More generally, paving the road for less hazardous methods or materials through design helps us encourage looser coupling and more linear interactions across spacetime (the importance of which we discussed at length in Chapter 3).

How do hazardous methods look? You likely have heard the folk advice, "Don't roll your own crypto" (originating from a time when crypto was still primarily associated with cryptography). Generalizing this advice is precisely what we mean by substituting less hazardous methods: you shouldn't roll your own database, logging pipeline, observability, and so forth, either. Hazardous methods manifest as injection from an attack perspective; SQL injection (SQLi), for instance, can be characterized as the result of rolling your own database query builder.

When should we substitute hazardous methods, ensuring we don't "roll our own" and use standardized tech instead? As we discussed in Chapter 3, when we don't need to differentiate at a software level, we should standardize and "choose boring." If our competitive advantage is in a particular facet of infrastructure or software, then we should invest more effort in those areas and potentially "roll our own," ideally considering design-based mitigations to potential hazards. For example, if industrial software company's differentiator is operating at scale, then it is worth the resource investment for engineers to figure out the multiregion, distributed nature of their systems. Or if an ad tech company's differentiator is constructing user profiles and refining them into usable segments, it is worth the resource investment to build and maintain a reliable machine learning system that can perform that function successfully.

We need to remember that a core ingredient in our resilience potion recipe is flexibility and willingness to change. We should always be curious about how we can construct a paved road for easier changes, whether faster deployment of resilience and security-related configurations or faster patching.

How do hazardous materials look in software? If the hot memory safety mess of C or C++ comes to mind, you aren't alone. Remember what we discussed in Chapter 4 about memory unsafety in the context of "raw materials" when writing code. It's safe to say that substituting C or C++ code for a memory safe language (of which there are many) would reduce such hazards. That isn't to say other languages are immune to safety problems that haunt us in other ways, but that belongs in a separate tome.

In general, any technology—whether libraries, code snippets, frameworks, and so on—that is harder to understand is more hazardous. "Boring" technology that is easier to mental-model, is better documented, and offers a supporting community is a less hazardous substitute.

Of course, we could try a design-based mitigation like restricting the ability for dinosaurs to reproduce by making them all female. But life, uh, finds a way. Better still is the ability to swiftly recover by design, a privilege lacking in other domains. The managers in *Jurassic Park* couldn't just kill and restart the dinosaur workloads automatically and on demand in the event of unintended behavior. Even defining intended behavior in the first place is impossible when dealing with featherful, breathing murder machines. We are blessed as computer people that we can design to build isolated, single-purpose components.

Choice architecture

How do we substitute less hazardous methods in practice? A popular tool from the behavioral economics sphere can help us out: choice architecture. Choice architects "have the responsibility for organizing the context in which people make decisions."[26] While it's scarcely used in status quo security, you've likely heard of similar practices under different guises. For instance, in consumer software, choice architecture is used to encourage repeat behaviors to improve user retention. In a resilience context, our focus will be on "nudging"—encouraging a particular decision making path for—users toward desired behavior through smart design.[27] Inculcating nudges in design can encourage security in a natural way, rather than feeling like an intrusion.

How do you start conceptualizing choice architecture in a resilience or security program? How do you reflect on user behaviors to inform the design of your nudges? Much of your security choice architecture will likely be aimed at nudging people *away* from making poor security choices, rather than toward a single, specific outcome. Not all poor security choices are the same. Generally speaking, humans tend to have unintended actions rather than inappropriate intentions. Of course, there are instances where rogue employees will pillage customer data for espionage purposes, or will, in a fit of rage, delete an entire database as retaliation for a perceived slight against them. However, for the purposes of your security programs, you should focus on curtailing unintended actions, because mistakes are within your control, while the intentions of users are not.

Understanding mistakes versus malice will help you focus your attention on the design of systems with which the humans interact—including software, devices, protocols, and work environments.

---

26 Richard H. Thaler et al., "Choice Architecture" in *The Behavioral Foundations of Public Policy*, (Princeton, NJ: Princeton University Press, 2013): 428-439.

27 Cass R. Sunstein, "Nudging: A Very Short Guide," *Journal of Consumer Policy* 37 (2014): 583-588.

Remember the concept of belief prompting from Chapter 2? You can also use this to model your end users' workflows in decision trees. Your employees have an objective in mind—like close the deal or deploy the new feature or pay suppliers. Assume they will do anything they can to achieve that goal, from easiest to hardest. Your first branch of the tree is whatever their workflow would be without any policy or mitigation at all.

Now, if you add a security requirement, how does their workflow change? The goal here is *not* to raise the cost of doing work (despite the infosec industry's best efforts!). The goal is to be curious about their experience and examine the problem at hand from multiple facets and perspectives. It requires performing user research to capture these workflows, but better now than blaming policy violations post-incident when there was no chance it wouldn't be bypassed. Once you feel confident you've identified and defined a user problem worth solving, you can use the decision tree to explore the second-order effects of your security program and visualize how you're changing work-as-done.

Defaults: The principle of least resistance

One of the more powerful tools in the "nudge" arsenal is the use of defaults—placing the ideal behavior on the path of least resistance.[28] A default means that users must opt out of that option or path, which substantially shaves friction caused by the user needing to opt in. A classic example of the power of defaults is making 401k contributions opt-in rather than opt-out. As shown by experimental evidence, automatic 401k enrollment results in 85% participation rates, a dramatic increase from the 26% to 43% participation before automatic enrollment kicked in.[29] In safety outside of security, newer cars lock by default when you walk away with the keys, which means human behavior no longer determines safety.

While the use of defaults as a tactic for encouraging more secure behavior isn't widespread in traditional cybersecurity programs, it can promote less hazardous methods or materials—like automating provisioning of vetted configurations in CI/CD pipelines as a form of default (like we touched on in Chapter 4). As a general principle, we should strive to provide teams with preferred choices of frameworks, middleware, orchestrators, authZ/authN patterns, and IaC tools with templates.

---

28 Laurens van Gestel et al., "Do Nudges Make Use of Automatic Processing? Unraveling the Effects of a Default Nudge Under Type 1 and Type 2 Processing," *Comprehensive Results in Social Psychology* (2020): 1-21.

29 James J. Choi et al., "For Better or for Worse: Default Effects and 401(k) Savings Behavior," *Perspectives on the Economics of Aging* (2004): 81-126.

By blessing these options by default, we endorse standardization and reduce choice overload for teams. We sow a more resilient and higher-quality default for the organization, even if some teams opt out and select other options. If we receive feedback that users are upset about security policies getting in the way of their work, this indicates opportunities for further user research (as discussed in the last section).

Incorporate Safety Devices and Guards

Safety devices and guards are the start of what traditional cybersecurity conceives as a security "solution" (although truly old-school security—think pre-'90s—viewed security as a design problem too).[30] These are mitigations that can be circumvented, forgotten, or defeated by users. If you deploy through a CI system, but have admin keys, you could deploy manually if you still really wanted to—making the solution at least partially reliant on human behavior.

GitHub's Dependabot is another worthy example of a safety device. The automatic updates with few-click deploys bump it up the Ice Cream Cone from a warning system (which we'll discuss next) as compared with similar tools like npm audit. With that said, Dependabot can help us (*https://oreil.ly/WTegx*) substitute less hazardous materials by design if it auto-approves identified changes and redeploys upon a successful CI run.

Rate limiting exemplifies how a solution is either a safety device or warning system depending on implementation. If rate limiting only generates an alert for a human to digest, interpret, and act upon, it's a warning system. If it actively limits or blocks requests, then it's a safety device. Harrowing tales from real breaches reveal the phantasmic nature of protection alleged by solutions reliant on human behavior. A cybersecurity incident at Uber in 2022 (*https://oreil.ly/OnL7g*) cited a human verifying a 2FA request that was not their own as the "cause" of the failure. Of course, 2FA is a warning system, not a safety device. The more pertinent question is: why was the attacker able to trigger an avalanche of 2FA attempts, aggravating the human into acquiescence? Rate limiting on the attackers' persistent requests would restrict a deluge of 2FA requests, either granting more time for responders to investigate the repeated "deny" responses from the real user or, if it automatically locked the account in question, forcing the attacker to scurry to other options.

Venturing into programming language land, the same configuration-dependent characterization of safety devices applies. A static type system is a safety device because programs that don't type-check don't compile, but a dynamic type system is a warning system—it makes us aware of issues, but requires our action to address them.

---

30 Donald MacKenzie, *Mechanizing Proof: Computing, Risk, and Trust (Inside Technology)* (Cambridge, MA: The MIT Press, 2004).

Type Checking in Programming Languages

Type checking involves the question of whether or not data flowing through the sentence is valid (if grammatically correct). Consider the sentences: "I fed Geralt fish" versus "I fed Geralt freedom." Geralt is of the type "cat." When you feed, you want something that can be fed into another type. Some languages—commonly referred to as statically typed languages—will tell us up front that "freedom" isn't compatible with the feed operation on Geralt. Others—commonly referred to as dynamically typed languages—will only throw an error when you try to do it.

If we instead try "I fed Geralt stars," how each language handles it may be different. Languages generally want to remove ambiguity, so they'll bind "stars" to something to avoid confusion. Nevertheless, "overloading" is possible, in which there are multiple interpretations of a term and conversions between types. At some point, the machine must resolve the ambiguity—and the way the compiler resolves this ambiguity may not be the way the human maintaining the code expects (as is true with integer promotion (*https://oreil.ly/KDcYT*) in C).

In Chapter 5, we highlighted several scalability signals that serve as salutary security signals too. One such signal is billing alerts, which also illuminate the difference between safety devices and warning systems. To restrict the amount of money attackers can spend on your behalf—like by siphoning your compute resources—per-account billing *limits* are stronger than billing alerts. At present, the major CSPs don't provide tools to limit spending by account or project and alert only when unusual activity occurs or thresholds are exceeded—and you have to configure those alerts yourself. Alas, these tools are inadequate to enforce a true backstop on spend.

Bolt-on security solutions—the ones we glue onto a system after it's built—are notoriously brittle and instigate more of the "baffling" interactions that confound us when failure occurs. Is it a network fault or a problem in our IDS? This befuddlement is exacerbated by a lack of documented knowledge about those tools, leading to excess friction in diagnosing production problems. We usually think of bolt-on solutions as appliances (whether physical or virtual), like a WAF that blocks SQLi or a firewall that blocks certain IP ranges. Embedded application and OS bolt-ons like ASLR, stackguard, or allocator randomization also exist.

When bolt-ons only warn us, they are warning and awareness systems, which we'll cover next.

Provide Warning and Awareness Systems

A warning or awareness system alerts someone about an event or behavior and allows it to proceed, whereas a safety device erects some sort of barrier between the hazard and the user (but not complete separation). Warning systems are not very effective outside of laboratory settings.[31] This is known in security as well. In the Target breach of 2013, the intrusion detection system generated an alert—but it was a generically named alert that was insufficient to stimulate human behavior and therefore did not lead to recovery. Another example is the futility of certificate warnings (and the rational rejection of paying attention to them by users).[32] Richard Thaler, winner of the Nobel Memorial Prize in Economic Sciences in 2017, even cites phishing warnings (*https://oreil.ly/GGjA9*) as "sludge"—an example of friction in design that leaves users worse off, a kind of cognitive detritus.

If we read a warning like "this file might not be trustworthy because it originated elsewhere," we'll likely dismiss it.[33] After all, we've used third-party files hundreds, perhaps many thousands, of times without incident. We want to use the file for some purpose and the reward outweighs the risk, which we perceive as quite low due to experience. If we read a warning like "updating firmware; do not unplug your computer," we take it more seriously, since it is not an action we perform often. There is little benefit to us unplugging the machine while it is updating and unusable anyway. The underlying principle is that warnings rely on the user believing the hazard exists. They will be ignored when the user does not believe the hazard exists (at least in that context or that moment).[34] As human factors researcher Marc Green astutely points out, "In other words, [warnings] are most likely to fail in the very circumstances where they are most needed."

We can characterize many security tools as a warning or awareness system: alerting, monitoring, endpoint detection and response (EDR), IDS, static application security testing (SAST), dynamic application security testing (DAST), literal warning boxes in user interfaces, testing, and so on. Few security tools are reliable enough, and therefore trustworthy enough, for engineering teams to run in blocking mode. The incentive mismatch between traditional Cybersecurity teams—whose top priority is security—and Software Engineering teams—whose top priority is to build, operate, and maintain systems in production—results in selection of security tools that can hog resources, panic kernels, or cause other crashes and bottlenecks when running in production. That paradigm does not nourish resilience.

---

31 Roger L. McCarthy et al., "Product Information Presentation, User Behavior, and Safety," *Proceedings of the Human Factors and Ergonomics Society Annual Meeting* 28, no. 1 (October 1984): 81-85; S. R. Arndt et al., "Warning Labels and Accident Data," *Proceedings of the Human Factors and Ergonomics Society Annual Meeting* 42, no. 6 (October 1998): 550-553.

32 Cormac Herley, "So Long, and No Thanks for the Externalities: The Rational Rejection of Security Advice by Users," *Proceedings of the 2009 New Security Paradigms Workshop* (September 2009): 133-144.

33 As one reviewer quipped, this is the "this product contains a chemical known to the state of California to cause birth defects…" of browser security.

34 David W. Stewart and Ingrid M. Martin, "Intended and Unintended Consequences of Warning Messages: A Review and Synthesis of Empirical Research," *Journal of Public Policy & Marketing* 13, no. 1 (1994): 1-19.

It may surprise you to read that tests, for the most part, are warning systems. Their typical implementation resembles monitoring more than they guarantee quality. They make us aware of potential issues, but do not take action on them (if they do take action that does not require human intervention, then it is potentially upgraded to a safety device). An unfortunate fact of the software status quo is that inordinate trust is placed in tests written by developers and unvalidated. Code review for tests is performed, but a deep enough review to challenge the correctness and effectiveness of the test is not performed nearly enough.

Dynamic analysis and static analysis tools are similarly warning systems. They usually warn us, but do not guard us. If static analysis tools do guard against a hazard—for instance, blocking a build when a vulnerability is detected—then they become safety devices. We might jump to the conclusion, then, that we should flip any warning system into block mode and leap up the Ice Cream Cone Hierarchy of Security Solutions. How simple! Not quite.

A solution like static analysis can output findings that are arcane to many software engineers; switching it to blocking mode will only result in confused software engineers who will try to bypass it, rip it out of their CI/CD pipeline, or reach out to the Security team (or whoever implemented the solution) to navigate what they should do. Sharing knowledge is just as vital when building security solutions as it is when considering software more generally, as we discussed in Chapter 4. Any safety device or warning system that relies even in part on human behavior should have the why and when clearly documented. We must give the users the necessary context to proceed in their work so we do not become security obstructionists.

As Betterment Staff Security Engineer Omar Biggle noted (*https://oreil.ly/-EfU4*) from experience:

> You can have software that's secure in the sense that it does the right thing if you know how to make it do the right thing, but it's only "safe" if it makes the decisions for you in a way that makes it very difficult to do the wrong thing and put yourself at risk. If a security tool identifies a vulnerability, but if the developer's first instinct is to turn it off because it's too burdensome, then it's futile.

Nevertheless, warnings seduce the security blunt end—or managers and organizations more generally across complex systems—because they are cheap and place more burden on the human, rendering them a convenient safety mitigation from the manager's perspective. They swiftly discover that warnings are ineffective, however, because they rely on human behavior in large part. What is the security organization to do? They wield the blunt, fearsome weapon of enforcement. By enforcing certain behaviors, the security organization can make warnings more effective, increasing their ROI—except, enforcement defeats their purpose and purported benefits, so the ROI is actually *worse*. Enforcement is not cheap and is, in fact, quite inconvenient, eroding the very characteristics that make warnings so tempting in the first place.

Such nonsense can be avoided by capturing a broader purview of benefits and costs when considering solutions—such as by considering opportunity cost—to challenge whether an easy and cheap solution is only easy and cheap until you must add enforcement to make it effective.

Respecting human attention when alerting

In the context of limited cognitive bandwidth and competing attention, alerts often come to mind as one of the most fraught areas. Ask any on-call engineer—whether security, ops, or SRE—and they're unlikely to lament how *few* alerts they receive. They are usually crumpled under the weight of too many alerts, many of which are deemed high priority, which naturally leads to cognitive fatigue. As Caitie McCaffrey once tweeted (*https://oreil.ly/afhWz*), "Alerts that always show up red[35] don't make your systems more reliable or secure. They just teach people to ignore alerts." If everything is labeled as important, nothing is important.

To avoid this stalemate, we should always consider what kind of behavior we're encouraging, what other cognitive demands will be present on the user, and how we can incentivize the user to turn their attention toward security. In 2019, there were reports (*https://oreil.ly/26TiT*) that a major defense contractor designed an aircraft safety system to flash a big red alert that proclaimed, "CYBER ANOMALY." Big red alerts may attract attention, but what does it tell the pilot? How should the pilot react? What should they investigate? Does it apply solely to life-or-death scenarios? Are they to assume there are never false positives? We should strive for clear, actionable alerts that respect human attention.

Eliminating distractions

In any workflow with security impacts, there will be times that require the utmost attention. Our goal is to eliminate distractions at these attention-imperative times. As the authors of *Behind Human Error* noted, "Our ability to digest and interpret data has failed to keep pace with our abilities to generate and manipulate greater and greater amounts of data. Thus, we are plagued by data overload."[36]

In one study at the intersection of behavioral science, UX, and cybersecurity, experimental evidence showed that there are significant costs incurred by network operators when switching attention between different areas in a network diagram.[37] The researchers found that improved action speed doesn't actually lead to faster task

---

35 As Bea Hughes rightly noted, we should stop alerting in red and green for the colorblind anyway.

36 David D. Woods et al., *Behind Human Error*, 2nd Edition (Boca Raton, FL: CRC Press, 2010).

37 Sean W. Kortschot et al., "Measuring and Mitigating the Costs of Attentional Switches in Active Network Monitoring for Cybersecurity," *Human Factors: The Journal of the Human Factors and Ergonomics Society* 60, no. 7 (2018): 962-977.

completion. One conclusion, borne out by other research on attentional demands, is that the number of actions should be reduced, rather than trying to improve the speed at which the actions are conducted. We'll discuss this later in the context of "What Would Gilbreth Do?"

While only some of you will be building products requiring visualizations of security or resiliency data, this principle is still important to keep in mind when creating processes or automating workflows. How many actions are required for the user to take when using a vulnerability scanning tool? How many actions are in your security review exemption workflow? How many clicks or keystrokes must the user make to use the corporate VPN or access internal shared drives? Again, we must respect human attention and treat it like the precious, finite resource it is.

Apply Administrative Controls Including Guidelines and Training

Administrative controls include the application of any sort of mitigation that attempts to control human behavior. Prescribing procedures and methods of work, policies, and training are all forms of administrative control. These are stopgaps at best, if not distractions that siphon resources away from more effective and reliable solutions (like those just described).

Policies are not a panacea. The infernal quadrant for Security Obstructionism (SecObs) solutions (*https://oreil.ly/iFOU3*) features many administration controls, including:

- Manual security reviews and change approvals
- Vulnerability management outside of developer workflows
- "Gotcha" phishing exercises
- Password rotation
- Avoidance of "shadow" technology
- Shutting down modernization efforts
- Internal education programs
- Self-service security, sans guidance

Unfortunately, compliance often requires policies; sometimes policies are the *only* thing required to meet a regulatory regime. Create them to satisfy out-of-touch auditors and compliance regimes if necessary, but do not rely on them as real security solutions. This category is the flimsy bottom of the cone for a reason. There isn't much resilience ice cream that can be scooped into a teeny, pointy end piece of cone.

The reality of work is that people are not thinking about hazards; they are thinking about getting their job done. They feel the hot breath of production pressures on their neck and are trying to fulfill their duties the best they can. Attackers are an afterthought, if a thought at all. Throughout their career, they've learned that incidents—especially those requiring disclosure—are rare while policies, guidelines, procedures, and training are shoved in their faces on a routine basis. Much like jaywalking in New York City, they flout the cybersecurity cops, and the rules those cops enforce, because they have places to be and things to achieve—and, on balance, the reward outweighs the risk. After all, why should they be the ones tasked with protecting the system from harm by attackers? Isn't that the Cybersecurity team's job? They're right, and that's what SCE and the revolution toward resilience aims to achieve.

When brainstorming ways to solve various security challenges, we use policies as an absolute last resort, a bandage or stopgap until we implement something far more effective. A Platform Resilience Engineering team has failed if the best solution they can conceive is demanding humans behave a specific way every time they perform an action. As Marc Green aptly explains: "Safety considerations just get in the way by making the task more difficult to complete and by forcing users into less efficient, controlled, conscious behavior. If a safety mechanism causes a significant inconvenience, the user will almost certainly attempt to find a way to circumvent it and to increase efficiency. This is human nature and is the *starting point* for safety interventions."[38]

Thus, we must think of policies as a tourniquet. They can be useful in emergencies to stanch acute bleeding, but they shouldn't be considered the primary mode of treatment. To co-opt the status quo security mantra of "defense in depth," policies are, at best, *supplemental* to design-based mitigations and any other mechanisms that do not solely rely on human behavior to succeed. The policy-based approach attempts to solve security problems by changing each individual's behavior—the soggy bottom of the Ice Cream Cone Hierarchy of Security Solutions—rather than eliminating or reducing relevant hazards by design. As patient safety researchers Kerm Henriksen et al. (*https://oreil.ly/qz00w*) frame the issue, "An approach aimed at the individual is the equivalent of swatting individual mosquitoes rather than draining the swamp to address the source of the problem."

Nevertheless, policies are seen everywhere and it would be unrealistic for us to advise scrapping all of them to pursue design-based mitigations, which, while offering a higher security return, do usually take longer to implement than policies (which can be written and proclaimed to the masses with relative ease)—although efficacy remains eternally elusive.

One thought experiment to reduce the dependency on policies is to restrict the security program to three rules or policies—which do you choose? Restricting it to three

---

38 Marc Green, "Safety Hierarchy: Design Vs. Warnings" (*https://oreil.ly/HIEQr*) (emphasis ours).

is a useful forcing function, but also aligns well with neuroscientific evidence that short-term recall ("working memory") performance is limited.[39] Let's consider an example of a developer working on a software project. If the number of security things they must remember when coding is more than their working memory capacity, then their recall accuracy will suffer. If there are fewer security things to remember than there is working memory capacity, then recall accuracy will improve.

Once you consider developers also must recall other things when coding, like advice related to code quality, then it's safe to assume the amount of available capacity is super limited. Thus, an eight-part secure development training module with ten pages each will overflow the brain at runtime. If the developer were a computer, they might crash, but instead our brains discard excess requests to fill our short-term storage and choose whatever is most salient—whatever information is "cued" most prominently during their work.

The point of scoping the number of policies or rules to three is to force yourself to reconcile your security program with the reality of the human brain. Once you've chosen your selective set of rules or policies, your next prompt is: Which of these rules or policies offer measurable success outcomes? What are the second-order effects of those rules or policies and how would you measure them? Basically, how can you capture the negative externalities (*https://oreil.ly/cxGXv*) that might arise from the rule or policy, especially those that might erode repeatability and maintainability?

 You can even create hypotheses and decision trees for security policies as a belief prompting exercise! For instance, "If we require developers to do X, they will likely do Y in response."

How can you make those three rules or policies repeatable, reducing friction as much as possible to weave them into everyday workflows and to make them easy for human brains to remember? Answering this will bring you closer to brainstorming design-based solutions.

Security awareness training is draining

Evidence of infosec's predilection toward believing policy violations to be the cause of failure manifests in the cacophony of security education and training programs. There are "security awareness training" exercises, videos, and even escape rooms, not to mention the existence of "cybersecurity awareness month" itself.

---

39 In neuroscience, there is still ample debate as to the precise structure of its limitations.

Restricting human behavior alone will never work. We can never force humans to fit the ideal security mold, no matter how much training we cram through their eyeballs into their brains. If we're ever tempted to try, we should treat that as a call to action to consider designing systems that minimize errors and inefficiency based on how people actually behave—their visual, cognitive, and even motor abilities. In a sense, we're trying to continually and gracefully recover from status quo bias—the tendency to keep doing things the same way they have always been done that we first introduced in Chapter 2.[40]

> The human tendency to adhere to the status quo rather than pursue alternatives is referred to as *status quo bias*.[41] When making decisions, humans do not simply choose which option would give them the largest benefit or the most minimal loss. Whether the option is part of the existing state of affairs influences our decision making—even if we are unaware of it doing so. This predilection for the status quo is especially apparent when making difficult decisions,[42] which, it is fair to say, describe most of the decisions we make in the realm of security, resilience, and technology more generally.

Enforcement itself is a byproduct of the focus on policy violations as a "root cause" of security failure. Disciplinary actions, legal investigations, cancellation of bonuses, and other tactics to hold people solely accountable for failures do not support the goal of modifying behavior. Instead, these actions breed fear, resentment, suppression of information, seeking other employment, as well as furtive, quieter workarounds if goal conflicts continue to pervade. As we keep stressing, humans are cunning at adapting to changing conditions. In a sense, they know when "standard" processes should be broken, or else they communicate to figure it out. Replacing ways of working with elaborate rules or software-based enforcement—a form of tight coupling—can cement us in a rigidity trap, making the system more brittle. The less trust we sustain in the system by design, the slower and more rigid we will become.

This isn't to say we should *never* provide guidelines on procedures. Marc Green captures the dynamic well: "This is not to say that warnings and procedures are always useless but rather that the best safety mechanisms do not rely on humans to act

---

40 Kerm Henriksen et al., "Understanding Adverse Events: A Human Factors Framework," in *Patient Safety and Quality: An Evidence-Based Handbook for Nurses* (Rockville, MD: Agency for Healthcare Research and Quality, 2008).

41 William Samuelson and Richard Zeckhauser, "Status Quo Bias in Decision Making," *Journal of Risk and Uncertainty* 1, no. 1 (1988): 7-59.

42 Stephen M. Fleming et al., "Overcoming Status Quo Bias in the Human Brain," *Proceedings of the National Academy of Sciences* 107, no. 13 (2010): 6005-6009.

contrary to their nature 100% of the time."[43] We do not want to be an ouroboros, exacerbating adverse situations by clinging to formality and "textbook" practices.

Other complex systems domains have studied the significant limitations of training. In healthcare, for instance, in the realm of cardiopulmonary resuscitation (CPR), skill retention from training is usually limited and the training requires frequent repetition, which isn't scalable.[44] The efficacy around security awareness training is equally dubious. For example, as the researchers conducting a large-scale and long-term phishing experiment found (to their surprise), "…embedded training during simulated phishing exercises, as commonly deployed in the industry today, does not make employees more resilient to phishing, but instead it can have unexpected side effects that can make employees even more susceptible to phishing."[45] Another paper found that phishing identification drops off as soon as six months after the training program.[46] Rather than invoking more frequent repetition of the training, as the paper suggests, why not assume that users will fail to identify all phishing emails and pursue design-based solutions instead? (After all, we've known about the hazard of phishing for decades—isn't it about time we do something real about it?)

When you are tempted to implement training, consider practicing experiments instead. Repetition and practice combined with immediate feedback is roughly how humans learn. "Acquisition of skills," as Nobel Laureate in Economic Sciences Daniel Kahneman says, "requires a regular environment, an adequate opportunity to practice, and rapid and unequivocal feedback about the correctness of thoughts and actions."[47] This sounds a lot like chaos experiments, right? Experimentation fuels a learning culture in a way training can never replicate, because experimentation is *interactive* while training is passive.

Checklists

Checklists are farther down the Ice Cream Cone Hierarchy of Security Solutions because they rely on human behavior to succeed. Although they should be relied on sparingly, they can be a bridge to the world of "secure by default" in SCE from the "security by awareness" world of traditional security. If we do implement a checklist, we should be thoughtful about human attention and not overwhelm users with

---

43 Marc Green, "Safety Hierarchy: Design Vs. Warnings" (*https://oreil.ly/HIEQr*).

44 Frank A. Drews et al., "Development and Evaluation of a Just-in-Time Support System," *Human Factors: The Journal of the Human Factors and Ergonomics Society* 49, no. 3 (2007): 543-551.

45 Daniele Lain et al., "Phishing in Organizations: Findings from a Large-Scale and Long-Term Study," *2022 IEEE Symposium on Security and Privacy (SP)* (May 2022): 842-859.

46 Benjamin Reinheimer et al., "An Investigation of Phishing Awareness and Education Over Time: When and How to Best Remind Users," *Sixteenth Symposium on Usable Privacy and Security (SOUPS 2020)* (2020): 259-284.

47 Daniel Kahneman, *Thinking, Fast and Slow* (New York: Farrar, Straus and Giroux, 2013).

dozens of items to check off. For example, if we create a checklist of potential design issues that could erode resilience to attack, we should keep it to the fewest number of prompts that encourage engineers to be curious and think through resilience properties before deeming a system ready for general availability (GA).

While checklists may seem like a simplistic device to employ in the complex realm of security, they can be valuable memory aids that refresh knowledge that naturally rots after training sessions. In the realm of healthcare, the benefits of checklists are backed by experimental evidence. For instance, the implementation of a 19-item surgical safety checklist led to a reduction in the mortality rate from 1.5% to 0.8%, in-patient complications dropped from 11% to 7%, and postoperative complications fell by an average of 36%.[48] In the realm of retirement savings, a checklist with eight reasons to delay redemption of benefits led to an 18-month postponement in redeeming Social Security retirement benefits.[49] Ultimately, it doesn't matter if it seems simplistic if it produces tangible positive outcomes.

What made these checklists work? They contain "simple, routine actions" that practitioners "may simply forget to follow because of time constraints, stress, or distractions."[50] When processes or policies become too complex or have too many steps, it will be harder for practitioners' working memory to keep up. Breaking down the actions to get from the starting point to the goal outcome into a series of steps that constitute ideal performance can help people—even experts—adhere to the optimal behavioral path. Even if we know the right way to do something or reach a goal, it can be difficult to remember it all in the moment. Crucially, these checklists must be in line with workflows—not on an internal wiki, but instead either in line with builds, commits, or PRs. Anything later or out-of-band means the checklist won't be followed in most cases.

With this said, if we do our jobs well as platform resilience leaders and engineers, checklists shouldn't be necessary. If we design a standardized authentication or authorization component that Product Engineering teams can leverage in their services, there's no need for a checklist reminding them of potential hazards when dealing with authN or authZ. The same goes for checklists about memory safety issues; if we reduce hazards by design, making it easy, say, for teams writing in C to compile into a WebAssembly binary (*https://oreil.ly/jmOhl*), then we no longer must rely on humans going through the checklist.

---

48 Alex B. Haynes et al., "A Surgical Safety Checklist to Reduce Morbidity and Mortality in a Global Population," *New England Journal of Medicine* 360, no. 5 (2009): 491-499.

49 Eric Johnson et al., "Preference Checklists: Selective and Effective Choice Architecture for Retirement Decisions," *Research Dialogue* 127 (2016).

50 Thaler, "Choice Architecture," 428-439.

Two Paths: The Control Strategy or the Resilience Strategy

To summarize, when we think about how to solve resilience and security challenges, there are two paths we can take: the control strategy or the resilience strategy. We compare them in Table 7-3. The control strategy designs security programs, and the elements within them, based on what security humans think other humans *should* do. From this control-centric perspective, what humans "should" do is give their full attention to a task every time; give every risk conscious consideration, notice and comply with every warning; adhere to rules, policies, and procedures 100% of the time; and remain willing to expend all resources toward this compliance (time, cognitive energy, money, etc.). Thus, the control strategy amounts to nothing more than wishful thinking.[51]

From the Security team's perspective, however, this strategy is extremely convenient; in fact, it might be better described as the "convenience strategy." The Security program can pursue cheap "solutions" that are easy to implement—like warnings, procedures, policies, training, and even some bolt-on security tools—and that also allow the Security program (who are very much the "administrators" and "managers" in this context) to blame users when an incident occurs. The Security team, or whoever is enforcing this control-based security strategy, gains convenience at the expense of everyone else's inconvenience. For example, the Security team may force developers to wrangle with slow, cumbersome appsec tools, gaining their own convenience at the expense of developers' inconvenience. They get to avoid the hard work of brainstorming design-based solutions and instead prescribe fanciful ways people should work, then blaming them when they fail to live up to those conceits.

Many organizations are fine with this ineffective paradigm, especially those with a blame-oriented culture (and those organizations tend to move slowly too). The way these organizations survive, however, is precisely because the humans within do not behave the way the Security program thinks they should. If humans followed all warnings, stated policies, procedures, and other rules 100% of the time, productivity would wane and perhaps even grind to a halt. Perhaps nothing indicates security theater (as we discussed in Chapter 2) more than the sociotechnical system relying on rule-breaking to thrive.

As much as we are passionate about resilience, safety, security, and whatever other labels you want to adorn the discipline in, we must remember that not everyone cares, and that is OK. Green is correct when he says, "People don't use products or environments in order to be safe. They use them in order to perform a task which allows them to reach a goal." When we forget that, we build solutions that try to transmogrify reality into a chimera—and we will always fail.

---

51 Marc Green, "Safety Hierarchy: Design Vs. Warnings" (*https://oreil.ly/HIEQr*).

Table 7-3. Differences between the control strategy and the resilience strategy to solve security

Control strategy	Resilience strategy
Plan security based on how managers think humans *should* behave	Promote and design security based on how humans *actually* behave
Humans should give full attention 100% of the time	Human attention is finite and a precious resource
Every risk should receive conscious consideration	Design the hazard out of the system, or reduce it, whenever possible
Humans should notice and comply with every warning	Avoid relying on human attention as much as possible
Humans should adhere to rules, policies, and procedures 100% of the time	Don't rely on humans to act contrary to their nature 100% of the time
Humans should be willing to expend resources toward compliance at all times	We should respect users' time, attention, cognitive energy, and priorities at all times

Any tool relevant to our computer systems work—whether a software library, API, toolkit, framework, virtual machine, and so much more—is "a tangible instantiation of designers' thinking about how, by whom, and in what settings it will be used."[52] In essence, all software reflects the designers' mental models of how humans will interact with it. Humans, however, are not deterministic, so those mental models are often violated. It is difficult to argue that the problem lies with the human user—reflected in the folk term *user error*—and not the designers' mental model. We can borrow from human factors engineers and leverage the term *use error*, which describes failures resulting from unintended interactions between a tool[53] and its user. Solving for "use error" will nudge you toward design-based solutions; solving for "user error" will lead you down the dark path of training, enforcement, and other solutions that rely on human behavior—the very thing the term implies is fallible.

When a user finds it easy to succeed when using a solution, it's an indicator of how closely the designers' mental model aligns with the user's reality. This returns us to the difference between "work-as-imagined" and "work-as-done." When work-as-imagined differs extensively from work-as-done, it means the hypotheses about how users, their context, and their interactions with the tool were not well-founded. So, when a user finds it challenging to succeed—or worse, easy to fail—when using a tool, that reflects a *design* problem, not a human problem. This is the importance of the "use error" framing; we must treat errors made by stressed and constrained users as the manifestation of system design failures.[54]

---

52 Robert L. Wears and Rollin J. Terry Fairbanks, "Design Trumps Training," *Annals of Emergency Medicine* 67, no. 3 (2016): 316-317.

53 While *device*—the more common term in human factors engineering—technically could include software based on the definition of "a thing made or adapted for a particular purpose," it means something specific in software land. Therefore, we use the term *tool* instead.

54 James Reason, *Human Error* (Cambridge, UK: Cambridge University Press, 1990).

What Would Gilbreth Do? (WWGD)

Frank Bunker Gilbreth was an engineer who was obsessed with finding the "one best way" of executing a task across different disciplines, starting with bricklaying. Gilbreth observed bricklayers performing 18 actions in their workflow and found a way to whittle it down to six.[55] Gilbreth can serve as our inspiration when performing user research and designing solutions. How can we find opportunities to reduce the number of steps or friction in our users' workflows? This can help us identify those coveted opportunities to support resilience while improving efficiency.

Hence, a fun heuristic is: What Would Gilbreth Do? (WWGD)

If a product is only successful when humans use it "correctly," then it is not actually successful. This is true whether the product is a children's toy, a SaaS app, or even a security policy. As anyone who has built products knows all too well, its users will surprise and flabbergast you with all the clever actions they take when interacting with the product. They will uncover workflows that boggle your mental model of the product. Security-as-a-product does not escape this dynamic; but traditional security refers to these unintended interactions as "violations" and punishes them rather than incorporating them into future product iterations. The dogmatic view that "users must be wrong" is the opposite of the curiosity we must cultivate in our security programs, and keeps your product from succeeding in the market—which keeps security from succeeding in your organization.

Blaming human error and slapping on behavior-related fixes is cheap and fast; we can convince ourselves that it is just an interim solution and we will get to contemplating design fixes later. But, as we see from the significant investment in policy enforcement, security training, and even warning systems (which require human operators to analyze the warning with accuracy and take the right action to succeed), these behavior-based bandages become distractions. Especially when we feel action bias after a security incident (as discussed in the last chapter), we want a fix *now*, even if it is ineffective. This pattern is "a sort of codependency in which a plausible but ineffective intervention offers the illusion of progress but reduces the pressure to find real, influential solutions."[56]

---

55 Arthur G. Bedeian, "Finding the One Best Way," *An Appreciation of Frank B. Gilbreth, the Father of Motion Study, Conference Board Record* 16, no. 6 (1976): 37-39.

56 Wears, "Design Trumps Training," 316-317.

Think back to the list of toil work seen in traditional cybersecurity programs in Chapter 5. These security mechanisms—largely administrative controls—do not respect the time of humans in the system. Having to perform that toil on a regular basis would drive any intelligent, driven person out of the security program.

Solution Design and the Thermodynamics of Effort

You could prioritize your own convenience by building software that achieves its core functionality without regard for how the end user will interact with it. Effort is instead shoved into the operational side of the software lifecycle; the end user must now perform the difficult thinking and acting in order to get things working in the way needed for their local context. In essence, you've freed more capital in your Effort Investment Portfolio by depleting capital in another team's or user's Effort Investment Portfolio.

Imagine a very simple cybersecurity tool; all its designers decided it should do is emit a "beep" on the computer whenever it detects a file matching a string known to be malicious. As the end user, you hear a beep…and then another beep…your day is now filled with beeps, but you have no idea why it is beeping and there is no obvious starting point for investigation other than performing the exact same task of scanning the whole filesystem against a list of strings associated with malware. The designers minimized effort in their own work, which means you are now overwhelmed by effort.

On the other hand, you can imagine a designer who wants to minimize all effort for the end user. To do so, the designer, at a minimum, must figure out how to expose all the information the end user might need to fix the problem—without making them expend cognitive effort to figure out precisely what's important. But, ideally, the designer will also need to figure out how to minimize the number of actions the user must perform, which likely means automating the appropriate response action when something malicious is uncovered. However, this means the designer must *also* ensure that anything detected as "malicious" is *actually* malicious so the user isn't blocked from performing their desired activity and so they don't have to "undo" the automated action. There is even more the designer must consider beyond that, but even with these few considerations we can see how much effort is now shoved onto the designer in order to spare the operator from it.

Green summarizes the trade-off well: "The design approach makes the designer responsible for product safety. Conversely, the warning approach downloads responsibility for safety on to the user, who is required to ensure that the product / environment works safely by avoiding accidents due to hazards inherent in the design."[57]

---

57 Marc Green, "Safety Hierarchy: Design Vs. Warnings" (*https://oreil.ly/HIEQr*).

Use case: Handling account takeover

Account takeover (ATO) is a pernicious, prevalent problem across nearly all organizations. Let's say we're worried about internal account takeover, like an attacker gaining access to developer or admin credentials. How does the Ice Cream Cone Hierarchy of Security Solutions apply to solving it?

Two-factor authentication (2FA), which many in cybersecurity might jump to first, is farther down the cone, a mixture of administrative control and warning system. Phishing vigilance—asking users to always be on the lookout for attackers' attempts to steal their credentials—is another traditional cybersecurity measure that is solidly on the flimsy end of the cone because it involves an administrator (usually the Security team) attempting to control human behavior. Distributed alerting (*https://oreil.ly/Pp9lV*), combined with 2FA, is another warning system that can serve as a backstop. Both of those are pretty far down the cone, however.

What can we explore higher up the cone? We can implement rate limiting as a safety device, with the added benefit of addressing numerous resilience concerns beyond ATO alone. Product teams could use rate limiting services to update global quotas and risk scoring per user account on every incoming request. Getting a little bolder, we could maintain a separate browser stack for internal applications enforced by proxy shenanigans to avoid XSRF on internal applications. For instance, developers must use a separate browser profile that doesn't visit normal websites. Of course, this is probably cumbersome and likely to disrupt workflows, which is exactly why we should keep moving up the cone to see what might be most effective.

Standardization can help us start reducing hazardous methods and materials. A standardized solution for login can help us reduce the number of "roll your own" login services. We can also create a paved road for logging and auditing, building internal tooling that makes it easier and safer.

Outside of paved roads and standardization, what other design-based solutions should we consider? We could implement immutable infrastructure (with an escape hatch in case of emergency[58]) so developers and operators can't abuse infrastructure credentials to access data. Isolation is our ally too; when operators do have to log in to infrastructure, isolation limits what they can access. Token-based authentication with automatic rotation means passwords are only sent to a single authentication system, and even intercepted credentials are a ticking time bomb in terms of ATO use (i.e., the credentials expire quickly, which attackers don't like).

We could also consider a per-tenant database strategy for SaaS applications that ensures emergency access only provides access to one tenant's data and that

---

58 "Immutability with an escape hatch" is a very reasonable approach. Immutability where you can potentially lock the firefighters out of a burning building for ideological purposes, less so.

application-level bugs can only lead to compromise of a single tenant's data. The rise of queues and "serverless" databases makes this design-based solution easier.[59] Such an approach would also enable the access model of users being able to share any piece of data they have access to with any other user (like in GitHub and Google Docs).

An even more secure-by-design approach is to instantiate per-tenant copies of...everything. In this approach, a router living in the front of the system checks access tokens and directs traffic to the copy of the application associated with the tenant. All the components in this copy of the application—the database, queues, storage buckets, and so forth—are associated only with that tenant. Such an approach works best with the auth model of logging into a large pool of data and where you very much do not want it to mix with other pools.

As you can see, accepting the status quo answer to "How do we solve ATO?" only gets us the brittle end of the cone. There isn't much resilience ice cream we could scoop into that. But when we venture up the cone, asking ourselves how solutions that are more design-based might look, we can innovate much more effective solutions that won't make users resent us for trying to control them (or, less cheekily, that won't pulverize organizational growth and productivity).

Experimentation and Feedback Loops for Solution Design

Flexibility and willingness to change is the last ingredient in our resilience potion recipe. We also talked about the importance of iterative change—and ease of change—in Chapter 3. When we design solutions to solve resilience problems, this principle holds true. How do we ensure we aren't dragged into "build something perfect to address all the things" hell? An approach emphasizing minimum viable products (MVPs) with iteration based on user feedback helps keep us nimble and open to change.

MVPs are helpful to get initial stabs at a solution in front of users to collect evidence of whether it satisfies your hypothesis (like "this service helps developers statically analyze their code"). If you're designing a mitigation that doesn't directly interact with users, an MVP can still be valuable to gather other forms of evidence, like performance penalties. It can also validate your hypotheses related to attackers, especially if you deploy it into a deception environment as discussed in Chapter 5.

---

[59] Usually, we build multitenant applications with a horizontally scaled copy of one application and a giant database that is logically partitioned. The application must understand which users can access which data, which is cumbersome and a magnet for errors.

Gathering Feedback on Your Solution Design

We recommend hiring onto your team someone who is well-versed in UX and is trained in user research and designing experiences. In general, there are four qualities to balance in solution design.

Utility
> Does the service or product solve the real needs of the real users?

Usability
> How quickly and easily do users figure out how to use the service or product to meet their needs?

Desirability
> Do users like using your service or product? Are they cautious when using it? Do they procrastinate about using it? Do they try to bypass it?

Aspiration
> Do users feel confident, accomplished, excited, safe, or other good vibes when using the service or product?

In the context of platform engineering, thinking about the first and second qualities may come more naturally than considering the third and fourth.

The next section describes how we can go from MVP to implementing the solutions we design so our customers can benefit from them.

Implementing a Solution

Once we've designed a solution, we want to see our customers adopt it and benefit from it. How do we encourage adoption and measure success? This section explores key considerations when implementing a solution.

Fostering Consensus

Product management is often about negotiation. Your customers have opinions on what solutions they want and how you should prioritize building them. Your Customer Success and Sales teams have their own opinions, as do engineers and product managers on other teams. And leadership definitely has opinions too. We need to gain consensus about our plans for solving resilience problems—from vision through implementation of a specific solution.

Success is solving a real problem in a way that delivers consistent value. In resilience platform engineering, success is no different. If a Security team at a midsize enterprise delivering a SaaS application is solving for a niche "threat" (like Spectre and Meltdown) while reducing the organization's service performance by 20% and productivity by even more, that is not success. Part of success is also fostering consensus around your decision. If you must implement something that is unpopular, perhaps due to unrealistic production pressures that would likely foment an outage, then ensuring organizational voices feel "heard" makes it more likely that the product will be adopted.

This doesn't mean we sacrifice security every time we receive negative feedback. It means we care about outcomes, not outputs, and that requires pragmatism, a focus on what will actually work in practice. All products, including security, are shared problems within an organization. Each stakeholder must feel they have a personal stake in whatever course of action is taken—a process called *building consensus*. For instance, if your Engineering team currently stores credentials in plain text and your proposed plan is to require multiround hashing instead, then discussing the why with relevant stakeholders early—such as the need to meet a compliance requirement to increase potential market penetration, like with PCI—will likely discourage them from digging in their heels when the time comes to implement the change.

Production pressures are eternal, relentless beasts. As much as we will try to satiate the organization's rapacity for frugality and efficiency, sometimes production pressures and resilience pressures will conflict more than align. Our goal is to support work, not obstruct it. This means that, if there is significant pushback to adoption of our proposed solution, we must listen and learn. How can we refine the design to assuage at least some of their concerns? Can we brainstorm a more incremental adoption strategy that eases them into new ways of doing work?

We've frequently described why clarifying the why in a system and its components is imperative. When our internal customers and other stakeholders don't understand why the problem is worth solving, why the solution is designed the way it is, and why the goal outcomes matter, they understandably challenge its value. "Why didn't you just do X?" is not an uncommon question to hear for a team when building solutions. In fairness, if you don't know why you didn't pursue other avenues, that's a problem. If you followed our advice throughout these chapters, though, you'll not only know the answer, but have documented it somewhere accessible and digestible to anyone interacting with the solution (including future maintainers of it).

Planning for Migration

In the excitement of building a solution for a real problem, it can be easy to overlook the need to pave the road for your customers to adopt or migrate to your solution. They're used to one way of performing work and now you're asking them to use something completely new, which typically comes with a learning curve. Remember, we don't want to be dictators prescribing solutions and patting ourselves on the back for a job well done while teams flounder or grouse. As Fournier quips (*https://oreil.ly/ A61iZ*), "The product work is not 'tell everyone you have Kubernetes now and they have to use it.' Instead, the product work is to identify different types of customers and figure out what will make it easy for them to migrate. What are the carrots you can provide to get people to do work that they don't care about doing?"

If we don't understand what is important to each of our customers, we will struggle to identify "carrots" we can dangle to encourage adoption. Consider the adoption of VMs, then containers, and, more recently, serverless functions. The headline value proposition was density (i.e., scalability) and reliability, but adopters of these technologies gained resilience via isolation too. When we go down the list of our user personas, which production pressures most resonate with them? Are there certain metrics they're trying to move this quarter or year? Is their work influenced by efficiency of accessing resources, like compute or storage? Are they obsessive about latency?

A lucid understanding of our relevant user personas' priorities and pains must influence how we present our solution to them. It's the same as when we are thinking through product marketing for solutions delivered to external customers. We wouldn't tout programmability as a value prop for a website-related offering to an internal marketing team; we'd focus on ease-of-use or speed-of-change, and we wouldn't frame these benefits in unfamiliar engineering terms (like change fail rate). Likewise, we would frame the value prop for a Product Engineering team in terms of the specific SLOs they prioritize for their service. We can't expect our internal customers to intuit how our solution will benefit them. Only through clear elucidation of targeted value propositions (and delivering on those value props) can we successfully dangle carrots.

Success Metrics

While many product-related metrics apply to platform engineering—who, after all, is building products for internal stakeholders—measurement can sometimes be trickier than in product engineering. If you are part of a resilience or security program with a market of all internal employees, that could be a market with constituents ranging from a few dozen to hundreds of thousands (or even millions!). Using metrics to inform product decision making will be easier when you have a sizable user base to survey.[60] Regardless of consumer base, metrics around usage and adoption are essential to track in platform engineering.

 Let's say our vision is to reduce security workflow volatility. Success might be described as, "In one year, engineering teams will spend only 5% to 10% of time on firefighting." Or it could be described as, "In nine months, 90% of security reviews will be automated."

Rather than focusing solely on your own metrics, as is traditional in Cybersecurity or Infrastructure teams, you should look at the metrics of other teams—your internal customers—in tandem to spot possible negative externalities. For instance, if your security review code coverage is increasing, check whether the Engineering team's lead time or deploy frequency metrics are being impacted. While anyone who took a Statistics 101 course will remember that "correlation does not equal causation," a worsening metric on the engineering side at the same time as an improving metric on the security side is a starting point for investigation. Maybe the Engineering team decided that playing a newly released video game was way more interesting than pushing code. By digging in further and speaking with those teams, you can ensure the problem is driven primarily by the video game, not your program. If the resilience (or security) program *is* causing a negative externality in software delivery performance or engineering productivity, then your investigation can help identify how your program can be improved to reduce friction.

The SPACE framework,[61] developed by DevOps and developer productivity expert Dr. Forsgren and compatriots, can help us elucidate these negative externalities as well as positive impacts too. The SPACE framework describes five categories of metrics that are relevant when measuring developer productivity: satisfaction and well-being; performance; activity; communication and collaboration; and efficiency and flow. Figure 7-4, from their paper, provides example metrics following this framework. If our internal customers are Engineering teams, identifying metrics from each category can help us gain a more complete understanding of our solution's influence on developer productivity.

---

60 Camille Fournier, "Product for Internal Platforms" (*https://oreil.ly/A6liZ*), *Medium* (May 9, 2020).

61 Dr. Nicole Forsgren et al., "The SPACE of Developer Productivity: There's More to It Than You Think," *Queue* 19, no. 1 (2021): 20-48.

Level	Satisfaction and well-being — How fulfilled, happy, and healthy one is	Performance — An outcome of a process	Activity — The count of actions or outputs	Communication and collaboration — How people talk and work together	Efficiency and flow — Doing work with minimal delays or interruptions
Individual — One person	• Developer satisfaction • Retention[†] • Satisfaction with code reviews assigned • Perception of code reviews	• Code review velocity	• Number of code reviews completed • Coding time • # commits • Lines of code[†]	• Code review score (quality or thoughtfulness) • PR merge times • Quality of meetings[†] • Knowledge sharing, discoverability (quality of documentation)	• Code review timing • Productivity perception • Lack of interruptions
Team or group — People that work together	• Developer satisfaction • Retention[†]	• Code review velocity • Story points shipped[†]	• # story points completed[†]	• PR merge times • Quality of meetings[†] • Knowledge sharing, discoverability (quality of documentation)	• Code review timing • Handoffs
System — End-to end work through a system (like a development pipeline)	• Satisfaction with engineering system (e.g., CI/CD pipeline	• Code review velocity • Code review (acceptance rate) • Customer satisfaction • Reliability (uptime)	• Frequency of deployments	• Knowledge sharing, discoverability (quality of documentation)	• Code review timing • Velocity/flow through the system

[†]Use these metrics with (even more) caution—they can proxy more things.

Figure 7-4. Example metrics from the SPACE framework (source: The SPACE of Developer Productivity (https://oreil.ly/le88h))

We said before that Platform Engineering teams should treat their customers' outages as their own. Incident data does not tell us much and can flirt with the dangerous metric of "mean time between failure"—the metric that occludes innovation. What matters far more than how many incidents occur, or even of what type, is *why* they occur and why they *don't* occur. Which factors are contributing to failure and which factors are contributing to success? If we don't understand these factors, we won't understand how our solutions are helping or hurting, nor what refinements might improve outcomes. As Erik Hollnagel, a resilience engineering researcher and senior professor of patient safety, says: "While compiling extensive accident statistics may seem impressive it does not mean that the system actually learns anything. Knowing how many accidents have occurred says nothing about why they have occurred, nor anything about the situations where accidents did not occur."[62]

---

62 Erik Hollnagel, "Epilogue: RAG—The Resilience Analysis Grid," in *Resilience Engineering in Practice*, 275-296 (Boca Raton, FL: CRC Press, 2017).

The benefits of reducing uncertainty are finite, but cybersecurity professionals have often turned to more measurement and more granular risk models as a coping mechanism. These tell us little about the reality of our systems—especially reality as it evolves in response to changing external and internal conditions.

SCE is a megadose of reality (and, we like to think, a chill pill too). The evidence each security chaos experiment generates provides you a mirrored shard of system resilience, from which you can piece together a mosaic reflecting your organization's security across its systems. Chaos experiments can uncover where your measurements don't measure up, from insensitive threshold alerts to monitoring data that lacks sufficient workload awareness to be useful.

Don't chase "secure" as a metric

In traditional cybersecurity, you'll sometimes hear people say that the ultimate measure of success is what percentage of your components are "secure." This tells us nothing of value; it amounts to busywork and guesswork. "Secure" is relative to your failure boundary and where your current operating point lies, as we discussed earlier in the chapter. The same exact components may be secure under some external conditions, but not others. Is a fully patched database with strong access controls "secure?" What if an attacker overloads it with requests, causing failover to a redundant database whose access controls aren't as strong? "Secure" is a hazy oasis shimmering at an interminable distance, not a realistic goal for systems.

As we said before, this is because resilience—and its subset, security—is something a system does rather than something a system has. And, just like any action or state of being, security is relative. We can say a bicycle gives us speed, but it can be either fast relative to walking or slow relative to taking the subway.

If you ask stakeholders what "secure" means in terms of their system, you're likely to receive wildly different answers. Developers may answer, "An attacker can't take the application offline for hours." An SRE may answer, "The application alerts on attempts to disrupt or take control of it and can quickly reprovision its underlying infrastructure to remove attacker presence." A CISO may answer, "There are no known or unknown vulnerabilities in the application's code or in its underlying components."

Focus on metrics that give us a holistic picture of the sociotechnical system. Resist the temptation to measure your success through vague, indefinable qualities that allow ample room to absolve yourself of accountability.

Chapter Takeaways

- At the "meta-design" level, we can sustain resilience through organizational structure and practices—transforming from a siloed security program into a platform engineering model ("platform resilience engineering").

- We must be aware of production pressures and how they tip sociotechnical systems toward failure. Production pressures involve the incentivization of less expensive and more efficient work, with quality (and security as its subset) as the typical sacrifice.

- A platform engineering approach to resilience treats security as a product with end users, as something created through a process that provides benefits to a market (with internal teams as our customers). Platform Engineering teams identify real problems, iterate on a solution, and prioritize usability to promote adoption. Resilience is a natural fit for their purview.

- Any product requires a long-term vision—a unifying theme for all your projects toward a defined end. The vision tells a story of what is being built and why.

- Treating resilience—including security—as a product starts with identifying the right user problems to tackle. To accurately define user problems, we must understand their local context. We must understand how our users make trade-offs under pressure, maintain curiosity about the workarounds they create, and respect the limitations of their brains' computational capacity ("cognitive load").

- Security solutions become less reliable as their dependence on human behavior increases. The Ice Cream Cone Hierarchy of Safety Solutions helps us prioritize how we design security solutions, starting with designing to eliminating hazards; substituting less hazardous methods or materials; incorporating safety devices and guards; providing warning and awareness systems; and, last and least effective, applying administrative controls (like guidelines and training).

- There are two possible paths we can pursue when solving user problems: the control strategy or the resilience strategy. The control strategy designs security programs based on what security humans think other humans *should* do; it is convenient for the Security team at the expense of others' convenience. The resilience strategy promotes and designs security based on how humans *actually* behave; success is when our solutions align with the reality of work-as-done. The control strategy makes users responsible for security while the resilience approach makes those designing security programs and solutions responsible for it.

- We should build minimum viable products and pursue an iterative change model informed by user feedback.

- We should gain consensus about our plans for solving resilience problems—from vision through to implementation of a specific solution—and ensure stakeholders understand the *why* behind our solutions. Success is solving a real problem in a way that delivers consistent value.

- To facilitate solution adoption, we must plan for migration and pave the road for our customers to adopt what we've created for them. We should never force solutions on other humans; if that is the only way to drive adoption, then it is a failure of our design, strategy, and communication.

- Measuring product success is necessary for our feedback loops, but can be tricky. If we design solutions for use by engineering teams, the SPACE framework offers numerous success criteria we can measure. In general, we should be curious about the factors contributing to success and failure for our customers.

- Any metrics related to how "secure" or "risky" something is, like percentage of "risk coverage," are busywork based on measuring the (highly subjective) unmeasurable. We need to measure our program's success—and any solutions we design as part of it—based on tangible, realistic goals.

CHAPTER 8

Security Chaos Experiments

Only in chaos are we conceivable.
—Robert Bolaño, *2666*

Experimentation seeks to derive new insights that were previously unknown about our reality, completing the feedback loop that is inherent in the scientific method. This dynamic cycle of discovery and learning is what drives scientific progress across every discipline. Experiments are the kindling for the eternal fire of our continuous learning, which is the only way as defenders we can realistically keep up with rapidly evolving environments. Experimentation is the focus of tier 2 in our resilience assessment from Chapter 2 for a reason: without simulating adverse scenarios to observe how our systems respond and adapt to deleterious conditions, we cannot conceive courses of action that can bolster systems resilience in a meaningful, measurable way.

SCE introduces the practice of rigorous experimentation that illuminates the resilience and security of a system in reality (not just in theory). As we discussed in Chapter 2, experimentation is far more than mere testing. Testing is the validation or binary assessment of a previously known outcome; we know what we are seeking before we go looking for it. In contrast, experimentation seeks to derive new information that was previously unknown, and these new insights inform our adaptations—the artifact of the final ingredient needed to brew our resilience potion. Injecting adverse security scenarios into our systems helps us understand how our systems behave and catalyzes opportunities to improve how we maintain system resilience. By running security chaos experiments continuously, we can evaluate and improve our understanding of the hazards lurking within our systems before they conspire into crisis situations. Experiments are our mischievous medicine to manage misleading mental models, revising them toward reality.

In this chapter, we'll describe the end-to-end process of conducting a security chaos experiment that roughly follows the EMPAK loop[1]—leveraging feedback loops to execute, monitor, analyze, and plan security chaos experiments based on a knowledge base—shown in Figure 8-1. We'll cover how to set experiments up for success with carefully considered prerequisites, designing a hypothesis, developing an experiment, and analyzing and documenting experimental evidence. Along the way, we'll provide guidance and lessons learned from early adopters that will help you anticipate potential hurdles and blunders, and ensure your experiments go smoothly.

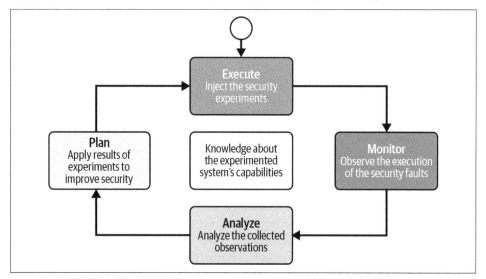

Figure 8-1. EMPAK loop presented by cybersecurity researcher Kennedy Torkura

Security Chaos Experimentation Applies the Scientific Method

You can think of the practice of security chaos experimentation as an application of the scientific method for deriving new information about the behavior and operational context of complex computer systems—information that was unavailable to us before. We call our resilience stress tests "experiments" because we perform a series of actions and carefully observe their effects to learn about system behavior—a classic experiment true to scientific tradition. Experiments grant us insights into possible outcomes when the system encounters the conditions we introduce. Since we're harnessing the scientific method, you should think of the practice as a feedback loop rather than a finite sequence of steps.

---

1 Kennedy A. Torkura et al., "Cloudstrike: Chaos Engineering for Security and Resiliency in Cloud Infrastructure," *IEEE Access* 8 (2020): 123044-123060.

Of course, scientific experimentation relies on repeatable procedures and logical analysis of results, which is what we'll espouse and explore in this chapter. How does one go about conducting science?

To start, you must ask a question about your reality. In the famed case of Isaac Newton, he might have asked, "Why did this apple fall from a tree and bonk me on the head? Why did it fall vertically downward rather than move upward or sideways?" With that question in mind, you develop a hypothesis. A *hypothesis* is a proposed explanation for our question, which we use as a starting point for investigation. A hypothesis could be: There is some kind of invisible force pulling the apple and other falling objects straight to the ground.

We pursue this investigation by conducting an experiment, which allows us to make observations that serve as evidence about reality. In Newton's case with the apple, his experiments required him to invent calculus as a side project (your experiments likely won't beget fundamental advances in mathematics, but you never know).

We then carefully compare the observations from our experiment with our predictions from our hypothesis, staying as objective as possible. For instance, we could find that a range of objects, like a feather, apple, and sword, indeed plummet straight to the ground as in our hypothesis, but at different speeds.

After this analysis, we can report and document our findings and use them to refine our understanding of reality—then iterate by asking new questions that lead to new hypotheses and new experiments. Newton performed precisely this process, refining his hypotheses over and over until he derived a conclusion supported by a wealth of evidence: Newton's law of universal gravitation.

This process is rightfully revered across scientific disciplines because it keeps you honest and in the fruitful mindset of continually revising your knowledge of reality. Likewise, pursuing the scientific method in the form of security chaos experimentation keeps us honest and in the mindset of continually revising our knowledge about our systems as they behave in reality.

Lessons Learned from Early Adopters

Before we proceed to the end-to-end experimentation process, let's lean into learning—the fourth ingredient in our resilience potion—by reviewing the hard-earned lessons learned by early adopters of security chaos experimentation.

Lesson #1. Start in Nonproduction Environments; You Can Still Learn a Lot

It's a "best practice" to run experiments in production, but rare is the organization that feels confident enough to start by simulating adverse scenarios in production. If you start in a test, development, or staging environment, then it's worth the effort investment to simulate real-world conditions as much as possible (like performing traffic replay). Creating production-like environments will benefit more than experimentation; higher fidelity makes testing more reliable too.

Lesson #2. Use Past Incidents as a Source of Experiments

By leveraging past incidents (that were remediated) as hypotheses, the value of experimentation will be more salient to your organization—and stakeholders across teams know how much that incident impacted the organization. How many customers were affected? Was revenue impacted? Did the Finance team have to work all weekend to get a contract for an expensive incident response retainer in place? Interviewing stakeholders involved in prior incidents helps you to harness this collective memory and convince executives why the practice is so valuable.

Even though the organization recovered from a past incident, the surrounding context has changed. Maybe the influencing factors have already manifested again. Perhaps the remediation we put in place isn't effective against variations on the previous set of conditions. This is why prior incidents are a pragmatic source to leverage as inspiration, since the organization wants confidence that it will not feel inordinate damage from a similar failure again.

Lesson #3. Publish and Evangelize Experimental Findings

When learning about chaos experimentation, people often think the technical challenges are the hardest part. But the technical parts are arguably the easiest to scale; expanding experimentation across the organization—from one team or service to many—becomes our biggest challenge. Culture is the barrier to adoption. The technical problems, including automating the experiments, are not nearly as vexing as gaining buy-in from internal stakeholders.

With this wisdom in hand, it's time to take your first steps toward applying the discipline by learning how to set experiments up for success, design hypotheses and experiments, conduct experiments, and analyze resulting evidence.

Setting Experiments Up for Success

To begin our experimental process, we need to allocate effort to planning, prepping, and socializing our intentions to the key stakeholders within our organization. Without buy-in from key stakeholders, we'll be seen as eccentric scientists trying to *add* chaos to our systems rather than learn from the chaos that already exists in our systems. By investing the effort in educating others on the value of security chaos experimentation, we can foster confidence and trust, granting us the organizational support we need for a successful experiment.

As you begin establishing a program of chaos experimentation, other humans in your organization might be wary about the idea of introducing "chaos." One way to anticipate this objection is to refer to it as "resilience stress testing" instead, as we discussed in Chapter 2. More generally, it behooves us to provide the proper context behind the experiment to make the justification evident—in a sense, creating a paved road for stakeholders to connect the dots as to why the experiment is worthwhile.

Framing Effects and Chaos Experiments

Different sets of stakeholders display variegated emotions when you start mentioning the concept of chaos engineering or SCE. Without proper context, chaos engineering might come off as an amusing divertissement or frightening friendly fire. Since its inception, chaos engineering has been tainted with the flagrantly farcical headline of "Breaking Things in Production." This has never been the case at any time in the history of chaos engineering as a practice, even in its infancy at Netflix. It has been and is always about "Fixing Things in Production."

Messaging is thus a core prerequisite to set your experiment up for success. We need to finesse facilitative framing, describing experimentation as a controlled, disciplined approach rather than "breaking things." We must mollify our organization by starting in a developing or staging environment, not production. We must ensure our goal outcome is unambiguous, that we wish to establish order rather than create chaos. We need to make it clear that we will target "known" scenarios and conditions rather than inflicting an "unknown," desultory, mindless mess. If we message the experiment as carefully considered proactive preparation designed to minimize impact, then other humans can gain confidence that we're not hell-bent on disruption—that we actually want to help make things better.

So, before you socialize the experiment, consider how different roles in your organization might perceive chaos experiments, including, but not limited to, the CIO, CISO, CTO, technical lead, product manager, SRE, and incident responder.

To elucidate the end-to-end process of a chaos experiment, let's learn by example. With the lessons from Chapter 7 in hand, we identify a poignant user problem and craft a user story based on it, like: "Ensuring authentication is consistent is hard for my Engineering teams. But if our critical services fail to authenticate incoming traffic, we might experience service disruption—or worse, downtime—and violate customer trust." Maybe there was even an incident where an important service failed to authenticate incoming requests properly or leaked unauthenticated data, making it imperative to solve this user problem.

Receiving feedback on this user story from relevant stakeholders can ignite initial consensus around the experiment. We can restate our user story as an invariant with which they're likely to agree, such as, "I want my entire infrastructure to handle authentication properly." What "properly" means will be domain-specific for each function, which is difficult to answer in an automated fashion—something worth emphasizing to stakeholders. But you're able to offer a solution to achieve this goal: creating an experiment that shows us which services automatically require authentication versus the services we *think* require it. That is, by conducting an experiment, we can challenge and expose inaccuracies in our mental models.

For a problem of this magnitude, we likely won't propose only one option when offering solutions to important stakeholders. At many organizations, fostering consensus means we need to give other stakeholders multiple options so they feel included in the process. To get there, we need to document the hypothesis we want to verify (which we'll talk about next) and why it's important to the business, which sets the context for the decision: which option is best?

We can write a basic description of the top three options, but we'd likely discuss each with other leaders first. For instance, our example user story pertains to a web application, so we'd likely consult the lead engineer for web frameworks. Not all of these options might be experimentation, either. If everything is written in Flask, we could analyze the source code and ensure all apps are using dedicated middleware for authentication—but, as part of documenting our options, we could identify the trade-offs between this approach and chaos experimentation to present a fair evaluation of the opportunities before us. If we don't use a standard service framework, or only have it in some places, then this option may be less compelling. But if we use a service mesh, we could instead pursue the experimentation option by replaying traffic and discerning which of our services and which of their endpoints accept unauthenticated traffic.

Let's assume we socialized the options with stakeholders and there were no firm objections to conducting an experiment (exciting news!). How do we proceed from here? The next step is to design the experimental hypothesis.

Designing a Hypothesis

Hypotheses are, in essence, assumptions we make about reality that inform what experiment we conduct. Designing a hypothesis starts with developing a model of the target system's "steady state" characteristics—its normal operational state—and its critical functions. Remember, understanding critical functions is the first ingredient of our resilience potion and is how we can craft the statement, "the resilience of what, to what, and for whom." If we don't know the target system's critical functions, we will struggle to evaluate the experimental evidence to determine whether those functions behaved as intended or not. An important step during this phase is to document the observable characteristics describing the normal operation of the system, including any relevant metrics. In our example, we want to look at the service's normal authentication behavior—how does the authentication middleware behave when conditions are normal?

After documenting the system's steady state behavior, we use that information to formulate a hypothesis of what *could* and *should* happen during our experiment as a starting point. Hypotheses typically take the form of: "In the event of the following X condition, we are confident that our system will respond with Y." In our example, our hypothesis is: "In the event of unauthenticated traffic, we expect our service endpoints will respond with an authentication challenge."

 We never run a chaos experiment that we already know is going to fail. If we know it's going to fail, we should just fix the known problem—and then run the experiment to verify the fix.

In general, there are five questions to ask yourself (or your team, if crafting the hypothesis collaboratively) as you design and document a hypothesis:

1. What do we expect to happen in the experiment?
2. What are the specific criteria and characteristics that support the hypothesis?
3. What is the scope of this hypothesis?
4. What are the variables?
5. What are our assumptions?

If you created a decision tree (or a few!) like we walked through in Chapter 2, then you're in luck! Each decision tree you create can serve as elaborate hypotheses that engender experimental ideas. In essence, the decision tree provides a blueprint for the types of experiments you should conduct to verify your system's resilience to the adverse scenario described by the tree. Each attacker node on the branch reflects an opportunity to inject that type of failure condition in your system as part of an experiment. Remember, we aren't looking to test Boolean properties here; we're looking to simulate adverse *scenarios* and *conditions* to see how our sociotechnical system behaves in response—both the machines and humans interacting in and with the system.

As we discussed in Chapter 2, decision trees must be refined over time to reflect evolving conditions. When we collect evidence from experiments or real incidents, we should update our trees. But because decision trees are a visual representation of our mental model about attacker behavior in our systems, they will be incomplete relative to reality. Rather than a reason for reticence, this incites an imperative for us to perform proactive experimentation to improve our mental models—and thus our decision trees—to the best of our ability.

Designing an Experiment

Once we've fostered consensus around the idea of an experiment and designed our hypothesis, it's time to design the experiment itself—writing an experiment that verifies the intended behavior. During this part of the process, we seek to uncover the behavior about which we're trying to learn. In our example, our goal is to discover parts of the system that aren't authenticating properly and where our mental models of system behavior are incomplete.

One experimental design consideration is *where* we conduct our experiment. We can inject adverse conditions in any part of the stack at any layer—wherever makes the most sense to verify our hypothesis. These places can include:

- Application frontend/presentation layer
- Backend
- Cache
- Database
- Hardware
- Infrastructure
- Logging system
- Middleware
- Network
- Operating system kernel
- Orchestrator
- Queues/message buses
- Routing/service mesh
- Service
- Storage

We should also consider what we expect to measure during the experiment. This includes the measurements, metrics, and signals we talked about in Chapter 5, as well as things like SLAs, service-specific KPIs, and internal tickets or customer complaints. Measurement grants us the confidence that we can scale the experiment to add scope, width, or breadth.

Another crucial design element is to carefully consider how the experiment could potentially produce adverse effects and prepare a plan to minimize the impact. In practice, two common tactics organizations use to minimize impact include injecting failure conditions on instances that aren't internet-facing and conducting experiments on instances with lower numbers of users. Many open source chaos engineering toolkits include an opt-in/opt-out model to indicate the boundaries for experimentation too (such as the tool ChaoSlinger, which we'll discuss in Chapter 9).

Overall, we recommend starting small and verifying expectations as you progress in your journey to ensure experimentation isn't generating negative externalities. While you might hypothesize that your system will successfully respond to an adverse scenario, it might fail instead—so you want to ensure minimal impact. For example, if you want to conduct an experiment on a web application firewall's specific types of failure modes—like well-crafted packet-based exploits—you might choose to initially conduct this on an application that is not business-critical or is in a nonproduction environment to ensure it does not foment customer-impacting problems.

As part of our experimental design, we should also invest effort to review and document fallback scenarios and procedures. By doing so, any stakeholders involved will feel more confident in their ability to respond in the event of an experimental hypothesis not being verified (i.e., our system fails to respond or recover in the way we assume). A fallback plan can also serve a value-added exercise to further characterize the expected outcomes of the experiment.

 It's important to design experiments in a way that reflects how real problems occur, wherever possible. Designing an experiment based solely on the most accessible methods or types of faults that are injectable is an antipattern. We're designing *scenarios* to inject, not testing faults. We can summarize this design principle as "derive versus contrive."

Finally, who should be involved in the experiment? Experiments are meant to be cross-functional due to the sociotechnical nature of our systems, so we must be thoughtful in planning who should take part in them. Typical stakeholders that might participate in conducting an experiment include SREs, security incident responders, product owners, and software engineers.

When getting started in running chaos experiments in your organization, it's integral to inform relevant stakeholders about what you're intending to do, why you are doing it, and when you plan to do it. Composing an experiment design specification ("spec"), to which we'll now turn, equips you to communicate the information your organization needs to feel confident in the experiment and prepare for it.

 Security teams beware. If your team has not built and run reliable production services, partner with a team that has. Please be humble and know where you need help. You will crush any grassroots momentum around experiments by getting the release and other service processes wrong—siphoning the lifeblood of organizational adoption. There's no shame in working with Software Engineering teams that have ample practice in this regard.

Experiment Design Specifications

Thinking through the considerations in the prior section informs our experimental design. To document our design—capturing the *why*, as we've stressed throughout the book—we can write a spec. Documentation is essential when we design, build, and exercise chaos experiments; it's one of the most overlooked and undervalued aspects of the process of crafting valuable chaos experiments, so this section will detail how to compose docs properly.

At the top of our spec, we should describe the goal of the experiment and how our design goes about realizing the experiment. With this context captured, we then describe the experimental phases. Let's think through how these phases might look in our example experiment.

In the first phase, we might describe how we'll build the MVP component for experimentation against a toy system that can show the signal we're seeking. In our example, this might be a basic service that validates authentication but can also be configured to ignore authentication. This verifies that our experiment can tell us whether our toy service isn't validating authentication properly (since we want to ensure its critical functionality is working before we conduct the "real deal").

For the second phase, we'll perhaps find a real service that is maintained by a friendly team that is eager to conduct the experiment (stressing the need, as discussed in the last chapter, to make collaborative connections in your organization!). At the risk of stating the obvious, we need to gain buy-in from at least one team if we want to conduct the experiment. Please don't conduct "surprise" experiments on other teams' services.

Our goal with the spec is for our organization to gain a luculent understanding of *why* we're conducting this experiment, *when* we're conducting and *where*, *what* it will involve, and *how* it will unfold. As we'll keep stressing, precise and exact documentation of your experiment nourishes trust with your organization.

Since chaos experiments should be based on the scientific method, your experiment design documentation could include high-level sections like:

1. Observation of the system's current steady state.

2. Question(s): What if this? What if we do that?

3. Hypothesis: Depict what we expect to happen in the experiment. What are the specific experimental criteria that will be executed? What are the variables?

4. Experiment: How will we conduct the experiment? What are our fallback plans?

5. Analyze: Summarize the conclusion. What is the outcome of our experiment? By analyzing and documenting the outcome, we can then layer on additional experimentation and choose a different subsystem or a different set of criteria variables.

 Documenting our experiment design proffers both short-term and long-term benefits. In the short term, we benefit from precisely scripted events and back-off plans. In the long term, documentation helps us automate experiments with logical scripting rules that create sequence and output, such as using Gherkin syntax (Given, When, Then, etc.). We'll discuss automating experiments later in the chapter.

The following is a list of some elements you might want to incorporate into your experiment design spec—but you need not include all of them. Your experiments should only be as light or heavy as your context demands. A smaller experiment conducted in a test environment may only require a subset of these fields.

Experiment source
    This could be a prior incident, public incident reference, decision tree, or game day exercise. You can include references like "historical incident having reference ID of 'X'" or "decision tree located at 'Y.'"

Relevant system
    This is the name of the product, service, system, or component where you will run the experiment.

Scope of the experiment
    In what environment will the experiment run—development, staging, or production? Are there any boundaries around the experiment (e.g., does it touch one service or span an entire tier of services)?

Identified stakeholders
List any relevant stakeholders, including those with whom you spoke as you socialized the experiment. Importantly, this should include the normal operators of the services in question.

Experiment launch date
Schedule a date and time to "launch" the experiment—to execute the proposed hypothesis by injecting the failure condition.

Experiment failure scenario story
"On a dark and stormy night, a product depended on a trusty Kubernetes NetworkPolicy to control traffic within the cluster and prevent accidental exposure of the Kubernetes API to the public internet."

Hypothesis
If possibility X occurs, then Y will happen because of X (e.g., "If sugar causes cavities, then people who eat a lot of candy may be more prone to cavities.").

Experiment intent
What do we expect to happen and/or learn from the experiment?

Experiment measurement
What is the steady state of the system under normal conditions that might be perturbed by the experiment? How will the experiment be measured?

Security and compliance regulatory control classification
Where possible, consider classifying each experiment against any relevant or applicable compliance frameworks (e.g., PCI-DSS, NIST 800-53, CIS Benchmarks, GDPR, CCM). This will enable the submission of experiment output as auditable evidence.

Design artifacts
This could include the experiment process flow diagram, architecture diagram, or decision tree.

Experiment prerequisites
Describe the prerequisites that must be checked before the experiment can begin. What authentication and access permissions do we require (e.g., network, service, or resource access)? What authorization do we require (e.g., users, groups, roles, and policies)? Do backups need to be taken?

Potential impact and scope
What are the possible side effects of this experiment? What are the experiment's opt-in/opt-out criteria?

Experiment injected faults detail

Describe in detail the conditions being introduced into the target system:

- Actions performed, such as disabling authorization, enabling anonymous authentication, disabling audit logging, ports misconfigured, and latency injected
- Exact parameters being manipulated, either programmatically or by a human operator, including parameter name, misconfigured values, and explanation

Experiment halt conditions

Describe under what conditions the experiments will halt its run.

Experiment dry run

Are there any checks that you have executed to validate the safety of running the experiment before you run it?

Experiment parameters

Does your experiment vary across runs? Can you change properties or variables to run the experiment? If so, document the configuration options that will be used in each run. *Note: this is a more advanced approach to experiment design; we recommend starting with static experiment configurations before parameterizing or randomizing your experiments.*

Experiment observations

These are expected outputs from the execution of the experiment. Questions to ask include: What outputs (e.g., logs, metrics) will be collected? In what method will they be collected? Where will outputs be sent to (e.g., disk, external server, S3 bucket)?

Post-experiment clean-up procedures

These are tasks that will need to be performed after the experiment has concluded to restore the system to a steady state or to clean up temporary artifacts. This may include cleanup, should the experiment have to be rolled back due to unforeseen circumstances (e.g., synthetic traffic, generated workloads, or duplicate nodes/containers/VMs/AMIs).

Before we conduct our experiment, we need to *notify* the organization of the experiment's release date—and share our spec with them—so they aren't caught by surprise when the experiment launches. A new experiment should follow a similar communications pattern as a feature release. We should notify teams of when the release will happen and announce an upgrade or maintenance window if need be (some organizations require it, and removing this requirement is not a battle worth fighting at this juncture in your SCE journey). We should inform key stakeholders of our rollback plan, both what it is and where they can find it. Because we aren't running the experiment in a vacuum, we should clearly communicate its impact and timing to internal teams so that when the experiment is conducted, all can unfurl fluently.

Chatbots in Chaos Experiments

We can even use chatbots to generate code for chaos experiments and can specify the programming language. Here is real output from ChatGPT as an example:

Here is an example security chaos experiment in Python for AWS. This experiment simulates a scenario where a security group rule is accidentally deleted, causing traffic to be blocked to an Amazon Elastic Compute Cloud (EC2) instance.

To run this experiment, you will need to have an AWS account and the AWS SDK for Python (Boto3) installed. You will also need to have a security group and an EC2 instance set up in your account.

This experiment can be modified to test other types of security incidents, such as deleting a security group rule that allows traffic from a specific IP range or deleting a network ACL rule that allows traffic from a specific subnet.

```python
import boto3

# Set up the AWS client for EC2
ec2_client = boto3.client("ec2")

# Get the ID of the security group and the EC2 instance
security_group_id = "sg-12345678"
instance_id = "i-12345678"

# Delete the security group rule that allows traffic to the EC2 instance
ec2_client.revoke_security_group_ingress(
    GroupId=security_group_id,
    IpPermissions=[
        {
            "IpProtocol": "tcp",
            "FromPort": 22,
            "ToPort": 22,
            "IpRanges": [{"CidrIp": "0.0.0.0/0"}],
        }
    ],
)

# Verify that traffic to the EC2 instance is blocked
try:
    # Try to connect to the EC2 instance using SSH
    ssh_client = paramiko.SSHClient()
    ssh_client.connect(
        hostname=instance_public_ip,
        port=22,
        username="ec2-user",
        key_filename="path/to/private/key.pem",
    )
except Exception as e:
    print(f"Failed to connect to the EC2 instance: {e}")
```

Conducting Experiments

Once we've finished our experiment's design spec, we can proceed to the "fun phase": building the experiment so we can conduct it. Much like a feature release, if we have clear, descriptive specifications, the building and releasing part becomes much easier. We'll skip over the finer details of building an experiment based on the spec because it's mostly just regular software engineering.

How does conducting an experiment look in practice? Let's return to our example of verifying authentication middleware. In our example experiment, we'll collect evidence of how activity in our authentication endpoints manifests in our logging and monitoring pipelines. Is our organization's chosen middleware present in everything we deploy? If not, we want to see what happens. Perhaps the middleware is misconfigured. Remember, a chaos experiment isn't about a "true" or "false" answer; we're generating evidence of behavior across the system to help us learn and to inform change.

Based on our initial scoping, we'll run this experiment on one service to discover to what extent we are or are not validating authentication properly—as well as the n-order effects across space-time from that behavior. Through repeated experimentation (which could be described as phase 3), we can reach a point where we're confident in the behaviors of a single service. Because the service isn't static, we want to automate the experiment to continuously verify our mental models as the service and the systems around it evolve.

Drawing from our lessons learned from early adopters, we aren't conducting this in production, either. Knowing how the service behaves in preproduction is still advantageous and actionable; it's better to know before deploying to production rather than performing a hotfix or a rollback.

All the preparation that went into our design spec pays off during this phase. We already have a release or change plan, which includes processes for SREs or responders if something goes wrong. What's left after the experiment is deployed (other than savoring our victory for at least a little bit)? We need to collect the evidence that will ignite our insights.

Collecting Evidence

For any experiment worth conducting, you won't receive a signal instantly once you deploy it. We want to learn over time, which means we must gather evidence over time. When do we determine we have gleaned enough data and potentially turn off the experiment? You guessed it—it depends! The nature of the experiment informs its duration, and whether you even need or want to turn it off. When you're beginning your experimentation journey, you may want to start with a time-bounded, more manual exercise: the game day, which we'll discuss later in this chapter. Once you and your organization are more comfortable with experimentation, you'll likely design experiments to run in "continuous mode."

Our preparation when defining the spec means we should already know what we're monitoring and what evidence we expect. Importantly, we want to collect experiment execution health logs. This involves printing each command, error, and output generated from both failed and successful experiment runs to ensure the experiment is running in a safe, healthy, and expected manner. In general, the types of data we want to capture include:

- Log data
- Experiment run errors
- Final experiment run status
- Run duration
- Run time
- Experiment failed error conditions
- Experiment clean-up operation status

 When we capture experiment feedback, how should we consider compliance? We recommend hashing and storing a replica copy of experiment output to ensure output integrity can be validated by your auditors, should you have them.

We also want to properly categorize outcomes (experimental findings) to drive action items—fulfilling the feedback loop we want as part of our resilience potion. Using outcome categories for experimental results can be a pragmatic way to measure experiment findings over time and keep things actionable. For security experiments specifically, typical outcomes can include:

Prevented
    The action is prevented, blocked, or disallowed.

Remediated
    If not prevented, it's remediated (triaged).

Detected
    If not remediated, it's detected (logs, alerts).

Outcome categories can tie back to our Ice Cream Cone Hierarchy of Security Solutions in Chapter 7 too. Design-based solutions that eliminate or reduce hazards by design likely result in the "prevented" outcome type. Warning systems will only result in the "detected" type. Identifying the degree of human intervention required can identify where there are opportunities for more design-based solutions. We want our humans to leverage their strengths—creativity and adaptability—so we must invest effort capital in improved design to ensure this is so.

Security chaos experiments do not:

- Validate a configuration; they exercise it.
- Check authentication privileges; they attempt to frustrate them.
- Validate network settings; they send real traffic.
- Check application policy; they interact with the application.
- Build a model from infrastructure templates; they build understanding from experimentation.

Once our experiment has lived a little in its environment, we can reap the experimental evidence to analyze—gleaning a better understanding of the system's resilience to adverse scenarios and how we can improve the system for future success.

Analyzing and Documenting Evidence

Our next step, following the scientific method, is comparing our observations to our predictions. As scientists, we must analyze our experimental results to validate and refine our hypotheses—verifying our mental models of the system, like each assumption we defined in a decision tree. Ideally, you should conduct an experiment review to discuss what did or didn't work as intended. Examining the experimental results from all facets—and bringing in alternate perspectives from other stakeholders—will help you more deeply understand your systems.

Let's explore how this unfolds in practice. The first step after we've collected evidence is confirming we collected the evidence we sought from the experiment. In our example, did it successfully verify and expose cases where authentication isn't working? Perhaps it exposed some endpoints as having misconfigured middleware; that is an opportunity for redesign. Perhaps it exposed that this adverse condition isn't making it into any of our warning systems—an opportunity to improve our observability pipelines.

The second step is to analyze the data with regard to the hypothesis. Did your assumptions hold true? Was the hypothesis correct? Did anything happen that you didn't expect? You should confirm that systems and processes (automated or manual) functioned as expected. In our example, do all the endpoints validate authentication correctly? For those that don't validate unauthenticated traffic correctly, what information do we collect about that traffic? Were there other failures associated with the injected failure scenario? Did we receive alerts elsewhere? Can we distinguish unauthenticated traffic from properly authenticated traffic in our observability tools? Did anyone report any issues through Support?

Capturing Knowledge for Feedback Loops

We will likely use quite a few tools to analyze evidence, but can synthesize the results into our collaborative information-sharing tool of choice, like a shared document or project ticket. Decision trees can help us report our findings too; you can update the decision tree (with versioning) by incorporating your newfound experimental evidence.

 Validate the feedback expected from your security and visibility tools. If you expect to receive an alarm or notification in your SIEM for lateral movement after a port is opened unexpectedly, that is part of the process and should be recorded. Similarly, if your security response automation tool has a playbook for an expected experiment, validate the automation of the response.

Creating a shared document or artifact in this manner completes the feedback loop. Most people groan about writing documentation, but its importance to sustaining a learning culture cannot be understated. Scientific progress is almost always the result of building upon prior knowledge; without those prior findings being documented, progress would be much more limited.

This document serves as a foundational artifact for an experiment review—which we explicitly don't want to call a "postmortem." At some companies, a postmortem can trigger heavy processes for many reasons. We want an experiment review that is lightweight, expedites learning, and catalyzes constructive changes. Importantly, the experiment review must be blameless. As we discussed in Chapter 6, finger pointing at humans is the fastest way to kill a learning culture. Point fingers at the decision tree as a neutral entity instead, if you must.

What we should be doing at this stage is asking a lot of questions, stirring curiosity and receptivity. Where were your hypotheses correct? What did you overlook or miss? Maybe an adverse condition didn't spawn the impact you expected. Maybe the policy controls you thought were being enforced seemed to be taking a nap.

If we're partnering with another team—like a user-facing service team in our example—we likely want to perform a "first pass" analysis to groom the evidence, distilling it into a summary with action items. In our example, what if the evidence suggests that a particular team doesn't seem to know how to use the authentication middleware? One action item could be to work with that team to implement the middleware appropriately. Or we could reach out to the team that delivered the authentication middleware to discuss opportunities for improving their documentation and design. If you're a Product Engineering team conducting the experiment yourself, it likely makes sense to designate one person on the team as the synthesizer of evidence.

The majority of experiments will fail the first time you conduct them in a unique target environment. Remember, our mental models about our systems are always inaccurate, especially when we haven't refined them with experimental evidence yet. So don't be surprised when numerous action items bubble forth. Having a clear sense of where to refine system design and operation is cause for celebration, not lamentation.

The process we've described thus far is what's needed the first time you conduct an experiment. If you run the experiment continuously after the initial run, you should automate it and wire it to an alerting system to continue collecting evidence. From there, you can continuously review the evidence to understand how the system's context is changing and whether there is evidence that your organization should make changes.

When we conduct an experiment, we may discover evidence of successful compromise in the past that was previously unknown to our organization. In our example, what if we run the experiment and discover authentication is totally open? We may search through our logs and find numerous cases of unauthenticated traffic being accepted. That's when you open up an incident ticket, no matter how daunting it feels or how despondent you feel. Remember, this is still a far more proactive means of discovering evidence of compromise than being informed by an external party. Much like planting a tree, the best time to discover a compromise was yesterday, but the next best time is now.

Document Experiment Release Notes

Once we've analyzed our evidence and conducted an incident review, we can communicate our findings. Experiments are designed to answer questions from human beings about complex computing systems. We must remember that humans prefer to consume information in the form of storytelling. Consider the story you are trying to tell when communicating results, especially to stakeholders who were not involved in the experiment, like executives.

When communicating with executives, a clear and actionable story will drive more change than a detailed, technical breakdown of the experiment. You should also connect the dots between action items and the organizational goals that are important to executives. Provide enough insight for them to understand the action items and approve as necessary. For other stakeholders, you can consider implementing a dashboard or other visualization dedicated to experiments. A dashboard can even add value to in situ experiments, like reporting failures or status changes during experiments.

After conducting the first experiment, reporting your findings, and remediating any action items, schedule time to rerun the experiment to validate the remediation actions were successful and the hypothesis is current. You can also iterate on your experiments. The more you conduct experiments reflecting the potential security failures in your tree, the more your teams can build new muscle memory for responding to incidents. Repeated practice of these experiments can make incidents feel boring instead of scary and stressful—and we all know that burnout and stress is a huge problem for incident responders in our industry.

It's of foremost importance to focus on the generation of value instead of chaos when first conducting experiments (and thereafter too). It's not worth expanding your practice until you can demonstrate how the experiments you are running are delivering value back to the organization. We will discuss effective ways of collecting evidence and presenting it in an impactful nature later in this chapter.

Automating Experiments

Once we've developed muscle memory around experimentation, we want to automate our experiments for continual use where we can. Automation lets us repeatedly conduct experiments in a precise and controlled fashion, ensuring we consider the same variables and can therefore manipulate them. Through automation, we can deepen experimental rigor and expand coverage over time. We also want to automate the analysis of experimental results and even the creation of new experiments if we can.

As we've elaborated at length throughout this tome, reality is constantly evolving. Change is inevitable. The experiment we run in Q1 will assuredly have different outcomes when we run it in Q4—or even next week when our organization releases a new feature or considerable change in our systems. We must assume that any and all changes impact our experiments.[2] To maintain confidence in our system's resilience to attack and other adverse conditions, our best recourse is to run experiments continuously via automation.

---

2 Casey Rosenthal and Nora Jones, *Chaos Engineering: System Resiliency in Practice* (Sebastopol, CA: O'Reilly, 2020).

Easing into Chaos: Game Days

If your organization is especially hesitant about conducting chaos experiments, game days can help you cultivate grassroots support for the practice. Game days are a more manual form of chaos experimentation that can offer a more comfortable starting point for your organization to ease into chaos. Generally, game days will have more temporal or spatial bounds than typical chaos experiments, being neither continuous nor automated.

Composing a game day isn't so different from the process we just outlined for composing an experiment. The game day practice consists of a session in which engineers work together and brainstorm various failure scenarios. They create a planning document that describes the system being tested, the proposed failure scenarios to be attempted (including steps that will be taken to simulate the failures), expectations of how the system should respond to the failures, and the expected impact on users. The team works through each one of the scenarios, documenting observations and identifying differences between expectations and reality. With these results, the team has real-world information with which to inform solutions that infuse and nurture resilience in the system.

In essence, we can gain organizational confidence in our capacity to conduct experiments by gingerly handling the end-to-end process. Once we, and relevant stakeholders, feel sufficiently confident in our manual approach to experiments, we can pursue the process described earlier in the chapter with the aim of automating our experiments for continuous resilience assessment.

Engineering leader Russ Miles describes several styles to run a chaos game day in his book *Learning Chaos Engineering*. One style is "Dungeons and Dragons": none of the participants are aware of the experiment's conditions. Another is "Informed in Advance": all participants are informed about the incident they will experience. We recommend reading Russ's book for more specifics on how to conduct game days.

Example Security Chaos Experiments

Now that you've read about the experimental process, you're perhaps buzzing like a hurried, hungry little bee hunting for the nectar of experimental evidence. Let's pollinate your imagination with some inspiration. The rest of the chapter catalogs example experiments across a few contexts: production infrastructure, build pipelines, cloud native environments, and Windows environments.

Security Chaos Experiments for Production Infrastructure

In this section, we'll translate adverse conditions in production systems or services into chaos experiments (Table 8-1), regardless of specific architecture (so it's applicable across "legacy" and "modern" systems alike). Most production infrastructure runs on Linux, and on Linux systems, everything is a file. From that perspective, security failure can be seen as any file creation, deletion, or modification that results in unintended, negative impacts on the system. As you'll see in Table 8-1, many experiments for production environments include injecting hazardous file-related behavior.

Table 8-1. Security chaos experiments for production environments

Chaos experiment	Question(s) answered
Create or modify scheduled tasks (cron jobs) via a file or program	How does your infrastructure respond to unanticipated tasks? How quickly are you able to detect and revert persistence mechanisms?
Create a user account via CLI	How quickly are you able to detect and revert new, unwanted users?
Create and execute a new file in a container	How does your container respond to new file execution? Does it affect your cluster? How far does the event propagate? Are you containing impact? How quickly is the activity detected?
Delete *.bash_history*	Is there any effect on your production operations when bash history is deleted? Can you detect when bash history is deleted?
Delete logfiles	Can your team(s) still diagnose a problem or issue in production when logfiles are deleted? Do you have backups of logfiles? Are those backups restored automatically? Can you restore systems without certain logfiles being available? Are you detecting the deletion of logfiles?
Disable access to DNS	How reliant are your systems on external DNS? Are you able to detect a potential DNS attack? Are you caching entries? Do you have a fallback in */etc/hosts*? Are you generating alerts if internal DNS entries point to potentially malicious IP spaces?
Disable resource limits (CPU, file descriptors, memory, processes, restarts)	Can an infinite script take up resources? Is there an automatic process for restoring resource limits? Are you able to take the system offline and reintroduce a new version with resource limits enabled, without impacting operations? Are you detecting when resource limits are disabled?
Disable security mechanisms (e.g., SELinux, AppArmor, endpoint protection)	Are you detecting when security mechanisms are disabled? How quickly do you restore the security mechanisms?
Dump process memory	Can you detect when attackers dump process memory as part of system exploitation? Do responders have the data they need to investigate it?
Execute sudo commands	Can you execute sudo in production? Is debugging disabled in production? Are you able to detect and audit when users execute sudo commands in production systems?
Exfiltrate large volumes of data (e.g., terabytes)	Are you detecting spikes in data egress? What signals are you using? Do anomalous billing spikes generate security alerts? How quickly are you able to shut down unwanted data exfiltration?
Flood each resource type on a host (I/O, memory, CPU, disk)	Are resource limits in place? How does the system handle resource flooding with limits enabled versus disabled? Are alerts generated upon excess resource requests?
Inject expired API tokens	Are any resources still accepting expired API tokens? Which resources are denying them? Is your monitoring triggered? Are you verifying signatures? Is your failover graceful? Are you producing standard API responses like 401 and 403?

Chaos experiment	Question(s) answered
Inject program crashes	Is your service restarting by itself after a program crash? How quickly are you able to redeploy after a program crash? Are you able to detect a program crash in production?
Load a kernel module	Can users load kernel modules at runtime? Are you detecting when kernel modules are loaded in production infrastructure? How quickly are you able to redeploy systems once an unwanted kernel module is loaded?
Modify /etc/passwd	Is /etc/passwd modifiable? Is there any impact of the modification on your operations? Are you able to detect attacker persistence?
Modify /etc/shadow	Is /etc/shadow modifiable? Is there any impact of the modification on your operations? Are you able to detect attacker persistence?
Modify AppArmor profiles	Are your AppArmor profiles modifiable at runtime? Are you detecting modifications to AppArmor profiles? How quickly are you redeploying affected systems?
Modify boot files	Are you detecting attacker persistence via modification of boot files? How quickly are you redeploying affected systems?
Modify internal firewall rules and access permissions	How quickly are you detecting unwanted changes to firewall rules or access permissions? How quickly are you reverting unwanted changes?
Modify root certificate stores	Are you detecting attacker persistence via modification of root certificate stores? How quickly are you redeploying affected systems?
Modify SSH authorized keys	Are you detecting attacker persistence via modification of authorized SSH keys? How quickly are you redeploying affected systems?
Run a network service scanner on a host in your infrastructure	Are you catching and/or restricting lateral movement? Do your internal systems crash due to the noise generated by the scanner? Does it generate any internal errors?
Run container runtimes at the "debug" log level	How does running at the debug log level impact the information exposed in your container to a user? Is any sensitive information logged? How do your logging systems handle additional data?
Shell into a container	Are users allowed to shell into containers? Are you able to detect what commands are run within a container? How quickly are you able to redeploy a container when an unexpected shell session is detected?
SSH into a noninteractive host	Is it possible to SSH into hosts that are designed to be noninteractive? Are you able to detect what commands are run on a noninteractive host? How quickly are you able to redeploy a noninteractive host in the event an unexpected SSH session is detected?
Time travel on a host (change the host's time forward or backward)	How are your systems handling expired and dated certificates or licenses? Are you relying on external NTP? Are time-related issues (e.g., across logging, certificates, SLA tracking) generating alerts?
Spawn unauthorized interactive shells	Can unauthorized interactive shells be spawned? Can you detect if the interactive shell occurs outside of normal process guidelines? Are you detecting unauthorized shells? If so, how long does it take for you to redeploy affected systems?
Write to files related to bash profile/rc	Are you detecting persistence mechanisms like writing files related to profile/rc? How quickly can you redeploy affected systems?

Security Chaos Experiments for Build Pipelines

There are quite a few ways that security failure can manifest in build pipelines specifically. What happens if there is an outage in your vulnerability scanner or other build-time security tools? Does it halt PRs being merged? Are releases frozen? Try forcing an outage in one of these tools—for instance, by using a faulty API token for the service.

Build pipelines—commonly manifesting as CI/CD pipelines—include a few different components: build and automation servers, code and image repositories, and third-party tools (which are often open source). We'll focus on build and automation servers and the tools that support CI/CD in this section.

The typical CI/CD pipeline operates in the following steps: a developer commits code to a code repository, it is built and tested by CI systems, and it is reviewed by one of the developer's peers. Upon approval, it will be merged and the updated service will be deployed by the CD system to the cluster where the service runs, often by pushing artifacts through image or container repositories.

In some pipelines, the developer will have direct write access to these image repositories and clusters—which could obviously lead to security failure. Furthermore, automation servers can often present a juicy target for attackers because they possess read and write access between image repositories and clusters.

In Table 8-2, let's explore some of the ways you can inject adverse conditions into your build pipelines.

Table 8-2. Security chaos experiments for build (CI/CD) pipelines

Chaos experiment	Question(s) answered
Add new users in authentication plug-ins, which access web consoles in automation/CI servers	Is authentication required to add new users? What happens when new users are added with web console access? Are you able to detect new users? Can you track their actions?
Approve commits with outdated/unapproved credentials	How does the system handle outdated/unapproved credentials? Are alerts generated when outdated or unapproved creds are used? How do these commits propagate through the rest of the pipeline?
Create and schedule new jobs via the automation server's script console (bonus points if done with anonymous access!)	Is authentication required to create and schedule new jobs via the automation server's script console? If not, are those changes detected or otherwise audited?
Decrypt stored passwords from the automation server's script console	Which users can decrypt stored passwords from the automation server's script console? Is any authentication performed?
Elevate the Jenkins service account to `sudo` or root access	Are there any restrictions on elevating privileges? Do you detect when the Jenkins service account is granted `sudo` or root access?
Enable anonymous read access in your automation server, then read build history and credential plug-ins	Are there any blocks to enabling anon access? Are you able to detect when anon read access is enabled? What is the access footprint of anon read-only users in the automation server?

Chaos experiment	Question(s) answered
Enable anonymous script console access and execute commands	Is there anything blocking anon script console access? Are there any limitations on commands that can be executed? Are you detecting command execution from the script console? If so, how quickly?
Enable autodiscovery in publicly facing servers	What impacts does autodiscovery have on your systems? What actions can be taken when autodiscovery is enabled?
Exfiltrate credentials via malicious AWS and GCP services (e.g., *storage.googleapis.com*)	Is any exfiltration allowed from your automation servers? Are you able to detect exfiltration via allowlisted services?
Grep and export *credentials.xml* and *jobs/.../build.xml* files	What restrictions are in place for accessing and exporting sensitive files? Are you able to detect access and export of these sensitive files?
Grep and reads of *credentials.xml*, *master.key*, and *hudson.util.Secret* in Jenkins	What restrictions are in place for accessing secrets in automation servers? Are you able to detect access and reads of secrets in automation servers?
Inject credentials into code	How do credentials embedded in code propagate through your build pipeline? How long does it take to detect credentials introduced in code? How quickly are they removed?
Inject credentials into configuration files (e.g., Git config files)	How do credentials embedded in config files propagate through your build pipeline? How long does it take to detect credentials introduced in config files? How quickly are they removed?
Inject credentials or keys into automation scripts	How do credentials or keys embedded in automation scripts propagate through your build pipeline? How long does it take to detect credentials or keys introduced in automation scripts? How quickly are they removed?
Inject credentials or keys into build logs	How do credentials or keys embedded in build logs propagate through your build pipeline? How long does it take to detect credentials or keys introduced in build logs? How quickly are they removed?
Inject expired OAuth tokens into builds	Are expired OAuth tokens still accepted in your build pipeline? If expired OAuth tokens are used, are alerts generated?
Inject old access tokens used for old apps	Are old access tokens accepted by old applications? Are you monitoring access activity in old applications?
Inject outdated service account keys to Jenkins jobs	Are outdated service account keys accepted by Jenkins jobs? Are alerts generated on attempts to use outdated service account keys?
Modify existing jobs and scheduling builds (bonus points if done with anonymous access)	Can users store secrets or credentials within environment variables? Are you detecting when jobs and builds are modified?
Overwrite build logs	Which users can overwrite build logs? Are build logs monitored? How quickly are unwanted changes to build logs detected and reversed?
Read build history in the automation server's script console	Can you detect users performing reconnaissance, including searching for credentials? Is there authorization to access build history?
Recursively clone a purposefully malicious submodule repository	How does your pipeline handle malicious hooks configured in submodule repositories? To what extent do they affect your pipeline and systems? Can you detect malicious repo configurations?
Reregister dead packages in use by your projects	Can dead packages be reregistered? What access to your pipeline or secrets is granted by dead packages? Are you detecting the resurrection of dead packages?

Chaos experiment	Question(s) answered
Run a crypto miner on your automation/CI servers	Are there resource limits on your automation/CI servers? Which users can run services on your automation servers? What signals are you using to detect crypto miners on your automation servers?
Run PowerShell commands in your automation server's script console	Which users can run PowerShell commands in the script console? Are there any authentication controls? What commands are allowed? Are you detecting the execution of PowerShell commands in the script console?
Wipe all code from repositories	Which users can wipe all code from repositories? Are there any controls to restrict code wiping? What signals are you collecting to detect ransomware? How quickly can you restore code to your repositories when they are wiped?

Security Chaos Experiments in Cloud Native Environments

Now let's explore common security failures in cloud native environments,[3] enumerated in Table 8-3, with an eye toward how these failures can be injected as adverse conditions into your systems for experimentation. Your organization may not have all these components or configurations in place in your systems, so treat this as an illustrative jumping-off point to brainstorm your own tests.

As we mentioned in Chapter 4, cloud native misconfigurations are significant contributors (*https://oreil.ly/BvY4P*) to security failure in cloud native environments, but they aren't vulnerabilities and don't receive a CVE identifier. Containers allowing anonymous access, unnecessary ports open on servers, orchestration management consoles exposed publicly, revealing stack traces when handling errors, or remote administration functionality being enabled are all examples of misconfigurations that can lead to security failure. While it's easy to see how these misconfigurations can contribute to security failure, other misconfigurations can be subtler. Outdated certificates are an obvious misconfiguration, but mishandled implementation of authentication can be harder to spot—while still capable of resulting in the same ultimate failure.

Table 8-3. Security chaos experiments for cloud native environments

Chaos experiment	Question(s) answered
Add a (massive) throttling limit to APIs	How does restricted communication affect your systems? Are there any relevant security tasks that can no longer be performed? How quickly are you detecting availability problems?
Disable noncritical roles and functions in an API	Is your API failing open or closed? Are any API endpoints hanging? Are they properly timing out? Are your triggers working and alerts being generated as intended? Does the API call still go through, even if there is no response or a malformed response?

---

3 We recommend looking through OWASP's Docker Security Cheat Sheet for other examples of failure within Docker containers specifically, available at *https://oreil.ly/nRkKX*.

Chaos experiment	Question(s) answered
Disable read-only access for filesystem and volume	What is the impact of being able to write to disk in your containers? How does an erosion of immutability affect other relevant security aspects of the system? How quickly are you detecting file or system modifications?
Disable resource limits (CPU, file descriptors, memory, processes, restarts)	What signals lead you to detect abuse of system resources? How quickly are you detecting spikes in resource utilization? How do you respond to a DoS?
Enable anonymous access in your orchestrator (e.g., the - -anonymous-auth argument in Kubernetes)	Is anonymous access enabled or disabled by default in your orchestrator? Are you granting role-based access control (RBAC) privileges to anonymous users? Are you tracking activity performed by anonymous users? How quickly are you able to disable anonymous access?
Enable inter-container communication	What is the impact of all containers being able to talk to each other? What information can one container disclose to another? How quickly are you detecting and reversing these changes (like - -icc=true in Docker)?
Enable swarm mode in Docker engine instances	Are you detecting unwanted open ports? Can other systems on the network access sensitive data via network ports?
Expose Docker daemon sockets (e.g., the TCP Docker daemon socket or /var/run/docker.sock)	How does unrestricted root access to the underlying host propagate in your container infrastructure? How quickly are you detecting and reversing socket exposure?
Expose microservices in the LAN from the same application	Are you able to detect lateral movement between containers?
Expose orchestration management interfaces/APIs	Are you detecting unauthorized access to publicly exposed management interfaces? How are you tracking changes made via management interfaces or APIs?
Expose traditional orchestration services, like NFS and Samba	Are you able to audit access to network shares? How quickly do you detect unauthorized access or modification of remotely hosted files?
Generate large loads in specific regions, like availability zones or datacenters	Are your APIs autoscaling? If they aren't, how quickly are you able to detect and restore functionality?
Inject orchestrator impersonation headers	Do you have limits on user impersonation? Do you have restrictions on what actions impersonated users can conduct? Are you tracking activity by impersonated users?
Inject unapproved lineages	How do unapproved base images in your image repositories propagate into your CI/CD pipeline? How quickly do you detect and remove unapproved images?
Insert known vulnerabilities	Where in your build pipeline are you detecting and patching/removing known vulnerabilities in components?
Mount host system directories (like /boot, /dev, /etc, /lib, etc.) as container volumes	How do changes to files within host directories impact your systems? How quickly are you detecting changes to sensitive directories?
Remove (or corrupt) random HTTP headers from APIs	How do your APIs respond to removed headers? Are you detecting when REST bodies don't match the intended content type specified in the header?
Remove resource segmentation	Which components can remove resource segmentation? How does lack of resource segmentation impact your systems? Are you able to detect when resource segmentation is removed?
Retrograde libraries and containers	Are you detecting the use of outdated libraries or container images? Where in your build pipeline are outdated components detected? How quickly can you restore more recent versions?

Chaos experiment	Question(s) answered
Run services as root in the container	Are you detecting containers that can facilitate full user privileges without a privilege escalation? Where in your build pipeline is this being addressed?
Run Docker containers with the `--privileged` flag	Are there any containers with all Linux kernel capabilities enabled? How quickly are you detecting invocation of the `--privileged` flag? What about for existing images?
Run unpatched container runtimes	How do unpatched container runtimes propagate in your build pipeline, from image repositories, to orchestration software, to hosts? What is your mean time to patch? Are you able to detect exploitation of vulnerable runtimes?
Simulate a lack of filtering sanitization on the edge	How do you handle data downstream internally? What is the impact of not having sanitization?
Switch schema format for internal APIs (e.g., if JSON is expected, return a 404 in plain HTML)	How do your systems react to new API schemas? How quickly are you able to detect and reverse unwanted changes to schemas?
Turn off API authorization	Are your internal APIs enforcing authorization? Are you able to detect race conditions? How quickly are you able to detect unwanted access to data? What signals are you using to do so?

Security Chaos Experiments in Windows Environments

Finally, let's list potential chaos experiments in Windows environments. While not the typical purview of chaos experimentation, Windows environments—especially of the on-prem, perimeter-model variety—are a popular hunting ground for attackers. One of the best design changes organizations could make to better prepare against these attacks is to migrate to an environment where you do not manage your own domain controller and you pay a service provider to manage it instead. Another great change is to migrate to an environment where contagion can propagate less—that is, where there is looser coupling between filesystems. Table 8-4 enumerates different adverse conditions in Windows environments and how they translate into security chaos experiments.

Table 8-4. Security chaos experiments for Windows environments

Chaos experiment	Question(s) answered
Access restricted data	What happens when a regular user attempts to access restricted data? Will you know when users attempt to access sensitive logs?
Attach an automated email forwarding rule	Are you aware of email forwarding rules that are set up? If suspicious forwarding rules are attached, will you be notified?
Bulk download of sensitive data	Will you know if users attempt to bulk-download or export corporate data from the shared filesystem? What mechanisms will notify you when this happens?
Check if remote execution is allowed on and from user workstations via PsExec/PowerShell Remoting	Where can remote execution be spawned from and to? Is the intended system policy in place? How does malware spread?

Chaos experiment	Question(s) answered
Clear Windows event logs	Are users able to clear the Windows event logs? Will you be notified when they do? How will you be notified and what steps are required to remain compliant in the event this happens?
Connect to a rogue WiFi access point that intercepts TLS	Will users see an error that their communications are being intercepted? Will you have a record when TLS certificate errors are suppressed?
Connect to internal corporate intranet sites over HTTP	Will corporate sites send sensitive data over HTTP, potentially leaving them susceptible to passive meddler-in-the-middle interception? Will you receive an alert if this happens? Do you have the data you need to investigate it?
Downgrade operating system components or browser	Do your users stay up-to-date on their software updates? What happens if they don't? Do your automatic updates work as you intend them to? How quickly can you upgrade in the instance of a downgrade?
Install a custom browser extension	Are browser extensions potentially stealing your sensitive data? Do you know what browser extensions users have installed?
Install a startup shortcut, schedule a background task, or create a dummy Windows service	Are new services and background tasks detected by your monitoring? How quickly can you identify new services and background tasks? How quickly can you remove them?
Load a webpage that wraps internal intranet pages in an iframe or uses a background form to POST to them	Are intranet pages vulnerable to XSRF or other vulnerabilities that could be triggered from an email or instant message? Do you receive alerts on them?
Log in to the domain controller interactively	How does the system respond to interactive logins on the Active Directory domain controller? Are the appropriate people notified that a "break glass" event has occurred?
Open a document with macros	What happens when a user opens a document containing a macro? Will the macro run by default or will users be prompted?
Redirect the VPN to connect to a rogue host to see if it validates the certificate	Is it possible for users to accidentally connect to a rogue VPN server? Will you be notified if this happens?
Run custom PowerShell or Batch file	Are arbitrary PowerShell or Batch scripts allowed to run in your environment? If so, do you have a record of which ran and when? Are all users allowed to run scripts or only users who are expected to do so as part of their job function?
Run custom software out of user documents or download directories	To what extent are users allowed to download and install new software? Will you be notified?
Use a password that was revealed in a data breach	Are you checking for breached passwords that attackers could use to log in as one of your employees or contractors? If a user reused a breached password, would you know? When a password breach occurs, do you force rotation of the appropriate passwords?
Visit internal intranet hostnames in a browser when disconnected from the VPN	Will users be redirected to a domain that could be registered by an adversary? Could it be possible to trick employees into thinking they are visiting a corporate intranet page when they're really viewing an attacker's phishing page?

Chapter Takeaways

- Experimentation is a cycle of discovery and learning, which is what drives scientific progress. Security chaos experiments are like applying the scientific method to software and systems security.

- Early adopters of security chaos experimentation learned three key lessons: first, it's fine to start in nonproduction environments because you can still learn a lot; second, use past incidents as inspiration for experiments and to leverage organizational memory; third, make sure to publish and evangelize your experimental findings because expanding adoption will become your hardest challenge (the technical work is comparatively easy).

- To set chaos experiments up for success, especially the first time, we need to socialize the experiment with relevant stakeholders. Investing in the right messaging and framing at the beginning will reduce friction later.

- The next step is designing an experimental hypothesis. Hypotheses typically take the form of: "In the event of the following X condition, we are confident that our system will respond with Y."

- Once we have a hypothesis, we can design our experiment so we uncover the behavior about which we want to learn. There are numerous considerations: where we conduct the experiment, how we measure success, potential impacts, fallback procedures, and more.

- Documenting a precise, exact experiment design specification ("spec") is critical. Our goal with the spec is for our organization to gain a luculent understanding of *why* we're conducting this experiment, *when* and *where* we're conducting it, *what* it will involve, and *how* it will unfold.

- Launching an experiment is not unlike a feature release. Our preparation in socializing the experiment, designing the hypothesis, and defining the experiment specifications makes this one of the easier phases.

- What evidence we collect when conducting an experiment is defined by the spec; we should already know what we're monitoring and what evidence we expect.

- The first step after we've collected evidence is confirming we collected the evidence we sought from the experiment. The second step is to analyze the data with regard to the hypothesis. Our goal is to compare our observations with our predictions—to verify and refine our mental models of the system, which informs what actions we can take to sustain its resilience to adversity.

- We should communicate our experimental findings through release notes. Most stakeholders don't need lots of detail; we should synthesize and summarize our experimental insights, highlighting any action items. Once those action items are performed, we can rerun the experiment.

- After your first experiment, or after you run an experiment the first time, you can automate it for continual use. Because our systems—and the reality around them—are constantly changing, we must continually generate evidence lest it grow stale.

- Game days, a more manual form of conducting a security chaos experiment, can help more hesitant organizations ease into chaos experimentation.

- There is no end to the kinds of security chaos experiments you can conduct in your systems. We enumerated many applicable to production infrastructure, build pipelines, service-oriented environments, and Windows environments.

CHAPTER 9

Security Chaos Engineering in the Wild

There is a growing community of security practitioners and organizations that are both advocating SCE and developing experiments through open source and other community initiatives. This chapter shares some of these stories from organizations that have successfully implemented security chaos experiments as a practice within their security programs.

Experience Report: The Existence of Order Through Chaos (UnitedHealth Group)

Authored by Aaron Rinehart

> "Big things have small beginnings."
> —T. E. Lawrence

UnitedHealth Group (UHG) and its technical service arm, Optum, provides healthcare products and insurance services to more than 85 million patients worldwide and is the largest U.S. health insurer.

As of February 1, 2023, UHG is ranked 11th on the 2022 Fortune Global 500 and has a market capitalization of $400.7 billion. The company is currently the world's largest healthcare company by revenue and the largest insurance company by net premiums.

In 2018, while serving as the company's chief security architect, UHG contained more than 380 business entities, operated globally, had annual revenue of $201 billion, and employed more than 270,000 employees worldwide.

The most prominent and difficult challenge that our organization faced at that time was incomplete technical documentation while conducting security architectural reviews. While we genuinely aspired to provide suitable security recommendations, we were never sure how accurate the inputs were. A poor depiction of the system made it extremely difficult to provide anything other than poor outputs as a result. Furthermore, when security design guidance was provided, there was no feedback mechanism for understanding whether it was implemented correctly or if it was operationally effective.

The primary need we were trying to solve for initially was to create a way to directly ask the systems basic questions about the state of their operational security after they had been deployed. The validation of security controls was the original problem set behind applying chaos engineering to security with ChaoSlingr, which is the SCE tool we created at UHG. It focused primarily on the experimentation on AWS infrastructure to bring system security weaknesses to the forefront.

When we first started working on ChaoSlingr we were experiencing several challenges throughout our security engineering lifecycle. The company began its long journey toward transforming the way we would build and deliver customer value and improved patient experiences through the modernization of our technology stack and processes.

Several major industries such as hospitality, institutional banking, airlines, insurance, and healthcare still rely heavily on legacy mainframe systems built in the 1970s and '80s (*https://oreil.ly/NbqE2*). If the company was going to succeed, it had to figure out how to digitally transform and extend the tremendous power of the mainframe in the process. The company began rapidly adopting new technologies and practices such as Agile software delivery, DevOps, Continuous Integration, and Continuous Delivery, and making the long, arduous pilgrimage to the public cloud.

The trigger that kickstarted the ChaoSlingr project came out of the journey to the AWS public cloud. As a company, this required a shift in mindset as well as technical skills to meet the challenge ahead. Throughout the technological diaspora underway at UHG, one of the many concerns the cybersecurity organization had was whether we had the right knowledge, tools, and skills to deliver our customers' healthcare workloads safely. ChaoSlingr was born out of this uncertainty. We decided that there was a need to proactively verify that the security we were building in the public cloud could meet or exceed our needs.

Shortly after beginning our odyssey toward the AWS public cloud, UHG began building the foundations of its Site Reliability Engineering (SRE) practice. Patrick Bergstrom became the organization's first Site Reliability Engineer. During our first conversation, Patrick started telling me about what it's like to be an SRE and his recent experiences at BestBuy, the consumer electronics retail corporation. He explained to me that one of the primary goals of an SRE is to improve the reliability of high-scale systems through automation and testing. He went further on regaling me with tales of breaking computer systems that most surely captured my interest as a cybersecurity professional. He explained to me that they would perform these "chaos engineering" exercises, which would introduce turbulent conditions into their operational computing environments with the intention of verifying that the systems behaved correctly.

After hearing about this novel engineering practice from Patrick, I rapidly began exploring Netflix's chaos engineering practices as well. Soon after, we began building a prototype piece of software to prove whether this new technical practice could be applied to improve our understanding of operational security. Not only was this a breakthrough toward improving our operational cybersecurity, but it also showed the company the value of thinking differently about the problems.

As a result of building ChaoSlingr, we not only released the company's first open source software project, but also introduced a new method of instrumenting security.

ChaoSlingr is a serverless SCE–focused tool written in Python Boto3 for AWS. The tool was originally modeled from Netflix's Chaos Monkey, but after a comprehensive analysis of Chaos Monkey's codebase, we realized that we did not need much of the functionality. The version we analyzed was built prior to the availability of several cloud native services and tool sets such as AWS Lambda. In the end, ChaoSlingr became a series of three AWS Lambda functions: Generatr, Slingr, and Trackr.

There is now a growing community of security professionals who are both advocating SCE and developing experiments through open source and other community initiatives. As general-purpose chaos engineering tools mature, those experiment libraries will include more security-specific experiments. Today, however, security professionals should still be prepared to design and build their own experiments through scripting or leverage existing open source software tool sets such as ChaoSlingr as a framework.

The Story of ChaoSlingr

ChaoSlingr, as seen in Figure 9-1, is a security experiment and reporting framework created by a team at UHG led by Aaron Rinehart (this chapter's author). It was the first open source software tool to demonstrate the value of applying chaos engineering to cybersecurity. It was designed and introduced as open source with the intention of demonstrating a simplified framework for writing security chaos experiments.

One experiment at UHG involved misconfiguring a port (which we refer to in Chapter 2). The hypothesis for this experiment was that a misconfigured port should be detected and blocked by the firewall, and the incident should be appropriately logged for the security team. Half of the time, that's exactly what happened. The other half of the time, the firewall failed to detect and block it. But a commodity cloud configuration tool did always catch it and block it. Unfortunately, that tool did not log it in such a way that the security team could easily identify where the incident had occurred.

Imagine that you are on that team. Your fundamental understanding of your own security posture would be shaken by this discovery. The power of ChaoSlingr is that the experiments prove whether your assumptions are true or not. You aren't left guessing or assuming about your security instrumentation.

The framework consists of four primary functions:

- *Generatr*, which identifies the object to inject the failure on and calls Slingr
- *Slingr*, which injects the failure
- *Trackr*, which logs details about the experiment as it occurs
- *Experiment description*, which provides documentation on the experiment along with applicable input and output parameters for Lambda functions

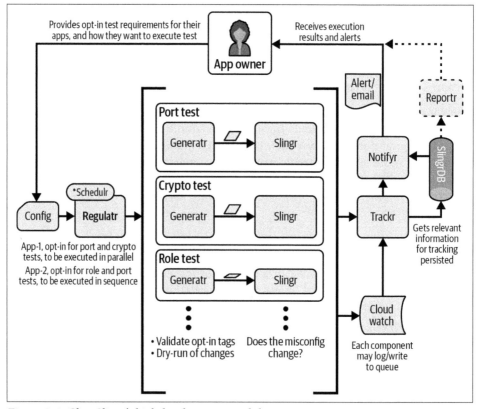

Figure 9-1. ChaoSlingr's high-level context and design

ChaoSlingr was originally designed to operate in AWS. It proactively introduces known security failure conditions through a series of experiments to determine how effectively security is implemented. The high-level business driver behind the effort was to improve the company's ability to rapidly deliver high-quality products and services while maintaining the highest level of safety and security possible.

The safety-critical systems that are being built today are becoming so complex and distributed in nature that no single entity can account for the entirety of its operational nature. Even when all the individual services in a distributed system are functioning properly, the interactions between those services can cause unpredictable outcomes. Unpredictable outcomes, compounded by rare but disruptive real-world events that affect production environments, make these distributed systems inherently chaotic. ChaoSlingr was developed to uncover, communicate, and address significant weaknesses proactively, before they impact customers in production.

Features of ChaoSlingr include:

- Open source
- Big Red Button, which automatically shuts down ChaoSlingr if it's not behaving or during an active incident
- Configurable timeframes and frequency of experiment runs
- Written in Python
- Runs as Lambda functions
- Autoconfiguration for setup written in Terraform script format

Step-by-Step Example: PortSlingr

When we decided to make ChaoSlingr open source, we recognized that we needed an example experiment that most engineers could understand. The example we came up with was a "misconfigured or unauthorized port change."

Our false assumption:

The cybersecurity industry has been solving this condition for the past 20 or more years, but somehow misconfigured ports are still a common occurrence. As security professionals, we felt confident that the firewall solutions that we had put in place were more than satisfactory at managing this kind of abhorrent behavior. We decided to test our assumptions by running a chaos experiment:

1. It turns out that our confidence was sadly misplaced—when we started running PortSlingr on our various AWS instances, we started to discover that our assumption was only about 60% true. Meaning that our firewalls only detected and blocked the misconfigured port 60% of the time; we expected it to catch and block the change 100% of the time. Remember, there was no actual incident as a

result of this experiment. However, we were essentially able to proactively identify a configuration drift issue that had occurred between different software environments and fix it before it caused any real harm to the company's systems.[1]

2. The second thing we learned was that our commodity cloud native configuration management tool almost always caught and blocked the change, which we did not initially expect.

3. The next thing we expected to happen was for both the firewall and configuration management tools to send log event information to our security event monitoring solution, which would trigger an alert to the security operations team. This operated as it was supposed to.

4. When the security operations analyst received the alert, they could not figure out which AWS environment the event came from. Most engineers' first response to this would be to think it is a trivial exercise to identify the source environment in AWS. All you need to do is map backward the IP addresses to the AWS environment the event came from. That process alone can take 15 minutes and that may not account for any Source Network Address Translation (SNAT) configuration in place, which intentionally hides the real IP addresses being translated from internal private AWS address space to publicly routable elastic network interfaces. The overall point here is that mapping back the addresses could have taken anywhere from 15 minutes to 2 hours. If the alert had been a real security incident or outage, it could have cost the company a significant amount of lost revenue and productivity.

5. Remember, this was not a real security incident, and we were able to proactively discover these inconsistencies within our security posture and fix them before they manifested into customer-impacting problems.

ChaoSlingr demonstrates how chaos engineering experiments can be constructed and executed to provide security value in distributed systems. In the time since its original debut as an open source software tool on GitHub, the organization has evolved its usage of the tool set and no longer maintains the repository. Despite no longer being maintained, the project can still be used as a great starting point for those who are newly adopting the craft. Many organizations utilizing ChaoSlingr have since forked the project and constructed their own series of security chaos experiments using the framework provided by the project as a guide.

As other enterprises adopt cloud native stacks and the DevOps model, their security programs must evolve to meet new demands such as the frequency of system-wide

---

[1] At the time we were performing these experiments, the company was in the midst of a cloud transformation effort and still very new to AWS as a practice.

changes enabled by Continuous Deployment. Traditional security testing, while valuable, is insufficient to meet these new challenges.

The mindset of the approach to security must also change. "System glitches" are the normal operating conditions of complex systems. Focusing on "human error," "root cause," or sophisticated attackers won't get you nearly as far in security as a better understanding of your basic security posture, in an ongoing way, with instrumented feedback loops. SCE creates these feedback loops and can expose previously unknown unknowns, limiting the surface area for attackers.

The tool ChaoSlingr proves that chaos engineering can be applied to cybersecurity. The experience of utilizing ChaoSlingr at UHG proved that there is value in this approach. When applied in a security context, chaos engineering has the potential to reveal valuable, objective information about how security controls operate, allowing organizations to invest security budgets more efficiently. Given that benefit, all organizations should consider when and how to implement this discipline, especially those operating complex systems at scale.

Experience Report: A Quest for Stronger Reliability (Verizon)

Authored by Troy Koss and Brian Bagdzinski

At the beginning of our technology boom, international media mogul Rupert Murdoch said, "The world is changing very fast. Big will not beat small anymore. It will be the fast beating the slow." My fellow SRE and I were working at a large telecom. Much like most technology companies, our systems were growing rapidly, new services and applications were spawning at a rate that seemed almost daily, economic pressures meant fewer and fewer resources, and the expectation for secure and highly performant systems was table stakes for a company with a reputation of reliability that a telecom must possess. We've seen Murdoch's thoughts play out time and time again. Those that have been able to deliver quickly while having a solid and reliable product offering have taken out some of the largest and most iconic businesses. Blockbuster was a thing before we had Netflix. Toys 'R Us was "The" toy spot before Amazon. We were struck with the question: what will it take for a large telecom to move fast, reliably? We knew that America's most reliable network needed the most reliable Culture.

Before we could embark on this journey to reliability, we had to take a look at our past and present to best understand how these concepts could be accepted effectively to shape our future. We looked to Google's Site Reliability Engineering practice as a logical starting point for inspiration. We were going to "Do SRE," whatever that means. Let's face it, we were different from Google; everyone is unique. Different business models, different products and services, different past, different teams. We knew we had to find a way to shape a pathway to successful SRE that was conducive for our company's profile. In the book *Seeking SRE* by David N. Blank-Edelman (O'Reilly, 2018), a critical antipattern to successful SRE is "Fixing the Ops Team." This is much more than having ops write some code to automate processes. Blank-Edelman explains how "successful SRE requires fundamentally reordering how the entire company or institution conducts business." Here's what we have in mind:

- How priorities are set
- How planning is conducted
- How decisions are made
- How systems are designed and built
- How teams interact with one another
- How we operate and think
- How we educate ourselves
- How our software operates
- How our software and infrastructure get deployed
- How we deal with incidents

SRE involves cultural changes to empower teams to optimize toward successfully delivering the metrics to delight their customers. Our challenge was to define a culture to promote SRE practices. Initially, the various dimensions we carved out as we created our north star included things like observability, resiliency, release engineering, continuous learning, and so forth. It was a distilled version of the many readings and educational materials extrapolated on the SRE practice. We started with adoption of these practices within our shared services group that ran common platforms across the enterprise. One example was our Kubernetes container implementation. For each dimension, we began to assess where the services were—not the typical scorecard, but rather out of the best practices that exist (e.g., having SLOs; capturing metrics, logs, and traces; having appropriate alerting; vulnerability scanning; treating infrastructure immutably).

As we began to do this, we immediately started seeing gaps in observability and monitoring. These shared platforms were meant to bake in all of the regulations and compliance a telecom requires, and to ease the burden for the many running their applications. We quickly began to see several problems that would be faced. We had limited insight to know for certain that we were meeting the standards and configuration we were putting in place.

The next struggle was knowing what our customer experience was; in this case, app teams using these shared platforms were the customer. There was a lack of SLOs, a good sense of how we were doing at any given point in time, or if we were meeting customer expectations. There was also a sense that we would become incapacitated by the goals we set, even if we had SLOs.

Finally, the number of support tickets and requests for aid grew exponentially; the teams surely knew it wasn't pleasant. It was difficult to untangle the complexity that was growing and to figure out where to even start an investigation when a problem arose. Was it a platform challenge? Was it an application implementation challenge? Depending on whom you asked, it was always the other team's fault. This complexity was breaking down the culture further, and the behaviors of engineers and developers were not embracing the blamelessness we were aspiring to have. We had to build confidence within our customers while feeling as though we were standing in quicksand of "more," "new," "bigger," "faster," "scale" that was sucking us into a pit of despair! You may be thinking, "How complicated could it really be?" Let's dig down a bit further.

The Bigger They Are...

Calling our company "large" would be an understatement. It was, and is, a behemoth: a Fortune 20 company that brought in $20 billion to $30 billion in quarterly revenue, served over 114 million retail connections, and housed some 160,000 employees. The technology needed to maintain something so vast grew into an elaborate spiderweb of interconnected services and infrastructure. It's not hard to imagine that we also had an equally immense Kubernetes footprint to match our sprawl. We had as many clusters as some businesses have nodes. Some large, some small, some with different requirements on location and data stored.

To paint a picture of the ecosystem we were dealing with, we had clusters hosted by AWS, Oracle Cloud, as well as on-prem datacenters. There was a mix of managed Kubernetes offerings, as well as self-hosted. We had both nonproduction and production deployments, each with East and West options. There was a mix of larger, multitenant clusters, as well as many which were more granular, single-tenant setups, each designed to meet specific security demands. This meant varying access permissions, data privacy boundaries, and eligible workloads. All in all, we were looking at supporting around 80 applications, totaling thousands of services, across hundreds of clusters split across multiple accounts and providers, several with 500 or more nodes during high-traffic hours.

All of this was assembled in roughly three years. Neither of us would recommend such an ambitious timeline. We faced many challenges, many of which could have been multiyear endeavors in their own right. Besides having to upskill all of our platform engineers on the technologies they'd now be supporting and innovating on, we had to reshape the practices and mentalities of our developers and adjacent tools teams. It's no surprise that we found ourselves with a large sum of tech debt: half-baked observability implementations that we lacked confidence in, a multitude of deployment strategies made by DevOps engineers who had come and gone, and some of the most painfully restrictive and slow developer experiences you could fathom.

Now, enter a newly formed SRE squad expected to tackle these challenges. The scope seemed excessive, even to us, but this was the cost of supporting many high-profile, highly sensitive parts of the business (more succinctly, point of sale, eCommerce, account management, and networking), many of which were at the mercy of the ebb and flow of product releases and promotional launches, demanding more and more scale to support the influx of customers. And in spite of everything already listed, there was a more difficult problem we had to face. It was the fact that we kept adding more. More clusters. More scale. More anomalies to troubleshoot. And ultimately more tickets and hours spent outside of normal working hours.

All Hands on Deck Means No Hands on the Helm

Every cluster spun up felt like it shortened the lives of our engineers. There was a great deal of stress associated with hosting and supporting our systems. Imagine that every year, around September, a brand-new, self-proclaimed revolutionary phone comes out. Well, you don't really have to imagine it. It happens. For consumers, this is the most exciting chunk of the year. For the engineers at our company, it means carving out the last two quarters for nothing but meetings, load tests, and code freezes. Months were spent in building confidence that we could handle what was coming, pushing aside all other work, like reducing toil or adding new features. We had a hunch that our confidence was artificial, since teams struggled to understand whether all their load tests were even indicative of real-life traffic patterns.

The engineers also struggled with other growing pains such as tracking down bugs introduced by cluster and component upgrades; bugs that loved to manifest inconsistently, escaping our existing observability. Nothing is more frustrating than having a hunch about why a problem is present, but lacking the tooling and processes to prove it.

One final point that stuck with us was how the engineers supporting our Kubernetes footprint were also partly responsible for bridging the gap between other teams, such as software delivery and security. Without being responsible for the entire stack, top to bottom, how could we support others outside of our group around proper architectural and design choices?

With the hope of living to see whatever technology replaces all our hard work, the team sought a way to help alleviate some of our struggles.

But large systems have run for decades and people have been writing scripts and maintaining them for years, so what's the deal? Why was this all such a challenge? Parts of SRE practices were already underway in a limited fashion. People already review availability, latency, performance, efficiency, change management, monitoring, emergency response, and capacity planning. Those are the tenets to SRE outlined in the original book by Google. I always joke that SRE brings us back on track from where poor outcomes from the DevOps movement took us away from asking, "Yay we're going fast, but is it even working?"

When we began socializing these dimensions and best practices, people immediately assumed we were used-car salespeople who just put a new paint job on a car. Google defines SRE as what you get when you treat operations as if it's a software problem. We had to take folks' minds down a path to imagine taking the challenges we face in designing our systems, networks, security, applications, and so on, and leverage software as a tool to tackle things. The problems outlined earlier aren't new. They existed for some time and were well known. The unfortunate reality was that the culture promoted solutions that were rudimentary and rooted in a traditional operations mindset.

Assert Your Hypothesis

It was time to change our approach. We ultimately made a decision to assume our assertions weren't right. That's correct. We made a strong position that everything we knew to be true about our clusters was a lie. One by one, we tackled large problem areas and determined we'd start over and make a hypothesis of what we thought to be true and make sure that we'd run a chaos experiment to ensure we were right. We went back to our roots, and reflected on our seventh grade science classes learning all about the scientific method (Figure 9-2). In the following sections, we'll discuss some of those problem areas and the hypothesis applied to help solve them.

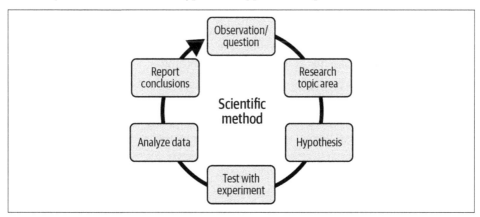

Figure 9-2. The steps of the scientific method

Reliability Experiments

As noted earlier, all of this started based on a desire to become more reliable. We began seeing that the more we saw these experiments unfold, the more knowledge we acquired and the less uncomfortable the teams began to feel. However, there was still some looming angst about the newer technology. While we had the aforementioned large footprint of Kubernetes, that didn't mean all of the teams handed a cluster were equipped with the experience necessary to run one (successfully).

We began devising an experiment to confirm our assertions of the cluster practices. There were two verifications for this: one was a Cluster Functional validation and another was a Pod Best Practice validation.

The first verification was introduced to ensure the cluster automation went smoothly before handing it off to a team. Without this verification, you won't know if new Kubernetes clusters are following best practices for initialization. Our parser had numerous failures in 2019 that were eventually traced back to upstream config changes breaking traffic routing to the backend services, halting all traffic coming out of all their clusters. New Kubernetes clusters created by automation or manual runbooks may not have been fully tested, so when an applications team starts to use it they often run across partial functionality or subtle problems. Existing clusters can have expected functionality degrade for all kinds of reasons, on one or multiple nodes, resulting in application failure.

> The hypothesis was that infrastructure teams that build or distribute Kubernetes clusters on a regular basis require a way to validate that the cluster is able to accept and run workloads.

An engineer wants to verify that they can deploy a pod, assign storage, and ensure other routine Kubernetes facilities are functioning on each node in their cluster. This gives them confidence that they should be able to conduct normal cluster operations, and if there is an issue, it helps accelerate troubleshooting.

The second verification is the Pod Best Practice experiment. Without this verification, applications wouldn't be deployed consistently over the fleet of clusters, resulting in haphazard operation, maintenance, and remediation practices, which will ultimately lead to increased outages, longer downtime, and increased confusion. In a microservices environment, developers with different degrees of Kubernetes operational knowledge contribute applications over time to a cluster. Lack of best practice configurations—like liveness and readiness probes, or resource requests and limits—can render an application unavailable during routine cluster operations, inhibiting scaling and complicating maintenance of a cluster. This verification ran a suite of compliance checks on all the deployments running on a system to confirm that they have all the best practices in place, including startup, liveness, and readiness probes; resource requests and limits; and more. An engineer wants to make sure that all their applications—or all the applications on a cluster they operate—are running safely in production and confirm that a deployment, scaling, or other activity will not create an outage. This also helped pinpoint everyone's favorite dilemma, which is "Who done it?" for narrowing down platform/infrastructure problems versus application issues.

Following is the simple output of our experiment:

```
Test                    | Status         | Errors             |
------------------------+----------------+--------------------+
health_check            |          Pass  | None               |
ready_state_check       |          Pass  | None               |
deployment_check        |          Fail  | Fail on node1      |
pod_communication_check |          Pass  | None               |
volume_check            |          Pass  | None               |
```

Even though these may not have been the sexiest of experiments, they provided assurance and security in the hands of more novice teams.

As a part of our reliability journey, we were eager to adopt SLOs to have an empirical way to measure the reliability of our systems as our customers perceived things. Our ambition to rapidly develop and ship new changes was also an area we wanted to constantly refine and improve. Most of the teams had little to no idea about SLOs, conflated them with SLAs, and didn't really have a good sense of how long it took to deploy changes. Again, we turned to chaos engineering and experimentation to guide us.

Pod deploy times affect the availability of services on a cluster, impacting upgrade, restart, and scaling times. Users need to know how long their artifacts take to deploy to a cluster to understand its behavior and set deployment time SLO expectations, and to address this, we made a verification for deployment time SLO estimation. Typically, pod startup times are calculated as the difference between the time when the pod was ready and when a pod was scheduled. However, when we are looking at pods that have been running before the verification started, there are scenarios where pods crash-loop, or a container in the pod might restart. In the scenario where a pod has restarted, the pod startup time is calculated as the difference between the time when the pod was ready and when the most recent container (that crashed) was restarted. We were able to get consistent and real perceived deployment times to accurately derive our SLOs! Instead of an even guess of "eh, 35 seconds," we could get a more accurate 26-second objective.

 The logical next step we took was to define another experiment with a hypothesis, founded on actual data, not guesswork: pods for applications that are deployed on my cluster should deploy correctly and within my deployment time SLO.

It would yield a report that showed the SLO attainment results comparing the actual deployment times against the configured SLO settings:

```
SLO Attainment: liveness-deployment

SLO Target   |   SLO Time (seconds) | Attainment    |  Violations | Result
-------------+----------------------+---------------+-------------+---------
50%          |                   25 | 90.0%         |           2 | PASS
80%          |                   30 | 100.0%        |           0 | PASS
90%          |                   31 | 100.0%        |           0 | PASS
95%          |                   32 | 100.0%        |           0 | PASS


Deployment Times: liveness-deployment

Deployment Name      |   # Deploys |  Errors |  50% |  75% |  95% |  99%
---------------------+-------------+---------+------+------+------+------
liveness-deployment  |          20 |       0 |   24 |   25 |   26 |   26
```

This was a pretty powerful moment for us as we demystified speculation and preconceived beliefs that you had to be actively using SLOs or be some elite tech company to begin conducting chaos engineering experiments to build reliability into your processes. On the contrary, chaos engineering was the gateway for us to learn about ways to make our systems more reliable.

Cost Experiments

No self-respecting large enterprise would ever let an opportunity to analyze cost pass it by. And such was the case at Verizon. While we were eager to start migrating toward Kubernetes and reap all the benefits of its scalability and features, it quickly became apparent that without proper discipline, the financials could spiral out of control. Running on this platform in a cost-effective manner is a delicate balancing act between the utilization and sizing of the hardware. If users set their expected CPU or memory requirements too high, or the platform team provides nodes that aren't geared toward the application's specific needs, you wind up with a lot of wasted space. Wasted space that quickly adds up into dollars. At the scale we were running, even small miscalculations could wind up costing tens of thousands a month.

An engineer needs to be able to determine if their requests and limits are set in a way that is a poor fit for their cluster, or if different machine sizes would be a better fit for their workload to be cost-efficient. We made a verification that takes a test fixture application with a designated set of resource requests, deploys replicas of it on the cluster, and visualizes the resulting deployment pattern. It can be configured to only deploy on existing nodes or only on scaled-up nodes from autoscaling activity.

The hypothesis was: How many application pods can fit on our nodes given their size and configuration, and how many of the remaining resources go unused when you can't deploy any more?

The treatment involved taking a given workload and scaling it out across a cluster at a growing rate, up to a limit. Once the scaling was complete, a report of excess CPU and memory on every node in the cluster was generated. Without this verification, platform owners struggled to understand the footprint of their application and how it directly impacts the size of the cluster, as well as the cost associated with running it.

While cluster sizing doesn't seem like a particularly complicated operation on paper— an administrator chooses machine sizes, then application developers configure resource requests and limits and deploy to the cluster—more often than not, we wound up with systems that were either memory-starved and had free CPU or vice versa. In some of the worst cases, we also had vastly overestimated requests that caused excessive and needless node scaling.

There was no easier way to reinforce the importance of running performant applications with properly scoped resource requirements than providing empirical evidence. Being able to demonstrate the behavior of the cluster by taking the exact parameters and configurations a team would be using, and ultimately what the bottom line was for that setup, was appreciated by both management as well as the platform teams being pressured to save money wherever possible.

This highlighted an ever-growing concern the engineers had been harping on regarding a large gap in the ability for developers to profile their applications. Now, with the data and the motivation of dollars saved, it was much easier to get the attention needed to assist teams with determining what an application *should* need while running on the cluster, instead of having them make arbitrary guesses.

The verification also contributed toward the internal debate between having clusters with a variety of applications, all with different sizes, versus those that housed only one, homogenous workload. Much like the "rocks, pebbles, and sand in a jar" metaphor, you can make better use of the space on a node by first filling it with the largest applications, then sprinkling smaller ones in the spaces that remain. Would the cost saved by better utilizing our infrastructure outweigh the benefits of smaller blast radiuses and tighter access controls? More food for thought within the teams.

Performance Experiments

In large enterprises, there are often many dependencies, both systematic as well as cross-team, or even across a line of business. These dependencies are often unknown, and even the ones that you *think* you know, you may or may not be able to control your interaction with them. We were facing the issue of many container images having unexpected behaviors in our pipelines during deployment. The team that ran the Artifactory container registry insisted there were no issues. There was a ton of speculation and frustration with developers and engineers as to why there were issues, but it soon fell back on the blame game. At this point, we'd seen this play out and it was time to address it with yet another chaos verification; it was the simplest way to make an objective assessment of the situation.

 The hypothesis was: If we took a series of test images of consistent sizes and deployed them over and over again, we'd have logical deployment times of an image of similar size.

We created 100 MB, 250 MB, 500 MB, and 1 GB images and let 'em rip. Want to take a guess at the results? The 1 GB image took less time than both the 250 MB and 500 MB images to retrieve and deploy. The 100 MB image took the longest. Something was clearly off. It turns out there was a networking issue that created an unexpected and anomalous behavior. What was most important was that we could show data to convey the story. It's all about challenging the hypothesis and seeing if your assertions are correct. Your production environment is filled with different rules, security groups, and firewalls you're at the mercy of. What looks good in nonprod, regardless of the drift control you have, leaves you vulnerable to unreliability. This verification became a staple to check on deployment delays and snags.

Remember that your ability to deploy also directly plays a role in your reliability, or lack thereof. If you need to get a fix out, you should have good confidence in the time it will take after the issue is locally discovered. We'll spare the details of the resolution for this specific issue, but it's worth noting that not only did we resolve this instance, but we were asked by the Artifactory team to run additional experiments in the future. Adoption had grown.

Risk Experiments

In 2019, JW Player discovered a crypto miner stealing CPU from them after getting onto their Kubernetes cluster via WeaveScope. This, as well as many other horror stories from within the industry, sent waves throughout our company, each time demanding a reevaluation of our security practices and standards. Within our Kubernetes ecosystem, we rely heavily on an agent running within the cluster to help combat incidents like this one. The tool's configuration is complex and a separate security team often manages its detection rules, block rules, and alerting. Unfortunately, as platform, application, and security teams make changes to their cluster and its configuration, security controls may no longer work as intended and may allow vulnerabilities to be created in the environment or block valid applications from running.

Our hypothesis was: If I deploy an application with known security vulnerabilities, it should be blocked. This blocking should happen in a timely manner, meeting our internal security incident TTD SLO.

This verification deploys a pod containing known vulnerabilities on a target cluster and determines if it is prevented from running by existing security controls. Additionally, it runs a control image to make sure security constraints are not blocking good pods from running. It reports the deploy status of both of these pods and surfaces the reason they were blocked to the user.

The goal is to assist a platform operator or security engineer in determining if the security measures on the system prevent the pod from running and whether they are adequately protected against running vulnerable containers. As a byproduct, any notifications, alerts, or other hooks that are typically triggered in response to a detected vulnerability are also verified. This also helps an application team confirm that any flaws they may inadvertently include in their application are being detected, and in which environment(s) they can rely on this protection, building confidence that they are safe.

The beauty of this verification lies in the ability to repeat it, continuously, as well as expand upon the different types of vulnerabilities being validated. While the rules governing our security agent are tested at creation, they are typically never revisited after that point. The last thing anyone wants is to find out that their security expectations aren't being met during an incident. This is precisely what we hope to avoid through this experiment. If we create a sample "bad" configuration for each rule that we enforce, and run that regularly, demonstrating that a cluster is still maintaining its security stance over time, the likelihood of unintentionally leaving gaps in our defenses is reduced considerably.

More Traditionally Known Experiments

You can probably tell our experiments were tailored to our environment with things that were proprietary to us. That's the best place to start—with something that provides business value and solves the pain and uncertainty plaguing your engineers and developers and where you have legitimate and real problems. This doesn't mean we stopped there.

Our role in simplifying the standard Kubernetes cluster bootstrapping with all of the baked-in corporate requirements allowed us to also make the experiment platform accessible to everyone. This allowed other common experiments to pop up. For example, we did a common app latency injection to ensure that our apps would respond as we expected them to. Keep in mind that this all took time, and it wasn't a simple little one-month-long project that got us a shiny accomplishment. It was a new way to understand our systems better than before and became a huge part of our evolution in adopting an SRE culture.

Changing the Paradigm to Continuous

Chaos engineering was working. We were making experiments as new challenges arose, teams were beginning to question their own understanding of the systems they were working on, and reliability was improving.

As a part of our journey to reliability, we started to really foster an awareness of toil, defined as unredeeming, manual, linearly growing work. Teams were calling out toil and doing what they could to find it and kill it. One of our leaders even went as far to say "know your enemy"—playing on the classic song from the famous band Rage Against The Machine. Even though we saw success from these experiments, we knew that there was inherent toil in manually invoking experiments. We knew the negative reactions were really pervasive when our teams started thinking of our chaos experiments as toil, or incessantly time consuming.

However, what they railed against was the amount of effort involved. Everyone loved how we were empirically able to prove our hypotheses, and they wanted to push further! But they found the act of manually evoking these experiments regularly to be difficult. They wanted to be able to run the experiments continuously and automatically. How could we trust ourselves enough to run these experiments all of the time, automatically?

It started in our lower environments with these experiments turned on and running by default. We found out quickly that it was important to have kill switches and safeguards in place. It was a good place to establish practical observability and monitoring with appropriate alerting and dashboarding. Those SLOs we mentioned earlier came in handy as we ensured our experiment did not impact our error budget and they became pseudo acceptance criteria to know our resilience that triggered during experiment action actually worked through the eyes of our customers. Once we felt comfortable within those lower nonproduction environments, we were able to elevate to production.

The advantage to continuous verification is truly being able to handle the unknown. Before, we were still not addressing what happens when we don't have focused efforts around mass traffic events where all hands are on deck. We then experienced all of the random unexpected bursts of traffic. It's the unknown or rushed business drivers that caused an influx of traffic and not enough time for huge focus. This would cause a huge pivot in attention and distract engineers. The key was being able to normalize and naturalize comprehension in safe and calm environments to gain confidence in knowing we can handle what's to come or respond in moments of crisis.

Lessons Learned

Chaos engineering is often characterized as "breaking things in production," which lends it an air of something only feasible for technologically elite or sophisticated organizations. In practice, it's been a key element in digital transformation from the ground up for a number of companies ranging from pre-streaming Netflix to those in highly regulated industries like healthcare, telecommunications, and financial services. Many enterprises are grappling with application modernization at an ever-increasing scale, and leveraging chaos-informed experimentation as a facet of their SRE practices can help them get their arms around the complexity of their systems. Understanding the complexity of distributed systems is foundational but critical to true observability. These practices can inevitably lead to clarity in metrics like SLOs, grounded in reality instead of guesswork.

Experience Report: Security Monitoring (OpenDoor)

Authored by Prima Virani

Security teams rely on high-quality logs and accurate alerts for a vast majority of security functions. In order to detect incidents and prevent negative consequences from occurring, teams need observable insights into where and when suspicious events are occurring. Suspicious event alerts, fueled by logs, are the most important sources of this insight. If the log pipeline fails, the alerting infrastructure automatically fails along with it.

Additionally, security teams are required to respond to and contain the incident as quickly as possible. Incident response teams rely on accurate, complete, high-quality logs, which not only help them find additional context around any event but also help identify appropriate countermeasures and provide evidence to present in court should the security event escalate and need to involve law enforcement.

There are two major points of failures that can impact an organization's security posture adversely:

- The organization doesn't have accurate log data to start with.
- The organization faces a glitch in the detection infrastructure, hindering them from gaining insights into an event. A "glitch" can be in any of these three parts of the detection infrastructure:
  — Logging
  — Alerting
  — Response

Failure in any of these can cause significant damage in the case of a successful attack. Just like any other challenge, there are many ways of approaching this potential failure in logging and alerting infrastructure.

One of the fundamental approaches to start solving for it is to verify that all logs are collected centrally and are consistently monitored for unusual access and/or activities. This, in addition to monitoring and alerting on log trends, can take a team's detection and response infrastructure robustness very far. With that, the team can observe unusual spikes and dips in the log flow on every pipeline from which a security information and event management tool (SIEM) receives logs.

To proactively check and identify breakages in the log pipeline and alerting infrastructure, it's important to schedule regular security chaos experiments to check that all the logs and alerts are being received and collected in the security logging and alerting tool sets as expected in a timely manner. In our experience, log pipelines are rarely tested after they are initially implemented. As a result, the teams often identify the breakages either completely by accident or during the unfortunate occurrence of a security event and/or incident.

Under these conditions, the team is trying to look for the particular log or alert and is unable to find it. Periodic chaos experimentation can help verify the health of these critical functions.

Again, going back to the example of the broken log pipeline, the engineering team was operating under the assumption that the logging and alerting infrastructure was working correctly. When assumptions like that are wrong, they can cause a company to lose millions of dollars on an hourly basis. Consider the July 2018 Amazon Prime Day outage where Amazon incurred costs of up to $33 million per hour while engineers scrambled to diagnose and triage the problem. That three-hour outage could potentially have been identified proactively using resilience techniques such as chaos engineering.

In conclusion, with (well-warranted) increasing emphasis on automation in detection and response, the infrastructure and tools involved in automation are rapidly becoming more complex. In light of this, we must seek new methods, such as chaos engineering, in order to better understand how these complex systems work, improve them, and anticipate the nonlinear nature of their unpredictable outcomes.

Experience Report: Applied Security (Cardinal Health)

Authored by Jamie Dicken and Rob Duhart, Jr.

The need for SCE grew organically at Cardinal Health, a global Fortune 20 healthcare products and services company based in Dublin, Ohio. With revenue of over $140 billion, Cardinal plays a critical role in the healthcare ecosystem.

At the executive level, securing the company's distribution centers, operations, products, and information was critical—not just for the company's reputation, but for the stability of the United States healthcare system. In addition to investing in teams to advise on and implement security controls, they authorized purchases of security products and tools to protect the business totaling millions of dollars. With such large investments, executives logically held high expectations of their effectiveness.

The SCE journey at Cardinal Health arose not only from the executive need for security validation, but from the Security Architecture team as well. That team, led by Robert Duhart, knew that theoretical security architecture would not protect an organization sprinting to the cloud. We needed an Applied Security model and we had a hunch that SCE could be the answer.

What Cardinal Health needed was "Applied Security"—a means to bring continuous verification and validation concepts of SCE to the organization.

Building the SCE Culture

In order to succeed in blazing a new trail, it was imperative that this new adventure begin with a culture of fearless exploration. SCE is an evolution of security and engineering thinking. Rather than building walls and hoping they won't be breached, SCE introduces disruption to maximize the security value within an environment. Given the state of the Cardinal Health cloud transformation, we decided that we were in need of a revolution in terms of how we approached our security practices.

The Mission of Applied Security

The concept of Applied Security was simple: test your security before someone else (an adversary) does. The name itself paid homage to the Security Architecture team's need to verify that the security measures or designs were appropriately applied, and carefully made no mention of things like "compliance" or "engineering" in order to minimize confusion with other established security teams.

In mid-2019, I (Jaimie) was hired by the newly formed Applied Security team to help shape and navigate this new territory. I had spent over a decade in building and leading software engineering practices, so the concept immediately resonated with me. To me, proactively instrumenting your security was exactly the same as proactively instrumenting your software application.

My first objective in getting started was to reconcile the business case used to create the team with the current expectations of my CISO, other Information Security teams, and Enterprise IT. After the first month, our mission became clear: identify unknown technical security gaps and partner with the organization to remediate them before they are exploited.

The distinction of "unknown" was made first because anything that was already known—that is, able to be entered into the risk register—already had the attention of our leaders, who could prioritize remediations. Applied Security wouldn't need to spend energy on those. Additionally, if the primary root cause or remediation was not a technical control, this remediation could be driven by our strong Security Awareness team whose responsibilities include security education and consultation. This means that instead of us spending time on addressing known issues or awareness or process gaps, we were able to remove those from our scope and count on other teams to drive those to remediation through their partnerships with department leaders.

The Method: Continuous Verification and Validation (CVV)

As exciting as it would be to just go nuts, get access to every system and every project, and just look for technical security gaps, we knew we needed a disciplined and repeatable process. In deciding what that process was, we identified three key goals.

First, our process needed to identify indisputable and critically important deficiencies. It did us no good to identify problems that the organization didn't agree were worthy of solving when considering the risk. Therefore, we knew we had to establish benchmarks that were relevant to our company and our systems. Those benchmarks could not be arbitrary, and they couldn't be considered to be merely theoretic best practices that practicalists could dismiss.

Second, our process needed to be thorough enough to see the "big picture" and detail the technical security gap. Whereas previous technical gaps had partial visibility to frontline employees, they lacked the detail to be entered into the risk register, which impacted their prioritization and remediation. For the Applied Security team to be successful, we had to not only identify the technical gaps, but integrate into the Risk team's remediation process—and that required thoroughness.

Finally, we had to ensure that the technical gaps we found and fixed were not unknowingly reopened in the future.

With these three goals in mind, we created a process called Continuous Verification and Validation (CVV). Simply put, on a regular basis we wanted to continuously verify that a technical security control was in place and validate that it was implemented correctly.

The CVV Process Includes Four Steps

Step 1

Establish the benchmarks by which gaps would be identified, called Applied Security Benchmarks (ASBMs). To give authority to our findings, we largely use the security standards set by our Security Architecture team and approved by our

CISO. If those standards don't yet exist, we partner with the Security Architecture and Security Operations teams to establish the recommendations, and we socialize the benchmarks with any relevant teams. This gives credibility to any gaps we identify, and establishes the requirement that either fixes need to be prioritized, or leaders must accept the risk.

Step 2

Implement continuous checks that our systems are adhering to the ASBMs. In many cases, we write custom scripts to verify the presence and proper configuration of security tools or design patterns, especially because we check adherence to Cardinal Health security standards. Before we write any code, we also evaluate both open source and commercial products and make an informed decision to build versus buy.

Step 3

Create a dashboard that illustrates the real-time compliance of all systems with the ASBMs. This dashboard serves two purposes: it allows us to get the big picture of a possible technical gap on demand, and it is a great communication tool when we speak to our leaders.

Step 4

If at any point adherence to the ASBMs decreases, we create an issue in our risk register. Thanks to the work our Risk team has done throughout the past five years, there is already a fine-tuned governance process that drives remediation and is incredibly effective. This means that the Applied Security team can then move on to implement CVV in other areas while remediations naturally occur in parallel.

While tremendous progress has continued and we've "taken the first hill," we recognize that victory in one battle does not win a war. We must continue "once more into the breach" and create a sweeping culture of SCE. As the organization shifts to an Agile and automated security mindset, the goal is to bring SCE into the fold at a larger scale and more broadly across teams. Our vision is that all teams are proactively testing their own security, discovering their weaknesses, and fixing issues before they ever get to production—effectively not even giving attackers a chance to exploit our systems. If a single five-person team has succeeded at proactively finding and fixing technical security gaps for a fraction of our tools, we know that an emboldened organization doing the same grants us far more reach and maximizes our chances for success.

Experience Report: Balancing Reliability and Security via SCE (Accenture Global)

Authored by Adriana Petrich and Francesco Sbaraglia

From our purview at Accenture, a global technology consulting company, we observed that SRE teams and cybersecurity teams are often only partially aligned in organizations. They are regularly perceived as opposing disciplines that host contradictions rather than follow a shared vision. SRE sits on one side, following the goal of ultimate reliability, while cybersecurity sits on the other, focused primarily on the protection of systems by having carefully balanced amounts of security controls in concert with a deliberate defense strategy.

The question facing many organizations is whether common design tensions, such as the trade-offs between availability, performance, and security, can indeed achieve a balance. One step we think organizations can take is training SREs to sufficiently recognize malicious cybersecurity behavior in support of organizational security issues. What will happen when a cyber attack impacts the reliability of the system? Alternatively, what will be the outcome of a reliability issue on security control effectiveness or attack readiness? What do you think would happen in these scenarios? Without clearly established cross-coordination, shared practices, and healthy communication patterns up front, it's likely that chaos will ensue and only create further friction.

One thing is sure: neither party can afford to suffer a loss of availability or exposure to a cyber attack. How can you secure what you do not know, and identify where your security gaps reside in extremely dynamic systems? Sometimes the best answer is the one staring you right in the face. In this instance it's putting the right mix of human beings together to focus on collectively improving each party's intended outcomes. We believe that the overlap of security and reliability reflects an opportunity for improving each of their respective objectives.

We can seize that opportunity by adopting SCE—an SRE practice that shines the spotlight on security matters through proactive security failure injection. The act of SREs performing security chaos experiments not only helps to discover unknown security gaps, but also shines the light on areas where performance trade-offs could be impacting security. With security chaos experiments, we use a scientific method loop—based on a steady-state hypothesis, continuous verification, and lessons learned—and implement mitigation to discover "unknown unknowns" by proactively injecting security failures.

The goal (and challenge) with SCE is to balance both reliability and security without neglecting one or the other. While the goals of reliability and security are often portrayed as divergent, it is a misconception that SRE practices and cybersecurity cannot work together. An SRE's primary objectives are improving end user outcomes through the creation of automation, measurement, and thorough analysis of historical incident postmortems. A cybersecurity engineer's primary objectives are to ensure that systems are operating in a secure operational manner through the implementation of automated prevention tool sets and proactive detection of insecure system threats.

At first look, both "are concerned with keeping a system usable" (School of SRE, 2020 (*https://oreil.ly/4ljtz*)). Given the nature of incidents and practices, SRE and security deal with pre-failure and post-failure situations—SREs, through reducing toil, address preemptive measures as security does with security gates or controls. Both cybersecurity engineers and SREs search for measures and opportunities to improve systems (even though they focus on different aspects).

Each practice not only has much in common, but these are all factors relevant to the need for chaos experimentation too. The attributes of shared end-to-end responsibility, the generation of valuable metrics used as feedback loops, and the ability to avoid and handle incidents set the foundation for SCE.

To successfully adopt SCE, we need to harness this overlap in objectives and practices. It's important to ensure that team members are incentivized to experiment and obtain support from organizational leadership. What else is needed to help enterprises adopt SCE? The next section will cover our roadmap for adopting SCE in the enterprise based on our experience.

Our Roadmap to SCE Enterprise Capability

In our experience in implementing this practice in enterprise clients, we have observed that enterprises face two key challenges: operational complexity and rapidly changing system infrastructure. The adoption of the public cloud has magnified this challenge by enabling systems to rapidly change and scale. In this constantly evolving and changing landscape, organizations are beginning to gravitate toward practices such as chaos engineering to build confidence in their ability to respond to unpredictable system outcomes as a result.

We have found that implementing SCE practices allows teams to proactively ensure that security tooling remains an effective countermeasure against certain types of attacks. It also affords the opportunity for engineers to validate incident response runbooks and sharpen their skills in executing them. When our clients performed chaos experimentation, we often saw an increased cooperation between teams as well as improvements in cross-discipline visibility. This allows for a healthier understanding of the operational state of the system and its ability to handle evolving threats.

Our roadmap for adopting an SCE enterprise capability is shown in Figure 9-3.

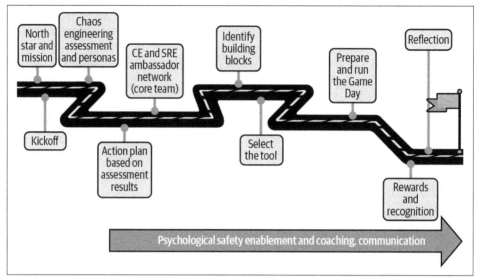

Figure 9-3. Our roadmap to SCE enterprise capability

Our Process for Adoption

Our process for helping enterprises adopt SCE practices involved breaking down the process into separate steps for incremental adoption. We also defined four building blocks that matter for a successful implementation:

1. *People, practices, and process*
   Transforming the SRE mindset toward SCE principles as security champions, and also conducting workshops to prepare executives for chaos experimentation by identifying potential impacts and areas of opportunity to kick off adoption

2. *Infrastructure*
   Conducting chaos experimentation at the infrastructure layer while considering scalability through capacity planning

3. *Platform*
   Improving security automation, deploying observability tools for monitoring and logging, and integrating third-party quality checks

4. *Applications*
   Extending experimentation to the application layer

Let's dig deeper into each of these.

People, practices, and process

There are many mischaracterizations on the public internet of what chaos engineering is. For example, a simple internet search of "Chaos Engineering" will result in multiple posts describing the practice as "breaking things in production" or creating randomness in your system akin to "monkeys in datacenters pulling plugs" when the reality couldn't be further from the truth. Combating these popularized misrepresentations of the practice up front can help ensure everyone is on the same page from the get-go.

The adoption of SCE requires a cultural shift and overall transformation in mindset. In our experience, some challenges to be aware of are a lack of psychological safety, misunderstanding of the practices, and overall awareness of the problems you're trying to solve for. Psychological safety can be an important factor to discuss up front to ensure that engineers are empowered for success and acknowledge it is safe for them to fail.

Embracing a blameless culture can provide a psychologically safe environment for people to feel comfortable to fail, to speak up, and to bring up ideas. Psychological safety is a key factor in ensuring teams are enabled to take interpersonal risks without fear and can creatively focus on fixing the system. Doing so will foster newfound empathy between teams in contrast to directing blame. Psychological safety means to build upon "trust culture" where people are able to address problems and where they can talk about such problems openly. A related mindset shift is accepting failure as normal. Enable teams to think with a broader horizon and establish ambassador networks that can evangelize the "failure is normal" reality.

From our perspective, psychological safety should incorporate people, processes, and practices, while also realizing that roles may need to be expanded to have an increased focus on operations. This can look different for each organization, but in our experience, we decided it's best that SREs join DevOps teams. We also recruited the required skills and established workshops to develop the necessary skills for our clients.

During these workshops, we have found it helpful to assess readiness by conducting an assessment to determine a client's desired outcome, identify key KPIs, and develop an understanding of their systems and the teams operating them. Based on the assessment outcomes, an action plan is put together.

As a follow-on to the readiness assessment, we conduct a whiteboarding session with the client's teams to discuss past incidents and targets that are likely used to create possible targets for our experimentation backlog. During this process, depicted in Figure 9-4, the team creates chaos experiments and scenarios to use to experiment upon the selected target(s). Each chaos experiment must have a rollback and abort plan. It follows a priority check and the evaluation of past incidents and targets. In this step, we decide which chaos experiment is best for the selected target. Typical selection criteria include a feasibility check for the experiment itself and risk potential. What follows is the creation of the experiments based on specific templates. Put all defined experiments in the chaos experiment backlog (20–30 experiments) and select a chaos experiment for execution. Once the experiment is selected and used, write down lessons that have been learned and do another whiteboarding session.

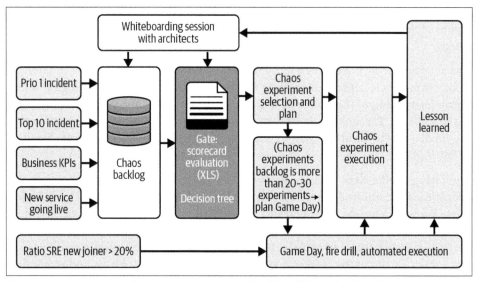

Figure 9-4. Accenture's chaos experimentation backlog ("chaos backlog") approach

Infrastructure and platform

Starting chaos experimentation at the infrastructure layer makes sense for most organizations since infrastructure components are common dependencies across teams. Chaos engineering experiments within the platform layer can have a larger effect on system reliability by addressing core components, their ability to properly scale, and their capacity to respond to disruptive events.

All chaos engineering products we tested have a wide-ranging number of precreated chaos experiments. We evaluated these tools using a scorecard-based approach to compare each of their benefits and ability to improve our KPIs.

During the process of adopting chaos experimentation, focus on Agile frameworks and approaches to implement a change. Consider what possible tools may become necessary, such as observability platforms, postmortem analysis, and automation management. When choosing tooling it's important to focus on capabilities that will enable deeper analysis of system failures, enable the creation or reduction of toil, and facilitate collaboration.

As part of the platform building block, we recommended prioritizing automation based on the number of incidents that occurred over a given time frame. If we identify three or more incidents occurring during a given time period, then SREs should spend their innovation budget (or story points) on automation that can fix relevant underlying factors.

Application

Application-level chaos experiments usually require more work to develop and prepare properly. Conducting chaos experiments at the application level usually requires extensive knowledge of software architecture design, so it's not always possible to use a preconfigured experiment template. But application-level experiments are critical for uncovering unexpected application behaviors during disruptive events as well as for improving SLOs.

Lastly, in our experience, once an experiment has been validated through a Game Day exercise, it is a best practice to automate the experiment going forward by continuously running it, such as by implementing it as part of your CI/CD pipeline.

Experience Report: Cyber Chaos Engineering (Capital One)

Authored by David Lavezzo

Capital One is a 25-year-old Fortune 100 company with a healthy addiction to technology. We're the first bank to report that we have exited datacenters and moved to the cloud. This technology transformation allowed us to push complex technology solutions rapidly, which was critical to allow the workforce to remain connected throughout COVID-19. With all this change came opportunities to build how we want—both in and out of the office—and with it came a lot of moving parts. With many different platforms, our teams make constant changes through our technology focus and constant drive to innovative improvements. As our tech stack evolves, so do the challenges.

What Does All This Have to Do with SCE?

Constant motion is chaos. Not in the sense of disorder or confusion, but in the sense of changes leading to unpredictability. No well-meaning security professional is spending their time wondering how best to degrade their systems; they're working out how best to fulfill the request of the line of business in the time they expect it, and doing it successfully so it looks good on their end-of-year performance review. This is relevant because by utilizing security chaos engineering to catch problems before they get into production and/or leveraged for badness, our teams are better able to know when changes are positive while making life a little more difficult for our offensive teams. So what happens when well-designed implementations cause unplanned change in critical systems we rely on?

What Is Secure Today May Not Be Secure Tomorrow

Software changes. The security community has developed and released countless tools to further their research and, as a result, start finding issues buried deep within the core that serves as the foundation of our infrastructure. Heartbleed, Log4j, Shellshock, and undoubtedly many more libraries that were safe because "open source means many eyes are on it" suddenly turn up on the "WE NEED TO CANCEL Q4" list. There are countless events where a previously known good library turned out to have a gaping flaw leading to Very Bad Days®. How can we plan for failure? How do we cut through marketing shenanigans and claims that vendor solutions will fix all problems, and make more informed decisions? Do we need more vulnerability scanners? We take traditional testing and sprinkle a bit of SCE into the mix.

Key takeaway: take decision trees (a.k.a. attack trees) and think through "if something happens in this spot on the tree, what is the worst that will happen?"

Better takeaway: looking at how we, as an industry, retroactively do security, I realized change was needed. But it needed to be proven to be effective.

How We Started

As exciting as it is to climb the cyber mountain, shout YOLO while pushing the big red button to watch the world burn, it's not the way to get support and build confidence, and that is exactly what is needed to succeed. Chaos is in the name of SCE, but it's anything but chaotic.

Cyber chaos engineering started out as a way to test vendor products in Capital One cyber engineering—to understand how new products actually worked and what we could expect out of them. Eventually it hit me. Do products actually need to be replaced? If something doesn't work, why doesn't it work? Is it a misconfiguration? Is everything configured as planned, but it just doesn't do what we think it does?

Operation at a High Level

1. Know your steady state, the baseline where all measurements start. There is no good, there is no bad, only the beginning of the journey.

2. Experiment, observe, and analyze. See what happens when you introduce new things to the baseline.

3. Identify gaps and deviations from the expected outcome. Does everything work how you think it works?

---

4. Improve the system based on analysis. Leverage existing partnerships to help everyone get better, making the entire program better.

5. Repeat continuously in production. Real systems need to be tested for real results. Just be careful.

Taking what we knew about our environment, the baseline, it made it easier to identify how a product fit within our space. It's OK if something is missed, as long as we realize it and drive to close that gap.

To reduce the appearance of being rogue wizards, I created a set of guidelines that in hindsight seem obvious:

- Create realistic deployment settings by working with additional stakeholders.
- Take what we know about the current environment and inject identical behavior into different environments.
- Record results and provide stakeholders with information used to make decisions of usability versus cost versus effectiveness.
- Work within requested time restraints.

How We Did This in Ye Olden Days

It was very manual, very unhip. I built a combination of PowerShell and bash scripts and used them for semimodular repeatable testing. I took the top 10 alerts we cared about and simply tested them to validate they still worked. They worked, but in unintended ways. I discovered a notable difference in expectations versus reality when it came to actually receiving the alert. Showing where we were versus where we thought we were was eye-opening and showed me why testing like this should exist and why doing it constantly was required. I learned you can do all the right things, follow all the best practices, and things can still fail. But we can fail in a controlled way on our terms and get them fixed.

How do we do this today?

Automation

It's not a secret that we love our APIs and love automation. Having a small team and trying to own the whole lifecycle clearly won't work, so how do we automate SCE? Rather than become a bottleneck on the road to production, we provide tooling to help engineering teams perform this work themselves through APIs.

We compile pre-vetted malicious actions covering specific use cases ranging from network to endpoint threats, and the access to retrieve the data identifying whether the security tooling detected and/or prevented the event. This allows them to self-test against their changes and understand their baseline versus changes meant to improve security *before* pushing to production. The goal is to reduce surprise as a result of unexpected outcomes from planned changes and avoiding expensive rework after being released to production. This cycle is shown in Figure 9-5.

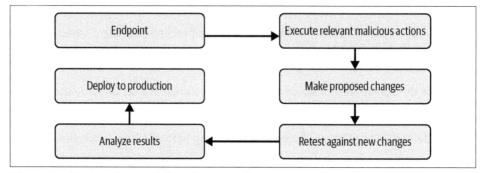

Figure 9-5. Engineering workflow change evaluation

Understanding change

The ability to understand the environment before and after a change is key to understanding if the change being made is altering the defensive capability of a platform and if it is, *how* it is being changed. The earlier it happens in the change process, the less impactful a bad configuration will be. NIST (*https://oreil.ly/tulh1*) has an old report on this with a focus on software engineering, but it's still applicable.

Once a system goes into production and the respective teams have moved to their next project, rework affects the entire project chain from that moment on, pushing back all other planned work and affecting projected deadlines. As an example, let's say you encounter one of the dreaded double negatives where you must enable a value to disable the setting. You know who I'm talking about. The setting is changed and you suddenly find yourself without a functioning key application that, while technically turned on, is no longer doing what it's supposed to be doing. It's still on and reporting that it's healthy, but is behaving like security at a sporting event doing pat-downs.

After discovery of the flaw, current work stops and root cause investigation must be performed. What caused it? Why did it change? Was the change authorized? Was it tested? Is the change by design? These could be really simple answers, but it takes time to answer when it happens later in the process after everyone has already signed off on the changes.

We leverage this process today when evaluating changes to things like endpoints and network security devices. The baseline behavior is recorded before planned changes, then re-recorded immediately after the changes to see what has changed and if so, was it in the way we expected.

Takeaway: automation of experiments during the configuration testing phases reduces risks of deploying undesirable configurations that increase deployment costs.

Using SCE for threat intelligence

It's no secret that simply existing as an entity makes you a target for attackers. Not only is it a key requirement to collect and understand the threats you face, it's extremely important to understand how you withstand attempts by adversaries to leverage these attacks. Saying something is enabled and working because it's turned on and configured is meaningless if it is untested. Assumptions are difficult to justify and do not build confidence that systems are working as expected. How do we build confidence in these systems? SCE+APIs. Yes, again.

Threat intelligence is serious business. With thousands of cyber attacks happening a day and endless telemetry generated from these events, there are never-ending sources of intelligence available to us. Rather than relying on hope that tooling will identify an indicator of compromise (IOC) (if it were to present itself in the environment), we take those threat intelligence feeds; identify applicable threats; map them to tactics, techniques, and procedures (TTPs); and experiment. Leveraging the understanding of what we know we've seen, we can hypothesize that a percentage of actions by an active threat actor will be identified. We will execute similar TTPs and evaluate whether our expectations were met and, if they were not, identify the cause of this gap.

This method helps prioritize what needs to be worked on and helps solve the ever-thoughtful "We don't know what we don't know." Using SCE for intelligence, we know exactly where we stand and what needs to be focused on next.

Identifying gaps

Holistically, it's less important to know that a specific tool is working than to know how an entire stack works.

Knowing something is blocked at a proxy will not let you know how the rest of the stack performs; being able to work backward is beneficial and helps us understand how things work in real life. An interesting exercise is seeing something blocked by a proxy, but still seeing activity afterward showing that it wasn't actually blocked. This is the exact reason layers are required; when not every layer works as planned. Atomic testing fits well here.

When gaps are discovered, we work backward to learn what happened. When observing an attack we look at the simple things. Do we see the logs on the system itself? Are they what we expect to see? Is it flowing to the data lake? Are there other factors that may be causing a delay in receiving logs? These are all questions we ask if something isn't working how it should be.

Things I've Learned Along the Way

Not everything works as planned.

I've learned that my understanding of how things work can be wildly different from how they actually work. Sometimes things just behave in unexpected ways. Policies that seem to be clear can actually have the reverse effect. Conflicting rules can produce a whole new world of opportunity of rabbit holes to fall into.

Blocked doesn't always mean blocked.

There are times when an appliance reports something as blocked, yet there is still data from the event happening afterward proving it didn't actually block, resulting in more work for teams. And that's OK. It's what layered defenses are for, because things don't always work as planned, especially in an environment that's constantly changing. Simply understanding how the environment works helps guide improvement roadmaps and capability enhancements that result in a stronger security posture.

You get popular. Also unpopular.

Success means you have successfully measured and observed how security tooling is actually functioning and are able to generate meaningful metrics showing where you are, where you've been, and where you should be going next. It also means you're making work for other people. Despite being immensely charming, it's made me unpopular.

Create partnerships.

You can't succeed if you don't make friends, and have I sure tried. Clear messaging is crucial. I've failed a bunch of different ways at doing this. Here's a short list of what people don't like: feeling bad, feeling attacked, getting surprises. Clear and open communication is a key component to succeed, especially in the beginning. When practicing SCE, it's important to provide data-driven evidence that teams are working on the right things and producing the results leadership expects.

We build partnerships by helping provide teams a data-driven way to prove their value. Old-school metrics bring more questions that are difficult to answer. If detected malware goes up, does it mean detections have improved, or have there been more attacks? If it goes down, is detection worse, or have there been fewer attacks? Does having all features enabled and installed on all systems mean it's effective?

In my opinion, no. While those are valuable, especially when determining the overall health of systems, they don't prove the defenses are effective. Besides knowing they're installed and enabled, we provide the data to know they prevent malware and constantly test against that known baseline.

A Reduction of Guesswork

Like any organization with sufficient staffing, there is always a point of concern when reading about the latest and best cyber attacks and whether the organization is exposed. In the old world, one would have to go on best estimates. You can look at data flow diagrams, network maps, and inventories while looking at configurations and/or rules, and make a guess on whether it would work. But there are better ways.

You can try it. We take our processes for experimentation and apply it in the same way. We take the threat, emulate it (if it's nasty we de-fang it, because running malware is generally a bad idea, especially if you're confident that you know what you're doing), and look at the results. We look and see if the reality matches our expectations and, if it doesn't, we start the improvement process. With the ability to quickly rerun the exact same scenarios, we're able to prove iterative improvement and provide a way to consistently retest against a baseline.

That same ability to quickly retest aids in platform tuning. Knowing the existing state allows the owner to understand the effects of tuning and whether undesirable behavior has happened. This understanding drives improvement of security posture and evidence that tooling is consistently working as expected.

Driving Value

People want their time spent on valuable pursuits and achieving business goals, while also being secure. Security compliance is one way to demonstrate a capability, typically done through sampling of events and presented as evidence teams are working on the proper things. However, there are issues with using compliance to drive security.

Being compliance-driven can mean that one is being measured by snapshots, proving at that point in time, things were working because there's an alert that proves it worked. It's also failure-adverse. Failure is necessary to better understand the real risks you face; avoiding it does a disservice to the teams tasked with securing an enterprise. So, how do we generate value while helping achieve goals?

SCE helps our peer groups provide data-driven evidence of the value they bring. We help prove that capability's function. Rather than looking at a point in time where something worked, they will know it has worked consistently and can prove it.

Conclusion

We're helping our teams become self-sufficient to identify what the security posture of their tooling is and improve on it. With our own work, we're able to continuously experiment and identify gaps in understanding while moving from theater to data-driven evidence of protection. This includes:

- Helping teams become more secure through self-guided tests
- Helping the enterprise be more secure through continuous experimentation
- Moving away from security theater to data-driven evidence on the state of security
- Understanding where you've been and where you're going, and what is needed to get there

Chapter Takeaways

- Adopting SCE requires a cultural shift and change in mindset.
- One by one, assert your hypothesis, validate your assumptions, and share what you've learned.
- Test your security before someone else does for you. Theoretical security doesn't work.
- Begin with a culture of fearless experimentation to learn what you don't know.
- Establish clear cross-coordination, shared practices, and healthy communication patterns between SRE and Security teams to achieve the right calibration of system security and reliability.

At a time when constantly evolving software and systems feel so vulnerable—fragile even—applying chaos engineering to cybersecurity feels not just apt, but imperative. When applied in a security context, chaos experimentation bears the potential to reveal valuable and objective information about systems security, allowing organizations to more verifiably ensure the stability and reliability of the systems on which they depend.

SCE—and even chaos engineering itself—is still an emerging and advancing set of practices, techniques, and tool sets. It's true that the shift in mindset is going to be tough for a few organizations initially, especially for those clinging to a traditional security ethos. But if we begin to challenge our assumptions, cultivate collaboration rather than silos, and learn through experimentation, we are certain to make a profound impact on an industry that so desperately needs it.

In conclusion, it is our belief that organizations charged with building secure, reliable, and high-quality systems will find the same value we have in applying SCE. We hope that you, the reader, will join us in building a community of practice and help advance the state of SCE.

Index

N

n-order thinking as belief prompting, 52
nation-state attack organizations, 118
National Park Service (NPS) on modularity, 195
Netflix
    authentication, 122
    "paved roads" created, 153
    security LEGOs, 76
    topology flow investments, 41
    Wall-E framework, 153
NetWire remote administration tool, 10
null baseline check for action bias, 243

O

observability activities, 210, 223-226
    attack observability, 228-231
        about, 228
        attacker tracing, 230
        chaos experimentation, 230
        deception environments, 228
        deception environments and small businesses, 229
        experimentation platforms, 230
        resilient system design, 229
    definition of observability, 224
    system signals and relevant attacks, 232
observing system interactions
    about, 159
    about tests, 163
    abstraction warnings, 177-180
        how to navigate abstractions, 178
    Configuration as Code, 160-162
    fault injection during development, 162
    Infrastructure as Code, 160-162
    operating and observing phase, 209
        (see also operating and observing)
OpenDoor experience report, 371-372
operating and observing
    about, 209
    activities in this phase, 210
    automation instead of toil, 234
    more scalable, more safe, 231-234
    observability, 223-226
        attack observability, 228-231
        definition, 224
        thresholding for safety boundaries, 227
    operational goals in SCE, 211-214

confidence-based security, 222
    DORA metrics, 217-219
    measuring operational success, 214-223
    Principled Performance Analytics, 222
    SLOs and SLAs, 220-222
    system signals and relevant attacks, 232
operator error in security culture, 26
    (see also human error)
opportunity cost and abstractions, 178
Optum experience report, 353-359
Oracle Cloud Infrastructure AttachMe vulnerability, 168
outcome bias, 257
ownership of security and resilience, 131
    database administration as DevOps, 132-134
Oxidation project (Mozilla), 142, 183

P

patches
    CI/CD for, 148-150
    Equifax breach, 148, 161, 255, 260
    infrastructure as code for, 161
paved roads created, 152, 291, 309
    testing requiring, 164
performance isolation, 116
performance tests, 166
Perrow, Charles, 27
persistence, 43
    monetized via crypto mining, 117
persona-based load tests, 172
phishing warnings, 296, 309
platform resilience engineering
    about, 267
    defining a user problem, 277
        prototype for usability, 285
        trade-offs made under pressure, 282-286
        user personas, 279
        user stories and journeys, 280
    defining a vision, 276
    explanation of platform engineering, 272-276
        blunt versus sharp end, 275
    Platform Resilience Engineering team, 272
        ideals sought in team, 273
        user stories for, 280
    production pressure effects, 267-272
    smaller organizations, 274

About the Authors

Kelly Shortridge is a senior principal engineer at Fastly in the office of the CTO. Shortridge is best known for their work on resilience in complex software systems, the application of behavioral economics to cybersecurity, and bringing security out of the dark ages. Shortridge has been a successful enterprise product leader as well as a startup founder (with an exit to CrowdStrike) and investment banker. Shortridge frequently advises Fortune 500s, investors, startups, and federal agencies and has spoken at major technology conferences internationally, including Black Hat USA, O'Reilly Velocity Conference, and SREcon. Shortridge's research has been featured in *ACM*, *IEEE*, and *USENIX*, spanning behavioral science in cybersecurity, deception strategies, and the ROI of software resilience. They also serve on *ACM Queue*'s magazine editorial board.

Aaron Rinehart is a senior distinguished engineer, SRE and Chaos Engineering at Capital One. He has spent his career solving complex engineering problems and transforming cybersecurity practices across a diverse set of industries: healthcare, insurance, government, aerospace, technology, higher education, and the military. Aaron has been expanding the possibilities of chaos engineering in its application to other safety-critical portions of the IT domain, most notably in cybersecurity. He began shaping the application of chaos engineering within cybersecurity during his tenure as the Chief Security Architect at a Fortune 4, UnitedHealth Group (UHG). Rinehart is a frequently requested speaker at respected media outlets and conferences, most notably RSA, O'Reilly's Velocity, Blackhat/DefCon, GOTO, OWASP Global, and QCon. He has been interviewed and quoted in various publications including *The Huffington Post*, ABC News, *TechTarget*, *DarkReading*, *SecurityWeekly*, *IEEE*, and *The Washington Post*.

Colophon

The animal on the cover of *Security Chaos Engineering* is an ornate hawk eagle (*Spizaetus ornatus*). Native to Central America and parts of South America, the ornate hawk eagle has a reddish-orange neck, a white throat, orange eyes, and a black-and-white chest. In addition, it has a crest (which indicates excitement depending on whether it is raised or lowered) and feathered tarsi (the tarsus is the part of the leg between the "knee" and the "ankle"). In general, the bird lives in forests and feeds on a variety of prey, from medium-to-large birds to small-to-medium mammals (and sometimes even reptiles).

Ornate hawk eagles have an extended commitment to their young from incubation to independence. Each clutch is only one egg. While the egg incubates for 44 to 48 days, the female sits on the nest while the male provides food for both the female and himself. Even when the egg has hatched, the male continues to provide food, dropping it close to the nest so the female can directly feed the young hawk eagle. Once the fledgling has started flying, the male takes over primary care of the offspring. The entire process, from laying the egg to letting the young ornate hawk eagle go, is a little less than two years, on average. Because of the time involved in raising their young, ornate hawk eagles tend to breed every other year.

The current conservation status (IUCN) of the ornate hawk eagle is "Near Threatened." Many of the animals on O'Reilly covers are endangered; all of them are important to the world.

The cover illustration is by Karen Montgomery, based on an antique line engraving from *Histoire Naturelle*. The cover fonts are Gilroy Semibold and Guardian Sans. The text font is Adobe Minion Pro; the heading font is Adobe Myriad Condensed; and the code font is Dalton Maag's Ubuntu Mono.